The Death of Reconstruction

The Death of Reconstruction

Race, Labor, and Politics in the
Post–Civil War North, 1865–1901

Heather Cox Richardson

HARVARD UNIVERSITY PRESS
Cambridge, Massachusetts
London, England
2001

Library of Congress Cataloging-in-Publication Data

Richardson, Heather Cox
    The death of Reconstruction : race, labor, and politics in the post–Civil
War North, 1865–1901 / Heather Cox Richardson.
      p.   cm.
    Includes bibliographical references and index.
    ISBN 0-674-00637-2 (alk. paper)
    1. Reconstruction—Public opinion.   2. Freedmen—Southern States—
Public opinion.   3. African Americans—Civil rights—Public opinion.
4. Public opinion—Northeastern States.   5. United States—Politics and
government—1865–1900.   6. Republican Party (U.S. : 1854–)—History—
19th century.   7. United States—Economic conditions—1865–1918.
8. African Americans—Civil rights—History—19th century.   9. Working
class—United States—19th century.   10. Northeastern States—Race
relations.   I. Title.

E668 .R5   2001
973.8—dc21   2001024212

For
Robert Francis Pontrelli,
Marshall Ambrose Pontrelli,
and
Eva Katharine Pontrelli

Contents

Preface

In my first book, *The Greatest Nation of the Earth,* I explored how free labor ideology shaped economic and political policies in the North during the Civil War. Legislation on banking and currency, taxation, agriculture, and railroads reflected the belief that man's God-given ability to create value with the labor of his own hands was the true basis of wealth and prosperity. This theory also molded Republican attitudes toward slavery, which by definition was the antithesis of free labor.

Free labor ideas changed the view that most Republicans had of the freedpeople, the 4 million African-Americans liberated by the war. Racism had been rampant before the conflict. Most virulent among Democrats, racist attitudes were widely shared even by Republicans as tolerant and benevolent as Abraham Lincoln. But the war years changed those attitudes. In 1861, Republicans believed that black workers were inferior to whites; by 1865, the industriousness of freedworkers migrating North and the heroism of the nearly 200,000 African-Americans who fought for the Union armies convinced Republicans that blacks were not the dull, animal-like creatures of racist myths. With their drive to educate themselves and their children, their desire to work their own land, and their eagerness to save for the future, they seemed to be ideal workers of the free labor model, who would rise and prosper through hard work. Most of the legislation of the early Reconstruction period—the Freedmen's Bureau Act, the Civil Rights Act of 1866, the Thirteenth, Fourteenth, and Fifteenth Amendments to the Constitution—was intended to foster and extend the free labor ideology among African-Americans.

Yet despite their initial postwar support for freedpeople, Northerners had turned against African-Americans by the turn of the century. By 1900, the North watched complacently as lynching and violence terrorized Southern blacks, as one Southern state after another disfranchised African-Americans and instituted a rigorous system of racial segregation in the form of the Jim Crow laws, and as blacks were forced into semi-slavery as sharecroppers. I wondered why Republicans abandoned their efforts to reconstruct Southern society and to remake former slaves into independent free laborers. What had happened in the thirty-five years from 1865 to 1900 to make Northerners forsake the freedpeople they had championed in 1865?

Previous historians have offered several explanations for what one called "the retreat from Reconstruction." Perhaps the most influential explanation was that of C. Vann Woodward, who in 1955 ventured the argument that after the Civil War, Southerners adopted racial segregation to split a political bloc of African-Americans and poor Southern whites that threatened the political supremacy of the white elite. Northerners capitulated to segregation, he argued, because they, too, were racists. After Woodward, many historians turned their attention to racism to explain why white Americans excluded their black countrymen from mainstream life. They dug into the Southern past, finding there such intransigent racism that Northern politicians were eventually forced to capitulate to it in order to build national coalitions that could win elections.[1] Other historians explained the region's abandonment of Reconstruction by pointing out that Northerners were exhausted after a devastating war, preoccupied with problems of corruption in their own section, and forced to dump their black allies overboard out of political expediency.[2] Taken together, historians since Woodward have painted a compelling portrait of the importance of white racism in the historical black experience and the development of American society, as well as of a confusing world of Northern corruption, spoilsmanship, and reform.[3]

Powerful though these explanations were, they did not appear to me to explain fully the Northern abandonment of Reconstruction. They seemed to present slices of the late nineteenth-century Northern experience that were not easily reconciled into a larger picture. While there is no doubt that nineteenth-century Northerners were unself-consciously racist, for example, had whites reacted to freedpeople solely on the basis of racism, they should have discriminated against both poor and prosperous African-Americans alike, and their attitudes should have been unaffected by specific events or pieces of legislation. This was not the case.[4] Similarly, while Northerners were increasingly preoccupied with corruption and civil service, they were even more attentive to Southern life and the black community. It remained unclear just how the disparate aspects of their experience fitted together in their own minds.

It seemed to me that, for an age before the advent of opinion polls and focus groups, newspapers, periodicals, popular books—even novels—might yield an understanding of how the Northern people at large viewed the dramatic changes in their society between the end of the Civil War and the beginning of the new century. After 1850, the American press mobilized the entire electorate, tying readers together as they read and responded to a variety of printed views. Government, private societies, and even individuals reported their actions and ideas to partisan newspapers whose editors tried both to reflect and to shape the views of their readers; people gathered at newspaper offices to hear the latest information; key editors presented the news for their readers and fed them articles interpreting events. Just how central the press was to public debate was clear in Congress; frequently speakers referred to newspaper articles as sources of their information on a wide range of topics. The public conversation of nineteenth-century Americans went beyond newspapers to popular tracts designed for public consumption. Politicians, reporters, travelers, and reformers all wrote essays, stories, novels, and travelogues to inform the public about current affairs. *Harper's Weekly* added another dimension to popular debate by publishing Thomas Nast's line drawings, which, the paper editorialized, "are of an allegorico-political character, at once poems and speeches. They argue the case to the eye, and conclusively. A few lines does the work of many words, and with a force of eloquence which no words can rival."[5] Even the illiterate could follow a story in Nast's pictures (as absconding politician William Marcy Tweed discovered when he was captured by a man who had seen a Nast caricature of him).

The circulation of newspapers exploded by midcentury, and I concentrated on those with large audiences. The *New York World* was perhaps the most popular paper of the time, with more than 500,000 readers, but even the *Washington Post*, which came from a city dubbed "the graveyard of newspapers," boasted runs of 15,000 copies per day. In the wake of emancipation there was rapid growth also of black newspapers in both the South and the North, and many issues of even local papers like the Colorado Springs, Colorado, *Western Enterprise* are extant, providing a window on black attitudes toward the questions of the day. "What would any American community be without its newspaper?" asked *Har-*

per's *Weekly*, which itself was called by a rival "one of the most powerful organs of popular opinion" and claimed an 1865 circulation of more than 100,000 a week. Reflected *Harper's New Monthly Magazine*, "It is not easy to gauge the exact influence of a daily or weekly paper in moulding public opinion; but there is no question that the press is the most powerful of all methods by which opinion is enlightened and swayed."[6]

The general press ran along surprisingly standard tracks. Unlike the smaller, specialized labor, business, or ethnic newspapers and magazines, the mainstream press concentrated on similar topics in all parts of the country. The *San Francisco Daily Alta California*, for instance, joined the *New York Times*, the *Chicago Tribune*, and other major papers in worrying about political turmoil over taxation in South Carolina. Their concerns were shared by many of the black newspapers. While offering different interpretations of newsworthy events, most newspapers focused on the same issues: money, the South, labor, the corruption of government. Examining a range of papers from across the North permitted a larger pattern to emerge from the complicated local politics of individual cities and states.

Shared perceptions of what was important reflected changing technology, as the booming telegraph news services standardized the press of the late nineteenth century. Since the powerful news services operated out of cities, and since the newly widespread railroads delivered city papers throughout the country, the prominent newspapers of the country usually set the terms of discussion about national issues.[7] Newspaper readers in rural areas would have access to stories about violent strikers, for example, despite the fact that they might have worried less about labor agitators than their urban counterparts. The major newspapers of the postwar North—the *Boston Evening Transcript*, *New York World*, *New York Herald*, *New York Times*, *Cincinnati Daily Gazette*, and so on—offer today's reader the opportunity to stand in the shoes of a Reconstruction-era American and observe distant events the same way a literate nineteenth-century Northerner would have.

Reading the popular press from the nineteenth century, I came to believe that the story of the relationship between freedpeople and white Northerners during Reconstruction was not only about race but also about the clash between two concepts of political economy. At the end of the Civil War, Northern Republicans believed in free labor—the idea that the nation had a unique political economy in which a person's labor could enable him to rise in a world where all had the same interest in increased production and national growth. After the war, adherents of an opposing vision of the nation's political economy compared America to Europe and argued that labor and capital naturally fought.

These competing theories of political economy were not new in 1865, but the dynamic economy of post–Civil War America made the conflict between them immediate and vital. Before the war, the majority of Northerners were farmers, small manufacturers, or employees of these two. It was easy for people in these circumstances to believe that an individual's efforts expended on natural resources produced value. The accumulating value of a man's production became the capital on which he supported himself and then rose higher in society. That workers and employers shared the same interest in increasing production seemed obvious in such a setting, for laborers thrived if their workplace succeeded and faced unemployment if it failed. Employers who worked closely with their employees had both personal pressures to treat them well and economic interests in retaining a skilled, contented labor force.[8]

The postwar years challenged this bucolic model of political economy as widespread industrialization transformed the nation. Businesses expanded over the nation's burgeoning transportation systems, beginning to operate under a new corporate structure that divorced a company's managers from its workers. By 1880, the new factories employed 5 million industrial workers, many drawn from the pool of immigrants who poured into the country after 1880 at the rate of more than 500,000 per year. Increasing mechanization meant that workers needed fewer skills and could be easily replaced by newcomers living in the ghettos of booming cities like New York, which, along with Chicago and Philadelphia, had well over a million inhabitants by 1900. Workers without job security, employed at below-subsistence wages, had a hard time believing in a harmonious economy in which hard work spelled success. Instead, they sought relief for accumulated grievances by taking to the streets; between 1880 and 1900, 6.6 million workers participated in more than 23,000 strikes.[9]

The conflict between the idea of a harmonious economic world based on free labor and the idea of class struggle pervaded late nineteenth-century politics and directly affected the question of African-Americans' role in American life. In their symbolic position as the nation's stereotypical workers, freedpeople were both strongest and most vulnerable. In early 1865, Northern Republicans confidently believed that Southern ex-slaves fit perfectly into the model of free labor society and would use their labor to develop the ruined South, accumulating capital to become self-sufficient and even prosperous. When acting as Northerners expected free laborers to, ex-slaves enjoyed great support. In the years after the Civil War, though, as workers who believed in a conflict between labor and capital challenged the prevailing concept of America's unique political economy, many interpreted the demands of the ex-slaves for land, social services, and civil rights as part of an attempt to subvert the American way. Northern anxiety about an expanding government in the hands of those unwilling to work, who would enact welfare-type legislation to confiscate the property of the true workers in America, fed the Northern obsession with strikers, the spoils system, the growing government, corruption, and communism. It also led to the Northern abandonment of those African-Americans who seemed to reject the free labor system of political economy in favor of exploiting government for their own ends.

Black Americans were not simply subsumed into the debate about white workers' control of government. In 1865, after all, Americans worried primarily about the South and the freedpeople, not about striking workers. Northern attitudes toward blacks shaped the national debate about workers as well as the larger debate over political economy, even as the controversy over the nation's true political economy affected Northerners' approach to African-Americans. In the years after the Civil War, fear of a perceived black rejection of the free labor ideal, coupled with anxiety over labor unrest, made the self-styled "better classes" abandon the midcentury vision of an egalitarian free labor society that included blacks as well as whites.

Changing Northern attitudes about African-Americans cut a broad swath across party lines. Republicans had organized around the free labor theory and joined with most Northern Democrats to fight the Civil War to protect the principles embraced by that theory, although members of the parties had profound differences about how a free labor society should operate. Within five years of the end of the war, Northern Democrats had begun to distance themselves from their party's Southern extremists and embrace moderate Republican ideas. In the election of 1872—which marked a seismic shift in American political thinking—

certain Democrats and Republicans joined together in the Liberal Republican movement, offering an attractive new "mainstream" whose enduring ideas dominated political discussion for the rest of the decade.
Defending a free labor society threatened by disaffected workers seeking
government support, this movement attracted adherents from both parties as well as splinter groups. By the 1880s, unreconstructed Southern
Democrats and "stalwart" Republicans—who adhered to an aggressive
radical approach to the South with an eye to maintaining political
strength there—lay at the two extremes of American politics. A large
body of Americans fell between these two poles, comprising a "mainstream" group whose evolving views stemmed from an original belief in
a free labor society.[10]

Northerners followed closely developments in the South and changes
in the lives of the freedpeople. What they read about in the press or
heard from political representatives, however, often misrepresented the
reality of black Americans' existence. Despite increasing Northern tourism to the South in the 1870s and 1880s, the lives of freedpeople remained foreign to most Northerners, and much popular writing of the
postwar years shows a skewed view of ex-slaves. Stories about blacks reflected the hopes and fears of Northerners who, incorrectly, perceived
the ex-slaves as actors in a world that mirrored Northern society.[11]
Northerners entwined their ideas about African-Americans with their
hopes and fears for the country as a whole. Northern attitudes toward
freedpeople became part of the general anxiety over the national government, which had grown so dramatically during the Civil War and which
continued to grow in Northerners' imaginations even more quickly than
it did in real life. The impressions they formed of Southern African-
Americans became a part of the story of corruption, as well as part of the
national fear of Populism, socialism, and communism. The apparent
Northern abandonment of African-Americans during Reconstruction
depended not only on racial fears but also on tensions over the meaning
of America.

I could never have written this book without the help of many fine
people.

My colleagues at the Massachusetts Institute of Technology and other
universities have been generous with advice and encouragement. I am
endebted to David Herbert Donald, Robert Fogelson, James L. Huston,

Pauline Maier, and Mitchell Snay for their close reading of the manuscript and their insightful suggestions for its improvement. David Blight, Thomas J. Brown, William E. Gienapp, Sally Hadden, Michael F. Holt, Nick Salvatore, and Michael Vorenberg helped me frame my themes, answered questions, and corrected errors.

My editors at Harvard University Press, Aida Donald, Julie Ericksen Hagen, Jeff Kehoe, Joyce Seltzer, and my friend Grace Won helped me to whip the manuscript into a book.

Research assistants Stephen Chen, Meghan Jendrickson, and Chandra Miller bravely faced microfilm machines to foray into newspapers and return with sheaves of photocopies. Christine Doyle Dee and Portia Vescio began as newspaper copiers but quickly became perceptive editors, inquisitive searchers, and friends. They left their marks on the pages that follow.

The wonderful librarians at Harvard University's Government Documents and Microfilms division have made the research for this project easier and more pleasant than it could have been. Stephen W. Tanner deserves special thanks for helping to shape my approach to this topic in a conversation early on about the *Senate Exodus Report.*

Generous fellowships from the Massachusetts Institute of Technology and Harvard University's Charles Warren Center enabled me to concentrate on this book. I owe special thanks to Claudia Goldin, Laurel Thatcher Ulrich, and the Warren Center Fellows for 1998–99, whose innovative work made me rethink my own.

Karin S. Daley afforded me the time to work by taking such good care of my children that I could write without worries. I cannot thank her enough.

My deepest thanks go to Michael R. Pontrelli for hoisting me over the rough spots.

With so much generous help, I should have produced a perfect book. That I did not is my fault alone.

The whole labor system of the [South] is in an utterly demoralized condition. How soon it can be thoroughly reorganized, and on just what basis that reorganization will take place, are questions of no easy answering. The labor question, and not reconstruction, is the main question among intelligent thinking men.

—Sidney Andrews, 1866

The View from Atlanta, 1895

African-American educator Booker T. Washington articulated the post-war Northern vision for the freedpeople in his famous address at the opening of the Atlanta Exposition on September 18, 1895. The address "excited the greatest amount of interest," Washington recalled, and "perhaps went further than anything else in giving me a reputation that in a sense might be called National." It led to his enduring popularity with many white Americans and his eventual vilification by opponents like prominent black leader W. E. B. Du Bois, who initially endorsed the speech, but turned against the ideas in it by 1900. A white committee in charge of the exposition, which was designed to showcase Southern industry, had chosen Washington, the principal and founder of Alabama's Tuskegee Institute, to "represent the Negro race" in a speech at the exposition's opening exercises, marking, Washington said, "the first time in the entire history of the Negro that a member of my race had been asked to speak from the same platform with white Southern men and women on any important National occasion." In the audience would be "the wealth and culture of the white South" and "a large number of Northern whites, as well as a great many men and women of my own race." A neighboring white farmer had jokingly warned Washington of what he already knew: he was in a "tight place." Washington deftly turned the famous Atlanta Exposition speech into a fitting document to represent the "Wizard of Tuskegee."[1]

Washington began his speech by reiterating what white Americans had known in 1865, that since one-third of the Southern population was black, "[n]o enterprise seeking the material, civil, or moral welfare of this section can disregard this element of our population and reach the highest success." Then, after acknowledging the late nineteenth-century understanding that, since emancipation, freedmen had sought to live without working, becoming politicians rather than "starting a dairy farm or a truck garden," he reminded his listeners of the hopes that Northern Republicans had held immediately after the Civil War, telling freed-people that they must settle down in the South, working "in agriculture, mechanics, in commerce, in domestic service, and in the professions." African-Americans, he said, must not "overlook" what Northerners had preached since the war era:

> that the masses of us are to live by the productions of our hands, and . . . we shall prosper in proportion as we learn to dignify and glorify common labour and put brains and skill into the common occupations of life; shall prosper in proportion as we learn to draw the line between the superficial and the substantial, the ornamental gewgaws of life and the useful. No race can prosper till it learns that there is as much dig-nity in tilling a field as in writing a poem. It is at the bottom of life we must begin, and not at the top. Nor should we permit our grievances to overshadow our opportunities.

African-Americans had proved that they could fit the free-labor model, Washington said, noting that thirty years before, straight out of the mas-ters' fields, they had owned nothing but "a few quilts and pumpkins and chickens (gathered from miscellaneous sources)," while at the exposi-tion they exhibited "inventions and production of agricultural imple-ments, buggies, steam-engines, newspapers, books, statuary, carving, paintings, the management of drug-stores and banks."

Washington echoed postwar Republicans when he admonished white Southerners to banish ideas of importing white labor and to work with "these people who have, without strikes and labour wars, tilled your fields, cleared your forests, builded your railroads and cities, and brought forth treasures from the bowels of the earth, and helped make possible . . . the progress of the South." With encouragement and educa-tion, he said, African-Americans would "buy your surplus land, make blossom the waste places in your fields, and run your factories." They were "patient, faithful, law-abiding, and unresentful." He called for "in-terlacing our industrial, commercial, civil, and religious life with yours in a way that shall make the interests of both races one."

As Republican wartime theory had also emphasized, Washington noted that all economic interests in society were harmonious, and must be treated as such. "Nearly sixteen millions of hands will aid you in pulling the load upward, or they will pull against you the load downward," he told his audience. African-Americans would either make up one-third of the "ignorance and crime of the South, or one-third its intelligence and progress; we shall contribute one-third to the business and industrial prosperity of the South, or we shall prove a veritable body of death, stagnating, depressing, retarding every effort to advance the body politic." Washington lauded the "constant help" of Southerners and Northern philanthropists, who saw that education for African Americans was critical to national development.

Despite his own impatience with segregated facilities in the South, in Washington's address he agreed with Republican postwar thought that such questions were immaterial.[2] "The wisest among my race understand that the agitation of questions of social quality is the extremest folly," he declared. Social equality would come not through legislation but with freedpeople's success as free laborers, "the result of severe and constant struggle rather than of artificial forcing." Such equality would be inevitable with economic success, for "no race that has anything to contribute to the markets of the world is long in any degree ostracized." Although he declared that African-Americans must enjoy "all the privileges of the law," he insisted that economic success was "vastly more important." "The opportunity to earn a dollar in a factory just now," he stated, "is worth infinitely more than the opportunity to spend a dollar in an opera-house."

As postwar Republicans had insisted, Washington claimed that with "the product of field, of forest, of mine, of factory, letters and art, much good will come," he said. Prosperity would bring not only "material benefits" to everyone but also "a blotting out of sectional differences and racial animosities and suspicions . . . a determination to administer absolute justice . . . a willing obedience among all classes to the mandates of law." The blossoming of the country under a national system of free labor would usher in the economic prosperity that would erase racial tensions.

Washington concluded his speech with words that could have come straight from Northern Republicans in early 1865, who had believed that the abolition of slavery and a national system of free labor would make America the greatest nation on earth. Economic prosperity and the end of racial tensions, Washington thundered, would "bring into our beloved South a new heaven and a new earth."

Americans North and South loved Washington's Atlanta Address. A correspondent for the *New York World* reported that the audience "was in an uproar of enthusiasm—handkerchiefs were waved, canes were flourished, hats were tossed in the air. The fairest women of Georgia stood up and cheered. . . . Most of the Negroes in the audience were crying." The *Boston Evening Transcript* reported that Washington's speech had "dwarfed all the other proceedings and the Exposition itself. The sensation that it has caused in the press has never been equalled." The editor of the *Atlanta Constitution* told a New York paper that "I do not exaggerate when I say that Professor Booker T. Washington's address yesterday was one of the most notable speeches, both as to character and as to the warmth of its reception, ever delivered to a Southern audience. The address was a revelation. The whole speech is a platform upon which blacks and whites can stand with full justice to each other." Washington recalled a walk through Atlanta during which he was so embarrassed by well-wishers that he returned to his boardinghouse; his trip back to Tuskegee was punctuated with stops at which admirers sought to shake his hand. Within a year, Harvard had conferred on Washington the first honorary degree it had ever offered to a black man; three years later, President McKinley visited Tuskegee with all but one cabinet member, paying tribute to Washington's "genius." Was Washington's address so popular in the North simply because it seemed to accept Jim Crow legislation when it declared that "in all things that are purely social we can be as separate as the fingers, yet one as the hand in all things essential to mutual progress," as Southerners assumed and as critics charged?[3]

In fact, Northerners lauded Washington's address because it recalled the positive Northern Republican postwar vision of a prospering South contributing to the national wealth thanks to the efficient labor of upwardly mobile freedpeople. Resurrecting this traditional image during a time of political and economic agitation by workers and Populists who wanted the national government to assume a role in American society legislating for the protection and benefit of workers, Washington seemed to be defending the old idea of free laborers producing under a government that only promoted growth. Washington's vision denied strikes and expected harmony between employers and workers. It called for laborers to depend solely upon themselves. The Atlanta Address promoted individualism at a time when Americans feared the growing strength of those demanding national welfare legislation.

Washington's address was not an attempt to curry white favor by sacrificing the ambition of African-Americans for equality. He certainly advocated the industrial education that appeared to be a step below professional education for African-Americans, as critics like W. E. B. Du Bois later charged, but reading his address as a capitulation to white racism does not take into consideration the previous three decades of debate about America's proper political economy. In his Atlanta Address, Washington publicly reappropriated for African-Americans the Northern image of the traditional laborer, who would begin his career in the fields or at a manual craft, and would rebuild the South as he became part of a constantly rising middle class.[4] Many black activists had rejected this image as unrealistic for any worker in late nineteenth-century America, and the majority of Americans no longer applied it to the mass of African-Americans, seeing them as disaffected workers who believed in societal class conflict.

By resurrecting this image, tapping into the political economy of postwar Republicans, Washington was actually making a radical and effective statement in favor of African-American power. Reclaiming the Republican vision of African-Americans as traditional mid-nineteenth-century workers, he was attempting to erase the negative images of political, civil rights, and labor agitation of the past decades that had conflated to place constant negative pressure on the black community. By disassociating themselves from the Northern white images of the 1870s, 1880s, and 1890s, Washington's African-Americans could reclaim the powerful wartime vision of black Americans who were important and integral parts of American society. Critical to the Northern view of the traditional laborer—the image that Washington insisted on applying to black Americans—was the idea that the traditional laborer would climb to a prosperity that dictated political and social prominence. By evoking this very strong stereotypical image of workers who succeeded economically, socially, and politically, Washington was making a powerful statement for the advancement of black Americans.

1
_____

The Northern Postwar Vision, 1865–1867

In 1861, Northerners fought the South to defend the general beliefs in free labor and independence that they had inherited from America's Revolutionary generation and which seemed to be under attack from an aggressive "Slave Power."[1] In 1854, the Republican party had formed as a Northern organization and codified the free labor ideal as its own political platform, although most Northern Democrats shared the free labor theory's basic tenets. Republicans followed political economists who argued that, thanks to its rich resources and largely undeveloped land, America's political economy remained close to God's natural plan for humanity. Every man, they believed, had been endowed by God with the ability to support and improve himself as his labor produced value from the raw materials found in nature. Young individuals started on the lowest level of American society, then improved their economic and social status by accumulating wealth over time. Considering America's still relatively undeveloped landscape, Republicans concluded that this meant individuals would begin as agricultural hands, then move into farming or, perhaps, mechanical trades, then rise to become independent landowners. Those with a secure basis in landed property had the option of becoming large farmers or investing in mercantile projects or industry, which would, in turn, employ other individuals just starting out. As the first Republican president, Abraham Lincoln, explained: "The prudent, penniless beginner in the world labors for wages awhile, saves a surplus with which to buy tools or land for himself; then labors on his own account another while, and at length hires another new beginner to help him."[2]

6

The vision of a society based on the labor theory of value encom-
passed almost every aspect of life; it was a worldview. Adherents of the
free labor idea believed first of all in the sanctity of private property, for
without the guaranteed right to the products of his own labor, no man
would desire to work. The free labor system also presupposed that all
benefited from increased production, since more staples would allow the
economy to diversify, permitting greater employment and greater investment in technologies that would magnify the value of a person's labor.
With ever-growing wages as men's production increased, a laborer could
consume more goods and eventually hire employees of his own, who
would continue in their turn to fuel a growing economy that buoyed everyone. Adherents of a free labor vision of political economy also believed that government policies must be carefully tailored so they did
not interfere with the natural operation of the economy. Fortunately,
they thought, all men within the system shared the same interests and
would therefore agree on proper measures to permit the free operation
of God's beneficent economy.

Although it recognized that individuals at different stages in their careers would enjoy different levels of prosperity, the free labor ideal was
egalitarian. Every man could rise, it dictated, so long as he was willing to
work hard. Followers of the free labor theory abhorred the idea of the
concentration of wealth, recognizing that monopolies of money or land
would force poor individuals to become permanent wage laborers, or, at
the very best, be forced to pay unreasonable prices for the land and tools
they needed to become independent. Adherents of the free labor theory
argued hopefully that because capital was constantly depreciating while
productivity increased, labor was constantly becoming more valuable,
or, alternatively, that capitalists would not squeeze their employees to
fatten their own pocketbooks, because employers recognized that their
interests were the same as those of their workers. Tailored to a world of
small farms and limited manufacturing, the free labor theory did not offer a true solution to economic consolidation or to below-subsistence
wages.

The free labor ideal required certain qualities in a worker. By the
1850s, prosperous or at least upwardly mobile Northerners of both parties had begun to perceive two types of American laborers. One fit the
free labor model, the other did not. On the one hand were the "good
workmen," who worked hard and skillfully, lived frugally, saved their

money, and planned to rise as individuals through their own efforts. These men strove for education and used their ballots intelligently to elect public officials who would protect property and the free labor system. Through their own efforts, good workmen gradually rose to become prosperous, often owning their own workshops and employing men themselves. If they failed to do so, they or their womenfolk usually became part of the "deserving" poor, to whom alms should be given. These impoverished individuals were doing their best to succeed in the free labor model but were prevented by infirmity or temporary setbacks. They retained high standards of morality and economy.

In contrast to the good workers were those who followed Democratic labor leaders, who looked to the history of England and to the theories of Ricardo and Malthus to argue that the condition of workers naturally declined over time and that polarizing wealth meant the creation of economic classes locked in inevitable conflict. Adherents of the free labor system saw these workers as inferior, disaffected; they were unreliable, unproductive, fond of drink, and inclined toward cooperative action against their employers. The "undeserving" poor, according to a New York charity society, paralleled the unreliable, unproductive workers. They were "indolent and vicious. . . . They love to clan together in some out of the way place, are content to live in filth and disorder with a bare subsistence, provided they can drink, and smoke, and gossip, and enjoy their balls, and wakes, and frolics without molestation."[3]

Aside from those workers flirting with labor organization, most Northern Democrats of the Civil War era shared the Republican devotion to free labor, but Republicans and Democrats parted company when they envisioned how the free labor ideal worked in society. Republicans believed that the economic and political interests of all Americans were the same, for all benefited from increased production. By 1865, they had begun to use the government to promote economic development. Democrats, in contrast, held firm to ideas of personal liberty, small government, antiauthoritarianism, and racism. While Northern Democrats agreed with Republicans about the importance of free labor, their racism made them limit the beneficiaries of that theory to whites. In addition, Democrats' antiauthoritarianism led them toward fears of conspiracy. They were quick to suspect both political and economic opponents of colluding to cause the destruction of personal liberty and independence of individuals through consolidations of capital or a strong government.

As a result, most Democrats saw tensions in American society between wealthy and poor, employers and employees, labor and capital, the people and the government. They also held firmly to the idea of a very limited national government.[4]

Within this general framework after the Civil War was a spectrum of political behavior stretching from conservative Northern Democrats, who hoped for a quick sectional reconciliation on terms as close to those before the war as possible, to radical Republicans, who planned for African-American equality and a complete revision of Southern society. In between these two poles were moderate Northern Democrats, conservative Republicans, moderate Republicans, and independents, who declared no political affiliation but tended to side with the moderates in both major parties. In varying degrees, those in the middle of the political spectrum called for only basic African-American rights while maintaining a limited government. After the Civil War, labor, agrarian, and other special interests sometimes organized politically and operated outside of this basic political framework, but while their ideas were noticed in national discussions, their opinions never dominated national debate.

In 1865, how did Northerners expect the 4 million ex-slaves, the South's primary laborers, to fit into this American system? Before the Civil War, Northerners of all parties had usually disparaged slaves, arguing that the system of slavery had stunted them. Slave labor was vastly inferior to white labor, they maintained, because slaves had no incentive to work. Like anyone else, a slave produced value when he or she worked, but the benefits of slaves' efforts were appropriated by their masters, who returned to the slaves only a pittance of the profits of the labor in the form of minimal food and clothing. Knowing that their efforts only padded the pockets of their owners, slaves slacked off. They had no incentive to work efficiently or to experiment with new methods to obtain better products. In time they become habitually shiftless and backward, unable to care for themselves because they had been trained out of self-sufficiency. Slave owners exacerbated the evils of the system by either misusing or wasting labor. Although the purchase price of a prime field hand was high before the war, Northerners maintained that, once purchased, slave labor was cheap. Slaves survived in conditions that white workers would scorn, and thus a slave labor force could be maintained for a fraction of the cost of free white labor. With such a cheap labor force, masters had neither to train their slaves to work efficiently nor to teach them new techniques to improve production. With no claim to the value he produced and no instruction to improve him, the slave was a feeble shadow of the Northern free white worker.[5]

Although Democrats continued to disparage African-Americans throughout the early 1860s, during the Civil War Southern battlefield victories made Northern Republicans change their perception of slaves as poor workers. Northerners had boasted that the war would be short, that one decisive battle would send Southern bullies scurrying back home while victorious Northern soldiers enjoyed their enemies' humiliation. But from the First Battle of Bull Run in July 1861, when Union troops ran back to Washington, D.C., in panic, through the end of the 1862 campaign, Southern troops won again and again. Searching for the cause of Southern victories, Northern Republican newspapers refused to attribute Confederate success to Southern superiority or Northern ineptitude, and instead attributed the Confederate victories to the extraordinary power of African-Americans to fulfill the labor needs of the South, leaving all white men free to fight. As early as May 1861, Republican newspapers reported that "negroes . . . have . . . been employed to do nearly all the labor of the war thus far," and, carrying this logic a step further, the *New York Times* attributed the fall of Fort Sumter to the work of slaves. "Without the black engineers and laborers that South Carolina impressed into her service," it announced, "Major Anderson might have remained in Sumter till doomsday." As Southern victories belied Northern expectations, Northern Republicans found the source of their enemies' strength in their chattel workers, who maintained food production and performed the manual work of the armies while their masters devoted themselves to fighting. The radical *Chicago Tribune* concluded that "four millions of slaves off-set at least eight millions of Northern whites," and the more moderate *New York Times* agreed that "the labor of every slave, . . . if he be put at the proper kind of work, and properly handled, is worth more than the labor of two white men."[6]

As they redefined slaves as good workers, Northern Republicans began to describe the distant bondsmen as quintessential examples of ideal workers who would work hard, support themselves, and gradually rise. When Democrats attacked emancipation measures by insisting that ex-slaves would be unable to support themselves, Republicans in favor of black freedom rallied around the idea that productive black workers would support themselves and contribute to American society. Focusing on African-American men, who were the plantation system's more valuable producers, Republicans rarely spoke about black women and children, who would more often require public assistance to survive. Party members repeatedly noted the production of African-Americans employed under the auspices of the Treasury Department on abandoned Southern lands. The *New York Times* reported that in 1864, freedmen of the New Orleans department earned $1,609,000 plus food and shelter, in addition to establishing almost 8,000 black children in school. Some individuals earned up to $300, proving, according to the *Times*, that the free labor system worked.[7]

During the war, this new Republican perception of slaves as good workers evolved to an understanding that African-Americans needed only jobs and wages to participate effectively in a free labor economy. While Democrats continued to insist that slaves could not work without white supervision, and that emancipation measures would "turn helpless children and superannuated persons out of house and home," Republicans advocating black freedom emphasized the easy transition many ex-slaves made to becoming free workers. From Washington came news that contrabands worked in hospitals and that many had been hired as servants by private families. The arrival of ninety-one ex-slaves in Philadelphia made some white people nervous, but many others rushed to hire "house servants and farm hands." Rumors of additional arrivals in the city increased requests for workers, and one local African-American leader concluded cheerfully that "a great scarcity of laborers exists in the country," making black workers welcome. While Easterners seemed to welcome ex-slaves, Western farmers, suffering under severe labor shortages by 1863, seemed desperate for their help, despite the region's deep racism. A paper from Indiana rejected a plan for colonizing ex-slaves outside the country because it objected to removing "4,000,000 of valuable laborers from America"; the *Cincinnati Daily Gazette* encouraged the arrival of black migrants from the South, and the *Chicago Tribune* suggested that the West should stop "depriving ourselves of the labor we need" and encourage the settlement of black people "so far as it may be necessary." Back East, Republicans noted that black labor was welcome and useful in the West, and suggested that "[w]hat is true . . . on a small scale, ought to hold good on a large one."[8]

A commitment to free black labor did not mean that Northerners had abandoned their racism. Democrats had relied on racist attacks on Lincoln and the Republicans in 1860 and by 1864 had reached a frenzied pitch of hatred. Coining the pejorative term *miscegenation* in that election, they insisted that the proposed Thirteenth Amendment abolishing slavery would bring swarms of bestial ex-slaves North to prey on white men's jobs and daughters. Anxious to de-emphasize the northward migration of freedpeople, Republicans of all stripes—even former abolitionists—insisted that freedpeople would stay in the South and make it prosper. The South could never expel its black population, the *Cincinnati Daily Gazette* commented, for "[t]he laboring population is bound up with the fate of the land, and must continue so, whatever their status," and even the radical *New York Daily Tribune* reported that "if Slavery . . . ended tomorrow, we are confident that even South Carolina would be in no hurry to expel from her soil the most industrious and productive half of her people."[9]

In daily life, most Northerners had little to do with the small, largely town-dwelling population of Northern African-Americans—fewer than 10 percent of all African-Americans lived in the North, and those who did concentrated in Northern urban areas—but racial hostility characterized the contact that did occur. Before 1865, Northern blacks led circumscribed lives. African-Americans were educated in segregated public schools if they were offered public education at all, shunted into low-paying jobs, denied the vote, barred from juries, denied civil rights, segregated in public facilities, and buried in segregated graveyards. State laws in Indiana, Iowa, Illinois, and Oregon prohibited black migration into those states. Racial violence erupted sporadically against African-Americans, and on a daily basis Northern African-Americans could expect even sympathetic whites to discriminate against them. Indeed, part of the initial drive for "free soil" in the Territories was the desire of some Republicans to keep African-American slaves out of Northern communities. Up in Maine in 1864, the white wife of a prominent abolitionist Union Army officer was typical of her time, complaining constantly about the black cook sent home by her husband even as she bemoaned the fact that her neighbors did not like "darkies."[10]

Despite their continuing dislike of African-Americans, in 1865, Republicans modeled their expectations of the newly freed Southern workers on their stereotypical image of ideal Northern laborers, believing that the ex-slaves would make their own way in the world. A leading Republican adviser counseled a minister traveling to South Carolina about how to approach the freedpeople. Francis Wayland warned Reverend Peck "that it is of the most questionable benefit ever to *give* to a person able to work." The process of raising freedpeople from slavery to freedom must be based "upon sound political principles," he explained, and while charity might benefit widows and orphans, it could only harm "a man with full health and plenty of work." Freedmen had to learn that "labor bears viable fruit," and that "all of their blessings are the result of their own labor." Revealing the redemptive power of the free labor ideal, Wayland concluded that "[n]othing will do more to elevate them into self dependent men than this." The idea that freedmen must work out their own fate in American society appealed to those who expected them to fail as well as those who believed in African-American equality. "Political freedom means liberty to work, and . . . enjoy the product of one's labor, be he white or black, blue or gray, red or green, and if he can rise by his own energies, in the name of God let him rise," declared ex-Democrat Andrew Johnson, before adding, "In saying this, I do not argue that the negro race is equal to the Anglo-Saxon—not at all." But so convinced were most Republicans that freedom would spell at least some sort of economic success for African-Americans that the Republican Congress in the spring of 1865 passed a bill incorporating the Freedmen's Savings and Trust Company.[11]

Republicans indicated their commitment to a naturally operating free labor system when they joined Democrats to reject the creation of a governmental bureau that would help freedpeople negotiate the difficult path from slavery to freedom. All but the most radical Republicans insisted that "the only way to treat these men is to treat them as freemen." Arguing that ex-slaves were no different than white men in hard times, one prominent Republican explained in 1864 that "[y]ou have got to give them alms, you have got to exercise acts of humanity and friendship to them for awhile. . . . They will be jostled as we are all being jostled through this life, but in a little while they will settle down into the position that Providence has designed that they shall occupy under the new condition of affairs in this country." Instead of a governmental bureau charged with the oversight of the freedpeople, Congress created a temporary bureau within the War Department for providing immediate relief to both white and black refugees made homeless and destitute by the war. Congress intended this "Freedmen's Bureau," as it was dubbed, only to carry the Southern population through the dislocation of the war; Southerners were expected to get back on their feet quickly. Republicans even denied the government's power to perform the overwhelming task of educating the freedpeople; private benevolent societies were recruited to help instead. With freedom, ex-slaves would become simply another group of workers in America's free labor society. "Our civilization is now untrammelled," stated the *Chicago Tribune* after the war. "In every part of our broad Union the laborer is worthy of his hire, and the rewards of industry wait on all who practice it."[12]

On January 31, 1865, a few months before the end of the Civil War, the House of Representatives erupted into wild cheering as Congress passed the Thirteenth Amendment to the Constitution, guaranteeing freedom for black Americans, and sent it off to the states for ratification. The new amendment prohibited slavery in America and gave Congress the power to enforce that decree with "appropriate legislation," a term that was left deliberately vague. By guaranteeing universal freedom in America, the Thirteenth Amendment completed Northern Republicans' vision of a nation based on free labor. It "perfects the great work of the founders of our Republic," triumphed the *New York Times*, enabling the nation to enter "upon a new stage of its great career . . . aiming at the greatest good and the highest happiness of all its people." Southern African-Americans would make "the broad fields that war has desolated . . . again blossom as the rose and reward the labor of the husbandman." A *New York Times* editor insisted that after the war free labor would make the South enjoy "such industrial progress as has never yet been witnessed in any country in the world"; the end of slavery would permit "an era of more perfect development in every sphere of industry." Congressmen agreed. "Under the inspiration of free labor," one Republican told the House, "the productions of the country will be . . . quadrupled" and America would become "the most powerful and populous, the most enterprising and wealthy nation in the world."[13]

The amendment was significant for another reason too; it was the first one in the history of the nation that expanded rather than limited the powers of the national government. Critically, the Thirteenth Amendment linked the African-American free workers to a stronger national government.

The surrender of Robert E. Lee and his army at Appomattox on April 9, 1865, brought a spiritual release and rejoicing to the North. The terrible sacrifice of more than 600,000 men had expiated the guilty sin of slavery, and it seemed that a chastened nation of free people could now stride forward to claim its great destiny as God's favored land, promising prosperity for all. But the heady relief of the war's end survived unblemished for only days. On April 15, 1865, black-bordered newspapers told the nation that Lincoln had been martyred. Less than a week after the end of the war, the promise of Reconstruction was already blighted.[14]

The last wartime Congress had adjourned in March 1865, before Lincoln's death, and Congress was not scheduled to meet again until December. This left Lincoln's vice president, Andrew Johnson, a free field of action for the first eight months after the war. A former Democrat from Tennessee, Johnson shared the Democratic imperative to reunite the nation quickly while keeping the government small and infringing as little as possible on the personal liberty of white Southerners. With a fundamentally different agenda than his Republican colleagues, Johnson worked frenetically to restore the Union on his own terms, before the Republican Congress he increasingly distrusted reassembled. Southern Democrats and Northern Republicans reacted speedily—and very differently—to his policies, both aware that the upcoming congressional session would likely change the political landscape of the country. From this unsettled summer came a definitive Republican vision of the new biracial nation as party members' general belief in the abilities of black workers became a conviction that the government must enforce a true free labor system in the South.[15]

Upon assuming the presidency, Johnson appeared to court the radicals, those vocal men who insisted on African-American political rights and a punitive course toward Southern whites implicated in the Rebellion.[16] To great applause, a week after taking office Johnson told a crowd that "the Government . . . is strong, not only to protect, but to punish. . . . Treason . . . is the blackest of crimes, and will surely be punished." But Johnson was a poor fit with radical Republicans. As a Tennessean crippled by a virulent prejudice against African-Americans, the former tailor opposed black rights; he also revered the idea of limited government and worried about Republican efforts to expand governmental powers. Quickly he began to moderate his tone in an attempt to build a coalition of Northern Democrats, Republican conservatives, and Southern moderates that would unite behind him on a more moderate program than radicals espoused.[17]

Johnson's moderation not only reflected his personal inclinations but also acknowledged that the Republicans could not create a new national political party on the radical platform of black rights. The Republican party had begun life as a sectional and a minority party—Lincoln, after all, had won the presidency with only a plurality of the popular vote in a field split four ways—and for the party to continue to be viable after the war, with the readmission of the Democratic South to the Union, it needed to broaden its base by taking a moderate position on Southern issues. This plan was hardly novel. Lincoln had hoped to develop moderate Southern support throughout the war with his generous Southern political policies, and his choice of former Democrat Andrew Johnson as a running mate in 1864, in place of the radical Republican Hannibal Hamlin of Maine, was in keeping with the Republican party's name change of that year. In 1864, the party officially became the Union party.

What was problematic to moderate Northern Republicans in 1865 was not the philosophy behind Andrew Johnson's policy but his means of implementing it. In May, Johnson announced his initial plan for "restoration," as he called the readmission of the Southern states to the Union. It made an oath of allegiance the only requirement for amnesty and restoration of property (not including ex-slaves, but including all confiscated lands that had been leased to freedpeople during the war) to all but high-ranking Confederate military or civilian officers. Reflecting his dislike of "aristocrats," Johnson also exempted individuals worth more than $20,000 from this plan. The president also called for the election of delegates to state conventions to frame new constitutions for seven Southern states and recognized provisional governments set up by Lincoln in four others. Ignoring suggestions that black soldiers or educated African-Americans should vote, Johnson limited the elections to white men who had taken an oath of allegiance, and required the conventions only to abolish slavery, nullify state ordinances of secession, and repudiate the Confederate debt. Then, in the months that followed, Johnson gave 100 pardons a day to the Southerners exempted from his restoration plan, eventually pardoning 13,500 Southerners out of the 15,000 who applied.[18]

Encouraged by Johnson's leniency, white Southern Democrats began in the summer of 1865 to resurrect their prewar society, or so it seemed to Northern Republicans. It may have been that Southern leaders were, in fact, pushing the South as far as they thought it would go, but their actions spelled treachery to the Republicans and terrorism to African-Americans. White gangs had been abusing and intimidating ex-slaves since the war ended, torturing and even killing freedpeople unlucky enough to fall into their hands; state organizations institutionalized the harassment. Some of the new state conventions refused to repudiate secession or the Confederate debt; Texas and Mississippi rejected the Thirteenth Amendment. Then, in the elections held under the new constitutions, Southerners elected ex-Confederates to a spate of state positions and sent Confederate congressmen, generals, colonels, and state officials to the U.S. Congress. Georgia went so far as to elect Confederate vice president Alexander H. Stephens to the Senate. The new Southern legislatures also passed "Black Codes," which dangerously mimicked slavery. In South Carolina, African-Americans could not work as anything but agricultural laborers without a license; Louisiana provided that freedmen commit to year-long labor contracts in the first ten days of January; Mississippi prohibited African-Americans from buying farmland. In most Southern states, freedmen found to be "vagrants"—that is, unemployed—were subject to arrest and subsequent bondage to landowners. A Republican visiting the South wrote that the Black Codes were "a striking embodiment of the idea that although the former owner has lost his individual right of property in the former slaves, the blacks at large belong to the whites at large." Although uneasy with the South's actions, Johnson had no choice but to side with white Southerners, his potential supporters, against the Republicans increasingly outraged by Southern events. When Congress reassembled in December, all of the Confederate states but Texas—which complied in February 1866—had received Johnson's approval for readmission to the Union.[19]

While Johnson spent the hot summer months trying to build a new conservative coalition that wanted a restored Union, small government, and a nominal acceptance of African-American freedom, a Northerner had been collecting information that would help thwart the president's plans. In May 1865, Johnson had asked Major General Carl Schurz, a prominent radical Republican who had cut his political teeth in the German Revolution of 1848, to tour the South and report on the postwar conditions there. Initially reluctant, Schurz quickly became concerned about the new president's lenient Reconstruction policy, and, prodded by his fellow radicals, Schurz agreed to conduct an investigation of Southern conditions. In July 1865, he began a tour of the South. His mission was nominally to gather information to enable the president to design an appropriate Reconstruction policy; he quickly began to see exactly what he expected to see, writing to his wife and to fellow radical Charles Sumner in August that "I have found all of my preconceived opinions verified most fully." Schurz traveled through South Carolina, Georgia, Alabama, Mississippi, and Louisiana, taking about three months. In addition to documenting the chaos in the South, his report to President Johnson outlined the radical Republican vision of and for the South.[20]

Schurz submitted his "Report on the Condition of the South" on November 22, 1865, after the South's attempt to reinstate quasi-slavery had become apparent. In the report, Schurz echoed the sentiments of Republicans of all stripes—radical, moderate, and conservative—that when talking of "reconstruction," it had to be remembered that "it is not only the political machinery of the States and their constitutional relations to the general government, but the whole organism of southern society that must be reconstructed, or rather constructed anew, so as to bring it into harmony with the rest of American society." Schurz worried that there was "among the southern people an *utter absence of national feeling.*" Southerners' insularity had kept the South from progress for fifty years, Schurz wrote; the region must be integrated into the whole Union to enable America to prosper. The South's "want of national spirit" was because "the southern people cherished, cultivated, idolized their peculiar interests and institutions in preference to those which they had in common with the rest of the American people." By this, Schurz meant that the South still remained tied to the antebellum world of slavery, with its consequent dependence on cotton and its hierarchy of wealth and society. What, then, according to Schurz, lay at the heart of the integrity of America and at the center of Reconstruction? "The negro question."[21]

Like other Republicans, Schurz believed that the key to the reunification of the North and South was the dominance of free labor, and he praised planters who were honestly trying to implement it by offering fair wages, stimulating the freedman's ambition, and offering education "to make him an intelligent, reliable, and efficient free laborer and a good and useful citizen." Planters like this were rare, and "almost invariably . . . far above the average in point of mental ability and culture." Schurz noted that those honestly engaged in free labor were satisfied with the freedman's work, and that Northern men who had come to the South after the war to grow cotton "almost uniformly speak of their negro laborers with satisfaction," proving that "the negro generally works well where he is decently treated and well compensated." He concluded that, if treated like free laborers, paid and respected, African-Americans would be efficient free workers.[22]

But Schurz's travels had convinced him that the vast majority of the Southern people could not yet adopt free labor "calmly and understandingly." In the first heady days of postwar freedom, ex-slaves had taken to the roads to search out loved ones who had been sold away, to reach cities where the Union army was distributing rations to starving refugees, or simply to test their freedom. This widespread black mobility had left planters without hands during spring planting season and confirmed the convictions of most whites that African-Americans would not work without physical compulsion and that a free labor system would fail with freedmen, who were unstable, ignorant of binding contracts, improvident, and lazy. This had been the justification for the Black Codes, by which Southerners tried to hold ex-slaves to labor for whites with violence and regulations. Schurz concluded that there was great opposition in the South "to the negro's controlling his own labor, carrying on business independently on his own account—in one word, working for his own benefit." A letter from Major General James B. Steedman, stationed in Augusta, Georgia, accompanied the report and confirmed Schurz's views: "the planters . . . have absolutely no conception of what free labor is." Another, from Charles H. Gilchrist, commanding colonel of the Fiftieth U.S. Colored Infantry, from Jackson, Mississippi, mused that talking with Southern white leaders reminded him of their prewar assertions that "the negro cannot take care of himself; capital must own labor," and so on. They had argued for so long that free labor would fail in the South, he wrote, "that it seems they have made themselves believe it, and every man acts as though they were bound to make it so; if it was not going to be the natural result."[23]

Although Schurz reported that it was imperative to convince Southerners that ex-slaves were good workers who did not want handouts from the government, he nonetheless placed his reliance on the government for Southern stability. Schurz reflected radical Republican opinion of late 1865 when he insisted that the government must stay in the South to foster free labor. Remove government protection of the freedmen, he wrote, and the South would resume slavery. He called for "a firm declaration on the part of the Government that national control in the South will not cease until . . . free labor is fully developed and firmly established." He bolstered his position with letters from army officers in the South who shared his views. Major General Peter J. Osterhaus of the U.S. Volunteers wrote from Jackson, Mississippi, in August: "There is no doubt whatever that the state of affairs would be intolerable for all Union men, all recent immigrants from the north, and all negroes, the moment the protection of the United States troops was withdrawn."[24]

Anxious to defuse the indictment of his policies inherent in Schurz's report, which would strengthen his opponents in Congress, Johnson sought another opinion about conditions in the South. At the end of November 1865, Johnson dispatched Lieutenant General U. S. Grant on a week-long tour of North Carolina, South Carolina, and Georgia. The veteran leader of the Union army was a moderate man who was determined to destroy the South's ability to make war but who bore no ill will toward his former enemies. Working with the radicals when necessary to protect himself or his army position, Grant's leanings were nonetheless against extremism, and he hoped to promote a peaceable reconciliation between the sections. A quick survey convinced the general that leading Southerners accepted the results of the war and wanted to return to "self-government, within the Union, as soon as possible."[25]

Much more moderate than Schurz, Grant rounded out the portrait of Republican expectations for free black labor. Grant praised those Freedmen's Bureau agents who "advise the freedmen that by their own industry they must expect to live," and who were finding them employment and enforcing contracts on both parties. But he worried that some agents had spread the belief that the lands of their previous owners would be divided among the freedmen, making them unwilling to sign labor contracts. "In some instances," Grant explained, "I am sorry to say, the freedman's mind does not seem to be disabused of the idea that a freedman has the right to live without care or provision for the future. The effect of the belief in division of lands is idleness and accumulation in camps, towns, and cities." And the end result of freedpeople's lack of foresight? "In such cases I think it will be found that vice and disease will tend to the extermination or great reduction of the colored race."[26]

In December 1865, Johnson greeted the Thirty-ninth Congress with a message announcing that he had "gradually and quietly, and by almost imperceptible steps, sought to restore" the Southern states to the Union. Newly elected Southern senators and congressmen waited to present their credentials and be seated. Johnson also treated the Congress to a disquisition on what he believed was the correct theory of American government. The key word in this explication was *limited*. "Certainly," he said, "the Government of the United States is a limited government, and so is every State government a limited government. With us this idea of limitation spreads through every form of administration—general, State, and municipal—and rests on the great distinguishing principle of the rights of man." In order to protect the purity of the national government and maintain its distribution of powers, so as to protect the liberties of individuals, Johnson told Congress, he hoped the Southern states could immediately "resume their functions as States of the Union." Johnson reminded Congress that "[t]he career of free industry" was open now to African-Americans, and that "their future prosperity and condition must, after all, rest mainly on themselves." The government must resist creating "inequalities." "Here there is no room for favored classes or monopolies," he explained; "the principle of our Government is that of equal laws and freedom of industry. . . . We shall but fulfill our duties as legislators by according 'equal and exact justice to all men,' special privileges to none." He concluded by wondering who would not ask God to guide the nation "onward to a perfect restoration of fraternal affection" so that the current generation could pass on to posterity "our great inheritance of State governments in all their rights, [and] of the General Government in its whole constitutional vigor."[27]

While most Republicans generally agreed with Johnson's theory of government, the reality of Southern Reconstruction under this theory convinced them that, in the face of Southern recalcitrance, a limited government might be less important than the power to enforce the Northern Republican vision for the South. The Republican Congress, in which moderates and radicals outweighed conservative Republicans and Democrats, had no problem dismissing Johnson's conservative message. Moderate and radical congressmen agreed that they would not seat the South's representatives and that Reconstruction must be a more thorough reworking of Southern society than Johnson had sponsored, even at the cost of a more active national government. By the end of 1865, all but the most conservative Northern Republicans shared a clear vision of the postwar South. Radicals emphasized that Southern whites must change, moderates emphasized that freedpeople must work, but all party members planned to use the national government to impose a free labor system in the conquered South.[28]

Northern Republicans who insisted on a free labor South spoke very generally of what that meant. Union soldiers in the South, to whom was left the task of explaining to freedpeople what the coming of freedom meant, described the minimum attributes of a free labor society. "You are now free," one soldier explained in 1865, "but you must know that the only difference you can feel yet, between slavery and freedom, is that neither you nor your children can be bought or sold." Another soldier added: "Shooting and whipping are done with." Speaking to a freedmen's convention in Georgia, a Union general added another point: "All you can earn is your own, you have the . . . right to be as rich as you can make yourselves by your own energy, industry, and economy." Actual labor arrangements at the end of the war were a chaotic mishmash of wage labor, contract labor, and sharecropping, as landowners and ex-slaves each tried to work out an acceptable system. But Northern Republicans, removed from the tumultuous reorganization of Southern labor, could speak in generalities.[29]

Their vision of a new free labor society in the South was based on a picture of the South as an undeveloped wilderness waiting for the efficient labor of free people to bring forth wealth. This image of the postwar South mirrored the primary stage of economic development that Republicans believed lay at the root of the American economic system. The South had remarkable natural resources, it was overwhelmingly agricultural, and it was populated with impoverished adults who were well trained to farm. Since Republicans had never acknowledged the role of start-up capital in economic development, they believed that the South had all the elements necessary to surge into remarkable productivity quickly. Pennsylvania judge and congressman William D. Kelley assured his constituents that the South was a rich land, "gorged with every mineral," full of fertile soil, and blessed with a good climate. In North Carolina, for example, he said, land would grow any vegetables, and "under these abounding stores of natural wealth" lay a belt of gold from forty to one hundred miles wide across the whole state "so richly interlaid with gold that a person with a common frying pan may wash the sands of many of the rivulets and make from one to three dollars per day." Slavery had prevented the realization of Southern wealth, but the introduction of the free labor system would bring the South, with its embarrassment of riches, into flower.[30]

Judge Kelley echoed the sentiments appearing in Republican newspapers. The South was "highly favored with natural advantages," a writer for the *Chicago Tribune* agreed, boasting mineral wealth, rich soil, timber, watercourses, good climate, and numerous harbors. But Southern attempts to avoid God's dictum that "In the sweat of thy face shalt thou eat bread" had brought punishment. Public sentiment branding labor as dishonorable had driven away immigrants and discouraged industry, education, and the growth of cities; "in a word, it was hostile to all those grand agencies in building up a country, which have been fostered with so much care in the East and in the West." "Labor," the author of the article reminded readers, "lies at the foundation of national progress, wealth and prosperity," and the introduction of free labor to the South would "ultimately regenerate a magnificent country long prostrate under the feet of an exacting iniquity."[31]

Only distance from the reality of Southern life permitted such an optimistic vision of the South's potential. The postwar South was certainly rural; a traveler could cover hundreds of miles of terrible roads without seeing an urban center, which, according to the census, could be a settlement of only 8,000. The South's cities were ruined, the fields were overgrown with weeds, much of the population was homeless and hungry. Even after time had allowed people to settle down, poor Southerners were mired in poverty, illiterate, and ill-nourished from their diet of salt pork, corn, and molasses. They lived in one-room cabins made of logs or rough lumber with unbattened cracks; they used a privy out back if they had one at all; they drank from a dug well or a nearby stream. Their imbalanced diet and unsanitary living conditions meant that poor Southerners suffered from diseases associated with malnutrition—pellagra, rickets, hookworm—which sapped their energy, and for which they received almost no medical care. But Northern Republicans downplayed these conditions in the postwar South, mentioning them only to blame the old slave system for degrading all but the wealthy portions of the population. Even when acknowledging the extreme poverty of the South, Northern Republicans insisted that the introduction of a free labor society would quickly revitalize the region.[32]

From their distant vantage point, Northern Republicans could contrast their rosy image of the South as a primitive paradise with their own rapidly changing region. Concentrating on rebuilding an agricultural South peopled by upwardly mobile field hands permitted them to ignore the growing tensions in Northern life. The war had tended to submerge class and ethnic struggle in the North under patriotism, but with the surrender of Lee's troops, stresses quickly reemerged. On their own doorsteps, Northerners had to contend with immigration and urban labor competition, with conflict between employees and employers, with popular anger at wealthy bankers and bondholders, and with prevalent racism. Democrats, with their rhetoric of capitalist conspiracies and support for the working class, could exploit these tensions, but Republicans, tied to a vision of a harmonious community, found the societal stresses troublesome. By focusing on the South, perceiving it as a sort of Elysium waiting to be developed by free labor, Northern Republicans could ignore their own problems.[33]

As Schurz indicated, Northern Republicans believed that what was necessary to rebuild the South and make it prosper was simply to transform its slave society into a free labor system. This meant not only replacing slaves with free workers but also making other fundamental structural changes in Southern life. First, the yeoman farmer, tilling a small farm, must uproot the plantation owner and his large estate. "The old plantation system is no longer possible," the *New York Times* lectured. "The planter must surrender his aristocratic notions and come nearer the standard of the Northern farmer. The system of vast estates must be abandoned and small farms take their place." This would serve the dual function of rejuvenating the Southern economy and replacing a hostile aristocracy with an independent democracy.[34]

Northerners also wanted to see the South diversify its economy. When a conservative gathering of South Carolina planters advised farmers to "cultivate less cotton and more breadstuffs; raise for their own use and for sale, horses, mules and stock of all kinds; cure their own hay, make their own butter and sell the surplus," the *New York Times* called the advice "excellent" and predicted that if it were followed it would rebuild the Southern economy. Indeed, the *Philadelphia Inquirer* attributed a respite from the postwar food shortages in the South to Southerners' grudging acceptance of the idea of crop diversity. Southerners "have learned that the first necessity of life is to eat, and that however promising pecuniarily the cultivation of cotton may be, it will not satisfy hunger." According to the *New York Herald,* in his tour of the South Judge Kelley urged Alabamians "to build rolling-mills, erect furnaces, employ water power . . . and to rotate their crops as we do in the North." In the freedpeople, he lectured, the South had a ready source of labor; Kelley looked forward to the day when black women and girls would spin in cotton mills, just as white women and girls did in the North.[35]

Some even went so far as to suggest that Northerners should replace Southerners in the South. A writer for the *Philadelphia Inquirer* reflected in 1867 that in a generation, when the South had become "thoroughly prosperous," Southern leaders would be "non-Southerners by birth, and the tone of society may be entirely different from what it is now. Northerners and persons of foreign birth will represent Southern interests; and the old aristocracy, for whose benefit the Rebellion was commenced, will have but little influence." Since Virginians were unwilling to work, the *Philadelphia Inquirer* declared two months later, "[t]he only hope for the 'Old Dominion' is the introduction of a hardy race of settlers from the North." Like-minded men in Boston organized the United States Mutual Protection Company to promote the occupation of "desirable plantations in the various Southern States" by "loyal citizens of the Northern States," "thereby infusing" into the South "a healthy and loyal element" while "promoting the pecuniary interests of the patriotic men who shall be instrumental in effecting this work."[36]

There was urgency in these Republican plans for Reconstruction, for the happy vision of a prosperous nation could not be realized until the South converted to free labor. Northerners wanted the South to develop an economic system that was compatible with the North quickly so that the nation could boom. With free labor rebuilding the South, "we rise as a new nation," thundered Pennsylvania congressman Kelley to the citizens of New Orleans in 1867, "sweeping from the rock-bound coast of the storm-lashed Atlantic to the golden shores of the sleeping Pacific," ready to rise and become the envy of the world. The *Philadelphia Inquirer* believed that Kelley spoke for the whole North; one of its writers later reiterated that, with thorough restoration and the cultivation of "a spirit of friendship," "the South . . . will blossom like a rose, and her property will mount to an aggregate far exceeding the returns of the best days of the South, before the Rebellion paralyzed her industry, reduced her resources, and enveloped her in the drapery of woe." Horace Greeley's radical *New York Daily Tribune* fairly palpated with the drive for a Reconstruction settlement, and even a writer for the conservative *New York Times* reflected that one could not "overestimate the results which will be produced in the rich cotton and rice fields of South Carolina and Georgia, and the river bottoms of Mississippi and Louisiana, with the application to them of the skill, energy, enterprise and industry which have made the stony hills of Massachusetts bloom like a garden, and converted the storm-driven plains of the Northwest into the granaries of the world."[37]

With the South and the North working together, the nation would prosper. What Northerners were striving for after the war, explained a writer for the *Philadelphia Inquirer,* was "a reunion of the people North and South—a reunion of hearts and a reunion of hands" to achieve "the prosperity of our people and the glory and honor of our common country." The *Boston Evening Transcript* agreed, calling for the sections to encourage "friendly relations" to promote commerce and industry, "by which the whole republic grows in greatness," and the *New York Daily Tribune* estimated that "a full and final settlement" which would "unlock [the country's] resources and set all its people to work" would "make hundreds of millions' difference in the product of this year's industry."[38]

Many Northerners were doing their part to reunite the sections. When the failure of Southern crops in 1866 left Southerners starving in the spring of 1867, even an exhausted congressman who had begged off from party engagements agreed to canvass for the cause "which appeals so strongly to every just and generous sympathy." Northerners contributed tens of thousands of dollars to a relief effort and declared a general collection day in Northern churches for the aid of "our unfortunate brethren" before the Senate committed a million dollars of federal money for Southern relief. Ex-Sergeant Gilbert H. Bates caught popular attention as he carried an American flag throughout the South, and the New York Firemen's Association bought a "splendid hose carriage" hung with Russian silver bells and carrying "one thousand feet of the finest hose, made to fit the water-hydrants of Columbia" as a present for a fire company in Columbia, South Carolina. One man wrote to the popular *Harper's Weekly* magazine that "the true men of the country" wanted to promote "genuine loyalty, universal brotherhood, and an enduring nationality."[39]

The hose carriage did not pacify South Carolina firefighters, who marched in Confederate gray under a life-size portrait of Stonewall Jackson at their annual parade in 1867 and had to be forced to salute the American flag.[40] Nevertheless, Northern Republicans were pleased to see that other Southerners were anxious to rebuild a prosperous peace with the North. As early as 1866, a few leading Southerners adopted the Republican idea that their economy must operate harmoniously, with all working together for the good of the South. Republicans made much of these men, carefully identifying as statesmen "New Southerners" like Georgia ex-governor Joseph E. Brown and ex-Confederate generals James Longstreet and Wade Hampton. The *Chicago Tribune* joined in lauding "a large and respectable element, consisting of those who, while they fought for the Confederacy, are now atoning for the past by giving their whole soul to the work not only of reconstruction, but also of physical, moral, and intellectual regeneration." "The industrious, thoughtful people of the South, white and black alike, to-day, are hopeful, in spite of political discouragements, as to their industrial future," wrote the *New York Times* in 1867.[41]

This general idea of American prosperity had specific economic meaning for Northern businessmen. Many had invested in the South before the war and hoped that their money would be repaid. Others saw the South as a prime field for investment but dared not risk capital in Southern ventures until the region's situation calmed and it rejoined the American mainstream. When Northern journalist Sidney Andrews traveled to the South in the fall of 1865, he noted that Northern creditors welcomed the business of Southerners who were trying to pay off prewar debts, who were, he said, responsible Unionists with a "keen sense of commercial honor and integrity." Northerners were anxious to help those who were trying to rebuild the South on a secure business footing. The *New York Times,* for example, lauded Northern capitalists who were joining Southern planters to plant with "best advantage and highest profit," pleased that Northern businessmen were "directing their attention to aiding planters and energetic Southern men in the reorganization of Southern labor, industry, and production."[42]

For all Northerners, the most promising sign of recovery from the South would be a good harvest, which would "gratify everyone with the certainty that our future is to be bright and prosperous," according to the *Philadelphia Inquirer.* Republicans believed that crops were the primary factor in economic growth; good crops would prime the economic pump and "set in active motion the sluggish machinery of trade."

"A successful harvest from Maine to California would add at least $1,500,000,000 to the wealth of the country," *Harper's Weekly* announced.[43]

But after the war the news from the fields was not good. The 1861 cotton crop was just under 4.5 million bales; the South did not return to that level of production until 1875. Heavy spring rains in 1866 curtailed planting, so the cotton crop of that year was small; Mississippi and Louisiana were additionally hurt in 1866 by flooding through the levees destroyed during the war. Then, at harvest time, the army worm arrived. By 1867, the South was devastated. Crops were planted that year, but Southerners needed the food sent by Northern relief societies to sustain them until the harvest. Then cotton prices fell to 14 cents a pound and cotton became more expensive to raise than could be realized on its sale. By fall 1867, the South and America in general were suffering "prevailing distress and business stagnation."[44]

The nation's economic slump was a natural product of the transition from a booming wartime economy to a peacetime economy, but its coincidence with the continuing Southern economic weakness and white Southern recalcitrance exasperated Republicans. They maintained that the South was not "blooming like the rose" because white Southern Democrats were terrorizing black labor and chasing away white Northerners who had brought capital and initiative to the South after the war. When the 1865 crops were poorer than expected under the South's new system of free labor, the *Chicago Tribune* blamed the situation on Southern whites who were unwilling to deal with the freedpeople. The *New York Times* agreed, noting that those working fairly with African-Americans were "now making large profits . . .—heavier than under slavery," and warning that those who abused the new free laborers were "laying up for themselves a harvest of retribution, in the disturbance of labor, internal quarrels, and the distrust and dislike of the civilized world." Reviewing the 1867 famine in the South, a writer for the *Cincinnati Daily Gazette* lamented that "[t]he late master is loth to admit that the negro is a freeman, and foolishly supposed that he could spite the world by starving himself." By spurning the first elements of a healthy economy, white Southerners, it seemed, were preventing their own recovery and forestalling the prosperity of the rest of the country.[45]

Northern Republicans abhorred the Black Codes and other indications—like planters' attempts to import Chinese coolies to replace the free black workers—that Southerners were clinging to the past. It was time to move forward to a new national prosperity, and Northerners scorned those whose primary goal was still to hurt the North. Continuing hostility to Northern immigration and disdain of Republicans was irritating enough, but worse was the Southern reluctance to deal fairly with black laborers. Northern Republican papers publicized with stories and graphic illustrations atrocities against freedpeople that began in 1865, when white Southerners as individuals and in groups began attacking freedpeople, intimidating, assaulting, and even killing African-Americans who tried to act upon their new freedom in any way that whites found threatening. The conservative *New York Times* initially warned only that the South's continuing abuse of African-Americans would bring on international disapproval, but riots in Memphis and New Orleans in 1866, where the police joined rioters attacking African-Americans and left at least eighty-six people dead, pushed even conservative Republicans to castigate the Southern whites who refused to accept the results of the war.[46]

By 1867, Northerners' patience was exhausted. Newspapers across the North used the vicious whipping administered to a black girl who had resisted when a white girl had tried to beat her as a symbol of the plight of African-Americans at the hands of white Southerners. In a nominal acquiescence to the letter of the law, whites had forced the African-American girl to apprentice herself to a white woman, who had then ordered her whipped. This incident exemplified the trials of ex-slaves all over the South. Southern whites bowed to the letter of the law, then perverted their actual behavior to approximate slavery. Noting that black people were still whipped and sold as punishment for crimes, a writer for *Harper's Weekly* lamented that "the freedmen are still pursued and sacrificed by the ancient laws of Slavery, and thus the rage of the baffled rebellion expends itself upon the most helpless and unfortunate of the population . . . no duty of this nation is now so solemn and paramount as to take care that the late slaves shall not be tortured." A writer for the *Philadelphia Inquirer* agreed that it would be terribly wrong "to trust the colored race to the tender mercies of their late masters," whose "every action" was marked by "savage vindictiveness."[47]

Republicans blamed the disruption of business and the South's economic stagnation on the white terrorists who tortured ex-slaves in 1865 and 1866, organized white gangs in the summer of 1867, and fed the growing power of the white-supremacist Ku Klux Klan from 1867 to 1873. A writer for the *New York Times* noted that capital shunned insecure situations; and the *Philadelphia Inquirer* disparaged Southern calls for immigration to the section. No doubt one could do well in the South, the paper agreed, but immigrants must be assured "peace, safety and independence." The South could beg for immigration, but Northerners and foreigners could not be induced to settle there until the South changed.[48]

While the Democratic *New York World* lauded the "brave planters" and their sons, who were doing their own work and "stimulat[ing]" the freedmen to great efforts, Northern Republicans were not pleased with Southern white Democrats, who, they believed, clung to the idea of restoring themselves to power politically and were surpassed in every way by African-Americans. Southern politicians were still "incendiary," calling for the resumption of rebellion and giving advice "injurious to the interests of both North and South." Southerners were clinging to "the lost cause" and complaining about their lot. When they refused to register and vote, they were being "stupid" and rejecting opportunities.[49]

The worst offenders, Northern Republicans agreed, were the South's young white men. In 1865, Carl Schurz's report and the letters reprinted in it indicated that the South's young white men were lazy and angry; the Northern press highlighted this theme in the years that followed. "The best thing that the South can do is, to go to work and compel the idle, worthless young men who lounge about village groceries and settlements, to take off their coats and astonish themselves by attempting to earn their own livings," admonished the *Philadelphia Inquirer.* The *Ashtabula (Ohio) Sentinel* agreed, reporting that whites outnumbered blacks in the South two to one but did nothing other than "howl for 'more labor,' being themselves nearly to a man idle." Reporting poor crop prospects from Virginia in 1867, the *Philadelphia Inquirer* explained that "[t]he 'first families' supported themselves, in old times, by selling their slaves; and now, when their trade is gone, instead of putting their shoulders to the wheel, are crying for aid." When Henry A. Wise of Virginia advised "the young men of his State to become farmers and do their own work," *Harper's Weekly* applauded his advice but not his motives. Wise counseled that by doing their own work "they will get rid of negro and foreign emigrant labor." *Harper's Weekly* sternly corrected

Wise by reciting a key rule of political economy: those who do their own work "will have greater means wherewith to employ such labor."[50]

It appeared that the North would have to force the free labor system on the South, and moderate Republicans who had initially dragged their heels at radical plans for government protection of ex-slaves more and more willingly turned to an increasingly active government to do so. A writer for *Harper's Weekly* summed up the changing Republican ideas about Southern Reconstruction. Recalling recent events highlighted in the press, he reflected that when Northerners who had moved to the South were forced to flee back home, when Union men in the South were tortured and killed, when an army general felt obliged to draw his gun to protect himself in a Texas railroad car, when courts and legislatures were controlled by rebels, there was only one solution. Either "the authority of the Government to protect citizens must be altogether abandoned in that region, or it must be enforced by the military arm until there is such a thorough reorganization of civil administration that life, liberty, and property are again uniformly safe."[51]

After the events of 1865 indicated that Southern whites planned the reinstatement of quasi-slavery, all but the most conservative Republicans determined to protect freedpeople as free laborers, attacking Johnson's policies and the Democratic regimes in the South. In the face of Johnson's return of property to ex-Confederates, Union officers tried unsuccessfully to confirm land titles to the freedpeople who had been working abandoned land; Congress passed a Southern Homestead Act to grant land to settlers who had cultivated it for five years. To stop white attacks on black rights, in 1866 Congress extended the Freedmen's Bureau, which had become an arbiter of labor disputes between black workers and white landowners, and enacted, over Johnson's veto, a civil rights law that guaranteed African-Americans the same rights for protection of person and property as whites. The new law defined African-Americans as citizens with the right to own or rent property, to have equal access to courts, and to make and enforce contracts. Forceful though these laws were, they nonetheless were moderate legislation, designed by moderates, to balance radicals' recognition of the African-American worker's need for protection with the conservative abhorrence of a powerful government.

When Southern intransigence continued unabated, Northern Republicans rallied behind the Fourteenth Amendment to the Constitution,

which placed in the nation's fundamental law the minimum requirements that seemed necessary to construct a free labor society throughout America. A vague and complicated amendment, the Fourteenth
Amendment was compromise legislation designed to guarantee the
rights and freedom of African-Americans while it also aimed to destroy
the power of the Southern aristocracy that presumably had led the South
out of the Union and that was thwarting Northern Reconstruction plans.
The amendment undermined the power of the white Southern leadership by repudiating the Confederate debt, prohibiting leading Confederates from holding office, and denying claims for repayment for emancipated slaves. At the same time, the amendment defined African-
Americans as citizens—placing this definition in the Constitution would
prevent later Congresses from overturning the Civil Rights Act of
1866—and declared that states could not deprive "any person of life, liberty, or property, without due process of law; nor deny to any person
within its jurisdiction the equal protection of the laws." It also nudged
Southerners toward black suffrage by threatening the reduction of congressional representation to any state that denied the vote to twenty-
one-year-old male citizens in good standing. The Fourteenth Amendment promised to defend African-American laborers without intruding
on state prerogatives for suffrage regulations or effecting any extraordinary program of land confiscation. In mid-1866, Congress made ratification of the Fourteenth Amendment a key requirement for each Southern
state's readmission to the Union.

In contrast to the uncooperative Southern whites, freedpeople seemed to
Republicans to be model free Americans, working hard to rebuild the
South as they climbed the ladder to economic success. Modern economists have established that the decline in Southern cotton production
after the war was attributable largely to a shrinkage in the South's effective labor supply as African-American women stayed at home and men
chose to spend less of their time in the fields and more with their families, in church, in school, and at leisure. The rural black population immediately after the war provided between 28 percent and 37 percent less
manpower than it had done when forced by slave owners to work at
maximum human capacity. But Northern Republicans did not see a dramatic change in the habits of black labor; they saw good free laborers
struggling to work their way up.[52]

Northern observers in the South after the war echoed the observation of Frederick Law Olmstead before it, when he reported the dreams of one Louisiana slave as if they were the stereotypical desires of a traditional free laborer to accumulate capital, buy land, and begin to farm on his own. If he were free, the man had explained, "I would go to work for a year, and get some money for myself," Olmstead reported, "—den—den—den, massa, dis is what I do—I buy me, fus place, a little house, and little lot of land." After the war, Northern observers repeatedly reported that "[t]he freedmen have a passion for land. Where a little can be obtained they are always purchasers." In 1865, journalist Whitlaw Reid quoted an old slave: "What's de use of being free if you don't own land enough to be buried in? Might juss as well stay [a] slave all yo' days."[53]

In the years immediately after the war, while Democrats insisted that ex-slaves were lazy ne'er-do-wells, the Republican press emphasized the great success of the South's enthusiastic and powerful black workers, whom Northerners perceived as a monolithic group characterized by poverty and a willingness to work its way up. African-Americans worked so well under the free labor system, the *New York Times* reported in 1865, that "within the former military lines of the United States there now reigns a state of order and industry among the freedmen which sets a good example to their employers, and one well worthy of emulation." "The result of free labor," concluded the *Cincinnati Daily Gazette,* "in a short time, will be the doubling of the aggregate wealth of the South." "The colored people are peaceably disposed, and, unless molested, will labor industriously for an education, and for the means of supporting life," opined the *Philadelphia Inquirer.* The *New York Times* agreed that "free negro labor has been neither unreliable nor unprofitable. . . . [T]he freedmen are willing to work when fairly treated and reasonably paid." The *Chicago Tribune* defended the freedpeople's "careful industry and habitual economy," reporting in 1867 that freedpeople had received fewer rations from the Freedmen's Bureau than whites since 1865, and that "during the past two years, they have gathered about them more creature comforts than are owned by the operatives of England, and last year hoarded in . . . savings banks . . . more than a quarter of a million of dollars." "The freedmen are showing their capability of becoming industrious citizens, [their emigration] would be a positive injury to the whole country," concluded the *Philadelphia Inquirer.* The *New York Times* agreed. America needed ex-slaves to restore "the productiveness and prosperity of the South." While white Southerners remained convinced that African-Americans were inherently lazy and stupid, Northern Republicans had come to view the freedpeople as exemplary workers.[54]

Indeed, Northern Republicans compared African-Americans favorably with white Southerners. "As a mass," a correspondent of the *Cincinnati Daily Gazette* wrote, freedpeople were industrious and sober while whites were indolent and drunken, African-Americans were "humble, but self-reliant; teachable, and yet firm; anxious to learn, but not driven about by every wind of doctrine. . . . They reject the idea of accepting the lands of their former masters, taken from them by confiscation; and their ambition is to buy, with their own hard-earned dollars, a little piece of land that they may call their own." Countering complaints that black plantation laborers demanded high wages for poor work, *Harper's Weekly* blamed white Southerners for teaching African-Americans that liberty meant laziness and suggested that it would take exorbitant wages to make up the large arrears of slavery. "If any colored man says a foolish thing," complained *Harper's Weekly,* conservatives instantly predicted a revolutionary bloodbath. But those same persons are "very careful never to publish any of the significant facts of the rapid advances made by the freedmen in every good direction." And no freedman was voicing "sentiments so atrocious as were constantly dropping" from "conservatives," both before and after the war.[55]

Indicative of African-Americans' determination to succeed was their marked enthusiasm for education. As soon as T. W. Sherman had captured the Sea Islands of Georgia and South Carolina, enabling Northern missionaries to open schools for the former slaves left on the islands, Northerners noted the determination of African-Americans to read and write. With the end of the war their enthusiasm for education became even more pronounced. "The thirst for knowledge among the blacks is extraordinary," reported the *Chicago Tribune* in 1867; "out of their scanty earnings they have built or bought 391 school buildings and support 1,000 schools." Northern Republicans interpreted this quest for education as proof of the freedmen's status as good Americans who wanted to rise. Education was fundamental for a person to understand his economic and political interests, and to enable him to use his labor intelligently and productively. "Popular education is the true ground upon which the efficiency and the successes of free-labor society grow," Carl Schurz sententiously declared.[56]

The Republican prescription for black success was the same one offered to white workers. Indeed, newspapers from the conservative *New
York Times* to the radical *Chicago Tribune* insisted that both black and
white laborers played the same role in American society. "Nowhere in
this free land has the question of labor anything to do with the fact that
different races exist within its limits," wrote the *New York Times* in 1865.
"Industry is a universal duty, resting as much upon one race as another.
It is the basis of all civil and social prosperity; and every inhabitant of
the country, whatever his color, whatever his extraction, is under the
same obligation to be something more than a mere consumer—something else than a mere drone in the hive. He is bound to contribute personally in some way to the general well-being." Two years later, the *Chicago Tribune* reiterated that the Republican party cared not about race
but about "the rights of labor. The question of race is merely an incident
of the situation, not by any means the object of the struggle in which the
respective parties are engaged."[57]

The worker's road to success was spelled out in popular success manuals, which promised economic prosperity to those who adhered to old-
fashioned, free labor values. This was the age of Horatio Alger, whose
first and most famous book, *Ragged Dick: Or, Street Life in New York with
the Boot Blacks*, ran as a serial in 1867 and was published in book form
in 1868. Not simply the archetypal story of a hard-working bookblack's
rise to prosperity, *Ragged Dick* was also a portrait of a nation in which
the poor and the wealthy shared the same values and economic interests.
In the story, the honest, plucky, and handsome Dick Hunter is helped
along by a series of older, benevolent businessmen who offer classic free
labor advice, which Dick absorbs gratefully. "All labor is respectable, my
lad, and you have no cause to be ashamed of any honest business," an
older businessman tells young Hunter, "yet when you can get something
to do that promises better for your future prospects, I advise you to do
so. Till then earn your living in the way you are accustomed to, avoid extravagance, and save up a little money if you can."[58]

Alger's business sage echoed popular postwar wisdom, which depicted a land of economic harmony and lauded financial success, as
great businessmen promoted the public good by increasing production
and making the wilderness "blossom like the rose" by using money liberally to develop national resources. In the first few years after the war,
Harper's Weekly ran a series of sketches of prominent Americans, explaining how individuals could attain such greatness. Financier and rail-

road magnate Daniel Drew "was trained on his father's farm to industry and frugality." With only a rudimentary education, he entered business at eighteen after his father had died "leaving little or no property." Young Drew made his financial start in cattle, then moved into steamboats, railroads, and banking. Nonetheless, Drew retained the basic free labor values of industry, "practical agriculture" (he maintained a cattle farm in New York), religion, and education. With significant words, *Harper's Weekly* concluded: "Mr. Drew is still in vigorous health, and, to all appearances, has many years of active labor before him." A similar story about banker Henry Keep explained that "[h]is careful habits soon enabled him to accumulate a small capital," which he managed to parlay into a fortune. It would take too long to recount all his triumphs, *Harper's Weekly* told its readers, "and yet, if these could be all written out, we should have an example of unwearying vigilance, intelligent energy, and far-seeing sagacity."[59]

Prosperity, it appeared, did not depend on birth, or wealth, or anything but a willingness to work, the ability to work intelligently, and the virtue of frugality. *Harper's Weekly* portrayed wealthy Americans as the children of poverty. A Wall Street king "was born in the boot of a stage; John Jacob Astor was born . . . in a butcher's stall; . . . Daniel Drew began life as a cattle-drover. Henry Keep appears to have been born in the poorhouse, and to have begun life as a runaway apprentice." It depicted even Cornelius Vanderbilt, heir to a Staten Island ferry business, as an impoverished child. *Harper's Weekly* explained that these men succeeded through their own hard efforts. "In ninety-nine cases out of every hundred greatness is achieved by hard, earnest labor and thought. . . . And thus it happens that the really great, the truly successful men of our country have been self-taught and self-made."[60]

Northern Republicans' counsel to freedpeople on how to behave like good free laborers sounded just like the prescription for white success. Speaking to a mixed-race audience as he toured the South in 1867, Pennsylvania congressman William D. Kelley echoed the *New York Daily Tribune*'s advice that communities of freedpeople should begin by farming, then gradually develop simple and then complex manufacturing. Kelley advised Southern freedpeople "to practice industry, to be just to all, to live in peace with all, to show themselves worthy of their freedom by their conduct, and to seek education." He also told them "to get independence for themselves by mechanical pursuits and by acquiring land."

According to the *New York Herald*, Kelley spoke directly to the freed-people in Montgomery, "reminding them that their freedom meant the right to toil for their living and get paid for it. . . . Freedom means that a good man is better than a bad man, and the smart man wins the race." He counseled ex-slaves to take care of their wives, educate their children, pay their taxes, and study national politics. Revealing the Republican expectation that African-Americans would begin at the bottom of the economic pyramid and work their way up, he encouraged mechanics to set up their own businesses and told farm laborers to try to get their own farms through the Homestead Act, by which the government offered western farm land for a nominal fee to anyone willing to settle and farm it. The *New York Daily Tribune* estimated that, if they worked hard, freedpeople "may all be thrifty free-holders and their own employers, owning a large share of the soil of the South, within the present century."[61]

To help ex-slaves to gain the skills necessary to become competent free laborers at the first stage of economic development, Republicans encouraged "manual," or vocational, education. At the same time they emphasized the idea of succeeding without government help by insisting that schools should be funded by private philanthropy. In 1867, the Republican press made much of "The National Farm-School, for colored orphans and for the children of colored soldiers." A well-connected New Yorker founded the school in March 1866 to be both a primary and an agricultural school. Pupils would receive an elementary education at the same time they were made into "practical and competent farmer[s]." The school had a 100-acre farm, worked in part by the students. The plan for the black students was strikingly similar to Republican ideas for young white men. School administrators hoped to send their pupils to the South or Southwest, where they could flourish on lands they took up under the Homestead Act. While able to accommodate only 50 children in the beginning, the school's managers hoped to take more than 200 when the necessary buildings were finished.[62]

Republican support for ex-slave workers did not indicate Republican support for workers who appeared to reject the idea of working their way up. The positive images of African-Americans after the war contrasted vividly with Republican portrayals of urban immigrant workers, for example, who were usually loyal to the Democratic party and were thus natural scapegoats for the Republicans. The Republican press caricatured Irish-Americans, for example, as the antithesis of good free workers. Thomas Nast's cartoons led the parade of devastating images that portrayed Irish-American laborers and servants as drunk, lazy, and stupid. Critically, the Republican representation of these workers attributed violence to those who did not fit the Republican free labor image. *Harper's Weekly* reveled in an Irish-American riot in March 1867, comparing the rioters to the terrorists of the French Revolution and recalling that Irish-Americans had "hunted and tortured and massacred the unfortunate and innocent colored population" of New York City during the wartime draft riots.[63]

Just as Republican support for freedpeople did not mean support for all workers, it also did not mean support for general advancement of all African-Americans. In their vision of the future, Northern Republicans kept their sights on the South and the fate of Southern freedmen, largely ignoring Northern black workers. The obvious reason for this omission was numbers. There were a great deal more Southern than Northern blacks, and their high percentage of the population necessarily made them greater players in the economic arena of that section. Equally important, though, was the fact that Northern blacks were systematically discriminated against in an established society, while Southern society was undergoing dramatic revision. It seemed easier to reorganize society in the South than in the North. Also important was the Democrats' use of racial conflict in Northern workplaces to bolster the demands of the "white laboring classes." With no politically palatable solution to offer to actual workplace discrimination—racist Northern workers would not stomach agitation for Northern black rights—Republicans preferred to ignore Northern issues and to concentrate on the South. In fact, when Republicans did talk about Northern black labor it was usually to explain how economic laws would eventually end employment discrimination without political intervention. Republicans found it much easier to imagine distant freedmen working their way up in the fields than to visualize reworking Northern society.[64]

Republicans had emotional as well as political reasons for concentrating on Southern African-Americans. The freedpeople offered Northern Republicans a traditional image of how they believed America's political economy should operate, in the face of a nation that was rapidly making that vision obsolete. Southern African-Americans were largely agricultural workers, which fit nicely into the Republican theory of political economy of the mid-nineteenth century, while Northern blacks tended to be manual workers in urban areas. While young men and women in the North were leaving their parents' farms for the big cities or the West as quickly as they could, mainstream Northerners could concentrate on "rearing" the Southern freedman instead, using the freedpeople to illustrate how the economy was supposed to operate. Northern Republicans nostalgically lamented the loss of an idyllic farming life; *Harper's Weekly* repeatedly printed idealized farm scenes, and the editor of the *Nation* puzzled that "newspapers and poets are all busy painting the delights of the agricultural life; but the farmer, though he reads their articles and poems, quits the farm as soon as he can find any other way of making a livelihood; and if he does not, his son does." The real problem in the nation, stated the *Ashtabula (Ohio) Sentinel* in 1869, was that no American wanted to work any longer: "He won't serve an apprenticeship to any manual art, or dig, delve, or mine, wash, cook, or plough, milk cows or bear children, if he can possibly get anybody else to do it for him." Farm girls sat idle and well dressed, "waiting to be married"; farm boys left home to "peddle . . . quack medicines" or clerk in a store. The one exception to this pattern, it noted, was the freedpeople, who did all the work in the South while the whites sat idle. By looking to the South's underdeveloped resources and its willing agricultural workers, Northern Republicans could continue to believe in the vitality of a traditional America where young people stayed on the farm and prospered gradually through hard work.[65]

"When the war was over the question, 'What shall we do with the blacks?' agitated the whole country," commented the *New York Times* in 1867. Everyone feared they would not work.

> Well, to the joy of his friends and the discomfiture of his enemies, the negro became an industrious laborer. It is true things did not work very smoothly the first year, but they were a great deal better the second, and this year the demonstration of the industry and fidelity of the colored class is complete. Throughout the South there is only one answer to the question as to how the negroes are doing: "Very well; better than could have been expected; better than ever before"—variant in form, but so strong in its cumulative evidence as to leave no doubt in the mind of any dispassionate observer.

Indeed, Republican newspapers were quick to highlight any good crop news from the South, attributing it to the free labor system. When the government ceased issuing rations during the summer of 1867, the *Phil-*

adelphia Inquirer reported that Southerners would have to take care of themselves, but that "[t]hey will be abundantly able to do so, for there never was such a crop of food raised in the South, even in the days of its greatest prosperity." Citing the crop returns for 1870, the *Chicago Tribune* insisted that "the abolition of slavery has not diminished the producing capacity of negro labor. [The figures] also show that, however numerous may be the exceptions, the labor of the South was last year most actively employed."[66]

From 1865 to 1867, Northern Republicans believed that African-Americans were going to be good workers in a traditional Republican vision of American society. But recalcitrant Southern whites, aided and abetted by a president who clung to the idea of a limited government, were systematically abusing African-Americans, cheating them of wages, assaulting them, and preventing them from accumulating property. Over the next three years, Northern Republicans would work to find a way to guarantee that white Southerners did not impede black Americans' efforts to join the free labor economy.

2
_____

The Mixed Blessing of Universal Suffrage, 1867–1870

Pleased by the former slaves' attempts to build a free labor society, by the end of 1866 Northern Republicans were angry and frustrated with the recalcitrance of Southern whites, who disdained the Fourteenth Amendment and refused to reorganize in good faith a society based on free labor. Trying to impose a free labor system on the South through legislation, and making ex-slaves free agents in that system, had clearly not been a complete solution to the Southern question. To explain why their simple plan had failed, Republicans fell back on their understanding of society.

Americans in the nineteenth century saw the economic world in political terms. The vote had long been understood as the only way a man could protect his economic rights. Unless a man could vote, he was at the mercy of any government that determined to tax his property, or even to confiscate it. Without property, he became dependent on others for survival. His economic dependence would destroy political independence, and the country gradually would fall under the control of the wealthy and powerful. Ultimately, then, suffrage in America was an economic right as much as it was a political one, and according ex-slaves the right to vote was the logical solution to the problem of protecting African-Americans as free laborers. But the enforcement of black suffrage necessitated a dramatic assumption of power by the federal government, and few Northerners were willing to venture such an expansion of government until they had utterly lost confidence in Southern whites' good faith efforts to build a free labor South that would work in harmony with the North.[1]

Immediately after the war, radicals like Carl Schurz advocated black suffrage on the principle of human equality, for the practicality of building up a Republican constituency in the South, and as a guarantee that the Northern plan for the South's conversion to a free labor system would be carried out. Southern whites could not be trusted to usher in a new economic system that would bring the South into line with the North. Freedpeople, in contrast, appeared to be loyal to the Union and the free labor system it represented. "In all questions concerning the Union, the national debt, and the future social organization of the South," wrote Schurz in his "Report on the Condition of the South," "the feelings of the colored man are naturally in sympathy with the views and aims of the national government." This was of special concern, since the addition of 4 million freedpeople to the census would increase the South's representation in Congress dramatically, threatening to increase the Southern Democratic presence in government. Schurz explained that the peculiar circumstances of the freedmen meant that their personal interests were identical to the interests of the nation. "When they vote only for their own liberty and rights, they vote for the rights of free labor, for the success of an immediate important reform, for the prosperity of the country, and for the general interests of mankind."[2]

Unlike radicals, moderate and conservative Republicans initially joined Democrats in disapproving of black suffrage. Both Democratic and Republican concerns about black voting lay in the American theory of a republican government. While Democrats based their opposition to black suffrage on their conviction that the American government was designed for white men, Republicans worried that black suffrage would distort different aspects of the republican government ideal. First, the argument for African-American suffrage ran counter to the traditional belief that, to understand his interests, a voter must be educated. Since teaching slaves to read had been a crime in the antebellum South, the vast majority of freedmen were illiterate. Opponents of black suffrage drummed on the point that the untutored freedpeople were unfit for the vote. Even the delegates at the 1866 Georgia Freedmen's Convention could not agree to endorse universal suffrage in the face of black illiteracy, and the Georgia Equal Rights Association and the *Loyal Georgian*, the state's only black newspaper immediately after the war, resisted universal suffrage. Instead they came out for "impartial" suffrage, which would permit property or education qualifications for voting, so long as they applied to whites and blacks alike.[3]

While the education question was troubling, the key stumbling block for Republicans was one they shared with Democrats: their conception of the federal government. In the American system, each state determined the qualifications it deemed necessary in its own voters, and on this principle of state power Democrats held firm. The idea of federal enfranchisement of African-Americans seemed to some a great magnification of the power of the federal government. In his first message to Congress, President Johnson argued that the federal government was unable to extend the franchise to African-Americans in states, and, for all their anger at his other actions, moderate and conservative Republicans, as well as virtually all Democrats, sympathized with his explication of constitutional precedent. "What right has Ohio and R[hode] Island to meddle with suffrage in V[irginia] and Florida?" asked Republican Edward Bates of Missouri. Until 1867, radical Republicans who supported black suffrage had to content themselves with the Fourteenth Amendment clause that encouraged state enfranchisement of African-Americans by threatening reductions in the congressional representation of states who denied or "abridged" suffrage to adult males.[4]

When Southern white abuse of African-Americans continued and Johnson's Southern legislatures refused outright to ratify the Fourteenth Amendment, however, formerly moderate Republicans began to shift over to the previously radical position in favor of government enforcement of black suffrage. Ensuring that freedpeople could help to write their own laws would guarantee that their rights were protected. As they watched former slaves suffer under white Southerners' oppression, moderate Republicans increasingly came to agree with Schurz that the vote for freedmen would be "the best permanent protection against oppressive class-legislation, as well as against individual persecution." A writer for the *Philadelphia Inquirer* explained "[t]hat full protection, and the enjoyment of the condition of freedom could not be insured to the blacks as long as they were disfranchised." Giving blacks the vote made it in white people's interest to treat ex-slaves "with something like fairness." "Equal rights are the sovereign salve for the soreness of different classes, races and interests," reported the *Cincinnati Daily Gazette*. The vote "would dissipate those discontents which, where classes are excluded from a voice in affairs, break into insurrection."[5]

While Republicans increasingly justified black suffrage by citing each man's need to defend his own economic rights, the theory that suffrage would protect the American system of private property came under fire after the Civil War. The vote was a social good so long as everyone understood and believed in the traditional free labor system, the idea of working his way up through hard work in a harmonious economic world. But by 1867, it was increasingly clear to Northerners that a labor interest, which most had previously seen as a minor group in American life, despite the vibrancy of the urban working community, was becoming much stronger. No longer could mainstream Republicans rest confident that all would vote to sustain a system based on the idea of an organic political economy in which all members worked in harmony.[6]

Almost as soon as the war was over, organized labor challenged the Republican belief that the nation was distinguished by the harmony of its economy, arguing instead that there was an inherent struggle between labor and capital in America. Repeated strikes, agitation for an eight-hour workday, and the proliferation of workers' organizations directly attacked the deeply held Republican belief in an organic society. In 1865, the *New York Times* felt obliged to remind those attending labor meetings that the interests of labor and capital were the same; in 1866, the *Workingman's Advocate,* a Chicago labor newspaper, told its readers that Republicans and Democrats "are the twin progeny of capital, conceived in sin and born in iniquity, so far as the elevation of the producing classes." The first national congress of the National Labor Union in August 1866 drew more than 60,000 people; its effort to organize workers to advocate their special interests drew the approbation of Karl Marx, who linked the Americans' efforts with his own at the International Workingmen's Association in Geneva.[7]

Workers' attacks on Republican ideas about political economy forced party members to reexamine their understanding of society, beginning with a redefinition of the American worker. Based on a preindustrial economy, wartime Republican theory held that almost every American who engaged in any sort of productive activity was a worker. Even wealthy capitalists were employing their capital—the fruits of their labor—in various pursuits that advanced the public good. But the war years had seen both the development of large-scale industry and increasing accumulations of wealth. Urban factories were employing larger numbers of operatives than ever before, and, increasingly, these "workers" were destined to remain wage laborers for the rest of their life rather than to use their unskilled positions to accumulate capital and prosper. At the same time, industrialists and bankers were starting to amass fortunes. So while Republicans continued to talk generally of the American "worker" as Everyman, usually a farmer or small business owner who would gradually work his way up the economic ladder, that definition was becoming obsolete. Party members also increasingly spoke of "workers" when referring to people who identified themselves as part of a labor interest and usually people engaged in long-term unskilled or semi-skilled labor.[8]

While party members continued to believe that their organization supported the average working man by using the government to clear the way for individual enterprise, workers' attacks on the Republicans' traditional understanding of what was good for labor made it unclear how the party would ultimately stand with regard to a labor interest. In 1867, the *Chicago Tribune* reiterated Republican support for the traditional American worker who fit into the free labor theory, while attacking organized labor in language that reflected the growing split between perceptions of traditional and disaffected workers. "More than half of the people of Illinois are capitalists, to the degree of competency or independence," it explained, "and more than half of the remainder are capitalists to the degree of comfort and insurance against want or distress." These citizens "obtained their property by the double process of working and saving," since, it explained, both were essential to success. Workers who did not succeed did not have legitimate grievances about wages or working conditions, rather they were profligate, "spend[ing] their earnings as fast as they get them" on "liquor, tobacco, amusements, . . . games . . . [and] fast company." "Envious of their neighbors' prosperity," they were "unwilling to copy their example of economy and industry." These dangerous men were "the fomenters and leaders of strikes," wanting "twelve hours' wages" for "six hours' work."[9]

The *Chicago Tribune* did not speak for the entire Republican party, which was not united against a labor interest. In the late 1860s, while most Republicans remained true to the core principle of a harmonious society of good workers, some prominent party radicals, such as Massachusetts representative Benjamin F. Butler and abolitionist leader Wendell Phillips, took the party's initial commitment to labor in the direction of class activism. By 1867, the most significant figure in the growing schism was the prominent antislavery politician Benjamin F. Wade of Ohio. Wade was himself from a working background—he had been a cattle drover and had worked on the Erie Canal before studying law and entering politics—and he was committed to both laborers and freed-people. His star had risen with the growing fight between Congress and President Johnson and culminated with Wade's leadership of the radical faction in Congress. In March 1867, the Senate elected Wade the president pro tem of the Senate, the next man in line to succeed to the presidency if Johnson should be removed.[10]

Some Republicans followed Wade's path and approached the question of black suffrage as a blow for the rights of American workers, even those workers who were poor, uneducated, and disliked. In January 1867, a writer for *Harper's Weekly* reminded readers that "[t]he basis of the State Governments must be the people of the States, not a class of them, and not those merely who have been hitherto considered the people." He advocated universal suffrage with only age and residency requirements, since educational restrictions in the South would leave political power "in the hands of a class, and that class the most hostile to the Government." In February, the popular Reverend Henry Ward Beecher argued that universal suffrage would educate the lower classes; the *New York Daily Tribune* printed his speech in its entirety despite editor Horace Greeley's own misgivings about universal suffrage. In April 1868, an article in *Harper's Weekly* reiterated that in America, "the people" meant everyone, even "what are called in other countries the lower classes, however really low in ignorance and degradation a part of the city population may be."[11] A writer for the *Cincinnati Daily Gazette* defended Massachusetts congressman Henry Wilson's call for universal suffrage, arguing that "60,000 who happen to be poor should not be subject to the will of 40,000 who happen to be rich." Connecting the widely discussed English Reform movement to expand the franchise with the black suffrage movement, *Harper's Weekly* concluded that the world was progressing to a new era of universal equality.[12]

Despite those radicals of Wade's stripe, however, most members of the Republican party did not endorse black or labor radicalism; conservatives and even some moderates had probably backed Wade for his important Senate position with the knowledge that his extreme stands would doom the removal of President Johnson and thus ultimately thwart radical control of the government. While radicals and some moderates argued for universal black suffrage on the grounds of majority rule, most moderates and conservatives were much more comfortable with the idea of impartial, but not universal, suffrage in the South. Even writers for the radical *New York Daily Tribune* and *Boston Evening Transcript* added their voices to those appearing in more moderate newspapers like the *Philadelphia Daily Evening Bulletin* and the *New York Times* in advocating impartial suffrage. Similarly, Carl Schurz uneasily suggested that suffrage qualification would be unobjectionable if it were applied even-handedly to both races.[13]

Growing Republican support for black suffrage did not indicate a general shift toward a radical belief in class conflict; rather it showed Republicans' determination to enforce a traditional system of free labor in the South. Since those Southerners who fit the model for the informed American citizen opposed the Republicans' plans, party members were willing to turn to the uneducated mass of workers to realize them. It was no accident that the achievement of black suffrage undermined more radical reforms that would have redistributed property in favor of the ex-slaves. Suffrage trumped discussions of confiscation of Southern lands and their redistribution to freedpeople. Even as the debate over black suffrage raged, Republicans joined Democrats in howling at confiscation proponent Thaddeus Stevens's "Grand Larceny Scheme" of confiscation. A writer in the radical *Chicago Tribune* sternly reminded Stevens that Northerners wanted "freedom and equality [to] be firmly established in the South . . . and that government shall be wielded by the friends of the Union," but nothing else. "Give the country reconstruction on the basis of universal suffrage, and it will require but a few years to change the whole structure of society in the South, without confiscation, without vindictive measures of any kind, and without even the disfranchisement of the rebel population," he prophesied. The vote, it seemed, would help to transform the South almost magically into a free labor society without launching America into dangerous new experiments in political economy.[14]

Standing firmly behind the efficacy of the vote to achieve economic equality, and realizing that they had to take a stronger hand with the South even at the expense of a stronger national government, congressional Republicans passed the Military Reconstruction Act on March 2,

1867, over Johnson's veto. The act called for the organization of Southern conventions to rewrite Southern constitutions. Critically, congressional Republicans had stipulated that the conventions' delegates would be elected by universal manhood suffrage; that is, the freedmen would vote. In addition, Congress stipulated that the new constitutions must include black suffrage. Thaddeus Stevens neatly summed up the arguments for black voting: "if it be just, it should not be denied; if it be necessary, it should be adopted; if it be a punishment to traitors, they deserve it." "The Military Reconstruction Act," Republican politician James G. Blaine later wrote, was of "transcendent importance and . . . unprecedented character. It was the most vigorous and determined action ever taken by Congress in time of peace. The effect produced by the measure was far-reaching and radical. It changed the political history of the United States. But," he concluded, "it is well to remember that it never could have been accomplished except for the conduct of the Southern leaders."[15]

While Northern Republicans were sanguine about African-American voters in the spring of 1867, the political actions of freedmen in the summer of that year made conservative and moderate Republicans begin to equate Southern ex-slaves with labor radicals who believed in class struggle. With the passage of the Military Reconstruction Act, Northerners and Southerners, white and black, scrambled to organize the freedpeople politically. For the ex-slaves, the summer of 1867 was a time of excitement and rejoicing as rallies and debates pulled them into the American political system. For some Southern whites, it was a time to attempt to create a new coalition with African-Americans; for others it was a time to unite as a "white man's party," intimidating and harassing freedpeople, who seemed to be rising above their station; for yet others, it was a time to disdain the whole process and to remain outside it. Moderate Northern Democrats accepted the finality of black suffrage even if they did not like it, and welcomed the idea "that the negro can no longer be the pivot of our politics" at the same time they began to construct the argument for the eventual destruction of black rights. More than anyone else, Northern Republicans welcomed the new black Republican voters in the South, but as they observed Southern activities in the summer of 1867, it seemed there was cause to be nervous about their new allies.[16]

As soon as the Military Reconstruction Act became law, some white

Southerners hurried to organize voters in the South. Much of what they said raised Northern Republican hopes for the region. "Mass meetings of white and colored citizens are being held all over" the South, reported *Harper's Weekly,* as leading Southern whites appeared to discard their opposition to Republican measures and tried to attract new black voters into their political camp. The white leaders at these rallies endorsed political equality for all and appeared to call for biracial cooperation to rebuild the South. At one rally on March 18, held in Columbia, South Carolina, prominent ex-Confederate Wade Hampton "advised the freedmen to give their friends at the South a fair trial, and if they were found wanting, it was then time enough to go abroad for sympathy. It was to their interest to build up the South; for as the country prospered, so would they prosper." Another white orator, William H. Talley, told the audience that "the white man and the colored man of the South have the same interest, the same destiny." Even the Democratic *New York World* judged that "the planters are rivalling the activity of the Radicals in appeals to the negro mind."[17]

The moderate Southern press followed the lead of these New Southern politicians, and the Northern press took note. As it approvingly reported that the *Charleston Mercury* was addressing black voters directly, the *New York Times* revealed its habituation to the idea of educated voters by missing the fact that few ex-slaves would actually be able to read the papers. The *Chicago Tribune* told readers that the Southern "press are all turning their attention to secure the negro vote"; it was "impossible to take up a Southern newspaper or read a Southern speech, without seeing that the negro has become the centre of attraction in Southern politics."[18]

Northerners initially learned from the press that the freedmen joined the white leaders in their hopes for the future. Two African-American speakers "evidently agreed with the white ones" at the Columbia meeting; one maintained that "the negroes would not rest until the whites were enfranchised" and the other argued that "the question to be considered in elections was not whether a candidate was black or white, but was he honest." A "large and enthusiastic meeting of whites and blacks" adopted conservative resolutions in Petersburg, Virginia; in the mayoral contest in Huntsville, Alabama, "the negro vote assisted to defeat the agent of the Freedmen's Bureau." In April, the *Philadelphia Inquirer* reported a conservative convention in Nashville, where an African-American orator and former Union soldier spoke like a good Republican. "Mr. Williams took the ground that the owners of the soil and the laborers were identified in interest, and should co-operate for the good of each other and the country." The *New York Times* maintained that freedmen would vote with their employers, "naturally act[ing] with those on whose capital they live. Their first and strongest feeling is that their interests are the same—that they must stand or fall, prosper or pine together." In May, six African-Americans even joined the Tennessee State Conservative Convention, which denounced Congress and the radicals and applauded the Confederacy, and September's Alabama Conservative Convention featured at least two African-American orators. Stories of cooperation between ex-slaves and former Democrats were prevalent enough to make radical Republicans feel obliged to scoff at interracial meetings, arguing either that the black attendees were there by compulsion or that the cooperating black leaders—even prominent ones like South Carolina's Beverly Nash—had no influence in the black community.[19]

The radical *Chicago Tribune* and *Cincinnati Daily Gazette* gibed at the sudden friendliness of white Southerners for freedpeople, sneering that "no sooner are the blacks placed on political equality, than the late masters discover that the strongest emotion of their nature is their love for the blacks," but other Republicans were more charitable. When Southern leaders addressed African-American meetings, a writer for *Harper's Weekly* complimented their "good sense." Of course the whites wanted to control the black vote, but this was only natural, and their new political leverage would enable freedmen to insist upon good treatment. The whites' courting of black voters was "the most healthy sign we have seen in the Southern States." It showed acceptance of the situation and would create a healthy party competition, which would regenerate the South. "The Bourbons who counsel inaction, and the zanies who nominate 'the white man's ticket,' will be left utterly in the lurch," the author concluded. "All that the friends of equal suffrage ask is a fair trial. They are willing to abide the result."[20] The Democratic *New York World* lauded Southern Democrats' attempts to woo the black vote and even suggested that, "if we do not . . . make any missteps," the Democrats could split the black vote in New York, which would "turn the scale" in a close election. Indeed, it seemed that "the negro may regard his rights as pretty well secured," opined the *Chicago Tribune*, "since the question is, which party in the South will now do most for him?" With the solution of "the negro question," the North and South would work together to place the South "on a basis of wealth and prosperity that will rival the great West."[21]

By April, a month after the establishment of black voting, Republicans widely concluded that black suffrage had virtually solved the dilemma of Reconstruction. The assistant commissioner of the Freedmen's Bureau in Alabama reported that the Reconstruction bills had resulted in "a general amendment in the treatment of the freedmen. . . . The sense of coming power brought immediate respect." According to the *Cincinnati Daily Gazette,* the ballot had ended the formerly frequent "outrages" on freedmen. "All things are working together for good," it concluded. *Harper's Weekly* agreed. "So sudden and amazing a vindication of the radical policy was scarcely to be expected," it wrote. "Instead of the slave code, the barracoons, the auction block, the paddle, the nine o'clock bell, the mounted patrol, the lurking, nameless fear . . . we have equal citizens meeting upon a common ground"; men "who were yesterday risking their lives and fortunes in a war to perpetuate slavery forever, are now calmly reasoning with the late slaves, and appealing to their common-sense and the ordinary motives of intelligent human beings." "The Reconstruction bill has been passed mainly in the hope to procure this accord," wrote the *Philadelphia Inquirer,* and it cheerfully viewed white attempts to woo African-American voters "as an evidence of the wisdom of the Congressional policy, which will do more to restore the South to peace and prosperity than any measure of reconciliation that could be devised."[22]

Unwilling to lose what had seemed to be a secure constituency, Republican politicos also began to organize the freedpeople, encouraging them to vote the party ticket to promote the Republican free labor vision. In the spring of 1867, Senator Henry Wilson of Massachusetts went to the South to drum up black votes for the Republican party. The "Natick cobbler" was a champion party organizer whose popular sympathy and style of oratory was "especially fitted" to gain black supporters," according to *Harper's Weekly* and the *Chicago Tribune.* For the most part, Wilson echoed the moderate Republican vision of a harmonious free labor society in the South, and, indeed, the *Philadelphia Inquirer* declared that Senator Wilson spoke for the North. The *Chicago Tribune* explained that "he is dreaming of a New England in the Carolinas and Georgia, in Alabama and Mississippi," so much so, in fact, that radicals were complaining that his speeches were "colored with . . . tenderness toward rebels."[23]

Wilson represented the Union League, which worked to organize freedmen in the South after the war, making Democrats snipe that Wilson was "perambulating the South" speaking to "ignorant negroes and mean whites." Hoping to expand the Republican party's support base, the Union League built on existing black social, fraternal, and religious organizations and used secret meetings to indoctrinate freedmen into politics. An organization designed to appeal to freedmen, it included black leaders as organizers and worked hard to address ex-slaves' immediate concerns. The Union Republican Congressional Executive Committee—the moderate congressional arm of the Union League that took control of Republican organization in the South in the spring of 1867— issued an address to the people of the Southern states calling for the restoration of the Union, free speech, free press, and free schools. It asserted that "the recognition of equal rights throughout the whole country secures peace, progress, and prosperity." It went on to claim "that the laboring man, whether white or black, needs the protection of law and the ballot, by which he secures equal laws and a just administration of them." It blamed the "backward condition" of the South on the "slaveholding aristocracy which has controlled it for two hundred years" and called for the Southern states "to accept universal suffrage, to establish public schools, and to enable the poor to become landholders as fast as possible."[24]

What Northern Republicans, with their monolithic view of black Southerners, did not see in early 1867 was that there was a dramatic rift in the black community between those with property and those who had none. Only a small fraction of the black population owned real estate or personal property; the vast majority were impoverished and landless. In North Carolina in 1870, for example, only 6.7 percent of all African-Americans held land, and most of those owned just a few acres. Only a very small number of African-Americans owned large plots of land; in North Carolina almost half of all black landowners held less than twenty acres. Prominent African-American leaders were usually freeborn, educated, somewhat prosperous, and biracial; in North Carolina in 1870, men listed in the census as "mulatto" were four times more likely than those listed as "black" to own land. Usually these prominent men practiced a profession, like the ministry, or farmed on land they owned.

Black leaders from this sector of the community tended to preach Republican political economy and the idea of working hard to achieve prosperity. The resolutions of the 1866 Georgia Freedmen's Convention, for example, in which urban delegates who made up "the intelligent mass of the colored population" outnumbered rural ex-slaves, stated: "That we discountenance vagrancy and pauperism among our people, and that we will make it our especial business to aid every one to obtain employment and encourage them to earn a competency by honest labor and judicious economy." While African-Americans who echoed the theory of Republican political economy received much attention from the Northern press, they were hardly representative of the entire Southern black population.[25]

Prominent African-Americans had very different needs and attitudes than the unskilled or semiskilled ex-slaves who made up the bulk of the South's black population and who were usually uneducated, dark-complexioned former field hands. Immediately after the war, as they worked for their former masters, who tried to reinstate an economic system as close to slavery as possible, the poorer African-Americans' first experience of free labor was devastating. They felt swindled and abused as their efforts gained them little or no money and the Black Codes recalled slavery times. With their often hostile employer-employee relationship superimposed directly on the old master-slave relationship, the majority of Southern freedpeople viewed the world not as an economically harmonious system in which all worked for greater prosperity, but as a struggle between the haves and the have-nots.

While Wilson and the white and black leaders of the Union League believed that they were voicing the true needs of the freedmen, who had to be incorporated into a harmonious free labor economy, the impoverished ex-slaves quickly realized that Union League organizers were unwilling to advance what seemed to be obvious solutions to the white Southern attempt to reinstate slavery, especially the confiscation of land. Union League leaders and prominent African-Americans rejected plans for land confiscation and remained tied to the idea of individuals working to achieve prosperity gradually in a harmonious economic system. When freedmen at the Virginia State Republican Convention called for confiscation, for example, white delegates shouted them down and instead started the convention's platform with: "Honor and reward to labor. Homes for the homeless who are willing to work."[26]

Popular orators from within the black community proliferated during the heady summer of 1867, and these men spoke for the ex-slaves, propertyless and exploited, who often called for both more immediate access to land and direct political representation to ensure that their interests were addressed. As early as April 1867, *Harper's Weekly* reported that a "decidedly radical" meeting of blacks was held in Charleston, South Carolina, adopting resolutions in favor of black suffrage and the right for black men to hold office, and opposing "large land monopolies." Northern papers continued to notice "radical" black meetings. On April 13, "a mass meeting of freedmen" in Augusta, Georgia, adopted resolutions "favoring the Republican party; the support of the widows and orphans of Union soldiers; the abolition of corporeal punishment; and the right of all colors to hold office." Conservative blacks and prominent white men at the meeting objected. One white speaker advised the freedmen "to be sober and industrious, and to exercise the rights of franchise judiciously; to avoid the wicked, designing men, who are in their midst to sow discord and strife," and stormed that if he had known the intended program he would not have attended. On the same day, a "Radical mass meeting of negroes" was held outdoors in Nashville, because no hall in the city was large enough to hold the crowd of five thousand "enfranchised freedmen" who "pour[ed] in from the country, afoot, on horseback, and in carts and wagons." As radical ex-slaves shouldered aside more conservative political leadership the Union League boomed; one organizer reported that in one week, 2,398 members had joined from one county alone. Significantly, many prosperous freedmen refused to join the league, and some black leaders even spoke out against it, charging that its Northern, white, grassroots organizers were frauds.[27]

Northern Republicans quickly realized that the Republican Union League attracted those who challenged the traditional Republican view of society. Not only did those league members believe in economic conflict within society, but they also displayed flashes of violence that Republicans associated with those opposed to the free labor ideal. In Charleston in March 1867, a Union League meeting to ratify the Republican platform quickly became a "radical" meeting, followed by a "negro torchlight procession" through the streets; the African-American usurpation of public space was itself a radical threat to those used to black docility. From an Associated Press (AP) story that other newspapers also picked up, the *Chicago Tribune* reported that "[t]he negroes made several attacks on the street cars, and took possession of one of them. The cars are now guarded by policemen. Considerable excitement prevails throughout the city, and there are grave apprehensions of further trouble." In April, the press reported that the sentiments of the African-Americans at the Virginia State Republican Convention were "for confiscation," and claimed that the convention burst into applause when a delegate proposed that "if Congress did not give the negroes lands, they should be taken by violence." In July, the *New York Herald* reported a battle between radical black Union League members and conservative whites and blacks in Franklin, Tennessee, that left four dead and twenty-three wounded.[28]

In addition to attracting disaffected African-Americans, the Union League captured the poorer white yeoman farmers of some Southern states who had traditionally opposed wealthier slaveholders, and who by late 1866 were facing starvation after repeated crop failures. Both impoverished and angry over the apparent return of their states to the prominent men who had led the South out of the Union, they called for debt relief and organized militarily to wrest control of Southern states from ex-Confederate leaders. The radicalism of both poor whites and ex-slaves frightened Northern Republicans. In May 1867, a hostile observer told the *Philadelphia Inquirer* that in Louisiana, African-Americans and poor whites alike were ignorant to the point of idiocy and yet were being registered to vote. He complained: "The colored man standeth forth in his dignity as a freeman, a citizen, a voter. And so doeth the 'white trash.' The old sugar planters and cotton raisers hold off in disgust and in silence at this state of affairs."[29]

It also became clear that some freedmen were cooperating as workers to win higher wages or better working conditions. The summer of 1867 saw strikes across the South, notably in Mobile and Charleston, where dockworkers and longshoremen successfully struck for higher wages. The organization of agricultural workers was even more striking, as the Union League encouraged freedmen to boycott conservative planters, seize crops if they were defrauded, slow down work, and squat on planters' lands. The *Montgomery Advertiser* reported that "[t]he Union Leagues lay down as part of their creed sympathy with labor against capital, and the Republican platforms generally do the same thing. In other words that they are the champions of the poor man as against the rich." Workers took to the streets in unprecedented numbers in the summer of 1867; the Associated Press reported in detail on riots in Richmond, Virginia.[30]

Democrats were quick to pick up stories of impoverished freedmen who were rioting for wages and either identify the interests of the ex-slaves with those of the white workingmen to complain that Republicans oppressed the poor of all races, or bewail increasing African-American radicalism. The *New York World* blamed Republican national economic policies for the general distress of the working population, and charged that the freedpeople were "as prosperous and hopeful as the corresponding white classes in the Northern States." The only thing that could help all American workers was a Democratic government that would "leave to the laborers of all sections a larger portion of their honest earnings." The *Baltimore Sun,* in contrast, concluded that "the unsettled habits and revolutionary training" of the African-Americans meant that their votes threatened disaster.[31]

Southern freedpeople appeared to be demanding powerful public positions to advance their agenda. In April 1867, *Harper's Weekly* reported that "several colored men" had purchased a South Carolinian newspaper "and propose conducting it as a negro organ." When the Virginia State Republican Convention met in Richmond on April 18, most of the delegates were black; only one white man was present at the South Carolina Republican State Convention in May, reported *Harper's Weekly.* Quickly, freedmen called for the right to hold office, both appointed and elected. "A meeting of Radical freedmen was held in Mobile on April 17," reported *Harper's Weekly,* "at which resolutions were adopted demanding for black men the right to hold office and sit on juries." African-Americans in Richmond, Virginia, called for government offices to be apportioned according to population; according to a hostile observer, freedmen in Mobile demanded that the police force be half black. The Associated Press reported that delegates to a political convention in New Orleans ended up marching through the streets; the "Radical rulers" of the city called for black police and a black mayor. These radical demands for black officeholders seemed to be heeded. *Harper's Weekly* noted, for example, "A negro named Theophilus Ash was elected one of the town commissioners of Plymouth, North Carolina, on April 20."[32]

By midsummer 1867, rumors came from the South that African-Americans had gone so far as to organize as a military force. Indeed African-Americans, often organized as Union Leaguers, armed to defend themselves in the summer of 1867. Hostile Democrats warned that ex-slaves were on the brink of revolt and bemoaned "the moody and suspicious estrangement which has taken the place of the friendly feeling heretofore existing between the slaves and their former masters." While discounting the idea of an armed black force, the *Philadelphia Inquirer* reflected, "It is not a matter of wonder that the hitherto oppressed blacks have come to an understanding for their own protection, in case the troops should be withdrawn and they be left to the tender mercies of their former owners."[33]

The appearance of black radicalism in the South forced Northern Republican observers to acknowledge the split in the black community. As conservative whites backed black conservatives for office to undercut black radicals, the rift became obvious. Repeatedly, newspapers reported the hostility of "the colored men" to more conservative black politicians. *Harper's Weekly* reported, for example, that a group of "colored men" "mobbed" black orators supporting a black conservative candidate in Georgia. In February 1868, a *Harper's Weekly* cartoon caught the new Northern awareness of class differences in the black community. Entitled "Aristocratic Distinction," it showed two well-dressed African-American men watching two Irish-American ragpickers. When one of the black men asked the other what the ragpickers did with ashes, the other answered: "Why, dey takes and dey sifts 'em out, and dey pick 'em over, and dey *sells 'em to de lower classes.*"[34]

The Northern worry about black radicals in the summer of 1867 enabled Northern Democrats to begin to develop a nuanced critique of Republican policy, replacing their former bald racism with a political argument that was not completely unattractive to conservative and moderate Republicans. While Northern Democrats continued to protest Republican efforts to "'organize a hell' in the South," prostrating "the Caucasian race" under "their own negroes," they also painted a picture of the corruption of government and economic bankruptcy based on the specter of black office-holding. When newspapers bemoaned the "corruption" of black voting and officeholders, they were not referring primarily to the direct bribery that has come to dominate the meaning of the word. Instead, they meant the corruption of the true form of their ideal democracy, in which all acted disinterestedly for the good of the country.[35]

Since the war years, Northern Democrats had argued that Republican policies sacrificed the poor to a Republican empire ruled by a favored class of party cronies. They argued that the war—fomented, in their view, by Republican abolitionists—demanded high taxation at the same time that it dramatically expanded government employment, and that Republican politicians then put their supporters into these new offices in an elaborate system of patronage. By 1865, 53,000 government workers were drawing about $30,000,000 in salary at the same time that the Union was saddled with a new $2.5 billion national debt largely in the form of bonds that the government had issued to fund the war. The public paid these expenses through new national taxes. Taxes crushed the working poor, Democrats argued, to provide money for both the Republican cadre of government workers and the wealthy, who drew interest on the war bonds they held.[36]

After the war, Democrats charged, Republicans trumped up stories of Southern atrocities to blind "dupes" to their "unconstitutional usurpations . . . class legislation . . . and . . . Treasury robbery." As an example of how the public was being looted to construct a Republican machine, the *Columbus (Ohio) Crisis* reported a new metropolitan police bill, which, it maintained, robbed the public of $30,000. Republicans had designed the bill, it claimed, "in favor of which one hundred non tax-payers had petitioned and against which two thousand tax-payers had remonstrated," to give jobs to Republican voters. "As certain loyal patriots were out of employ [sic], they should be rewarded with fat stealings, wrung from unwilling tax payers," the *Crisis* explained. In the postwar anxiety over the ballooning federal government, Democratic arguments occasionally attracted Republicans; in January 1867, for example, the *New York Daily Tribune* wailed that the Republican party had placed into power "thieves and swindlers" who had "robbed the Nation."[37]

Military reconstruction simply increased the bill and consolidated Republican power as it further expanded the government, Democrats said. In July 1867, the *Baltimore Sun* estimated the cost of the federal employees to be deployed in the South under the new plan at $110 million and echoed the warning of the *National Intelligencer* that military reconstruction paved the way for absolute Republican despotism. The *Sun* also reported that Congress might fund radical Republican newspapers in the South, and that a man speaking ill of Congress had been summarily arrested and fined $300, both signs that Republicans were consolidating their absolute control of the government. The *St. Paul Pioneer*

Press blamed inflation on the "radical party," which had increased taxation and the national debt "by feeding thousands of lazy, idle negroes, supporting a huge standing army, 'reconstructing' negro States, and other extravagant party projects."[38]

In July 1867, the Democratic *New York World* greeted the second session of the Fortieth Congress by effectively joining the theory of the "spoils system" with Democratic racism to construct a powerful opposition to black voting on the basis of political corruption. The *World* warned that black voting and the consequent assumption of offices by black men to whom politicians owed patronage posts would mean that African-Americans would come to hold almost all of the political offices of the South. The *World* foresaw "negro governors, negro mayors of cities, and negro occupants of every grade of office State and municipal." African-Americans would covet the salaries of public office, hoping to avoid the more productive but difficult work in the fields that paid lower wages. The Mobile hopefuls for the police force, for example, wanted the positions only "because it would distribute $60,000 among that class. Everywhere the Freedmen's Bureau has inculcated the idea among the blacks that political privileges mean profuse donations of unearned money and opportunities to pocket things generally—a belief, by-the-by, that obtains largely among their Radical preceptors." Even if black voters elected white officers, the *World* told readers, the outcome of black voting would be government "completely under the control of negroes."[39]

Explaining that "[w]hether their officers are black or white will make little difference, since they will be answerable to black constituencies," the *World* maintained that black suffrage would corrupt government by enslaving it to the poor, who would use it against those who held property. "When the government, that is, the taxing power, represents the poverty of the community, and not its property, there will be a constant tendency to rob property of its rights," it explained. Nontaxpaying freedmen and their Republican representatives in the legislatures would liberally vote new taxes, while the taxpayers, disfranchised after the war, would have no power to enforce economy. Heavy taxation would create full treasuries, which would naturally lead to "squandering prodigality" and the temptation to and opportunity for large patronage lists and corruption. Without oversight by taxpayers, governments dependent on black constituencies "will be among the most wasteful and corrupt that ever existed," the *World* warned. It argued that its position was not based on racism: "This will not result from the fact that the rulers are negroes, but from the fact that they are men," it contended.[40]

Referring to some black radicals' oratory in 1867, the *World* anticipated that the "pretext" under which black governments would "rob and oppress their late masters" would be that uncompensated slave labor had produced the wealth of the South in the first place, and that it rightfully belonged to the freedmen. Under this idea, black governments would "perpetrate robbery," making "extravagant expenditures" for schools, churches, hospitals, and other charitable institutions. The *World* even foresaw changes in real estate tenure "so as to render it worthless to its white owners, and make it the easy prey of negro rapacity." In May 1867, the *World* charged that Republicans had "effected the most sweeping change ever introduced into a political organization" solely to perpetuate their power. It accused "brawlers" like Pennsylvania congressman Judge William D. Kelley of planning to rule Southern whites "by means of the blacks, to array the two races in enduring hostility to each other, and to vest the control of intelligence, education, and property in the hands of ignorant freedmen, manipulated by cunning demagogues."[41]

This Republican plot had dangerous implications for the nation. A minority working for favors could swing the balance of an election. For example, the *World* explained, a small number of advocates of the eight-hour day, "or other special legislation," could give the election to a candidate that promised them what they wanted. "So with the negro vote. The promise of police places and $60,000 will carry the entire vote of Mobile for a Congressman, or Governor, of either party; and so with all other offices in every section of the South." Eventually, the *World* insisted, African-American voters would elect the next president, who would be beholden to their interests.[42]

Democratic newspapers hammered home the idea that freedpeople wanted offices so they could confiscate wealth and live without working. The *Baltimore Sun* charged that African-Americans demanded the vice-presidential spot in the next election and a majority in the Southern state governments. The *New York Herald* warned of "the excesses of Southern black Republican political ascendancy," for, it argued, the black vote would control the Republican party and African-Americans were incapable of self-government. The *Herald* foresaw race war, anarchy, and bloodshed. A North Carolina correspondent to the *New York Herald* insisted that radical measures had demoralized freedmen, making them expect to get "their subsistence from the whites after the latter have worked hard" and anticipate that the government "will do for them whatever they demand." Lazy ex-slaves, he reported, had "confiscation on the brain." A Tennessee correspondent agreed, claiming that radical Republicans were teaching ex-slaves that the legislature would divide property among them to recompense them for their days in slavery.[43]

This attack brought scathing responses from radical Republicans that African-Americans were, in fact, backing only the best candidates for office, and noting that most of those "best" candidates were white. Radical Republicans continued to support the vote of the ex-slaves, arguing that freedmen were controlled by "an intelligence that will not be deceived, and an instinct that will not lead them astray." They had competent leaders and, even better, "native good sense and homely shrewdness," which protected them from those who would deceive them. They were politically savvy and "eager for instruction." A writer for the *Chicago Tribune* went further, suggesting that events were overturning white convictions about African-American inferiority. "Now it becomes doubtful whether the negro is so inferior, intellectually, after all, as he was represented to be a few years ago. The yoke of slavery has been lifted from his neck; the great revolution has made him the political peer of his late master, and it is by no means certain that he will not soon show himself the intellectual peer."[44]

But conservative and even some moderate Northern Republicans linked the Northern Democrats' argument about black government to their own fears of the Southern black radicals who seemed to believe, as labor radicals did, that labor must fight capital. Conservative and moderate Republican concerns focused not on the creation of a Republican empire based on African-American votes, as the Democrats did, but on the idea that freedpeople seemed to mimic disaffected laborers who refused to work for their own success. If such men controlled legislatures, as the Democratic argument suggested they could, they might easily change the nature of American government, denying the sanctity of individualism and creating an interventionist government that redistributed wealth.

Leading the voices of conservative Republicans, the *New York Times* was much more moderate than the *New York World*, but nonetheless worried that radicals were demoralizing the freedmen, "encouraging them in idleness" as they led ex-slaves to expect to prosper through government handouts rather than hard work. "A marked change has taken place . . . in the disposition and conduct of the Richmond negroes," a correspondent from that city reported to the *New York Times* in May 1867. No longer "orderly, civil, industrious," or "anxious to prove themselves worthy of" emancipation, they were "growing insolent, unruly, domineering, [were] selecting dominance instead of equality." The *New York Times* contrasted radical African-American orators—"fat and sleek, clad in irreproachable alpaca sacks and shiney trousers," well taken care of by "demagogues who use their presence and their utterances for their own purposes"—with good African-American workers of the Republican vision, men with families who needed food, shelter, and clothing. "These and their little ones," the *Times* lamented, "ask for bread and receive the ballot; they desire work and are invited to the hustings." "But for political propagandists," the paper contended, "the two races to-day would only know the change in their relations, by their mutual gains materially."[45]

When election troubles coincided with the continued food scarcity in the South, conservative Republicans worried less about white reluctance to accept black labor than about the black workers themselves. Conservatives feared that instead of working hard in the fields, ex-slaves were organizing and concentrating exclusively on political power. The author of a letter printed in the *New York Times* in January 1868 wrote that "[t]he negro will not work, or cannot be relied on in the fulfillment of his contract." He stated that the cotton crop could not be picked in South Carolina and Georgia because "the negro was absent, attending to speeches and elections." Another writer concluded that free labor was a failure in the South, but that freedpeople would have worked well if it had not been for "the political agitation of the Radicals." Gleeful Democrats made much of the Republican *Economist's* prediction that political agitation during the harvest would hurt crop yields.[46]

Afraid that African-Americans were expecting that political power would guarantee their economic salvation, Republican newspapers felt obliged to reiterate the true laws of political economy. The *New York Times* reminded freedmen "that the interests of the two races are the same:—that the policy which ruins the whites will ruin them. . . . [I]f, by riots, disorder or idleness they check the general prosperity, they also check their own." Agreeing with the *New York Times* in warning freed-people "against troublesome demagogues who pandered to bad appe-tites to obtain the colored men's votes," the *Philadelphia Inquirer* showed an increased Republican emphasis on education, to give African-Ameri-cans a true understanding of political economy. According to the *Phila-delphia Inquirer,* freedmen must "labor diligently to educate themselves, and rely upon their own exertions for homes, instead of expecting to get those of white men by confiscation." Even the radical Republican press joined the education bandwagon. The *Chicago Tribune* advocated educa-tion for blacks because "large masses of ignorant people, no matter how well they may be disposed naturally, constitute a dangerous element in any community," and the *Washington Chronicle* called for an increasing emphasis on education "to bring the long oppressed colored race to a standard which shall make them intelligent, industrious and patriotic citizens." *Harper's Weekly* concluded that "[n]o subject can be more in-teresting at this time to the people at large than that of the education of the Southern people, black and white; for through the education of the masses the permanent and thorough reconstruction and unity of the country is to be finally attained."[47]

Their frequent use of the term *demagogue* to describe political leaders of the freedmen indicated Northern Republican apprehension about the potential use of the black vote. The concept of the demagogue duping a mob was a very powerful image immediately after the Civil War. Most Northerners believed that demagogues had led the South out of the Un-ion, and that demagogues were leading labor agitators in the North, con-vincing working men that labor and capital were opposed and inciting them to attack the wealthy. That demagogues harangued the freedpeople rhetorically tied black political activism to two other groups that had de-nied the free labor ideal.[48]

Conservative and moderate Republicans increasingly perceived poor black workers in the South as disaffected, and the peculiar circum-stances of 1867 dangerously magnified their power. Many white South-erners protested Reconstruction legislation by refusing to register to vote. "The consequence is, that the blacks are registered to a man, while so many of the whites have neglected to do so that in several States the blacks can carry the Congressional elections and have control of the State Governments. How they will act in such cases perhaps the whites will discover; but if they fear the consequences, why did they neglect the opportunity?" wondered the *Philadelphia Inquirer.* As the registration numbers piled up, it began to look as though black voters would out-number white voters across the South. Ultimately, as about 750,000 African-Americans and 635,000 whites registered in the ten unrecon-structed Southern States, blacks were a majority in South Carolina, Mis-sissippi, Louisiana, Florida, and Alabama. But the impressions of the time exaggerated the numbers: according to *Harper's Weekly,* African-Americans outnumbered white voters in eight of the ten Southern states, and in the two others, loyal whites would join the ex-slaves to put down the Southern Democrats. This was a mixed blessing. On the one hand, Republicans were pleased that loyal voters would outnumber the dis-loyal ones. On the other, they worried that the South would be con-trolled by the ex-slaves, who had lately shown a distressingly radical tendency. *Harper's Weekly* noted, for example, that the county that in-cluded Nashville, Tennessee, had enrolled only 1,600 whites "against" 4,400 blacks. This was majority rule with a vengeance.[49]

The apparently growing strength of radical freedpeople seemed to parallel the efforts of white workers in the North; it sometimes literally paralleled it as newspapers ran columns on the South and on Northern workers, side by side. Agitation for an eight-hour day made the radical *Chicago Tribune* accuse its advocates of trying to reform "all existing laws of political economy, by making capital a disgrace rather than a credit to its owner"; similarly, the *New York Times* concluded that the eight-hour day was an attempt of communists "to get the first wedge of their theory introduced into our industrial system by statutory enact-ment." In August 1867, the National Labor Congress called for a politi-cal party "to be composed of the laboring classes," that would nominate its own presidential and vice-presidential candidates, signaling a new phase in workingmen's attempt to influence the government. The *New York Times* railed at the National Labor Congress, insisting that real workers were buying businesses and becoming employers rather than agitating. Within days of reporting that summer's violent riot of Union Leaguers in Tennessee, the *New York Herald* entitled an article on strik-ing workers "ALMOST A RIOT IN BROOKLYN."[50]

Although white labor unions downplayed their shared interests with African-Americans, emphasizing instead their fear of black competition, and black Americans' reaction to labor radicalism was mixed, radical Re-publicans' advocacy of both African-American rights and labor interests identified the two in the minds of those who believed in the free labor ideal of a harmonious economic world. Benjamin F. Wade, for example, was famous as a champion of the working man and as one of the nation's leading supporters of black rights. When he made the logical step from the Republican party's general support for labor to the idea that labor and capital were locked in conflict, he illustrated the intellectual link between black freedom and labor radicalism. In July 1867, in Lawrence, Kansas, Wade told an audience that the theme of the nation was the struggle between labor and capital. This was precisely the vision of society popularly attributed to labor organizers and popularly discredited by moderate and conservative Republicans in favor of the idea that, in America, there was no class conflict, since everyone rose together as they worked toward economic prosperity. Wade's solution was exactly what more moderate Republicans feared from disaffected laborers: "Property is not equally divided, and a more equal distribution of capital must be wrought out," he said. Such a speech by a man like Wade joined radical black activism with organized labor interests.[51]

"Important Speech by Senator Wade," shouted the *Washington National Intelligencer,* and the public certainly agreed. *Harper's Weekly* denied that Wade was preaching revolution and claimed that he had simply voiced "what every student and observer of modern civilization very well knows, that the capital and labor question is one of the most vital of all subjects." But while *Harper's Weekly* put a brave face on Wade's speech, the *New York Times* was appalled, snarling that Wade "springs from the domain of American republicanism to the region of French socialism," and that he "assails the whole industrial and business fabric of the country, and sends forth propositions involving a general division of lands and goods, the limitation of capital, and the more ample recompense of labor—all by acts of Congress." Only three months later, aware that the radicalism of Southern black workers had become a major issue for the fall elections, and cringing at Wade's increasingly radical reputation, *Harper's Weekly* had to agree. Although one had to admire the "sincerity of [his] convictions and the ardor of [his] eloquence," it said, he did not have "good sense, which is the indispensable quality of a party leader."[52]

The actual elections of 1867 calmed the fears of most moderate Northern Republicans, although some conservatives continued to worry that Southern representatives elected by black voters would support "agrarianism . . . confiscation . . . [and] revengeful legislation." On August 1, 1867, African-Americans in Tennessee were the first blacks to vote for a governor and members of Congress; they acted with "a dignity, a moderation, a decorum which their best friends dared not to hope," claimed a writer for *Harper's Weekly.* Three-quarters of the delegates elected in the fall to the Southern constitutional conventions were Republican; the rest were labeled Conservatives. About 45 percent of the Republican delegates were Southern whites, 25 percent were Northern men who had moved South after the war, and 30 percent were African-Americans. Southern whites were a majority in all conventions except those of South Carolina and Louisiana, where African-Americans dominated. Black delegates to the conventions came from the elite of the black community; about four-fifths of them were literate, almost all were professionals or farmers who owned their own land. While Democrats insisted that Republican policies were estranging the races in the South, and some conservative Republicans agreed that the freedmen had elected "ignorant nominees of their own color, or white rascals who woo and win them by preaching the gospel of laziness and license," Republican newspapers emphasized that Southern whites had joined freedmen to vote for the new biracial, progressive world developing in the South.[53]

Like Southern blacks, the majority of the nation rejected radicalism in 1867. On the table were issues like the impeachment of Andrew Johnson, the future of black suffrage, civil rights legislation integrating schools, and, of course, a call for land redistribution. When men like Wade were turned out of the Senate in 1867, Massachusetts Republican Nathaniel P. Banks reflected that the election was "a crusher for the wild men," and Maine Republican James G. Blaine wrote to a colleague: "[The losses] will be good discipline in many ways and will I am sure be 'blessed to us in the edification and building up of the true faith'—I feel, I have for some time felt, that if we should carry everything with a whirl in '67 such knaves as Ben Butler would control our National Convention and give us a nomination with which defeat would be inevitable if not desirable."[54]

The reasonable and measured outcome of the 1867 elections despite the terrorist tactics of extreme Southern conservatives confirmed mainstream Republican support for black suffrage. Party members insisted, according to *Harper's Weekly,* that "the whole body of the people of the Southern States" should "be consulted in the formation of the new governments of those States." That plan had the "undoubted disadvantage" of admitting uneducated men to the suffrage, but this evil was outweighed by the "inexpressible benefit" of having a majority or large minority of the population loyal to the government. A *New York Times* correspondent recalled that the nation had watched anxiously to see what voting would do to the freedman. Relieved, he reported that African-Americans had advanced dramatically in education and "in morals—in honesty, truthfulness, and chastity." The *Chicago Tribune* added that as farmers, wage laborers, soldiers, and now voters, freedmen had "shown themselves fully competent and altogether worthy to be citizens of a free republic."[55]

In the *Fortnightly Review*, Frederic Harrison explained the Republicans' promotion of majority rule in the South, even when the majority was uneducated. In an opinion quoted approvingly in *Harper's Weekly*, he said, "What is wanted in the mass who vote is the desire for the right result, freedom from selfish motive and willingness to trust in wise guidance."[56]

Frederic Harrison's words were apt, for despite their continuing defense of black suffrage, by 1868, conservative and moderate Republicans were getting worried that the voting masses in the North threatened the survival of free labor society. In 1868, poor white Democratic voters followed George H. Pendleton of Ohio into the Democratic "rag baby" camp, which implicitly endorsed the idea of a national class struggle by calling for the repayment of war bonds in depreciated currency rather than in gold, deprecating black suffrage and the Reconstruction amendments, and arguing that the Republican party was deliberately prostrating the working man to build up a national empire. Asserting that there was an economic conflict in American society between rich and poor, the Democratic campaign of 1868 seemed to lay siege to the free labor ideal.

The key to the Democratic platform was popular dislike of taxation, on which Democrats capitalized by insisting that it caused the struggle between labor and capital that had become apparent after the war. Since the war, Democrats had criticized the "wealthy bondholders" who were tapping dry the poor laborers who had to pay interest on war bonds in inflated gold while their own wages were paid in depreciated paper money.[57] The *New York World* constantly hammered home the idea that "[t]he manufacturers, speculators, and money-dealers grow rich, and the industrious poor are still further impoverished."[58]

According to Democrats, the taxes that crushed the poor not only funded wealthy bondholders but also paid for a growing army of Republican officeholders who promoted black rights solely to stay in power, by rousing sympathetic Northerners and avaricious blacks to support them. New York Democratic leader Horatio Seymour maintained that holding troops in the South cost more than $150 million a year and that the yearly price tag for Reconstruction as a whole was $300 million. Democrats blamed the high taxes necessary to support Southern Reconstruction for bank and business failures in 1866 and 1867, and argued that the high taxes needed to fund bonds in gold would mean that workers would "have to be taxed to the extent of several hours a day more, for indulging in the supreme pleasure of setting the negroes free, and turning them loose to starve, to die and rot." Firmly believing that America should be a white man's government, Northern Democrats attacked the black suffrage that kept Republicans in power, maintaining that freedmen were radicals threatening race war in the South and that the new constitutional conventions in the South meant "to subject the State[s] to negro supremacy." Thanks to Republican policy, Democrats charged, "[t]he poor whites of the country are to be taxed—bled of all their little earnings—in order to fatten the vagabondish negroes."[59]

The Northern Democrats' portrait of Southern black radicals scheming to control the South got confirmation from repeated Associated Press stories that depicted freedpeople as revolutionaries. AP reports from the South in 1868 were so incendiary that, by the late summer, Republican newspapers charged that all the Southern AP reporters belonged "to the worst class of ex-Rebels," twisting events to fit their own agenda. Indeed, in August the AP reported, for example, a Republican celebration in Atlanta that turned into a black riot; it also noted that the South Carolina legislature was attempting "to turn all the schools in the State over to the negro School Commissioner," a racist interpretation of reasonable administrative reorganization. A month later it reported a riot of three hundred African-Americans in Augusta, Georgia, who allegedly marched "to overawe the citizens and kill the leading Democrats of the town and vicinity," who would, of course, be overwhelmingly white. This story was more biased than usual; despite the AP reporter's indictment of the violent freedmen, at the end of the day only five whites were wounded, while seventy-five to one hundred African-Americans lay dead.[60]

When the Democratic Convention met in New York on July 4, 1868, it nominated for president and vice president New York's former governor Horatio Seymour and former Union general Francis P. Blair, Jr., on a platform that encapsulated the argument that Republicans were using the support of uneducated African-Americans to create a Republican empire acting in the interests of a favored few. The platform endorsed the plan for repaying war bonds in currency rather than specie; declared the Reconstruction laws "a flagrant usurpation of power . . . unconstitutional, revolutionary, and void"; announced that suffrage should be regulated by the states; and called for "the reform of abuses in the administration, and the expulsion of corrupt men from office."[61]

The Republicans offered a different vision, emphasizing their belief that there was no class conflict in American society because America's true system of political economy fostered economic harmony. During the campaign of 1868, Republican newspapers repeatedly spelled out to workers how the economy worked, reiterating that everyone in the nation had the same interests. They argued that there was, in America, no such thing as a wealthy, bondholding class, as the Democrats charged. Instead, they said, "the bondholders, as a class, are mechanics, laborers, salaried officers, and tradesmen, rather than rich men and capitalists." The war debt was contracted with every class of men in America, Lincoln's secretary of war Edwin Stanton told an audience in Carlisle, Ohio, and would be repaid to all of them; wartime financier Jay Cooke spelled out his bond sales in great detail, insisting that his largest group of investors came from those of average income.[62]

While some Republicans, like Thaddeus Stevens, whose radicalism included workers as well as African-Americans, supported the repayment of bonds in currency, moderate and conservative party members argued that the Democrats' program would destroy the harmonious American economy. It attacked the interests of wealthier men, forcing them to send their investments overseas and thus decreasing the money available to hire American workers. If the Democrats pushed their program through, the business of the country would be "prostrated," and everyone would suffer together. Suggesting that repudiation was a Southern plot to injure the Union, *Harper's Weekly* reported that "it is the duty of every faithful citizen" to convince advocates of currency redemption that their course is wrong. The *Chicago Tribune* went even further: the conflict was between "right and wrong . . . good and evil."[63]

Moderate and conservative Republicans combated economic radicalism even within their own party, holding tight to the idea that all economic interests in American society must operate harmoniously or the very basis of America's political economy would be destroyed. In May 1868, moderates failed to convict President Johnson on articles of impeachment, in part because his successor would have been Senate president pro tem Benjamin F. Wade. A sharp observer reflected that "many who would be glad to have Johnson put out of the way shrink from the consequences of giving the control of the Executive department of the Govt. to Benj. Wade." Not only was he "a man of an intemperate character," but also "he says our greenbacks are the best currency in the world and advocates the addition of 100,000,000 to the present stock at once." Recalling the infamous Kansas speech, John Bigelow noted that "last year . . . [Wade] . . . made a speech in the west in which he was understood to recommend a redistribution of property occasionally by law. . . ."[64]

Reemphasizing the labor theory of value as the true key to economic prosperity, in June 1868, the *New York Times* insisted that "it is often said, and always truly said, that no person needs to be idle in America who is willing to work." During the campaign, Republicans made much of the impoverished backgrounds of their now-prominent leaders. Democrats "make professions of being friends of laboring men," Henry Wilson told an audience in Philadelphia, but "I know some little about the toiling men of this country," he continued. Using his poor childhood and his exodus from home at age ten to earn his living as proof of his humble origins, Wilson told his audience that he knew "something of that policy that lifts up the working man. I am one of the men who believe that God made this world large enough for us all, and that there is a community, instead of hostility, of interests among men." Thanks to the Republicans, who shared Wilson's vision, "the last generation have made greater progress than ever was made by the working-men of any country or of any age." Prominent Republican Galusha Grow agreed, saying that in America a man "can rise and attain a position of honor . . . no matter where [his] birthplace or [what his] condition."[65]

In contrast to their defense of traditional free workers, Republicans excoriated workers who combined to oppose capital. *Harper's Weekly* acquiesced in the Democratic complaint that Southern black labor was disorganized, but so, it said, was Northern white labor. The North was suffering under "a deplorable disorganization of labor and a decrease of productive industry." Workers fomented "agrarian doctrines," and labor unions struck for high wages just as business was depressed. Instead of engaging in productive labor, men tried to find government jobs, which in turn just fattened the tax list. *Harper's Weekly* called for "the inauguration of measures that shall stimulate production and induce the vast army of idlers, plunderers, and beggars to turn their attention to the farm, the work-bench, and the counting-room. If they could be made to work, the annual income of the country would at least remain equal to the expenditure." The *Philadelphia Inquirer* put specifics to *Harper's Weekly's* general charges; it highlighted the death of a nonstriking worker at the hands of strikers, and blamed legislators toadying to workers for the passage of the eight-hour law in Pennsylvania.[66]

While they attacked labor radicalism, Northern Republicans who had begun to shy away from the apparent radicalism of the ex-slaves returned to their defense in the spring of 1868, when conservative Southerners tried to stop the adoption of the new state constitutions by organizing terrorist groups like the Ku Klux Klan to intimidate pro-constitution men from going to the polls. Republican newspapers reported Klan murders of Unionists and supporters of black political rights. Even more dramatic than newspaper stories were the drawings in *Harper's Weekly* of white Southern outrages on freedpeople. The graphic drawings of lynchings and stories of terrorism against African-Americans and the whites working with them made it appear that the South was trying to destroy Northern plans and reject Northern demands, bolstered by President Johnson and Northern Democrats. Republicans insisted that they must work to rebuild the nation firmly "upon the impregnable foundation of equal rights."[67]

This done, the North's vision of a biracial South could still be realized. *Harper's Weekly* held on to the idea that many Southern whites were willing to work with African-Americans, but suggested they were afraid to do so because of the Southern extremists. It noted that in Alabama, even with the alleged intimidation in the preelection weeks, the total vote for the constitution was 90,483, and that 18,553 of those votes came from white men. The *Chicago Tribune* reported that intelligent Southerners disdained the Northern Democrats' opposition to black rights and recognized the citizenship and equal rights of ex-slaves; men like Wade Hampton, it reported, seemed to be working to create a new progressive South. Democratic insistence that Republicans sought to impose "negro rule" on the country were met with scathing replies that the argument was "silly," not only from Northern radicals like the staff of the *Chicago Tribune* but also from Southern moderates like Georgia's ex-governor Joseph E. Brown, who continued to hope for a biracial conservative party in his state. "Nobody really fears negro supremacy in a nation where, of thirty-five millions of people, there are only four millions of African descent," the *Chicago Tribune* snapped. "The idea is a preposterous absurdity."[68]

When the Republican Convention met in Chicago in May, it nominated General Ulysses S. Grant and Indiana politician Schuyler Colfax on a platform that called for a unified nation based on the theory of free labor and the economic harmony it implied. The platform denounced the repayment of bonds in currency as "a national crime," endorsed the congressional plan for Reconstruction, and called for black suffrage in the South, leaving suffrage issues to state control in the North. It also noted favorably "men who [had] served in the rebellion, but who now frankly and honestly co-operate with us in restoring the peace of the country and reconstructing the Southern State governments upon the basis of impartial justice and equal rights," many of whom, like Joseph E. Brown of Georgia, were delegates to the Republican Convention. Recognizing the power of the Democratic critique of Republican rule, though, the platform's framers also called for the rapid reduction of taxes, the "strictest economy" in government, and the "radical reform" of "corruptions," which, it carefully specified, were "shamefully nursed and fostered by Andrew Johnson."[69]

During the campaign, moderate and radical Republicans held up black workers as model Americans who should have the right of suffrage, contrasting them with white workers who were following the Democrats into repudiation and labor organization. Northern Republican newspapers continued to portray African-Americans as good workers. They emphasized that freedpeople were educating themselves at their own expense. The assistant commissioner of the Freedmen's Bureau in Alabama reported not only that African-Americans had the same natural capacity as whites, but also that "the remarkable interest" of freedpeople in education was growing. With children in school, "the parents lay aside primers every where [sic] to be studied by themselves during the intervals of labor." *Harper's Weekly* continued to run drawings of African-Americans that showed hard-working, well-dressed, and good-looking people. In July, when Congress permitted the disbanding of the Freedmen's Bureau, the *Chicago Tribune* explained that this decision was "high testimony to the good character and behavior of the blacks." Thanks to their "good behavior, thrift, eagerness and aptness to learn," their advance had been "simply marvelous," and fully proved "the wisdom of admitting them to all the rights of citizens."[70]

Republicans used the South to illustrate how things prospered when all worked together. In the spring of 1868, business began to revive across the nation. The Southern economy improved as cotton prices rose from 15.5 cents a pound to 24 to 25 cents a pound. *Harper's Weekly* reported that "negroes are inclined to make contracts; and the once despondent and apathetic are preparing to go to work to raise cotton and corn with as much animation as though they were just commencing life." Increasing Southern prosperity helped the North, too, *Harper's Weekly* reminded readers, as Southerners bought their supplies from the North. The *Philadelphia Inquirer* repeatedly emphasized the auspicious crop predictions from the South, reprinting a Louisiana sugar planter's opinion that "[t]he freedmen are working better and more cheerfully than at any time since the war." The newspaper concluded, "The negro as a laborer seems to do very well; all that he can and does require is, that he shall be honestly treated."[71]

Responding to Northern Democrats' racist assaults on black voting, Republicans pushed the idea that the cause of freedmen was the cause of the American worker, since both prospered under a true free labor system. Resurrecting their prewar attack on Democrats, Republicans argued that the theory that dictated white supremacy in the South would lead to the oppression of all free workers. Democrats wanted to give to Southern "patricians" "the right to vote for the working and laboring people," explained the *Chicago Tribune*. "The liberty of the freedmen is in danger, and because they represent labor in the South, the liberty of all other laboring men" was threatened, too. "Discrimination made against the laboring element because it is black, will not cease to be made when a large proportion of it becomes white." Workers needed the ballot to protect themselves from "the men who have all the capital, who own all the land, who are habituated to rule and who are despotic from the long exercise of unchecked power." Senator J. W. Patterson told an audience in Philadelphia that Democrats said they were a poor man's party. "God is the poor man's party," Patterson contradicted, "and he is the party of the poor without respect to race or color. And imitating our Divine Master, we propose to be the party and the friends of the poor without respect to race or color," unlike, as he spelled out, the Democratic servants of Southern white leaders.[72]

The moderate new state constitutions in the South helped Republican portrayals of African-Americans as good solid Americans. Eschewing radical reforms, the new constitutions established universal manhood suffrage and provided for state schools for both whites and blacks. They also involved Southern state governments in social welfare, and, for the first time, established state boards of public charities, instituted prison reform, and decreased the number of capital crimes. While the new constitutions raised property taxes dramatically, especially those on large landholders, to fund the states' new functions, Republicans downplayed this. That the constitutions also disfranchised only a few, rather than all, ex-Confederates indicated the essential moderation of the new legislatures. By August, even the *New York Times* defended African-Americans, arguing that black representatives had neither legislated against property or order, sought special privileges, tried to confiscate land, nor compelled white women to marry them. Instead, they had been "extremely moderate and modest in their demands," had "been scrupulous in their respect for all the rights of property," had worked hard to elevate the "degraded classes," and had "in all respects given proof of a capacity to take part in the carrying on of a Republican Government, that can but astonish those who know the condition in which they have till lately been kept." After defending black suffrage, Ohio congressman J. M. Ashley maintained that "the freedmen do not expect to control Southern politics; and they could not gain this supremacy, if they would." The government had done what it could for them, he said, and "[e]verything now depends upon the freedmen themselves—upon their perseverance, their patience, and, above all, upon their intellectual and moral progress."[73]

Insolent Southern Democrats inadvertently helped the Republicans' sympathetic portrayal of deserving black workers. Majorities in seven Southern states—Alabama, Arkansas, Florida, Georgia, Louisiana,

North Carolina, and South Carolina—adopted the new constitutions and elected Republican legislatures and state officers, despite white boycotting of the polls, intimidation of black voters, and violence. The legislatures convened and ratified the Fourteenth Amendment, thus completing the terms for readmission to the Union. Although radicals feared for Republican freedpeople when national power left the states, Congress readmitted the whole group of seven states in June 1868. Almost immediately the white Democratic members of the Georgia legislature argued that the black legislators were ineligible for office under the Georgia constitution and expelled them. The bad faith of the white Georgians, who clearly counted on a Democratic president in 1868 to sustain their actions, contrasted painfully with the dignity of the expelled members. The story of one expelled man who pointedly wiped the dirt from his feet when he left the chamber told volumes in Republican papers and fueled sympathy for Southern African-Americans.[74]

The election of U. S. Grant as president in November 1868 indicated that the path of Reconstruction would be one that reflected the Republicans' vision of a harmonious free labor world. On the one hand, Grant's election rejected the economic radicalism that pitted poor against rich. Grant had run on a hard-money platform, and his election firmly put down the Democratic paper money faction. The election results also repudiated a powerful labor interest, white or black. Moderates triumphed that freedmen had voted without dominating the election, and cooperative white Southerners had also felt welcome at the polls. "What . . . has become of the negro supremacy which has been one of the bugaboos of the campaign?" asked the *New York Times*. There was, it said, no sign of "the ruthless disfranchisement of whites, or the intolerable mastery of the blacks" that Democrats had predicted.[75]

On the other hand, the North had utterly rejected the conservative policies of Andrew Johnson, and it seemed that the South now recognized that it must accept Northern terms of Reconstruction and get the business of rebuilding under way. "The Congressional policy of reconstruction is seen to be the policy of a vast majority of the people, who have determined, by their votes, that the South must accept this or nothing—must reach this standard, or remain forever under ruinous disability," mused the *Philadelphia Daily Evening Bulletin*. And this determination would be a blessing for the whole nation, it added. Once the South had been reunited with the North, the South's commerce would revive, agriculture would boom, resources would be developed, and the laboring population would increase through immigration to the section. Northern trade with the South would grow, and in the harmony of this new era the army would be withdrawn from the South. Then, "the great Republican party will have the proud satisfaction of knowing, by positive proof, that it has been right all through this contest, and that the principles and policy advocated and sternly adhered to, have at least secured permanent peace to the country."[76]

This pleasant vision quickly seemed to be becoming reality. In December 1868, the *New York Times* noted that conditions in the South were improving, and that Southerners were now convinced that they could easily achieve material prosperity and were earnestly striving to do so. It reiterated in January 1869 that "a healthy prosperity" was growing in the South. "The bulk of the people in the reconstructed States are realizing the reward of labor; they are fast emerging from poverty and depression, and are prepared to profit by the lessons of a painful experience." "Things wear a greatly improved aspect," the newspaper concluded.[77]

It also appeared that white Southerners had accepted the political conditions necessary to make the South prosper. The *Washington Chronicle* and the *Philadelphia Press* reported in February 1869 that ex-Confederates were pouring into Washington for Grant's inauguration, "mingling freely with their former friends . . . comparing their martial experiences. . . . [I]t is wonderful how completely the ex-rebels yield to the double fiat of the bullet and the ballot." While Northern Democrats disparaged fusion movements in the South—one in Virginia was "a personal bargain" whereby prominent white men offered support for black suffrage in exchange for "the sweets of power"—Republicans were more hopeful. The *Philadelphia Daily Evening Bulletin* reported that new movements "headed by the wisest, best and most liberal men" in Virginia, South Carolina, and Louisiana provided for acceptance of congressional Reconstruction, including black suffrage. The *Philadelphia Inquirer* reported not only that the victory had heartened Unionists in the South, but also that Democrats were anxious to please the president-elect. The *Washington Chronicle* and *Philadelphia Press* concluded that Johnson's encouragement and the hope of a Democratic president in 1868 had bolstered Southern Democrats, but Grant's election had made even "the most ultra secessionists" recognize defeat and prepare to become "peaceful and law-abiding citizens."[78]

Grant's election appeared to put in place the Republican plans for the South that Johnson had thwarted. In early 1869, a National Convention of Colored Men met in Washington, D.C., to discuss the conditions of African-Americans, with special attention to the political and social problems of Reconstruction. *Harper's Weekly* depicted the delegates as well dressed, orderly, and handsome African-American men accompanied by fashionably dressed female guests. On January 19, at the close of the convention, a committee of twelve went to congratulate Grant on his election. He thanked them and told them that the laws would protect African-Americans. Then he went on to emphasize that "[t]hey should prove by their acts, their advancement, prosperity, and obedience to the laws, worthy of all the privileges the Government has bestowed on them; and by their future conduct prove themselves worthy of all they claim."[79]

It appeared that the only thing that was left to ensure African-Americans a fair chance in the South was the right of suffrage, since the Georgia legislature's expulsion of black legislators had proved that current guarantees were insufficient. When the third session of the Fortieth Congress met in the months between Grant's election in November 1868 and his inauguration in March 1869, Republican congressmen passed and sent off to the states for ratification the Fifteenth Amendment to the Constitution. The new amendment fixed into the nation's fundamental law the principle that all men should be able to vote to protect their own interests.

After the 1868 election, Congress reassembled on December 7 and refused to seat the new congressmen arriving from Georgia. The next month, George S. Boutwell of Massachusetts introduced a proposed amendment to the Constitution from the House Judiciary Committee, on January 11, 1869. The amendment established the right of suffrage without regard to race, color, or previous condition of servitude, and provided for federal enforcement of that right. Four days later, while the "superior intelligence" and "business-like manner" of the black members of the "Colored Suffrage Convention" were attracting "much attention," according to the *New York Times*, William M. Stewart of Nevada introduced to the Senate the Senate Committee on the Judiciary's own, more radical version of the amendment, which protected "the right of citizens of the United States to vote, and hold office" regardless of "race, color, or previous condition of servitude." These amendments were the starting point of a long debate during the short session of Congress. While Republicans intended the Fifteenth Amendment in part to enfranchise Northern blacks, whose cause had failed at the Northern polls in the elections since the war, the main thrust behind the amendment was to protect Southern freedmen from white Southerners who refused to accord them the rights of free workers.[80]

Reflecting popular support for black suffrage, the House passed its joint resolution fairly quickly, on January 30, by a vote of 150 to 42, agreeing to use the federal government to protect suffrage without regard to race, color, or previous condition of servitude.[81] In contrast, radicals in the Senate were not content with the limited protection offered by the House's amendment and fought hard for two additional ideas: black office-holding and universal suffrage. Their attempts were not welcomed in the Republican party at large, for Republicans were increasingly uneasy about the connection between black voting and the idea of disaffected laborers subverting the government. When some radical Republicans argued that the House amendment was too limited because it allowed states to pass laws restricting voting on grounds other than those specified, more moderate Republicans maintained that this was one of the more attractive aspects of the plan. While admitting that universal suffrage in the South had "not produced the disasters which many apprehended," and even that "[t]he freedmen, suddenly invested with prodigious power, have on the whole exercised it with moderation," the New York Times came out for impartial suffrage. It reflected that universal suffrage in New York City had been "unfavorable" and that such a principle "in some communities is fraught with peril." The Times spoke for moderate and conservative Republicans, but even radicals Wendell Phillips and Robert Dale Owen protested that the Senate had gone beyond the necessary reform.[82]

While the Senate dropped its demand for universal suffrage, it was less willing to forgo guarantees of black office-holding and passed an initial version of the amendment with this provision intact. The example of Georgia had made clear the need for federal protection of office-holding, but Democratic explications of the corruption inherent in black office-holding had attracted Northern Republicans concerned less about color, as Democrats were, than about the control of government by those who believed in a conflict between labor and capital. Democrats continued to harp on the evils of African-Americans in office, charging in January 1869 that African-Americans were tools of plotting Republicans, and also suggesting that they were bloodthirsty savages responsible for the racial violence that was convulsing Haiti, Jamaica, and Liberia. Some Republicans, concerned about the corruption of government if workers controlled it, resisted black office-holding. "Do our public offices, high and low, stand in such desperate need of negro assistance as to render it imperative to give negroes the right to hold them?" demanded the *New York Times*. Others argued that the right to hold office was inherent in the right to vote and so the clause was unnecessary. Eventually even radicals unwillingly let this provision go to secure the passage of the rest of the amendment.[83]

Democratic opposition to the amendment was more muted than Republicans had expected. This was in part because Democrats understood that Northerners now endorsed black suffrage, and in part, perhaps, because Democrats hoped to earn enough favor from President-elect Grant to induce him to take a moderate approach to Reconstruction. Democrats' main objection to the measure focused on its centralization. Their conviction that the amendment would destroy a critical aspect of state sovereignty—a state's right to determine its own voting qualifications— attracted the support of Republican conservatives like James Dixon of Connecticut and James R. Doolittle of Wisconsin, who agreed that the Republicans were moving steadily toward centralization. "The question . . . is not merely a question of suffrage," Connecticut's Dixon argued, "but . . . it goes to the very founding of republican government." Failing, of course, to persuade the Republican majority of their convictions— one argued that "the time had come when the power of the General Government should be felt over every foot of its territory to protect all classes of citizens in their rights"—Democrats tried to ridicule the bill by calling for women's suffrage and for giving the vote to all children over twelve.[84]

"It must be done," insisted William Stewart of Nevada, the Senate sponsor of the amendment. "It is the only measure that will really abolish slavery. It is the only guarantee against peon laws and against oppression. It is that guarantee which was put in the Constitution of the United States originally, the guarantee that each man shall have a right to protect his own liberty." With public opinion behind them—"[t]he principle of this amendment is unquestionably right," reflected the *Phila-*

delphia Daily Evening Bulletin—and after a conference committee hammered out the differences between the House and the Senate, Congress passed the Fifteenth Amendment on February 26, 1869, and sent it off to the states for ratification.[85]

The congressional passage of the Fifteenth Amendment seemed to Republicans to usher in a new era of peace and prosperity. "How much we have gained since Lincoln spoke at Gettysburg!" triumphed the *Washington Chronicle*. "In November of 1863 we had a theory of liberty, a hope of equality, a dream of justice to all men. In May of 1869 that theory is a fact, that hope is fulfilled, that dream is a reality." As 1869 wore on, Northerners exhibited increasing friendliness toward their old enemies, even their actual battlefield foes. At the end of May, the first national Decoration Day, or Memorial Day, saw veterans decorating Confederate as well as Union graves. In August, the Gettysburg Memorial Association invited former Union and Confederate officers to the battlefield to mark out the lines of the battle. More than a hundred Union officers and many Confederates accepted the invitation for an informal reunion.[86]

With its passage by Georgia—whose readmittance to the Union depended on a positive vote—the Fifteenth Amendment was ratified on March 30, 1870. It seemed to be the culmination of the effort to enable African-Americans to join the American political economy. After the amendment's ratification, Frederick Douglass gave a speech entitled "At Last, At Last, the Black Man Has a Future": "The black man is free, the black man is a citizen, the black man is enfranchised, and this by the organic law of the land," he thundered, and "one of the most remarkable features of this grand revolution is its thoroughness. Never was revolution more complete."[87]

It seemed that America had finally achieved black equality. In 1870, the *Chicago Tribune* rejoiced that the passage of the Fifteenth Amendment and the subsequent readmission of Virginia, Mississippi, Texas, and Georgia to the Union meant the end of governmental action on behalf of African-Americans. From that point on, legislation would be general, treating all races alike. Black Americans had been "merged politically with the rest of the people" and therefore could be singled out neither for attack or defense. "Hereafter he has to run the race of life, dependent, like all others, upon his own energy, ability, and worth." On this, the Republican *Chicago Tribune* and the Democratic *New York*

World could agree. Nothing more could be done for African-Americans than to make them the political equals of white men, the *World* reflected. More attempts on their behalf would simply reintroduce inequality between different races. With full political equality established by the Fifteenth Amendment, the freedman had been "raised as high as he can be put by any other action than his own. . . . Nothing more is possible. . . . [T]he rights of the negro can never again be an issue in our national politics." Prominent Republican politician and novelist Albion W. Tourgée concluded: "It was all over,—the war, reconstruction, the consideration of the old questions. Now all was peace and harmony. The South must take care of itself now. The nation had done its part; it had freed the slaves, given them the ballot, opened the courts to them, and put them in the way of self-protection and self-assertion. The 'root-hog-or-die' policy . . . became generally prevalent. The nation heaved a sigh of relief."[88]

With the Fifteenth Amendment out of the way, Northerners turned back to the apparent corruption of the nation's government. Democrats continued to harp on "the monstrous corruption and extravagance" of the Republican party as it poured tax money into its constituency to secure votes. While Republicans were not losing sleep about the creation of a Republican empire, they too worried about the creation of a government directly involved with the populace. Democratic accusations dovetailed with the concerns of Republicans about the growing national government, to the point that the Democratic *New York World* could approvingly quote a speech by radical Republican Elihu B. Washburne, chairman of the House Committee on Appropriations. Washburne worried about the "demoralization" of government thanks to "the expenditures of vast and unheard of amounts of public money; . . . the giving out of immense contracts by which sudden and vast fortunes were made; the inflation of the currency, which engendered speculation, profligacy, extravagance, and corruption; . . . the intense desire to get suddenly rich out of the government and without labor; and the inventions and schemes generally to get money out of the Treasury for the benefit of individuals without regard to the interests of the government." Noting calls of the Republican *Cincinnati Daily Gazette* for an end to railroad subsidies, since they bred corruption, the *New York World* insisted that "[t]he chief questions in our present politics are those which relate to the raising and disbursement of the public money."[89]

Between 1867 and 1870, Northern Republicans fought for universal suffrage to enable ex-slaves to protect their interests in a hostile South. But while they eventually forced the ratification of the Fifteenth Amendment, the fight for suffrage took a toll on Northern Republican support for freedpeople. Southern African-American radicalism in the summer of 1867 had enabled Northern Democrats to launch an attack on ex-slaves that attracted conservative and moderate Republicans. Northern Democrats argued that Republicans were using black votes to construct an empire that would perpetuate Republican rule by catering to African-Americans. To this idea Republicans added their growing anxiety about those who believed in class conflict. Moderate and conservative party members began to worry that voting African-Americans would harness the government to the service of disaffected workers, who hoped to confiscate the wealth of others rather than to work their own way to economic success.

In 1870, these fears were still inchoate, but they were prevalent enough to make Northern Republicans refuse to support the protection of black office-holding in the Fifteenth Amendment. They were also enough to make the growth of the government suspect among members of both parties, who feared that a large government meant corruption, as individuals accepted government posts and patronage rather than engaging in productive labor for their subsistence. In 1870, it appeared that black suffrage was not the simple route to a universal free labor system that it had seemed to be in 1867.

3

Black Workers and the South Carolina Government, 1871–1875

The ratification of the Fifteenth Amendment did not in fact end Reconstruction, for, as *Harper's Weekly* had pointed out three years before, a critical question remained: How were freedmen going to get land? Land was, after all, "a vital element of substantial citizenship" and the key to starting the climb up the American economic ladder. Southerners were taking care to make sure freedmen did not acquire it. In Georgia, for instance, nearly all of the valuable public land was taken, and even where it was available, *Harper's Weekly* noted, "the late masters, in settling their labor accounts, take good care not to leave money in the hands of the laborers." "Yet land is essential to their proper status as citizens, and how shall they obtain it?" wondered the magazine. That question puzzled Northerners, and helped the seeds of suspicion planted by black radicalism to flower as Northerners watched events in the South over the next five years.[1]

With all the elements of a successful free labor system in place in the South by 1870, Republicans enjoyed the spectacle of freedpeople succeeding as free workers. Lauding freedmen who mirrored the stereotype of white workers and began accumulating property by working on the land, in 1871 the *Boston Evening Transcript* noted that Mississippi freedpeople who were "penniless" in 1865 owned more than $200,000 worth of property in 1870, proving that former slaves were perfectly able "to take care of themselves." In twenty-three Mississippi counties in 1869, "the black tenant-farmers produced 40,561 bales of cotton, while the crop of the whites in the same counties was 27,893." The following year, the black farmers increased production to 50,978 while the white farmers produced only 20,893 bales. The *Chicago Tribune* was only a bit more cautious, noting that free labor was producing almost as much cotton and much more food than the South ever had before, but suggesting that machinery, fertilizer, and "the general improvement of agricultural industry and personal thrift among the people" would improve production even more. It foretold that when political disturbances ended in the South, intelligently employed workers would produce "double and treble the values and quantities ever produced by enforced labor in the best days of the system." "The blacks never worked harder or better under slavery than they do now," recorded the *New York Times* in March 1871. They were buying farms, educating their children, and taking their wives out of the fields, it continued, and still producing a cotton crop equal to that of 1860. "The laboring force of the . . . South is stronger than it was before the war . . . and undoubtedly much more intelligent and prosperous." In March 1871, Northern Republicans welcomed the five new African-American representatives seated with the new national Congress, maintaining that "their presence in that body, vindicate[d] the safety to the Union which is incident to the broadest freedom in political privileges."[2]

Although most Northern Republicans maintained that freedpeople were good laborers, working hard to move up the economic ladder, Republican newspapers also revealed the survival of a popular concern about a black labor interest anxious to gain its demands through organizing and influencing legislation rather than working. Increasingly, Northern Republicans emphasized education for ex-slaves to make them proper citizens. In January 1871, for example, a writer for the *Boston Evening Transcript* reiterated the call for financial aid to freedpeople's schools on the grounds, he said, of "debt" and "self-defence." "We owe it to the negro to lift the weight of ignorance from him which we imposed, and from the day that we gave him the right of suffrage we owed it to ourselves to render him fit to use it." The newspaper emphasized the eagerness of freedpeople to learn, and quoted a freedman: "What help you give us in the next five years, while the dullest negro is roused to a new ambition . . . will send us further on our way than any urging or spurring afterward."[3]

Northern Republicans were increasingly anxious about the attributes of American workers in general, a concern highlighted by the escalating organization of labor in the nation. At the end of 1870, a writer for *Scribner's Monthly* reviewed the labor agitation of the past few years. It complained that men used to do "a good honest day's work for stipulated pay." They used to spend years training to become competent or skilled workmen; cooks and chambermaids took pains "to learn the duties of their places, and faithfully to perform them." "There was a time," he sighed nostalgically, "when one workman more skillful than another received freely his right to better pay than his bungling and unskillful neighbor—when there were motives to excellence in handicraft which made all workmen strive to do their best." But now it was "painfully evident and notorious" that a change had taken place. Labor had been "demoralized" by "the discussions, and combinations, and 'movements' of the past few years." Employers were paying high wages for inferior work; incompetent and impudent servants were making housekeeping "a terror." "The good workman has lost his incentive to be better than his companions, and the poor workman grows poorer by being raised, without effort of his own, to an equality of wages with his superiors." Demagogues, who were "a nuisance to society at large," had demoralized labor by their "senseless" cry "against the despotism of capital." The real despots over the workers were labor organizations, "determining whether they shall labor or not, reducing wages to uniformity without reference to skill and faithfulness," and leading workers away from "wholesome moralities." Workers should concentrate not on agitating for better wages but on making themselves worthy of them, the author concluded.[4]

The growing American tension over workers and the nature of the nation's political economy heightened dramatically with the establishment of the Paris Commune, which controlled the city of Paris from March to May 1871 in the wake of the Franco-Prussian War. The completion of the transcontinental telegraph cable to Europe in 1866 allowed Americans to receive daily dispatches from the Continent. Aware that the American public had grown to like telegraphic reports during its own war, newspaper editors splashed onto their front pages and into human interest stories every development of the Paris Commune.[5] Propertied Americans were horrified by the news from Paris; it seemed to show a world in utter turmoil. The commune was a "wild, reckless, irresponsible, murderous mobocracy"; its philosophy, both Republican and Democratic newspapers reported, "is atheism, materialism, the negation of all religion; their political programme is absolute individual liberty, by means of the suppression of government." Many newspapers maintained that the world of the "communists" was so perverted that even women forsook their natural role and became viragos, bent on murder. Taking up this theme, the *Chicago Tribune* highlighted the danger lurking under the deceptive surface of Commune society, calling attention to "the decent and lady-like appearance of some of the women, who are perfectly well-dressed, and who have been caught pouring petroleum into cellars, or firing from windows." Newspapers dwelled on the numerous executions and the destruction in Paris, emphasizing the disorder of a society in which lower-class women murdered and upper-class men died. A Boston newspaper quoted George Sand's pronouncement that the Commune had "inspired an intense disgust in the minds of the most ardent politicians, even those most devoted to democracy."[6]

Ignoring the real structure of the French uprising, most Americans who were already nervous about workers were horrified by news from Paris; it seemed to show a chaotic world in which disaffected laborers had grabbed control of government with the plan of confiscating all property. Republican and Democratic newspapers alike complained that "their political economy consists essentially in the dispossession . . . of the present holders of capital, and in assigning the coin, instruments of labor and land, to associations of workmen; their historical theory is that the nobility and the bourgeoisie have each had their reign, and that the turn of the proletariat has now come. They exclude all that is outside the working class from society, considering it as socially and even physiologically effete." The deeds of the "Communists of Paris" came from the "communistic idea 'that property is robbery,'" according to the *Philadelphia Inquirer;* and the *Chicago Tribune* noted that, in Europe, support for the Commune came from workers who were contemptuous of capitalists and landowners. As productive workers, the Communards were defective: "The Commune was possible only because the youngest generation is without energy and wholly enervated," the *Boston Evening Transcript* reported.[7]

Following several years of labor agitation in America, the events of the Paris Commune made many Americans fear that workers' organizations would attempt rebellion in America. Speculations about impending revolution surfaced throughout the spring and summer of 1871; the popular *Scribner's Monthly* warned its readers in italics that *"the interference of ignorant labor with politics is dangerous to society."* The great Chicago fire in October—coincidentally the same month that the National Labor Union had planned to hold its first national political convention, although it had been postponed—revealed just how frightened many Americans had become. Some argued that the fire had been part of a laborers' plan to burn American cities. Providing what he considered proof that the Chicago fire had been set, one man concluded: "These facts show us the enemy we have to fight. The diabolical combination of the Communists to overturn capital and revolutionize society uses fire as its most effectual weapon. The conflagrations of Paris and Chicago should be warnings to the world." Famous reformer Charles Loring Brace wrote that "in the judgment of one who has been familiar with our 'dangerous classes' for twenty years, there are just the same explosive social elements beneath the surface of New York as of Paris."[8]

As Northerners worried about revolution, they began to pay a great deal of attention to the International Workingmen's Association, which had organized in 1864 in Europe and had come to America by 1867. In December 1871, the *Boston Evening Transcript* worried that "the Internationals" were trying to foment disturbances in New York. Their aim was the "disintegration of society." "They are agrarians, levellers, revolutionists, inciters of anarchy, and, in fact, promoters of indiscriminate pillage and murder." It maintained that "[t]he ideas of the Internationalists are subversive of all the regulating principles which bind together the American social state." The *Philadelphia Inquirer* warned its readers that Internationals were waging war against capital and property, and that anyone who had either would be compelled to divide it with "those who have little or nothing." Communists, the *Philadelphia Inquirer* charged, believed that $365 was enough to render a man a criminal capitalist. They planned war on America's "landed aristocracy," which it said was almost entirely "small farmers, who are admirably represented, twice a week, in our market houses, peddling their butter, cheese and vegetables." It was clear that this effort would attract only "the poorest of the poor, men too idle, vicious or improvident to be of any use to themselves or any public cause to which they may be allied," and who would attack America's small farmers and mechanics. Republicans insisted more and more stridently that labor radicals were "incapable of understanding that there should be, and that, under proper conditions, there is a harmony of interest between . . . [capital and labor]; and that everything is to be lost and nothing to be gained by a mutually destructive war between such powerful agencies in human affairs."[9]

The increasing popular fear of labor radicals made Northern Republicans distinguish even more strongly between two types of workers. They deplored those represented by the Paris Commune and the International, who insisted that capital and labor were antagonistic. These workers, it seemed, refused to produce and instead planned to confiscate the property of their betters through violence. An increasing dislike of these poor, disaffected laborers showed up in a subtle change in mainstream understanding of the free labor system. In the 1860s hard work brought success, but by the 1870s success itself proved someone's worth. "Success, as a general rule, is the measure of ability," announced the *Boston Evening Transcript*. "The amount of success to be achieved . . . is generally allowed to be in proportion to the intelligence and executive ability brought to bear upon [economic pursuits]."[10]

Republicans lauded those they believed were the true producers of the country, who accepted the idea of an organic society and who obligingly worked their way up the free labor ladder. In America, according to the Republican *Philadelphia Inquirer,* the enemy of the Internationals was simply any "mechanic who honors religion and law, and by a superior skill, industry and economy acquires a little property, or who comfortably feeds, clothes and educates his children." The *Cincinnati Daily Gazette* agreed that workers would become capitalists themselves not by "burning down factories or attempting to take forcible control of them," but by working hard and saving. Calling "these truths" "trite," the article's author nonetheless felt it imperative to reassert them in view of "the efforts made to convert a portion of the American people to the Communist doctrines, which recently received such a terrible exemplification in Paris."[11]

While most Northern Republicans disliked workers who threatened the organic nature of society, even some Northern Democrats were becoming uncomfortable with labor interests, despite prominent party members' championing of the idea that laborers were a distinct class entitled to government protection. By June 1871, August Belmont, the well-to-do chairman of the Democratic National Committee, remarked that Republicans were making political capital out of the Democratic drift toward the common man by accusing the Democrats of "revolutionary . . . intentions." While centrist Republicans took the lead in attacking labor organizations, the moderate and extremely popular Democratic *New York World* also quietly criticized "self-seeking demagogues and self-appointed orators" whose harangues hid "the real wishes of the working-men," who, it said, had no special interests except the widely popular eight-hour law. Prosperous Democrats were as nervous as Republicans about workers who saw society as an inherent struggle between rich and poor. Many of them would consider new political affiliations after 1871, as prominent Democratic politicians supported "the laboring classes" at the expense of the wealthy.[12]

Events of the early 1870s fed Republican fears that disaffected workers could try to gain property by taking over the government instead of working, and some Northern Democrats began to share this anxiety. Together they formed a group that clung to the idea that the true American system depended on a harmony of interest between labor and capital and that championed those workers they saw as traditionally productive. In April 1871, the New York *Times* predicted that "[p]ossibly the very extravagances and horrible crimes of the Parisian Communists will, for some years, weaken the influence of the working classes in all countries. The great 'middle-class,' which now governs the world, will everywhere be terrified at these terrible outburst [*sic*] and absurd[ities], they will hold a strong rein on the lower."[13]

South Carolina, whose elected government had a majority of African-American legislators from 1867 to 1876, became the stage on which Northerners examined an America controlled by workers. Although it was not actually true, Northerners accepted the idea that the freedmen, America's most stereotypical laborers, were running that state's government. This meant that discussions of South Carolina contained an intersection of class and race that debates about most other Southern states did not. As politicians manipulated images of the South Carolina government to suit their own interests, Northerners gradually came to accept the idea that black workers were plundering South Carolina landowners in a class struggle against capital.[14]

The actual story of South Carolina's Reconstruction government offered little foundation for the image of it that Northerners came to hold. In 1868, a constitutional convention consisting of seventy-six African-Americans and forty-eight whites rewrote the state's constitution. The new constitution gave the vote to all men, removed property qualifications for office-holding, and called for the popular election of judges and officials. The new legislature met in July 1868; it contained eighty-eight African-Americans and sixty-seven whites. To raise the funds to rebuild the state, this new legislature passed new tax laws. Before the war, taxes in South Carolina had been levied on personal property and had fallen largely on professionals, merchants, and bankers. Landed property was drastically undervalued for tax purposes. The new legislature levied taxes on all property at its full value, making landowners, especially large landowners, confront higher taxes at a time when their cash was at an all-time low. At the same time, the legislature endorsed land reform, and, failing to attract congressional support for a $1 million loan to purchase land for freedpeople, it used state funds to buy land for resale to settlers—usually freedpeople—on easy terms.[15]

While the South Carolina legislature was itself a perfect illustration of the rift in the South's black community, Southern Democrats did not perceive it that way. The black representatives in the South Carolina legislature came primarily from among the state's prosperous, light-skinned, African-American professionals who owned property and aspired to economic affluence. These men did not, in fact, exert themselves for the poor working man, echoing instead the idea that workers and employers must either rise or fall together. Angry whites refused to see that the South Carolina legislators repeatedly rejected measures designed to protect black laborers, and they continued to perceive the black office-holders as the spokesmen for poor field hands. Many disfranchised ex-Confederates writhed in racist agony at the "crow-congress," the "monkey-show," the legislative "menagerie," and accused it of prostituting an expanding government to the interests of the freedpeople.[16]

Northern Democrats were sympathetic to white South Carolinians' complaints on racial grounds, but Northern Republicans paid little attention to the specifics of the South Carolina struggle until late 1870. In the wake of the white backlash against the new conventions and state constitutions, which led to political assassinations and terrorism, the South Carolina legislature authorized a new state militia in 1869. In the spring of 1870, the incumbent governor began to rebuild and arm the militia as a political force to help him hold power against both Democratic and other Republican opponents. When white men refused to serve with freedmen, the militia effectively became black. By election day of 1870, the militia contained more than 90,000 men. In the election, reformers consisting largely of ex-Confederates charging the current administration with corruption ran against the Republicans. After the reformers lost, bitter men, organized as the Ku Klux Klan, took vengeance on freedmen for the results of the election.[17] The armed African-American militia fought back. In late 1870 and early 1871, Northern Republicans were horrified by reports of the anarchy in South Carolina.[18]

In March 1871, most Northern Republicans seemed genuinely confused about who was for and who was against violence for political gain. Democratic politicians insisted that the South was peaceful and less violent than the North; Republican politicians maintained that South Carolina was a bloodbath. While they condemned terrorism, most Northern Republicans were willing to believe that many Democrats wanted to restore order. When the Republican governor of South Carolina met with leading Democrats to try to stop the violence, Republican newspapers reported that the meeting was generally positive, and that the Democrats complained only of "the insolence of the colored militia."[19]

While disliking the violence on both sides in South Carolina, Northern Republicans remained committed to black rights in the state and refused to accept the Democratic argument that black voting necessarily meant a government in thrall to black interests. When prominent ex-Confederate general J. B. Kershaw told the South Carolina governor that the Ku Klux Klan represented "the just indignation of a plundered people," and maintained that the way to restore order was for "the scoundrelly carpet-baggers from the North and the rascally scalawags of the South to resign the offices they had usurped, and leave those States in the hands of Southern gentlemen," Northern Republicans exploded, and defended the right of African-Americans to serve in government. The *Chicago Tribune* commented, "so far as Kershaw and his set are concerned . . . it serves them right to be ruled by their own negroes and such white vagabonds as their negroes can be gulled into electing to office." The *San Francisco Daily Alta California* quoted a Democratic South Carolina newspaper's opinion that it would be better to rebel and thus force a military occupation of white men than to continue under a government of "negroes and white incarnate fiends." The California newspaper maintained that "a restless element of South Carolina, always in a minority," did not like any government that it could not control. Less than a month after Kershaw's speech, and in the midst of Northern reaction to it, Congress passed the Ku Klux Klan Act to protect Southern African-Americans from white terrorists.[20]

The Ku Klux Klan Act of 1871 was the last firm Northern Republican defense of African-Americans, because moderate Northern Republicans were about to change their outlook on Southern questions. In March— the same month the Communards took Paris and the governor of South Carolina met with Kershaw—a new attempt of white South Carolinians to rid themselves of their hated government offered political capital to antiadministration Northern Republicans. Their formulation of South Carolina's problems resonated powerfully with moderate Northerners in general.

Conservative South Carolinians opposed the legislature not only out of racism but also because they believed that their government was controlled by the lower class. The state had had a relatively successful labor movement after the Civil War, and by 1869, South Carolinians had real reason to believe that the state legislature was dominated by labor interests. In contrast to the North, these interests appeared to be represented by the Republican party, whose adherents had been those loyal to the Union during the war. Thus they were predominantly freedmen. After successful organization in Charleston by African-American workers in certain trades—notably the longshoremen, whose strikes gained them their demands in 1867, 1868, and 1869—Republican leaders organized a state labor convention, which met in Columbia the day after the legislature convened in 1869. Prominent Republican politicians Robert Brown Elliott; W. B. Nash; Franklin Moses, Jr.; Francis L. Cardozo; and Alonzo J. Ransier led the convention of more than three hundred delegates, almost all of whom were African-American.[21]

The politicians at the convention emphasized the harmony of interests between capital and labor, but some delegates, according to an unfriendly reporter, wanted the convention "generally to take a position directly and willfully hostile to the whole employing class," calling for "Higher Wages, or Strikes and Revolution." The convention ultimately called for only moderate legislation in favor of labor, hoping to protect workers from fraud, regulate work hours, and begin government aid to farmers for the purchase of land. But even these mild measures were enough to support the Democratic accusations of 1867 that, if allowed to vote, African-Americans would plunder white property. Ex-Confederate Democrats bristled at the apparent attempt of the black lower class to use the government against them. A British observer attuned to class nuances reported from Charleston in November 1870 that, with many white South Carolinians disfranchised, "a proletariat Parliament has been constituted, the like of which could not be produced under the widest suffrage in any part of the world save in some of these Southern States."[22]

When the state began to collect a new tax that had been levied by the new mostly black legislature, the Charleston Chamber of Commerce met in March 1871 to protest. It called for a taxpayers' convention to meet in Columbia on May 9. The delegates to this "Tax-payers' Convention" were nearly all staunchly Democratic ex-Confederates who had been bitter in their opposition to African-American suffrage on racial grounds. Former Confederate officer James Chesnut, Confederate general Martin Witherspoon Gary, and former Secretary of the Confederate Treasury G. A. Trenholm, among many others, took leading roles in the convention. A sympathetic Southern newspaper cheerfully recorded that the body included: "four ex-Governors, two ex-Lieutenant-Governors, three ex-United States Senators, five ex-Congressmen, one ex-Chancellor, one ex-Secretary Confederate Treasury, forty-three ex-members of the House of Representatives, sixteen State Senators, eleven Generals, and five Bankers." But while the protesters were familiar, their tactics had changed. The convention had taken its cue from Republican fears of disaffected workers in society, and instead of harping on race, it emphasized property issues.[23]

This new strategy played perfectly to disaffection within the Republican party. For at least a year, Northern Republicans disillusioned by Grant's tariff policy, his effort to annex Santo Domingo, and his cronyism had been considering a reform movement. They hoped to coalesce with moderate Northern Democrats, who were nervous about workers, embarrassed by the Tammany Hall corruption scandals, and anxious to cast off their affiliation with unreconstructed Southern Democrats. At the powerful *New York Daily Tribune,* Horace Greeley joined other disgruntled Republicans in believing that the time had come to dump Grant, mollify the South, and move the nation forward to claim its great destiny as a united people. Greeley's important newspaper made the Tax-payers' Convention the occasion for the opening salvo in an attack on Grant.[24]

Those opposed to Grant championed the Tax-payers' Convention not only because of the political advantage it offered but also because its version of events in South Carolina illustrated the sense of many Northern moderates that the nation's political economy was in danger. In the midst of the coverage of the Paris crisis, Northerners of both parties who did not identify themselves with a labor interest were keenly aware of the struggle in their own country between adherents of the old idea of an organic society and those who believed in a political economy of class struggle. Mainstream Northerners watched anxiously as urbanization and industrialization encroached on the antebellum rural world, creating a class of unskilled or semiskilled workers, often foreign-born, who seemed locked into their low-paid positions. Interpreting the problems of low wages and chronic underemployment as indications of the workers' own poor performance, Northerners who did not identify with a labor interest were increasingly frightened of workers who appeared to be flouting the traditional rules of success through hard work. Mainstream Americans were anxious to weaken the growing power of these workers, who seemed to threaten traditional American society.

When the New York Daily Tribune's "special correspondent" in South Carolina delivered a front-page article on May 1, 1871, entitled "Political Problems in South Carolina," he read the Northern struggle over political economy into the racial struggles of the South. Printed in a newspaper that had always been a staunch supporter of African-American rights, the article joined Northern Republican fears of those advocating a political economy based on class struggle with the Northern Democratic opposition to black voting on the grounds that African-Americans would be the decisive voters in key elections. By uniting these two ideas, the author suggested that African-Americans would indeed wield political power for their own interests, as Northern Democrats charged, and that those interests were based on the presumption of class struggle.[25]

The author admitted that "party lines are race lines in South Carolina," but described this "typical Southern State" as a victim of disaffected workers, who believed in class conflict. Integrating racism into the language of political economy, the author explained that most of South Carolina's population was made up of "negroes, who as a class, are ignorant, superstitious, semi-barbarians. . . . They are extremely indolent, and will make no exertion beyond what is necessary to obtain food enough to satisfy their hunger. . . . Upon these people not only political rights have been conferred, but they have absolute political supremacy." Lazy African-Americans elected to office demagogues—carpetbaggers or African-Americans—who controlled their followers by harping on themes of class warfare and legislating wealth away from prosperous hard workers—"the intelligent people of the State"—and giving it to the indolent. This picture of South Carolina linked government corruption with "the rule of a class just released from slavery, and incompetent, without guidance, to exercise the simplest duties of citizenship." The correspondent concluded: freedmen "are the governing class in South Carolina, and a class more totally unfit to govern does not exist upon the face of the earth."

The correspondent wrote that the white party in the state was already angry at the perceived corruption of the new legislature, which, like its predecessor, seemed bound to the labor interest. Whites found the new taxes "[a] final cause of irritation." "The rate of taxation was largely increased over that of previous years, and the property-owners honestly believed that they were robbed to support the extravagance of the 'Nigger Government,' which they so cordially hated." The article stunned Democrats North and South by revealing that some Northern Republicans were willing to accept Southern Democrats' opposition to African-American rights so long as their complaints were framed in terms of a conflict over political economy rather than race.[26]

While covering the actual convention, Greeley continued to develop the idea that the struggle in South Carolina was about the survival of a society based on hard work and economic harmony. He ignored its evident racism—one speaker argued that "the negro is mentally a child," whom he equated with "the idiot" and "the fool"—and presented the Tax-payers' Convention as a moderate and sensible response to a crisis over political economy. The nation's most prominent Democratic newspaper, the *New York World,* presented the issue of South Carolina's misgovernment solely in terms of race. The Republican *New York Times* suggested that the higher taxes reflected South Carolina's large postwar population, admitted some corruption, and blamed the Ku Klux Klan for disrupting the country. But the *New York Daily Tribune* highlighted the convention's report, which, tailored to a Northern audience, worried about workers plundering the government treasury, talked of the confiscation of property through taxation, and insisted that South Carolina whites hoped to work with freedmen to reform the state government. The *New York Daily Tribune* maintained that the convention was "remarkably temperate, dignified, and free from any manifestation of political feeling." A few days after the convention, it lamented that "[t]he most intelligent, the influential, the educated, the really useful men of the South, deprived of all political power, . . . [are] [t]axed and swindled by a horde of rascally foreign adventurers, and by the ignorant class, which only yesterday hoed the fields and served in the kitchen." When a reader wrote eloquently to defend the legislation of the South Carolina government, arguing that wise laws defended the laboring man, Greeley caustically voiced his "regret that men wise enough to pass such laws should not also have proved honest enough to abstain from the wholesale corruption that has made the present State Government a stench in the nostrils of the tax-payers."[27]

Horace Greeley was a powerful man, and his slant on South Carolina would have carried weight on its own, but defenders of the freedmen unwittingly aided him by suggesting a connection between African-Americans and the sort of workers represented by the Paris mob. Massachusetts senator Benjamin F. Butler and former abolitionist Wendell Phillips, the anchors of the Republican faction devoted to the interests of labor, appeared to deny the very basis of the Republicans' vision of American society by arguing that there was a conflict between labor and capital. In shocking rhetoric designed to recall the ongoing French crisis, Butler—who defended the Commune—warned that the freedmen might retaliate against men represented by the Tax-payers' Convention and the Ku Klux Klan if pressed too hard. If they did, he prophesied, South Carolinians "may, perhaps, be shocked and stand aghast with horror."[28]

Phillips was less delicate even than Butler. At a labor reform convention, he called for "the drum-head conviction and the gibbet" for all those protesting against the Reconstruction government, since they instigated the Ku Klux Klan. A few weeks later he publicly censured Greeley for encouraging freedmen to follow the traditional route to prosperity for which Republicans believed freedpeople, like all Americans, were destined. Phillips condemned Greeley for telling "the landless, still persecuted negro . . . 'Go to the Western prairies; root hog, or die!'" "Mr. Greeley suggests for the future nothing but his dreary political economy and devotion to the pursuit of material prosperity," Phillips complained, but "[t]here is much yet to do in the sphere of human rights."[29] Horace Greeley was the editor popularly credited with offering to young white men the very famous advice, "Go West, young man," and he was one of the key architects of the entire Republican view of a free labor political economy that allowed all who were willing to work the ability to prosper. Phillips's attack on him suggested to mainstream Republicans that freedpeople denied this Republican vision of society.

Picking up where Butler and Phillips left off, Greeley completed the association of South Carolina freedmen and the sort of workers represented by the Paris Communards. On a tour of the South in the early summer of 1871, he reported to his newspaper a revealing interview with Democrat Robert Toombs, a former Confederate secretary of state from Georgia. Black suffrage meant that "a great lump of ignorance and vice had been made part of the governing class," Toombs declared, and even education could not help. He explained, "Reading and writing did not fit a man for voting. The Paris mob were intelligent, but they were the most dangerous class in the world to be trusted with any of the powers of government. A property qualification was what was necessary for a stable government. Only those who owned the country should govern it, and men who had no property had no right to make laws for property-holders." Toombs's real fear was that "the lower classes of white men— the dangerous, irresponsible element" would join with African-Americans and, being in "the majority, and being able to control the State, would . . . attack the interests of the landed proprietors."[30]

Within a week of this article, the *Chicago Tribune* reminded its readers that a situation like that of South Carolina's directly threatened the North. The Tammany Hall scandals were in the wind, making it clear that Boss William Marcy Tweed's ring maintained their lucrative hold on the New York City government by distributing patronage to immigrant and poor voters. *Tribune* editor Horace White maintained that New York and South Carolina alike were plagued by bad government elected by a vicious constituency. His reasoning reflected the new theory of political corruption, and revealed the erosion of Republican support for black suffrage. In the atmosphere of a battle against a corrupted government, Democrats emphasized that the vote of the common white man was the best defense against the corrupt leaders elected by ex-slaves, while Republicans increasingly argued that it was the poor white man, misled by demagogues who harped on the theme of class warfare, who placed corrupt men in power. According to the *Chicago Tribune:* "New York is abandoned by her property-owners to the role of one set of adventurous carpet-baggers and vagabonds, because her men of character and responsibility have not time to take charge of the city government . . . South Carolina is ruled by carpet-baggers and irresponsible non-property-holders for other reasons."[31]

The Tax-payers' Convention fizzled, disbanding with only a call for economy in the South Carolina government, but it had successfully

merged Northern Democratic and Northern Republican concerns, establishing the proposition that, in South Carolina, disaffected workers who
rejected the organic view of society and believed instead in class struggle
controlled the government with an eye to redistributive legislation. That
the governing South Carolinians were freedmen, whose race further degraded the image of disaffected workers, only made many Northerners
increasingly anxious about workers' participation in the government.

This formulation of South Carolina politics resonated with non–
working-class Northerners, who had good reason to fear the growing
power of those they believed to be subverting America's political economy. In the fall of 1871, a widely reported contest put Benjamin F. Butler
in the news. The round, balding, mustachioed Butler was infamous for
his spoilsmanship, shifting his allegiances and using government patronage shamelessly to maintain his own power as he did the bidding of
any constituency willing to back him. In 1871, he led a prolabor organization in seeking the Republican nomination for governor of Massachusetts. With the enthusiastic support of Wendell Phillips, Butler
mobilized labor reformers and the industrial towns in the Bay State to
back his candidacy. Mainstream Republicans like Henry Wilson, Charles
Sumner, Henry L. Dawes, and George F. Hoar joined forces against him
and made sure of the election of their candidate, but no one missed the
power of Butler's organization. At the *Nation,* E. L. Godkin worried that
"those who crowd the tenement-houses and workshops of manufacturing cities" were corrupting American government. He wrote that Butler's
candidacy represented "the organization, prematurely and under false
colors, but still the organization of such a commune as America would
now supply." He mused that few "will not allow that it came dangerously
near to success."[32]

Way out in California, a Republican newspaper in San Francisco
mused about the future of the American government. "If this Government is ever overturned it will be from below," it reflected. Congress operated in the open, while state legislatures could not be publicly super-
vised. "It is in the State Legislatures that the greatest dangers lurk. Their
general decadence has been the theme of discussion for years. Every
Legislature that assembles, no matter where, seems to be worse than its
predecessor." South Carolina, it appeared, was a case in point.[33]

The Tax-payers' Convention's overt attack on black workers, suggesting
that they rejected the free labor ideal of an organic relation between la-

bor and capital that enabled a hard worker to prosper, encouraged a Northern Republican reevaluation of freedpeople. To make successful the accusation that freedmen were plundering South Carolina, opponents of the legislature had to replace the image of freedmen as good, productive workers participating in America's free labor system with a picture of them as bad workers bent on confiscating wealth without work. Indeed, the correspondent for the *New York Daily Tribune* in South Carolina made a notable reassessment of Southern labor in his article "Political Problems in South Carolina." He wrote of "the great mass of the negroes . . . the plantation 'field-hands,'" who were not only indolent but also "given to petty thieving to great extent." Holding "absolute political supremacy," they elevated their own leaders and reduced white people to "thralldom" as they enacted their own legislative program.[34]

Greeley continued to develop the theme of the disaffected black worker in his newspaper, attributing to African-Americans the same negative qualities pinned on white organized labor by its enemies. In May and June, he lamented that the African-American man did not save his money, instead buying useless things on credit, "a fashionable bonnet and pair of gaiters for his wife, perhaps or a gaudy necktie and oroide pin for himself." Another article maintained that black sharecroppers were responsible for their own poverty. "The negroes, keeping no accounts and not very careful in their habits, usually found, on settlement, that they had eaten up their crop while it was growing and were often in debt after it had been sold and accounted for." Picking up the popular image of "communists" who argued about economic theories while their wives struggled to feed the children, Greeley contrasted the lazy black men with their wives, whose "industry" was "noticeable." He continued, "They wash, sew, work in the vegetable gardens near the city, keep stalls in the market, and sell fruit, candies, cakes, and lemonade on the streets, seated usually upon the sidewalk with their feet in the gutter, and their goods in their laps or spread out by their sides. Many a lazy fellow who hangs about the City Hall steps day after day, waiting for a job of corporation work, is supported by his industrious wife." The emphasis on women's productivity was useful only as a foil for the lazy men, for in June, Greeley's paper chided lazy black women for shunning field work.[35]

Unwilling to work, these African-Americans relied on government jobs handed out by those politicians who relied on their support. The *New York Daily Tribune* continued to accuse black men of rejecting plantation work for the jobs provided by Southern city governments. Northern Democrats were quick to add to the growing sense that freedmen were rejecting the free labor ideal, insisting that they were leaving the fields and thus ignoring the fundamental stage of advancement in a free labor society. In September 1871, the *New York World* told its readers that freedmen were abandoning farms, "where they would be useful to themselves and to society; where they would increase and multiply, and gradually accumulate property, and advance in civilization and knowledge," to go to cities and take government jobs, paid for by "taxes on the property holders."[36]

A strike of black workers in Washington, D.C., in June 1871 enabled Greeley to portray African-Americans directly as the type of labor agitators that Americans increasingly disliked. According to the *New York Daily Tribune*, "a large number" of black workers applied for jobs with a Washington railway company and accepted the offered wage of $1.25 per day. When they showed up for work, however, they demanded $2.00 per day for eight hours of work. When the director offered them $1.50, "only about a dozen" went to work. As the work was "proceeding too slowly," it was contracted out, and the contractor then primarily hired white men at $1.25 to $1.50. "About 300 colored men" tried to prevent the white men from working. In addition, "[t]hreats were made by the strikers to the colored men at work, that if they did not strike, they (the strikers) would kill them." The upshot of the disturbance was this: after having forced all black workers to quit the railway, African-Americans gathered to organize, while the contractor said he could find "plenty of good white men to work for $1.50 a day, and that he [would] not employ colored men at any price." The ex-officio president of the Board of Public Works added to the story by writing a letter declaring that $1.50 was a fair wage and that the Board of Public Works "[would] not yield to violence, nor countenance any attempt to intimidate or interfere with honest laborers by mobs or gangs of armed men." The *New York Daily Tribune* recorded that "thousands" of other workers—black and white—"would be glad to come and work for the wages offered," and it said that the public wanted the "lawless mob" to be handled with force. When the struggle ended peacefully, Greeley's paper correctly concluded: "The experiment of free colored labor has been watched by all parties with great interest," and that many were "ready to seize upon the distorted reports which came from Washington as evidence of the incapacity of freedmen as laborers."[37]

The *New York Daily Tribune* worked to reinforce the idea that African-Americans should eschew politics and confine themselves to the traditional American route to success. In September 1871, it commented that freedpeople in Tennessee "have taken a sensible and practical way of showing each other, as well as their white neighbors, what progress they have made in the useful science of agriculture." An agricultural exhibition near Nashville showed the "very creditable" products of African-American farms. "The black men are learning rapidly enough that they are abundantly able to make their own way in the world, and to fill the useful positions of producers as satisfactorily as their white brethren. One such exhibition as that at Nashville, organized and carried out by colored men, is worth more to the race than a score of negroes in Congress," the paper preached.[38]

Freedmen unwittingly bolstered Northern fears that they rejected the free labor system. In October 1871, the National Colored Convention assembled in Columbia, South Carolina. When its delegates repudiated the new political reform movement in the South and adopted resolutions calling for the preservation of the reconstructed state governments, they seemed to align themselves with the disaffected Southern workers allegedly plotting confiscation.[39]

In January 1872, newspapers reported that "At no time since the close of the rebellion has there been greater interest than now in the political and financial interest of South Carolina." Indeed, the election year of 1872 injured even further the image of black workers, as reforming Republicans and Northern Democrats popularized their formulation of disaffected black workers subverting government to their own ends. By 1872, Greeley had irreparably split with Grant and knew that the president was vulnerable to accusations that the men in control of his reconstruction governments planned to confiscate wealth rather than work for wages. Through January and February the *New York Daily Tribune* harped on the corruption of the South Carolina government.[40]

Then, in March, Greeley printed a report from South Carolina by James S. Pike, a disillusioned former radical Republican politician. After interviewing men with financial interests in South Carolina—notably former Confederate general Wade Hampton—Pike published an article entitled "A State in Ruins." His article tied together the Democratic formulation of the corruption of politics inherent in black voting with the Republican anxiety about disaffected workers. It highlighted both

Hampton's complaints about the state's "oppressive taxation" at the hands of black legislators and their carpetbagger allies and his insistence that laborers did not want to work. The next month, an editorial in the *New York Daily Tribune* maintained that, while freedmen had not utterly failed under freedom, "they might and should have done much better." They had to own land to have their freedom "assured and perfect," the paper reiterated, but complained that they had not bought land because they had spent their money "in drink, tobacco, balls, gaming, and other dissipation." Had they not wasted their capital, the editorial insisted, "they might have bought therewith at least Ten Million acres of the soil of their respective States which would have given each family an average of ten acres of mother earth; and the free and clear owner of ten acres need never stand idle or accept half wages."[41]

Greeley's attacks on freedmen became central in the 1872 race for the White House. In early May, disgruntled Republicans and "New Departure" Democrats, who hoped to replace Grant, organized the Liberal Republican party and gave their presidential nomination to Greeley. While New Departure Democrats emphasized their belief that Republicans sought to create an empire through patronage and corruption, powerful Republican newspaper editors who shifted away from regular Republicanism instead developed the changing image of black workers. Murat Halstead of the *Cincinnati Commercial*, Horace White of the *Chicago Tribune*, William Cullen Bryant of the *New York Evening Post*, and Edwin L. Godkin of the *Nation* all swung over to Greeley's camp and adopted his rhetoric about unproductive black workers looting the Reconstruction governments, while they emphasized that white Southerners were helping the South to prosper.[42]

Liberal Republicans' attacks on African-Americans were not simply rhetorical attacks on Grant as the mentor of the freedmen; they also reflected the Republican dislike of powerful Northern labor interests. Labor organizations seemed particularly restive in 1872, and Liberal Republicans seemed preoccupied with reporting strikes and attacking organized labor. At the *Chicago Tribune*, White continued to take his cue from Greeley, and, standing staunchly against politicized labor organizations, he complained in January 1872 that "those who style themselves 'the working classes'" needed to be taught "a few sound truths of political economy." "Now that their representatives are becoming more and more prominent in politics, their lack of such knowledge is painfully evident." The *New York Daily Tribune* noted that a worker attending a Labor Reform Convention in Connecticut rose and "hint[ed] that, if the wrongs of the American laborers are not righted, he will resort to the revolutionary violence of the Paris Commune." Two weeks later, White reiterated that South Carolina had been run deeply into debt by improvident men, and called for wealthy South Carolinians, who knew how to manage property, again to hold office.[43]

In contrast to the Liberal Republicans following Greeley's lead, stalwart administration Republicans dealt with disaffected workers by reaffirming the party's commitment to a harmonious American political economy. They courted workers, nominating as vice president longtime friend of labor Henry Wilson, letting Wendell Phillips and labor leader S. P. Cummings draft a "labor plank" in the platform, welcoming Butler back into the party, and staging a National Workingmen's Convention in New York to nominate Grant and Wilson. Republicans also continued to defend freedmen as good workers starting their climb to prosperity in the fields. A correspondent to the *Cincinnati Daily Gazette* maintained that the South was producing more cotton than ever, and that "[a]ll the predictions about the idleness of negroes and evils of negro suffrage have proved grossly false. The negroes have done their part, and they have done it with no disposition to assume anything on account of their political privileges."[44]

Despite stalwart Republican support, the actions of the freedmen themselves in the 1872 election seemed to many to prove that they indeed opposed the free labor ideal and threatened the American system. The Fifteenth Amendment went into effect in March 1870, making the 1872 presidential election the first in which the national government could enforce black suffrage. Northerners stood poised to judge freedmen's participation in the government. The choice of candidate was a difficult one for many African-Americans, since their old champion Horace Greeley now led a party of Northern reformers, including men like former abolitionist Charles Sumner, who had joined with their traditional enemies, the Democrats. Both advocating the increased services of the Reconstruction governments and recognizing that Greeley's policy would probably mean the restoration of Democrats to power in the South, most African-Americans voted for Grant and the Republican party, following Frederick Douglass's famous dictum: "The Republican party is the ship and all else is the sea."[45]

While voting for Grant was the logical choice for freedmen, voting for the regular Republican ticket in the South meant supporting politicians who had been widely accused of corruption. Then, too, some freed-people felt so strongly about the dangers of Greeley's policy that they attacked Greeley's few black supporters in the South, leading the *Boston Evening Transcript* to accuse them of "mob violence." Forced to choose between suicidal reform and the tarnished government that offered them political survival, freedmen chose survival and earned condemnation from a wide range of Liberal Republicans, Democrats, and conservative and even some moderate Republicans.[46]

African-American congressman Robert Brown Elliott from South Carolina revealed that even some of the black community was turning against those African-Americans portrayed as desperate for patronage to sustain them. Elliott had been lionized in the press for his intelligence, presence, honesty, and oratory, and was a national symbol of the black "better classes" who had assimilated the free labor ideal along with its values of education, religion, temperance, and diligence. Defeated in his bid for senator, he maintained that the successful candidate had bought his election from African-Americans who valued the emoluments of office-holding more than good government. "I can bear defeat," he said, "but the humiliation the thing has brought upon our colored race—that's what hurts me. Our race is now on trial before the world as to its fitness to govern. . . . The colored men . . . are in large majority in the Legislature, and then for them to deliberately sell out by wholesale is a blow that we can't get over for years. It is a blow at our integrity, our honesty, our manhood. . . . What will the world think of it?"[47]

Liberal Republicans lost the election, but their campaign popularized the idea that most freedmen were determined to rise without work, and legitimated in Republican thought the Democratic idea that black voting inherently threatened to corrupt the government.

The Liberal Republican debacle of 1872 and the almost immediate death of a devastated Horace Greeley were a bitter dose for those who opposed Grant, and their vitriol popularized the image of disaffected workers controlling government for their own ends. In January 1873, Whitlaw Reid, who had replaced Greeley as editor of the *New York Daily Tribune*, sent James S. Pike to South Carolina to write a series of articles about the state. While Pike recorded that he "was moved to visit S. Carolina from the extraordinary circumstances of its political condition," he and Reid probably intended his articles to add more fuel to an anti-Grant movement, and, to some degree, to punish the African-Americans who had deserted their old champion and voted overwhelmingly for Grant. Belying the idea that the South Carolina trip was to be a fact-finding tour, almost all of the themes of the new series had already appeared in Pike's 1872 article. While Northern black leaders recognized Pike's portrait of South Carolina as injurious to the African-American population, many Northern whites were predisposed to believe his story. The articles attracted so much attention that Pike expanded them and published them in December 1873 as *The Prostrate State: South Carolina under Negro Government*. The book was widely reviewed, it sold well, and it had a dramatic impact on the image of freedpeople in American society. The series, and later the book, fleshed out the idea that African-Americans had rejected the laborer's traditional path to success and were instead attempting to rise by controlling politics to confiscate the wealth of their betters.[48]

Pike's articles drew the attention of the entire nation, which by 1873 was not only preoccupied with South Carolina's troubles but also riveted to a political crisis in Louisiana in the wake of the 1872 election. There, stalwart Republicans had denied the election of a reform governor and appealed to the president for support. A Republican court installed the Republican candidate, William Kellogg, into office, but opponents insisted that their candidate, John McEnery, had been the popular choice and organized militia-type units known as "White Leagues" to defend his right to the governorship. As the rival factions fought for control of the state, Northern Democrats and Liberal Republicans believed that the Kellogg faction was a prime example of an undemocratic government forced on the people by a cabal bent on holding power by catering to a black mob. Then, in December 1872, the sitting Republican governor was impeached, leaving the office in the hands of the acting lieutenant governor, prominent black stalwart P. B. S. Pinchback. Seeing an African-American become the state governor confirmed the worst fears of anxious Northerners. The Liberal Republican *Nation* pilloried Pinchback as "a fine specimen of the rising colored politician" of the South. It accused him of usurping power, and argued that the "cock-fighter and gambler" "has literally nothing under him but Federal bayonets and an injunction."[49]

Carefully excising from his travel notes positive references to African-American legislators, Pike began his report with a description of society turned "bottom-side up." "The wealth, the intelligence, the culture, the wisdom of the State," "men of weight and standing in the communities they represent," had been displaced in the legislature by "the most ignorant democracy that mankind ever saw, invested with the functions of government." Pike's black "democracy" wore "coarse and dirty garments of the field; the stub-jacket and slouch hats of soiling labor." African-American legislators, Pike argued, who were elected by their peers, had jumped far ahead of their earned position in Southern society.[50]

According to Pike, the freedmen refused to follow a traditional path to success, preferring instead to plunder the true producers of the state. Pike reminded Northerners that South Carolina was "an elysium for an agriculturist." Plantation land "in good working order" could be had for two dollars an acre, and cotton was an extremely profitable crop which required only "easy and enticing" labor. "It would . . . be difficult to know where an agriculturist could turn to find so good a prospect of reward for his labors," he wrote. Surely, in a land like this, any one willing to work his way up in a traditional way could do so easily. But instead of working for their success, impecunious laborers destroyed capital with confiscatory tax laws. The representatives of wealthy Charleston, for example, were chosen by "swamp negroes," he said. Pike reprinted a report of the South Carolina Tax-payers' Convention of 1871 lamenting that "they who lay the taxes do not pay them, and that that they who are to pay them have no voice in the laying of them." He quoted a speaker from the convention saying that African-Americans had been given "the privilege, by law, of plundering the property-holders of the State, now almost bankrupt, by reason of the burden of taxation under which they labor."[51]

Pike's picture of labor confiscating capital elaborated on the connection between bad workers and a bad government, and was designed to strike terror into the hearts of Northerners who feared that disaffected workers could capture the American government. Echoing the 1867 *New York World,* Pike quoted a South Carolina judge's opinion that demagogues had convinced freedmen that "[Southern] lands properly belonged to them, and not to their former masters." Pike agreed with the Tax-payers' Convention that the tax burden "is calculated, even if it be not intended, to bring about a wide-spread confiscation of property."

Twice he quoted a white man's report that African-American senator Beverly Nash had campaigned with a speech arguing: "The reformers complain of taxes being too high. I tell you that they are not high enough. I want them taxed until they put these lands back where they belong, into the hands of those who worked for them. You toiled for them, you labored for them, and were sold to pay for them, and you ought to have them."[52]

Pike's prescription for South Carolina reiterated the traditional Republican plan for individual advancement. After eulogizing a group of freedpeople who had successfully developed their own plantation, he encouraged philanthropists to commence a true blueprint for Reconstruction. A model plantation worked by ex-slaves would demonstrate the attributes of adequately paid free black agricultural labor, lift from poverty "the best portions of the colored population," "pave the way for their social and moral elevation; and thus perhaps might be laid the foundation of a revolution in the character of the race, that would lead to the most benignant results," he concluded.[53]

In 1873, Northerners were especially susceptible to Pike's portrait of dangerous workers in control of society. The Panic of 1873 threw many out of work, and they took their grievances to the streets in the form of strikes and protests. In April, for example, while the *New York Daily Tribune* ran Pike's articles, the *Cincinnati Daily Gazette* published "Anarchy and Bloodshed in the Indiana Coal Regions," which recalled the Paris Commune when it claimed that the women in Indiana "have thus far proved the most desperate element."[54]

Another article, titled "A Frightful Riot in Louisiana," went further, explicitly talking of disaffected workers trying to control government. Historians have called the Colfax Massacre the bloodiest single instance of racial carnage in the Reconstruction Era, but newspapers at the time described the horrific white massacre of African-Americans as self-defense against pillaging ex-slaves who had cloaked themselves in authority. According to dispatches reprinted in the *Cincinnati Daily Gazette,* Captain William Ward, a white legislator in the discredited Kellogg government, protested his removal at the hands of a judge and organized a force of freedmen and "a few white men of his own complexion," took possession of the Colfax courthouse, and took over the government. A Democratic newspaper from Missouri reported that the "mob" then "went on to use their powers violently until finally, intoxicated by an immunity of lawlessness, they began to hunt down those who were obnoxious to them, sack their residences and pillage their plantations. Several men were obliged to flee the parish." African-Americans who feared such disaffected men joined the clamor against them; O. J. Butler, "an intelligent colored man" and "a respectable merchant," told the *New Orleans Picayune* that "there are colored people . . . who sadly deprecate the occurrence; and, in fact, many of them, like myself, have been compelled by threats of violence to leave the place." Ultimately, the White Leaguers rallied for "self-defense" against the "reign of terror," set fire to the courthouse, and shot the men running from the flames. Eighty to one hundred of the Kellogg supporters died.[55]

Even workers who did not take over towns expected to take over the government, the press reported. The *Nation,* for example, worried that "much of the manual labor required by cities, States, and the General Government" was procured on "thoroughly communistic principles." It quoted the report of a government official who complained that favored mechanics, "who, as a rule, exhibit little interest in the performance of their duties and have no responsibility whatever," received higher wages than "gentlemen of education who occupy positions of trust and great pecuniary responsibility in the different bureaus." The *Nation* concluded that: "all discrimination against head-work in favor of hand-work, in spite of the mystic blatherskite which is poured forth so freely on this subject, is a discrimination against civilization itself." As New York "workingmen" rallied to protest the government report and adopted resolutions "denouncing members of Congress and the Legislature of the State for dereliction of duty to the cause of labor," even the radical *Boston Evening Transcript* bemoaned the "communism" creeping into America. Snarled the *Chicago Tribune,* "The spirit of Grangerism, Workingmanism, Communism, Grievanceism, or by whatever name the present fever among those who assume to themselves the title of 'the industrial and producing classes' may be termed, appears to be growing apace throughout the United States."[56]

More prosperous Northerners reacted to these stories by attacking organized labor and rallying around the idea of traditional American workers. The *Philadelphia Inquirer,* for example, told its readers about the murder of a nonstriker, kicked to death because he refused to join a strike; it attacked carpenters' demands for hour reduction by arguing that this rejected the American labor system; and it reflected that a new

Illinois law to prevent strikes "protects the rights and interests of the skilled and steady workmen, puts an end to the too long damaging dictation of the blatant demagogues that have for years profited from their self-chosen positions guardians [sic] of the rights of laborers." The *Cincinnati Daily Gazette* published "The Fallacy of Strikes," reiterating in the article that "[m]en have the right to claim certain wages for themselves, . . . those of whom they demand these rates . . . have an equal right to decline to grant them, and other workmen have an indisputable privilege to take the places of those who will not come to terms." The newspaper expected that society would bring to heel "malefactors" who tried to enforce their demands by "abuse, threats, or actual violence." By 1874, the *Chicago Tribune* was telling readers that the International was making the United States "the battle-ground in the war that Communism is waging upon society," and it warned: "We must no longer close our eyes to the dangers the International threatens."[57]

Presenting Southern African-Americans as analogous to disaffected Northern laborers, Pike's picture of South Carolina became the dominant one in discussions of freedpeople in 1873. On the one hand, Republicans still lauded ex-slaves like those represented by a "convention of colored men" in Texas. The *New York Times* reported that black Texans owned "taxable property, mostly real estate, valued at $2,076,000" in only twenty-one counties. This proved, the paper claimed, that freedpeople, emancipated eight years before in absolute poverty, had "quickly acquired habits of forethought and thrift, and were mastered by a desire to become rooted as proprietors in the soil to which they had been attached as slaves."[58]

On the other hand were increasing fears that disaffected black laborers sought to control the government. Growing numbers of Northern newspapers picked up their tone from the *New York Daily Tribune,* even if they lost the clear edges that that paper gave its argument. Some Republicans continued to insist that stories of Southern freedpeoples' laziness and mismanagement of government were concocted by Democrats, but that insistence got much less press in the North than evidence that African-Americans in general demanded political appointments in exchange for votes. When the Colored People of Ohio met on August 22, 1873, to declare the political independence of African-American voters from the Republican party and to protest what many of them saw as discrimination in appointments to government offices, many white men interpreted their protest as proof that freedmen wanted to hold government office simply to be able to live without working. The story of the meeting was widely reprinted, and widely condemned. Reporting that Grant had sent a "mulatto Colonel" to Ohio to manage "his colored brethren," the *San Francisco Daily Alta California* said that "[t]he colored men of Ohio have discovered that numerically they are entitled to one-twenty-fourth part of the offices," and demanded them in exchange for supporting the Republicans. The *Philadelphia Inquirer* used the meeting as an opportunity to condemn office-seeking in men of any color. The *Boston Evening Transcript* reported on both the Ohio convention and a similar one in Baltimore. Even the *New York Times* believed a story that "a number of colored politicians" had formed a secret society "for the avowed purpose of supporting only colored men for political offices," and joined other Republican papers in denouncing the movement.[59]

Northern Republicans and Democrats found common ground in their deprecation of black workers who sought to change the government. At the end of 1873, the *Boston Evening Transcript* mused that "the divisional lines of the Republican and Democratic parties are now . . . indistinct." African-American congressman R. B. Elliott sounded like a Democrat when he explicitly told a black audience in South Carolina that "they were responsible for the thieves who had plundered the State into bankruptcy, since they had elected them to office." They must reform immediately, he admonished, warning that the national Republican party was ready to cut loose "upon the slightest provocation from the corruption now existing in the South, and unless you do something, and that speedily, they will be compelled to cut off the rotten branches." Things were grim indeed when, from her new home in Florida, Harriet Beecher Stowe herself, abolitionist author of *Uncle Tom's Cabin,* claimed that freedpeople did not work as hard as Northerners because the South's long growing season meant that "there really is not need of that intense, driving energy and vigilance in the use of time that are needed in the short summers of the North."[60]

In the fall of 1873, even the staunchly pro-Grant and pro-freedmen *Boston Evening Transcript* ran a letter from Tennessee originally printed in the Democratic *New York World* arguing that "the blacks, as people, are unfitted for the proper exercise of political duties. . . . The rising generation of . . . blacks needed a period of probation and of instruction; a period . . . long enough for the black to have forgotten something of his condition as a slave and learned much of the true method of gaining honorable subsistence and of performing the duties of any position to which he might aspire." A man writing about Louisiana summed up the increasingly prevalent attitude about freedmen at the end of 1873. "It takes four negroes to do the work of one, on an average, and that which they do is done in a slovenly manner," he wrote. "Those negroes at work are between thirty and sixty years of age, and the younger decline to work almost entirely, but aspire to office, and have too much blue blood in their veins to stoop to any manual labor . . . they are made to believe that they will, with the aid of the white scallawags [sic], soon be masters of Congress."[61]

Prominent Northern minister Henry Ward Beecher read Pike's book and, perhaps unconsciously, took the argument a step further. Linking together all black and white laborers who rejected the free labor system, Beecher wrote in his *Christian Union* that the only solution to the situation in South Carolina was "the speedy achievement of rule by the classes who ought always to rule."[62]

South Carolinians opposed to their state government found the changing Northern sentiment about freedpeople encouraging, and recommenced in January 1874 to attack their legislature. Complaining that the new taxes were "much heavier than in any preceding year," property holders met in Columbia and called for the reassembly of the Tax-payers' Convention. The angry assembly recommended that the convention "ask [Congress] that [South Carolina] be remanded to a territorial condition or be placed again under military rule." At the meeting, the Northern press reported, "a number of speeches were made—one of them by a colored man—all declaring that the assessments have been outrageously high and that the people will not stand the abuse any longer." After the meeting, its executive committee unanimously resolved to recall the Tax-payers' Convention on February 17, in Columbia. Over the next two months, discussions of the South Carolina Tax-payers' Association became so widespread that by the end of March, a Pennsylvania congressman told the House of Representatives that the desires of the South Carolina protesters were "a matter of public notoriety."[63]

What did the reconvened Tax-payers' Convention actually do? In

March 1874, it sent to Washington a delegation with a memorial citing the plunder of the state as a basis for the remanding of South Carolina to military rule. The members of the delegation included quite prominent Southern Democrats, including four former governors and one former Senator. The delegation members visited the vice president, cabinet officers, and prominent congressmen. Henry L. Dawes of Massachusetts presented their petition to the House of Representatives on March 31, stating that it was "signed by gentlemen of such character as precludes the idea that it is frivolous or without any such foundation as would justify such an investigation."[64]

Reminding Congress that "the history of the country teaches that taxation without representation is tyranny," the petition claimed that a similar system of "monstrous oppression" existed in South Carolina. The petition maintained that in South Carolina, "those owning the property have no voice in the government, and those imposing taxes no share in the burden thereof." Declaring that, in many cases, extravagant taxation consumed "more than one-half the income from the property taxed," the petitioners argued that the South Carolina "government is arrayed against property." Echoing Pike, the petition maintained: "It has been openly avowed by prominent members of the legislature that taxes should be increased to a point which will compel the sale of the great body of the land, and take it away from the former owners," going on to argue that this policy was designed—misguidedly—to "promote the elevation of the black population, and the acquisition by them of the lands thus virtually confiscated." The *Philadelphia Inquirer* reported that the petition "bore the signatures of a large number of prominent and influential citizens."[65]

It took only a day for opponents of the Tax-payers' Association to take up the gauntlet. As the first order of business on April 1, 1874, African-American congressman Joseph H. Rainey of South Carolina presented to the House the response of the Republican Central Committee of South Carolina to the Tax-payers' petition. Rainey noted that the men signing the memorial were "prominent politicians of the old regime." The reply maintained that the taxes were not burdensome, and were imposed for the good of the state. It also declared that the Republicans, not the Tax-payers' Association, "represent the substantial interests in the State, as they represented the great majority of the people." Grant sided with the Republican Central Committee, of course, as did the House Judiciary

Committee when it declared that Congress had no authority to address issues within states. The petition was dropped.[66]

Although Grant recognized the petition as a political attack and blamed the extremism of the men comprising the Tax-payers' Association for the freedpeople's consolidation against them, the 1874 Tax-payers' protest had struck a chord in the North and received attention way out of proportion to its apparent import. The Tax-payers' Association had framed its complaints in such a way that the North would hear them, had enlisted a Massachusetts man to present them, and had asked the unthinkable. South Carolinians, citizens of the state that had begun the Civil War in defense of state's rights, had asked the federal government to assume control of their state. The demand was shocking—the North snapped to attention—and the fight over black participation in the government was to be fought in a national forum over the issue of taxation.[67]

For Northerners, the real issue at the heart of the Tax-payers' protest was whether adherents of a traditional vision of a harmony of economic interests or proponents of a new belief in class struggle should control American government. Significantly, the national battle over the South Carolina legislature was not fought over the issue of race; the opponents of the South Carolina government were careful to include prominent African-American voices in their protests. The *San Francisco Daily Alta California* revealed that, to Northerners, their imagined African-Americans in the South Carolina government had come to represent a whole stratum of American society. In a peculiarly Western image, it lamented that "[t]he old line of honest men have [sic] disappeared; gone like particles of gold in a bushel of sand, sunk out of sight, hidden by the common earth above them. Now the carpet-bagger, the scallawag [sic], the mean white trash and the ignorant freedman, constitute the top material, and the decency is out of sight."[68]

The image of South Carolina as a world of workers running amuck was one around which both moderate Democrats and Republicans could unite. While Democrats avoided complaining directly about workers controlling government and tried to emphasize the color dimension of the property issue, the *New York World* nonetheless editorialized against the removal from power of Southerners who were "trained to deal with great questions of public economy, sound financiers and rational statesmen." The *New York Times* asserted more strongly that poor workers were ruining South Carolina. Following every move of the reorganized Tax-payers' Association, it asserted that, in South Carolina, "[t]he preponderance of the political power is in the hands of non-tax-payers, who refuse the tax-payers a fair representation for their protection." The *Philadelphia Inquirer* reflected that "[t]he present legislation may be in the interest of a class . . . which has been elevated from the depths without experience how to act." While race was always a part of debates involving African-Americans, at the heart of the 1874 fight was political economy.[69]

The 1874 fight was over which version of political economy would dominate America. For many years—especially the past three—Americans had been learning to distinguish between workers who accepted the concept of a harmony of interests in society and those who believed in class struggle. In February 1874, a writer for the *Boston Evening Transcript* distinguished between the two types of workers in a description of German immigrants. Some, he recorded, were "solid, honest, thrifty, taking an adieu of their country, in company with their wives and children, as industrious as themselves." The others were caricatures of the disaffected worker that revealed just how profoundly this sort of individual threatened American life. They were "of less inviting appearance," "wifeless and childless" socialists who discussed "strange theories of government" and who denied the very basis of civilization by "arguing that the relation of husband and wife is but an 'historic product,' . . . 'that the woman who freely gives her love to any man is not a prostitute but the woman of the future.'"[70]

In 1874, the fight over African-Americans permitted this division to be illustrated with real force. A typical letter to the *New York Times* from a Virginia correspondent made clear the distinction between good and bad workers by concentrating on African-Americans. On the one hand were "too many negroes, as well as whites," who were "lazy, self-indulgent and improvident." They worked at farms or tobacco factories in the summer, but wasted their money (and "valuable time") in "weekly railroad excursions." With winter came unemployment as factories closed and farms lay fallow, and the workers were "almost reduced to starvation or beggary." These freedpeople took their rightful place in American political economy: "This improvidence, which leaves them victims to hunger and cold for several months in the year, largely accounts for the great mortality among them." It was workers like these that the *Boston Eve-*

ning Transcript reported were policing the Louisiana bayous in January 1874, stopping all work until they received higher wages. "Citizens," the Boston paper reported, had petitioned the governor for help, stating: "Our section is in a state of terror and alarm. All work is suspended. Armed bodies of mounted men enter our premises in spite of our remonstrances, and threaten the lives of all at work."[71]

On the other hand were African-Americans who were "sober, well-behaved, and tolerably industrious . . . quiet, orderly, and polite . . . the best servants in the world when well paid and well treated," reported the Virginia correspondent to the *New York Times*. With the self-respect that supports "all personal elevation and advancement," these freedpeople were washing, dressing well, improving their homes, saving for the future, and educating their children. They were "fast becoming owners of the soil all over" Virginia, and were "now farmers in their own way on their own account." In Richmond many had "houses and . . . bank accounts, while some are already wealthy." "My washerwoman, good old soul," the writer continued: "is mistress of the comfortable house in which she lives, besides owning several tenements which she rents out. She also owns hacks, wagons, carts, and horses—and yet her industry is such that she still plies her trade of laundress." Similarly, an old "plasterer and white washer" of his acquaintance owned "twenty or thirty houses, big and little, in the city," but continued to live in "his modest suburban cottage."[72]

Newspapers lectured freedpeople on their duties as free laborers, encouraging them to struggle for "education and intelligence, and character and property," to lead "lives of sobriety, honesty, industry, frugality and courtesy." Even the rhetoric of the press distinguished powerfully between unacceptable and praiseworthy African-Americans. Newspaper articles discussed disaffected African-Americans as a mass. They were usually Southern freedmen, faceless, nameless, and never quoted directly. In contrast, newspaper reporters accorded acceptable African-Americans individuality and respect, using their full name and often a specific physical description or even a picture. This type of African-American, who was almost always upwardly mobile, was frequently allowed to speak at length in direct quotations. Even the *Chicago Tribune*, for example, lauded a prominent African-American who claimed that ex-slaves were succeeding as free workers in America and pointedly rejected an alternative vision for the nation's workers. "All that we ask,"

John Jones insisted in a speech excerpted at length in the *Tribune*, "is to be paid the regular market price for our work. I thank God that there are no Communists among us, demanding other people's labor and blood. We work for all we get, and do not propose to quarrel with our neighbors because they may have more than we have."[73]

In South Carolina some called for "a chosen noble band" to sit in the to enforce its honesty, but despite this suggestion of a Ku Klux Klan–like organization, even in South Carolina many believed that the fight about taxes was not about race. When the taxpayers of Richland County met on January 12, 1874, the *Charleston News and Courier* reported:

> There were several colored men present, and one of these, William Winthrop, an industrious carpenter, addressed the meeting. He said that the question of taxation was separate and distinct from politics; that he was a Republican, and did not wish to be thought otherwise, but that the colored man and the white man were ground down alike by the oppressive taxation imposed upon them, and he was willing to join with the whites in an honest non-political effort to obtain mutual relief. He was repeatedly cheered by the convention.

At least one South Carolinian argued "that the rule of the negro in South Carolina is a phase of the struggle between Labor and Capital;" and a "mechanic" noted that the Tax-payers' Convention was made up of the "old cliques and Bourbons" who were not welcoming men like him even if they, too, paid taxes.[74]

On March 14, 1874, a month after it ran cartoonist Thomas Nast's portrait of a "Communist" labor organizer as a skeleton inviting a working couple to violence and death, *Harper's Weekly* tapped Northern racism to demean bad workers who seemed to want control of the government. To illustrate an article about the South Carolina legislature, the magazine printed Thomas Nast's now famous cartoon depicting two caricatured African-American legislators gesticulating and yelling at each other, while two unsavory white legislators watched. Above the group is slim, classic "Columbia" warning: "You are aping the lowest whites. If you disgrace your Race in this way you had better take Back Seats." In May, letters from South Carolina reported that "the sheriff and the auctioneer were about to complete the work of the negro elector and the carpet-bag office holder," selling prime land "for taxes." The proceeds would pass "from the swarm of collectors to the larger swarm of thieves, who imposed the taxes and impatiently wait to realize them."[75]

In April 1874, the editor of the *Nation* used the association of African-American voters and disaffected workers to attack what he believed was the growing power of workers in America. Excluding from his remarks African-Americans who were industrious, intelligent, and well behaved, editor E. L. Godkin explained in "Socialism in South Carolina" that "the average of intelligence among the rest is very low—so low that they are but slightly above the level of animals." He insisted that freedpeople were plundering the property holders as farms were sold to pay taxes and plantations were broken up to provide jobs and homes for indigent freedpeople. "The sum and substance of it all is confiscation." Godkin relied on racism to make this reorganization of society even more chilling, describing "the rich Congo thief on top and the degraded Anglo-Saxon at the bottom" of society. Finally, Godkin spelled out for his readers the lesson of the Palmetto State. "This," he trumpeted, "is what socialism has done for South Carolina." Raising the image of House leader and spoilsman Benjamin Butler as a leader of both workers and African-Americans through his extensive patronage system, Godkin reported:

> The taxpayers . . . are now actually engaged in begging General Butler, the greatest socialistic demagogue of our day, to have a little mercy on them. It is not a mistaken instinct which leads them to him, for they know very well that the South Carolinian imitators derive their power from the steady-moving and merciless machinery which fills the custom-houses and post-offices with his tools; and it is this machinery which makes socialism in America the dangerous, deadly poison it is.[76]

Edward King's famous 1873–1874 series for *Scribner's Monthly*, "The Great South," encapsulated the now mainstream image of dangerous black labor attempting to manipulate government to gain property. A journalist who had come to prominence when he covered the Franco-Prussian War and the Paris Commune for the *Boston Morning Journal*, King published "The South Carolina Problem: The Epoch of Transition" in June 1874, right after the Tax-payers' protest. In it King told the public that, after the war, freedpeople had believed that they should use their ballots to get property, and so had elected officials who confiscated land through taxation. In vengeance for slavery, King wrote, "Swart Demos" meant to wrest the lands from white people. He defended opponents of black suffrage: "It is not taxation nor even an increase of taxation, that the people of South Carolina object to; but it is *taxation without representation,* and *unjust, tyrannical, arbitrary, overwhelming taxation,* producing revenues which never get any further than the already bursting pockets of knaves and dupes." Freedpeople, charged King, were "cumberers of the soil; their ignorance impeded, their obstinacy throttles; their idleness will in time annihilate all chances of [South Carolina's] resuscitation. . . . They . . . revel in . . . idleness . . . yield easily to corruption . . . are immoral and irresponsible; . . . not at all unfriendly in spirit towards the whites, their old masters, yet by their attitude in reality they do them deadly harm."[77]

Thanks to the rhetoric of the South Carolina Tax-payers' Association Northerners who feared a labor interest had come to accept Southerners' contention that the mass of freedmen were a disaffected lower class plotting to confiscate the wealth of their betters through government aid. Despite its inaccuracy, the image of an uneducated mass of African-American voters pillaging society was one of the most powerful ones of the postwar years. In 1874, even the *Boston Evening Transcript* warned that "if ignorance shapes the laws, wise men will not long live under them, nor will the State thrive." In March 1875, when 2,000 black workers underscored the relationship between African-American labor and the government by marching to the White House to protest low wages, Grant refused to receive them. That same year, the *San Francisco Daily Alta California* reflected that, although South Carolina was in fact a prosperous state that "would compare favorably with any in the South," a man who "had read the report of the horrible rule of negroes and carpetbaggers . . . had been convinced that [in South Carolina] . . . industry was paralyzed; that the lazy negro was eating the bread of idleness; that the disheartened planter sat in listless despair; that the bankrupt merchant looked upon his empty shelves and cursed."[78]

At the same time, mainstream Northerners retained their support and admiration for those African-Americans who were continuing to rise in a traditional, individualistic way. The *New York Times,* for example, told its readers in May 1874 of "three colored men—Manuel Persons, Moses Persons, and Addison Lewis"—who had bought a 200-acre Tennessee farm for $3,800 over three years, despite their initial lack of capital and the need to support their families. In 1875, while condemning freedpeople who squandered money on "very ancient and shabby buggies, sham jewelry, and geegaws of all kinds," a journalist for James G. Bennett's *New York Herald* eulogized the Georgia freedpeople who owned "nearly four hundred thousand acres of farming real estate, besides city property" and who paid taxes "on over seven millions of property, of which nearly four hundred thousand acres are real estate."[79]

From its geographical vantage point in the distant West, the *San Francisco Daily Alta California* could comment insightfully on the stereotyping of African-Americans in the postwar years. In 1875, it reflected that extremists on one side had "fallen into the habit of imagining Pompey, ex-slave, freedman and voter, as a lazy personage who sleeps in the daytime, steals chickens and pigs at night, votes early and often, and lives off the toiling whites." Extremists on the other side drew another picture. "In the latter, Caesar Augustus works passionately from sunrise to sunset, letting go of the plough only to wipe the dew of honest toil from his forehead, and catch, meanwhile, a glimpse of the spelling-book tied to the plough-handle; that he spends the evening studying by the light of a blazing pine-knot; that he votes conscientiously, but at the risk of his life; that he is the constant prey of unprincipled whites. Humble, virtuous, studious and laborious, he is a dusky paragon." Disparaging these overdrawn caricatures, the *Daily Alta California* nonetheless tracked growing black landownership and accumulations of capital, and it concluded that black prosperity would break down the racial component of voting lines.[80]

Afraid of what they believed had happened in South Carolina, a critical group of Northerners hailing from both parties was coalescing around the previously Republican idea that a harmonious society of people following a traditional path to prosperity through hard work was the true American way. The Liberal Republican movement had failed, but its ideas flowed back into both the Republican and Democratic parties, creating a shared body of ideas. At the same time, the Liberal Republican years had created an enduring independent political voice that continued to grow for the rest of the century as more and more newspapers and their readers, who saw themselves as members of what they called the "better classes," tried to throw off political obligations and hold true to the ideas of limited government beholden to no special interests, equality of rights, individualism, and hard work. In 1875, the *San Francisco Daily Alta California* reiterated that "real substantial, enduring prosperity will be reached on the basis of solid hard work," and that advice was repeated by independents and members of both parties throughout the nation. These mainstream Northerners held tight to the American system of success, which seemed to be threatened by workers who, believing in a class conflict, were attempting to control the nation and confiscate wealth through legislation.[81]

Progressive Democrats joined those who spoke for a harmonious political economy based on good workers and even suggested that right-minded people of both races could coexist happily, as Republicans had originally insisted. In 1879, in an article cheerfully reprinted by the *New York Times,* the Democratic *Beaufort (South Carolina) Tribune* reported that Beaufort County had a black majority but maintained that its laboring population was "peaceful, quiet, orderly, and very prosperous," and that whites and blacks lived together in unity, harmony, and accord. While it complained that African-Americans took "most of the office of profit and trust that are dependent upon the popular vote," it asserted that "the most influential leaders among the blacks were in favor . . . of putting forward better tickets for the support of all classes than were unfortunately foisted upon them." The *Beaufort Tribune* believed "that the negro population of our Sea Islands are as hard working, as civil, as orderly a class as are to be found in any land, and as long as they are as productively useful as they are now, we see no reason why they should not have some representation in our Legislatures." Similarly, after political chaos in Arkansas, a businessman in the state reported in 1875 that "[m]en, women and children are really at work, black and white, and all are at peace now, and on the best of terms. . . . The past hard times have given us severe lessons in economy and industry, and now that our political troubles are over, they are looked upon as for our ultimate good, and so all our people are more hopeful than at least for years past."[82]

This increasing consensus between moderate Democrats, independents, and Republicans reflected a political realignment in the country. At the end of 1874, the Democrats captured Congress for the first time since the war. Even in South Carolina, the Republicans had split over the issue of taxation and corruption, although stalwart Republicans had managed to hold on to the state for another two years. After the election, the staunchly Republican *Cincinnati Daily Gazette* could not entirely deplore the result; it congratulated the party because "corruptionists who made their way into power in the Republican party have been almost entirely spewed out by the people." The *Boston Evening Transcript* agreed, triumphing on January 1, 1875, that "[t]he year just closed has witnessed a practical union of the best men for the purpose of elevating the tone of official life, and driving those into retirement who would debauch the people and degrade the Government service to their own level." It looked forward to "enlightened, economical, and just civil administration." Southerners and Northerners were reconciling over the issue of true government. "The chords of true patriotic feeling are in process of being touched by angel fingers," the *Boston Evening Transcript* cooed.[83]

Two years later the South was "redeemed" by many of the same men who had led the Tax-payers' Association, and not all Republicans objected. When Wade Hampton's Red Shirts swept to power as reformers in South Carolina in 1876, African-Americans were visible enough in the organization for Hampton's men to request federal troops to help protect the "Black Red Shirts" from black opponents. While Hampton's African-American supporters apparently were poor men who joined him for emotional reasons or out of economic need, many Northerners accepted the conservative portrayal of them as "respectable colored men." These Northerners believed that the South had indeed been redeemed as reformers swept from office corrupt Republicans who had mustered a lazy black constituency by calling for class legislation. Symbolically as well as practically, in 1877 President Rutherford B. Hayes stopped using U.S. troops to protect Southern freedmen, who no longer seemed to Northerners to be free laborers in need of government support. Instead, Hayes turned the military against workers engaged in America's first national strike. Many feared that this uprising, the Great Railroad Strike of 1877, was "the beginning of a great civil war in this country, between labor and capital."[84]

4

Civil Rights and the Growth of the National Government, 1870–1883

Northern Republican disillusionment with African-American attitudes toward social issues compounded the Northern association of Southern freedmen with labor radicals who advocated confiscation of wealth. Taking place during and immediately after the South Carolina tax crisis, the civil rights debates of the 1870s seemed to confirm that African-Americans were turning increasingly to legislation to afford them the privileges for which other Americans had worked individually. Civil rights agitation did more than simply flesh out an existing sketch of disaffected black workers, however; it suggested that advocates of African-American rights were actively working to expand the national government to cater to those who rejected the free labor ideal.

"Civil rights," in the immediate aftermath of the war, meant something different than it gradually came to mean over the next several years. *Harper's Weekly* distinguished between "natural rights" to life, liberty, and "the fruits of . . . honest labor," and "civil rights," which were critical to a freedperson's ability to function as a free worker. Civil rights, it explained, were "such rights as to sue, to give evidence, to inherit, buy, lease, sell, convey, and hold property, and others. Few intelligent persons in this country would now deny or forbid equality of natural and civil rights," it asserted in 1867. The 1866 Civil Rights Act, written by the man who had drafted the Thirteenth Amendment, Illinois senator Lyman Trumbull, was intended to secure to African-Americans "full and equal benefit of all laws and proceedings for the security of person and property as is enjoyed by white citizens." It guaranteed only that the legal playing field would be level for all citizens; state legislatures could not enact legislation endangering a black person's right to his life or his land. By 1867, hoping to woo conservative Republican voters into the Democratic camp and to undercut the justification for black suffrage, even moderate Democrats claimed to be willing to back civil rights for African-Americans "with every token of sincerity . . . from a free and spontaneous sense of justice."[1]

"Social" equality was a different thing—it was a result of a person's economic success rather than a condition for it. It was something to be earned by whites and blacks alike. Directly related to economic standing, a man's social standing rose as he prospered. A good social position also required that a person possess other attributes that the community valued. A place in upwardly mobile American society required religious observance and apparently moral behavior, as well as the habits of thrift and economy dictated by a plan for economic success. This gradual social elevation became a mirror of gradual economic elevation through hard work as a traditional free laborer.[2]

Immediately after the Civil War, as Democrats insisted that black freedom would usher in social mixing between races and intermarriage, almost all Northern Republicans emphatically denied that emancipation was intended to have any effect on social issues and reiterated that African-Americans must rise in society only through the same hard effort that had brought other Americans to prominence. In 1867, a correspondent to the radical *Cincinnati Daily Gazette* from Louisiana painted a complimentary portrait of Louisiana African-Americans, then concluded that they had neither the expectation nor the desire for "social equality, that favorite bugbear." They would ridicule any attempt to break down social distinctions by legislation, knowing that the government could give them only political equality, the writer claimed, quoting his informants as saying, "Our own brains, our own conduct, is what we must depend upon for our future elevation; each one of us striving for himself and laboring to improve his mental and moral condition." Adding credence to the correspondent's representations, the Georgia Freedmen's Convention of 1866 resolved, "We do not in any respect desire *social* equality beyond the transactions of the ordinary business of life, inasmuch as we deem our own race, equal to all our wants of purely social enjoyment."[3]

As the Republicans enacted legislation promoting the interests of Afri-

can-Americans, however, racist Democrats insisted they were forcing social interaction to promote African-Americans artificially, at the expense
of whites. When the Civil Rights Act of 1866 took effect, Democrats
charged that the Republican concept of black equality before the law
meant Republicans believed that blacks and whites were entirely equal.
The *New York World* predicted interracial marriages; the *Columbus
(Ohio) Crisis* insisted that a black orator in Richmond had told his black
audience to "vote for the man who will bring you into his parlor, who
will eat dinner with you, and who, if you want her, will let you marry his
daughter." In 1868, *De Bow's Review* argued that negro suffrage meant
that African-Americans would "next meet us at the marriage altar and in
the burial vault," where they would "order the white ancestors' bones to
be disinterred and removed elsewhere, and their own transferred into
these hitherto held sacred white family sepulchres."[4]

In response to Democratic attacks, in 1868 the *New York Times* reiterated that Republicans planned only for African-Americans to share the
rights and opportunities of typical free laborers. It maintained that "reconstruction did not fly in the face of nature by attempting to impose
social . . . equality," it simply established political and legal equality.
These rights would eventually "obliterate" social prejudices as white
men sought black votes. The next year the *Times* approvingly reported
that abolitionist agitator Wendell Phillips had said that "the social equality of the black race will have to be worked out by their own exertion."
Frederick Douglass put out the best idea, it continued later, namely: "Let
the negro alone."[5]

Republican insistence that social equality would work itself out as freedpeople worked their way up to prosperity could not provide an answer
for the overwhelming discrimination African-Americans faced. While
many black and white Southerners accepted the established patterns of
segregation, those practices meant that African-Americans' public life
was inferior to that of their white counterparts. Black people could not
sit on juries in most of the South, they could not be certain of transportation on railroads or accommodation at inns, their schools were poor
copies of white schools. In addition to creating a climate of constant harassment for African-Americans, discrimination, especially discrimination in schooling, seemed to hamper their ability to rise economically.
The Fourteenth and Fifteenth Amendments had made all Americans

equal before the law, but they could not guarantee equal access to transportation, accommodations, or schools, and while many ex-slaves accepted conditions as an improvement on the past and dismissed civil rights bills as impractical, those African-Americans who had worked hard to become members of the "better classes" deeply resented their exclusion from public facilities. "Education amounts to nothing, good behavior counts for nothing, even money cannot buy for a colored man or woman decent treatment and the comforts that white people claim and can obtain," complained Mississippi Sheriff John M. Brown. Prominent African-Americans called for legislation to counter the constant discrimination they faced.[6]

African-American proponents of a new civil rights law to enforce nondiscrimination in public services had a champion in the former abolitionist Senator Charles Sumner of Massachusetts. An exceedingly prominent man, the tall, aloof Sumner was the nation's leading champion of African-American rights after the war and had advocated a civil rights measure supplementary to the Civil Rights Act of 1866 since May 1870, when he introduced to the Senate a bill (S. 916) making the federal government responsible for the enforcement of equal rights in public transportation, hotels, theaters, schools, churches, public cemeteries, and juries.

But Sumner's sponsorship of a civil rights bill immediately made more moderate congressmen wary of it; his enthusiasm for black rights frequently made him advocate measures that seemed to remove African-Americans from the free labor system and make them favored wards of a government that was expanding to serve them. Only two months after the ratification of the Fifteenth Amendment had reassured moderate Republicans and Democrats alike that they had done everything possible to make all men equal in America, Sumner told the Senate that black men were not actually equal enough, but that his new bill would do the trick. When it passes, he said, "I [will] know nothing further to be done in the way of legislation for the security of equal rights in this Republic." His bill was referred to the Committee on the Judiciary, which indefinitely postponed it in July 1870.[7]

When Sumner told the Senate six months later that he would press to a vote a new supplemental civil rights bill, Northern Democrats and Republicans both made it clear that they believed the bill offered African-Americans not the equal rights necessary to become free laborers but favoritism, handing to them the social prominence for which others had had to work. As such, they could not support it. African-Americans had been given the same rights as other free Americans, and now they were able to hold their own in the race of life. More legislation would offer them advantages no other group in America enjoyed. The Democratic *New York World* chided that Sumner was "the worst enemy the negro has." "Through terrible blood-spilling and with many a weary tug and groan it has been brought to pass that Cuff is given 'a white man's chance.'" Now Sumner was imperiling the whole experiment, the paper said, by "loading it down with social equality enforced by law."[8] The Republican *Chicago Tribune* agreed with the *New York World,* using a story about the bumper Southern crops of 1870 to reiterate that African-Americans must follow a traditional path to social equality:

> We look far more to the prosperity of industry at the South than to the legislation of Congress for the building up of a state of public feeling favorable to the advancement of the negro in social rights and equality of privileges. He now has all that law can confer, viz.: equality of legal rights, together with the ballot and the right to hold office. The rest depends on opinion and custom, which are principally controlled by pecuniary interest. If the free black laborer develops into the successful cotton-raiser, his wages will form the measure of his growing freedom, and it will not be many years before he will be found owning his plantation, directing heavy operations in capital, and employing many hands. The road to the negro's social equality lies through his capacity for work and his ability to give direction to the labor of others.[9]

Despite the notable lack of enthusiasm for it, in December 1871 Sumner reintroduced a civil rights measure as an amendment to a general amnesty bill for Southerners. Even the *Boston Evening Transcript,* which staunchly supported Sumner and radical legislation, reemphasized that economic growth, not legislation for freedpeople, was the panacea for the South. It preferred to push amnesty, it said, which would stabilize the South, enabling its economy to prosper, and permitting both races in the region "to amalgamate with the nation in its unity and share its glorious fortunes and destiny."[10]

Not only did the bill itself seem to confirm that politicians hoped to harness the African-American vote by offering the black community extraordinary rights, but also Sumner's own political circumstances in

1872 linked the bill directly to the growing popular fear of demagogues catering to African-Americans to amass power. The headstrong senator had fought with President Grant over the annexation of Santo Domingo in 1870, ultimately losing not only the battle but also his prestigious seat at the head of the Foreign Affairs Committee. Even worse, his stand had made party members choose between him and the president, and most of them had begun to drift away from Sumner toward the White House. By 1872, Sumner was anxious to reassert his role as the leader of black voters, and skeptics noted that his sudden resurgence of interest in civil rights might renew his ties to the black population, helping to rebuild his waning strength. Sumner, who sometimes showed astonishing political naïveté, made his efforts to swing black voters into his camp palpably obvious to opponents in the late spring of 1872, when he accused Grant of snubbing African-American leader Frederick Douglass by refusing to invite him to dinner with white men. Douglass was forced to defend a private comment and, after rebuking Sumner for "parading . . . fugitive remarks," to side with Grant, asserting that the president had simply overlooked his invitation to the White House. With Democrats charging that "as a political element . . . the colored people of America belong to-day to our Senator from Massachusetts," the political convenience of Sumner's civil rights advocacy played perfectly to the idea of a demagogue convincing the idle freedpeople to look to a growing government for support while he rode to power on their votes.[11]

Sumner's civil rights bill did not command any more congressional support than it had popular support. Republicans failed to pass his measure in February and May 1872, then later in May, when Sumner was out of the chamber, they suddenly passed an emasculated version of it with the school and jury clauses excised and leaving enforcement to state courts. The furious senator accused the Republicans of sacrificing black rights and tried to recall the party to the commitments of its earlier days, but to no avail; the House allowed even the weakened bill to die.[12]

Irreconcilably divided from the Grant camp, Sumner threw his lot in with the Liberal Republicans, and then he, too, abandoned the civil rights question, confirming critics' suspicions that the issue had been simply a political ploy to attract African-American political support. With the new party's ties to the Democrats and hopes to win over the white South, it had to drop any demands for legislation that benefited African-Americans. In the summer of 1872, Sumner was virtually silent on the subject; in a very long public letter to African-Americans about their pending choice between Grant and Greeley, he devoted only one short and very general paragraph to calling for civil rights legislation.[13]

The rhetoric of the 1872 election campaign confused civil rights with social interaction and further weakened the civil rights cause by continuing to associate it with the idea that disaffected African-Americans who were unwilling to work were demanding extraordinary rights, egged on by demagogues who catered to them in exchange for votes. Echoing Democrats, Liberal Republicans emphasized the corruption of democracy as the administration maintained power by promising special interest legislation to indolent African-Americans. Trying to defend Grant and stalwart Republicanism from charges that Southern Republican regimes supported corruption and laziness in the ex-slave population, administration Republicans distanced themselves from the idea of a civil rights bill. Even Republican newspapers that supported equal rights for African-Americans emphasized that they should simply be judged by the same criteria as whites. More radical papers like the *Boston Evening Transcript* placed "the recognition of the equal civil rights of all classes" at the very end of a list of the South's needs. Sumner's apostasy in deserting Grant also tarnished the hopes for a civil rights bill, as angry stalwart Republicans were now suspicious of everything he did.[14]

As Sumner embodied the image of a demagogue controlling the freedpeople, President Grant offered to all but conservative Democratic Northerners a seemingly model approach to social interaction with African-Americans, rejecting blanket legislation in their behalf but according respect and social equality to members of the black "better classes," who had worked hard to earn their prominence. He did not appear to support civil rights legislation, halfheartedly declaring during the campaign only that he favored "the exercise of those rights to which every citizen should be justly entitled." Once safely elected, he announced in his inaugural address that "[s]ocial equality . . . is not a subject to be legislated upon, nor shall I ask that anything be done to advance the social status of the colored man except to give him a fair chance to develop what there is good in him."[15]

Opposed to special legislation, Grant instead appeared to accord rights to deserving individual African-Americans. In July 1872, prominent black leader Frederick Douglass was able to tell a crowd that he "never was received by any gentleman in the United States with more kindness, more cordiality, I may say with more confidence—never felt more at home in the presence of any gentleman—than I have in the presence of Ulysses S. Grant." After using his inaugural address to undermine civil rights legislation, Grant invited a number of prominent African-Americans to the inaugural ball. The Liberal Republican *Nation* overcame its dislike of the president and applauded his approach to racial equality. It argued that the conjunction of his words and actions "mark an epoch in the national feeling toward the colored race," confirming that "the war period [has] ended for whites and blacks alike." From now on there would be no excuse for continuing "old party divisions," and no reason to believe that "on general questions of public policy there will be any greater unanimity among the blacks than among the whites." Reconstruction was over now that the nation could boast "West Point cadets dancing in the same set with the wives of colored Congressmen."[16]

While stories surfaced during 1873 of continuing reactionary violence against black voters and attacks on African-American civil rights, others told of Southern willingness to let African-Americans rise in Southern society according to their own abilities. The *Boston Evening Transcript* noted a Virginia politician's race baiting and wearily asked if the inhumane and unjust discrimination on the basis of race and color were never to be settled, but the *Philadelphia Inquirer* chose to highlight instead the speeches of two prominent Louisiana politicians who declared that Southern whites and blacks had "a common country, common interests." While "the difference of races" might be an "insurmountable obstacle in the way to harmony and a mutual, equitable understanding," they said, the duty of white Southerners was to make sure whites and blacks enjoyed the same rights and privileges. It was a freedman's own business to establish his social status. "As he makes his social bed he must sleep on it. We must not 'taboo' him or place any obstructions in his way. Give him a free field and a fair chance," they concluded. The *San Francisco Daily Alta California* pleaded in February for sectional peace to promote prosperity and was pleased to declare in August that in South Carolina, where actually the Ku Klux Klan had only recently been driven underground, "the public rights of the freedman, as secured to him by the Constitution . . . are frankly acknowledged by all classes of citizens."[17]

At the same time that hopeful Northerners saw a laudable willingness among white Southerners to permit hardworking ex-slaves to succeed, Northern anxiety about black political activity and its role in the corruption of the American political system grew. The spring of 1873 saw officials in the discredited Kellogg government in Louisiana protesting their removal and taking over the Colfax courthouse with a group of black supporters. The resulting backlash left not only eighty to one hundred rioters dead but also a popular fear that freedmen would riot to assume control of the government. Then, after the Colfax Massacre, a "large assemblage of colored citizens of Boston" gathered, they said, to "demand protection at the hands of our Government because we served it and its people when as slaves we tilled their soil and cultivated their fields without fee or reward," because they "were led to the slaughter" as Civil War soldiers, and because they voted for Grant in the last election. In the summer of 1873, nervous Northerners reported rumors that African-Americans were organizing to elect only black men to office or to demand a greater share of appointed offices. Only two weeks later black representatives from Louisiana's Kellogg government defended their organization to a "colored mass meeting" in New York City as the party that truly represented ex-slaves. While some African-Americans were working hard to succeed, others seemed more determined than ever to demand subsistence from an expanding government.[18]

Civil rights agitation directly fueled the fear that inexperienced black officeholders would subvert the government by catering to the demands of disaffected black workers. Once again Democrats emphasized that black officeholders were the rabble of the population, unnaturally elevated to public office, where they agitated for racial issues and held a captive constituency in the thrall of Northern radicals who plotted a Republican empire. Republican newspapers worried less about a Republican empire than about officeholders jumping from the fields to legislative office, where they would prostitute the government to the demands of the undeserving, who apparently wanted the social as well as the financial benefits of hard work simply handed to them. The *Boston Evening Transcript,* for example, exclaimed over an undistinguished local black delivery boy who moved to South Carolina after the war and became a legislator and judge, and, finally, speaker of the state assembly. It also published a wire story that noted that "Mr. Davis, the colored candidate for lieutenant-governor of Mississippi, was formerly a barber."[19]

Northerners' worry that disaffected African-Americans hoped to dominate government to promote their own interests dovetailed with the increasing visibility of African-Americans agitating for a civil rights bill. Northerners had become accustomed to seeing radical legislation pushed by the powerful white friends of the freedmen, led by Charles Sumner, but African-Americans were now speaking for themselves. Increasing black assertiveness had led some Southern legislatures to pass civil rights laws: South Carolina passed one in 1869; Texas in 1871; and Mississippi, Louisiana, and Florida in 1873. In 1873, Northern newspapers featured African-Americans themselves, in the North and the South, assertively demanding federal protection for their right to equal treatment by public companies, juries, and, most of all, by public schools. In April, at an anniversary celebration of the ratification of the Fifteenth Amendment in San Francisco, orators from the city's strong African-American community "condemned the Supreme Court" for refusing to support desegregated schools, denounced African-Americans who failed to "assert their constitutional privilege," and demanded "the right to have their children admitted to the public schools." Some African-Americans agreed with the argument that they held the decisive votes in political contests and warned that "if a Supplementary Civil Rights Bill did not pass, there would be no more black Republicans." African-Americans across the nation pressed for a civil rights bill; in September 1873, African-Americans called for a national convention to meet in Washington on December 9 "to impress upon Congress the necessity of passing a Civil Rights bill." They complained that "the votaries of color-prejudice, insult, degrade, and outrage thousands with seeming impunity," denying African-American men and women access to hotels, schools, and public transportation. "These are facts common to nearly all sections of the country, and the strong arm of national law is needed to correct them. We want Congress to give us a 'Civil Rights bill' with such penalties as will teach humanity to the imbruted, and compel the tyrant to loose his hold on the poor," they declared.[20]

During the first four months of 1874, at the same time that the rejuvenated South Carolina Tax-payers' Association recommenced agitation, the national discussion of a new civil rights bill branded the measure a deliberate attempt to expand the government and harness it to the special interests of African-Americans who refused to work their way up in society and demanded extraordinary government benefits. On December 1, 1873, after public encouragement from African-American groups, Charles Sumner had reintroduced a civil rights bill to supplement the 1866 Civil Rights Act. It specified that no public institution or company could exclude persons on the basis of "race, color, or previous condition of servitude." This bill would affect inns, transportation companies, theaters or "other places of public amusement," cemeteries, juries, and, critically, the public schools. Jurisdiction over cases arising under this bill went to federal courts and officers. In short, the bill would remove discrimination by color from any public or publicly supported institution and place the power to enforce that equality in the federal government.[21]

On December 16, 1873, two weeks after Sumner introduced his bill to the Senate, Benjamin F. Butler, whose name had become synonymous with spoilsmanship and the manipulation of ignorant constituencies with the promise of legislation in their favor, introduced a virtually identical bill to the House. After a brief debate, Butler committed his bill to the House Judiciary Committee, which eventually reported it back with a substitute that struck at the very essence of civil rights by providing for segregated schools. It said that if any state "shall establish and maintain separate schools and institutions, giving equal educational advantages in all respects, for different classes of persons," it would be in compliance with the proposed law. An Alabama Republican carried separation further, introducing a bill that would segregate not only schools but also inns, transportation, theaters, and everything else covered by the bill in the first place. Although many suspected that widespread opposition to the bill would guarantee that it would never actually see the light of day again, the stage was set for a heated national debate about African-Americans and civil rights.[22]

Republican congressmen felt "that it was the colored members' fight, and that they were able to take care of it," leaving prominent South Carolina black representatives Alonzo J. Ransier and R. B. Elliott to lead the fight in the House, while the National Convention of Colored men, meeting in Washington on December 9, issued a public address supporting the bill, and "respectable" African-Americans across the nation echoed their call for civil, but not social, rights.[23] Elliott's speech on the bill was widely acknowledged by Republicans to be "first-rate," and to speak well for African-Americans in the government. Ransier said there was no freedom at the South without such a measure, and a white representative from Virginia proved his point by defying "anybody to assert that the ne-gro is the equal of the white man," then ignoring House protocol to in-sult the black congressman directly.[24]

The exchange between the white Virginian and Ransier exemplified the grounds on which the bill's supporters advocated it. Proponents of the measure emphasized not the absolute right of all Americans to equal treatment but rather the protection of "respectable" African-Americans from mistreatment by lower-class whites and from inclusion in the ranks of those less "respectable" than they, those distinguished by the charac-teristics popularly associated with the disaffected workers: poverty, bad habits, bad manners, violence. On Southern railroads, especially, segre-gation meant that African-American men and women of the "better classes" could be forced to ride in smoking cars with rowdies, and blacks who purchased first-class tickets rebelled at their forced proximity to those beneath them. The pro–civil rights bill *Philadelphia Daily Evening Bulletin* sympathized with their outrage, and reflected that the bill would not have been necessary "if the prejudices of a vast number of the people had not resulted in the continued exposure of respectable negroes to in-sult and injury." It objected to "an offensive distinction against a per-fectly reputable class of citizens."[25]

African-Americans from the "better classes" deliberately dissociated themselves from disaffected workers and the poor Southern freedpeople lumped with them, standing firmly for inclusion in the ranks of the American mainstream. An African-American woman wrote to the *New York Daily Tribune,* outraged that her ticket for an expensive theater seat had been refused and that she had been encouraged to sit in a cheaper seat. She concluded: "Permit me to say that I belong neither to the 'white trash' or 'colored people' of the South, but am a free-born native of the State of Ohio, as were my parents before me." While this woman proba-bly supported the civil rights bill, other prosperous African-Americans feared that sweeping legislation would lower their status by mingling the entire American population together, rather than permitting the maintenance of class distinctions that removed prosperous black Ameri-cans from both white and black lower classes. These people hoped to gain more rights not through a law that would benefit everyone but through private action on their own behalf. Black "tax-payers" in Rich-mond, Virginia, for example, "addressed a respectful petition to the Judge of that Court asking that intelligent negroes be permitted hereafter to sit in cases where the accused is of their color." While prosperous African-Americans disagreed about the civil rights bill, they agreed that there were distinctions within the black community and that their interests were not the same as those of poorer blacks.[26]

White opponents of the bill did not see it as an attempt to prevent discrimination against prosperous Americans; rather, they believed it catered to the ambitions of the worst freedpeople to expand the government so it could let them have the benefits of a free labor society without actually working. While white Southerners and conservative Northern Democrats focused largely on the "social" equality, or racial mixing, they saw in the plan, moderate Northerners of both parties primarily disliked the idea that it would dramatically expand the power of the American government in the service of African-Americans who seemed determined to gain the benefits of prominent social standing without having to work hard to achieve it. Democratic opponents of the bill hammered on the idea that it was unconstitutional and would increase the power of the federal government to the point that it would obliterate the states. They had opposed Reconstruction legislation as an attempt by Republicans to create a "consolidated empire" in place of "a confederation of sovereign States," but had found some relief in their understanding that the Fifteenth Amendment would end the Reconstruction legislation that they worried was centralizing the government. Now a new bill had appeared to challenge that belief. The Democratic *New York World* nodded to the good intentions of the bill's framers but insisted that the bill would take critical functions away from the state governments, which were the only ones who could decide "whether negroes, or Chinamen, or Indians shall be allowed to buy and occupy boxes at the opera, or to dine at the *tables d'hôte* of steamers and hotels, or to send their children to the public schools, or to get themselves buried or cremated, as the case may be, in common with their white fellow citizens." If the national government assumed the power to decide these questions, it wrote, the state governments might as well be dissolved.[27]

Conservative, moderate, and even some radical Republicans agreed with the Democratic opponents of a strong national government, fearing that big government would mean sinecures, patronage, taxes, and an enervated populace that would forget how to engage in productive labor. The Thirteenth Amendment was the first one to convey powers to the federal government rather than limit them, and the amendments and legislation since then had seemed to many to illustrate a dangerous trend. While Democratic rhetoric attacked Republicans as the agents of centralization, as early as 1867 a writer for *Harper's Weekly* had countered Democrats' accusations by explaining that Republicans wanted only to end slavery and political exclusion, both of which endangered the country. "This is the kind of centralization which the country demands for the common safety of all the States; more than this it neither asks nor would tolerate," he concluded. In 1873, a Republican Supreme Court handed down the *Slaughterhouse Cases,* which checked the trend toward centralization by declaring that only the very limited rights of national citizenship were protected by the Fourteenth Amendment. The court insisted that the equal protection clause of the amendment applied only to legislation that specifically discriminated against African-Americans, like the Black Codes, leaving to state jurisdiction the ubiquitous discrimination by businesses and individuals. Democrats actually used the *Slaughterhouse Cases* to oppose the civil rights bill.[28]

The civil rights bill demanded the expansion of the national government; members of both parties decried it. When Sumner introduced the bill to the Senate, the Associated Press reported that Republicans Orris S. Ferry of Connecticut and Lot M. Morrill of Maine agreed with Democrats that "the bill was unconstitutional. . . . Such a bill never had and never could pass." In May, both the radical-leaning *Philadelphia Daily Evening Bulletin* and the conservative *New York Times* admonished that "the right of States to govern themselves is as dear to the people as it ever was. And it ought to be dear to them, for when they abandon it they will have utterly forsaken the system of government established under the Federal Constitution." On July 4, 1874, prominent radical Republican Israel Washburn of Maine alerted an audience to the "unquestionable danger" of "the general and apparently irresistible tendency of things in the direction of *centralization.*" With the civil rights bill pending, this founder of the Republican party expressed alarm at "the disposition of Congress to extend its jurisdiction over questions and concerns heretofore acknowledged by all parties, to pertain, rightfully and exclusively, to the states." He worried that people sought federal relief "for all ills and evils, for all inconveniences and accidents . . . Whatever State legislation, or individual or corporate enterprise and capital are inadequate to accomplish, or unwilling to undertake, the federal government is confidently asked to promote." Famous during his congressional service as "the Watchdog of the Treasury," Washburn worried about the federal government's increasing expenditures and warned his audience that the government must keep appropriations to constitutional objects.[29]

As Washburn indicated, Republicans linked growth of the government to higher taxes, which they disliked almost as much as their opponents did. Democrats hammered at the tax issue, not only out of long-standing principle but also to make political points, as Republicans had controlled the government since 1861, when taxes began to rise dramatically to fund the Civil War. But Democrats were not alone. Republicans opposed taxes almost as vociferously as their opponents. The *New York Daily Tribune,* for example, joined the *Cincinnati Daily Gazette* in insisting that the government must "cut . . . down expenditures to the lowest possible level" to avoid taxation, and the *Worcester (Massachusetts) Spy* agreed that Congress must "impose such stringent measure of economy as will obviate the necessity of increased taxation."[30]

By the mid-1870s, almost everyone accepted the argument advanced by Democrats in 1867 to attack the idea of black suffrage, that politicians used the monies garnered from taxation to give government jobs to or even to bribe their worthless constituents. This patronage system seemed to turn the government into a growing welfare bureau for those too lazy to work. A writer for the *Cincinnati Daily Gazette* bemoaned the difficulty of decreasing the size and expenses of the government. In both private and public affairs, he said, "there is always a pressure to increase the number of employees. Every Congressman has his friends and insists upon placing them, whether needed or not. On the contrary, every person discharged, and every reduction in compensation, meets with strong opposition." Indeed, the "spoils system" was central to politics in the nation, as politicians tendered growing numbers of offices to their supporters in return for votes and financial contributions to their political machines. Applying the idea of patronage and the spoils system to African-American voters only fueled the idea that a growing government would have a dangerous relationship to disaffected Americans.[31]

Compounding the general concern over a growing government in thrall to disaffected workers' interests was the popular belief that the federal government was providing special treatment for African-Americans who were not working their own way up, unaided, as free workers should. Only four years before, after all, Republicans and Democrats alike had agreed that the passage of the Fifteenth Amendment must be the end of all legislative efforts for the freedpeople, since it reached the limit of constitutional legislation in their behalf. The next year Charles Sumner had raised hackles in both parties by declaring that yet another step—a civil rights bill—would complete the legislative program for equality. Now another bill had appeared, and Northerners wondered when the legislation would end. Unfavorably comparing African-Americans with Jews, who combated ubiquitous prejudice without the help of the federal government, Republicans as well as Democrats argued that it was time for African-Americans to stand own their own, making their own way as all other American workers had done. "Is it not time for the colored race to stop playing baby?" the *Chicago Tribune* asked its readers. "The whites of America have done nobly in outgrowing the old prejudices against them. They cannot hurry this process by law. Let them obtain social equality as every other man, woman, and child in this world obtain it,—by showing themselves in their lives the social equals of those with whom they wish to consort. If they do this, year by year the prejudices will die away." The *Tribune* concluded by warning: "If they press the passage of this bill and succeed, day and day that prejudice will grow deeper and more bitter."[32]

Legislation that benefited African-Americans seemed to mainstream Northerners to encourage their dependence on the government for help rather than cement their adherence to free labor principles. Even as the Panic of 1873 caused unemployment and terrible hardship among workers in all sections of the country, Northern Republicans and independents firmly rejected the idea that the government should respond to individuals' demands for aid, fearing that such ideas mirrored "the revolutionary and Socialistic doctrines of the French Revolution" and declaring that it was not "the proper sphere of Congress to enter on a general system of providing for pauperism." But the government did, in fact, distribute rations to a flooded area of the South in the spring of 1874, and newspapers reported that the aid was "demoralizing" local African-Americans, who refused to work so long as the government would support them. Government aid was so demoralizing, the *Boston Evening Transcript* reported, that even some freedpeople in areas not touched by the flood demanded "that they should have a share of the provisions sent up for the relief of those in the inundated districts."[33]

The civil rights bill seemed to many to be the work of stalwart Republican demagogues who were trying to attract the votes of disaffected freedmen. Significantly missing the fact that it was affluent and not indigent African-Americans who wanted the bill, in January 1874 the *New York Daily Tribune* told its readers that emancipated slaves had ambitions for social equality only when "instigated by evil and designing white men." The *New York Daily Tribune* harped on the idea that the supporters of Republican political machinery in the South were "thieves," members of an "undesirable and unprofitable class," to whom the party provided jobs in exchange for votes. Even the staunchly Republican *Boston Evening Transcript* reported, "There is, . . . and always will be, a class of low, designing politicians, who by appealing to the prejudices and jealousies of the negroes will use their political power in opposition to any measure designed to give the whites ascendancy."[34]

Civil rights legislation seemed to many Northerners a destructive capitulation of demagogues to the whims of ex-slaves, in fact threatening rather than promoting African-American equality in a misguided effort to placate frivolous black sensibilities. The most troubling aspect of the new bill for Northern Republicans and independents—who remained racists despite their general support for black equality—was its provision for integrated schools. Northern Republicans argued, as Southerners and Northern Democrats also did, that mixed schools would destroy free schools in the South. Unwilling to have their children associate with the freedpeople, Southerners would cease to fund public schools at all, driving the region even further into ignorance.[35]

The insistence on integrated schools even at the expense of destroying the existing system seemed to sacrifice real progress for imagined gains. Only about half of the South's children attended school in 1875, and in 1880 70 percent of the black population remained illiterate; but to white Northerners of the "better classes," the glass seemed half full. They had read about the growing and increasingly successful school system in the South since the end of the war, learning that 10,000 African-Americans in Virginia had learned to read in 1866, and that, in the following year, New Orleans had appropriated $75,000 for black schools, despite the city's segregated system. In 1868, the assistant commissioner of the Freedmen's Bureau in Alabama reported that "the blind hostility against [black schools] which was at first apparent has almost wholly disappeared." In the spring of 1873, the highly popular tours of singers from Hampton Institute in Virginia and Fisk University in Nashville, Tennessee, publicized the biracial support for these expensive schools. In October 1873, the *Boston Evening Transcript* reported that Kentucky had constructed its first black high school building, for 600 students, at a cost of $25,000. By February 1874, readers of the *New York Daily Tribune* read the report of a friendly Southerner that taxpayers had previously opposed funding schools, but "[n]ow the public schools are everywhere. The system is more perfect in some States than others, but it is being rapidly perfected in nearly all."[36]

African-Americans who attacked what seemed to be a thriving system that would permit black children to gain an education and achieve real equality appeared willful. They seemed to reach for an artificial equality based not on worth but on legislation, and were willing to destroy real gains for false elevation. In 1873, the radical *Boston Evening Transcript* published a report from Washington, D.C., that chided black leaders who wanted to break up the city's "excellent system of colored schools" to consolidate them with white schools. The African-Americans had met and "demanded" admission to the local white schools, adding, according to the *Boston Evening Transcript,* that they were "outraged in exclusion therefrom, and from that we will never rest until we secure admission therein.'"[37]

Northern Republicans, independents, and Democrats all complained that African-Americans wanted the civil rights bill not to redress a real deficiency in their legal treatment but out of a childish opposition to segregation as "a mark of degradation put upon the blacks." "It is not a practical question with them," the *New York Daily Tribune* explained, "but a matter of sentiment upon which they are naturally sensitive." Disdainful of African-Americans who demanded rights, the *Cherokee Advocate* from Oklahoma Territory summed up this version of opposition to the civil rights bill: African-Americans maintained that separate schools were "an insult and an insinuation of disgrace to the colored people." The Reconstruction amendments made the ex-slave "equal in all things before the law to the white man," mused the paper, but "[c]an any law put down the insinuation of which he complains?"[38]

Not only did Liberal Republicans and Democrats make the connection between government aid to African-Americans and a corrupt political system; increasingly all but the most stalwart Republicans did, too. The Republicans had been badly hurt by the 1872 election debacle in Louisiana, in which stalwart Republicans had denied the election of a reform governor and administration appointees had installed the Republicans on the grounds that black voters had been kept from the polls by intimidation. "Scarce a particle of all the trouble, recklessness and ruin" that had blighted Louisiana "would ever have been heard of," insisted the *San Francisco Daily Alta California*, if the state were "free from the miserable wretches who . . . ingratiate themselves with the colored people, and who have used them and their influences against their old masters and the real good of the State." Louisiana, it seemed, was a clear case of stalwart Republican refusal to bow to the popular will in order to stay in power, and clear evidence of the reciprocal relationship between poor black voters and attempts to consolidate political power. Moderate Republicans anxious to maintain control of the government without depending on the Southern black vote recognized that they had to deny this association convincingly enough to retain wavering Northern voters.[39]

By 1874, most Republicans were ready to cut the freedpeople's ties to the government in order to force African-Americans to fall back on their own resources and to protect the government from the machinations of demagogues pushing special-interest legislation. When Mississippi Republicans asked President Grant in January 1874 to use the administration to shore up their state organization, the *Philadelphia Inquirer* enthusiastically reported his refusal. Grant "remove[d] his segar from his mouth and enunciate[d] a great truth with startling emphasis," according to a writer for the newspaper. The president said it was "time for the Republican party to unload." The party could not continue to carry the "dead weight" of intrastate quarrels. Grant was sick and tired of it, he told listeners. "This nursing of monstrosities has nearly exhausted the life of the party. I am done with them, and they will have to take care of themselves." The *Philadelphia Inquirer* agreed that the federal government had to cease to support the Southern Republican organizations of freedpeople and their demagogic leaders. The *New York Daily Tribune* approved Grant's similar hands-off policy in Texas, thrilled that "there [was] no longer any cause to apprehend that another State Government will be overturned by Federal bayonets."[40]

Benjamin Butler's role as the House manager of the civil rights bill only hurt its chances, for he embodied the connection between freedpeople and a government in thrall to special interests. The symbol of the "corruption" of American government, Butler was popularly credited

with strong-arming the House into recognizing the Louisiana representatives backed by the Kellogg government, which was generally believed
to be an illegal creation of Louisiana's largely black Republican party,
supported not by the people of the state but by federal officers. Honest
men wanted to destroy "the principle which Mr. Butler and his followers
represent," wrote the *New York Daily Tribune* and others, "the force in
our politics of which he is the recognized exponent, and of which thousands of our politicians of less prominence are the creatures." "Butlerism" meant gaining power by promising an uneducated public patronage or legislation in their favor, and all but the stalwart Republicans and
Democratic machine politicians hoped for the downfall of both Butler
and what he represented.[41]

Despite the fact that it was prosperous African-Americans who advocated the bill, it appeared to opponents that the civil rights bill was
an extraordinary piece of unconstitutional legislation by which demagogues hoped to hold on to power in the South, and thus in the nation,
by catering to the whims of disaffected African-Americans who were unwilling to work. The proposed law seemed to offer nothing to the nation
but a trampled constitution, lazy freedpeople, and a growing government corrupted into a vehicle for catering to the undeserving.

The civil rights bill would probably never have passed the Senate had
it not been for the sudden death of Charles Sumner on March 11, 1874.
Before he died, Sumner charged fellow Massachusetts senator George F.
Hoar to "take care of the civil-rights bill,—my bill, the civil-rights bill,
don't let it fail." Even Republican enemies of the bill eulogized the "great
man"; the *Chicago Tribune* reflected that "there is no man, friend or enemy, who does not pause to pay respect to the memory of Charles Sumner." African-Americans across the country mourned Sumner's death
and called for the passage of his "last and grandest work," and on April
14, 1874, from the Committee on the Judiciary Senator Frederick T.
Frelinghuysen reported Sumner's civil rights bill protecting African-
Americans from discrimination in public facilities, schools, and juries.
The committee's amendments placed firmly in the national legal appara-
tus responsibility for overseeing violations of the proposed law. In caucus on May 8, some Republican senators objected to "certain features" of
the bill but expressed a desire to act "harmoniously" on the measure. In
the next caucus, the Republicans decided to support the bill without
amendments.[42]

After an all-night session of the Senate, a handful of African-American men in the galleries applauded as the Senate passed the bill on May 23, 1874, by a vote of twenty-nine to sixteen. Rumors circulated that the president had "some doubts about signing it" if it should pass the House, and many Republicans indicated they would not mind the loss of the bill. "Respect for the dead is incumbent on us all," snarled the *New York Times,* "—but legislation should be based on a careful and wise regard for the welfare of the living, not upon 'mandates,' real or fictitious, of the dead." Referring to the apparent African-American control of Southern governments, the *Times* asked whether the freedman "stands in need of protection from the white man, or the white man stands in need of protection from him." The House Judiciary Committee could not agree on its own civil rights measure and decided to replace its bill with the Senate's. The House then tabled the bill for the rest of the session, despite the continued urging of "leading colored men" that Benjamin Butler get it taken up and passed.[43]

Far from allowing Northern fears to abate, the summer of 1874 reinforced the idea that disaffected African-American workers were trying to control the government in order to gain through legislation what others had earned through hard work. On the heels of the Tax-payers' agitation and the civil rights debates, and in the months preceding important congressional elections, renewed violence tore through the South. The press warned of an imminent "war of races" in the South, and the wires reported violent incidents in which black mobs led by demagogues tried to take power. The fact that casualties were almost always from the Republican side was explained by the argument that white Democrats had risen in self-defense against vicious demagogues and their ignorant supporters. During the August elections in North Carolina, for example, wires reported that all was calm in Wilmington until "James Heaton, a Republican politician, created a disturbance and successfully resisted the power of the city to arrest him for some time, being backed by a negro mob of several hundred. The whites took no part in it. The negroes now fill the streets and the excitement runs high." In the evening, according to reports, 100 African-Americans fought with 30 whites, leaving 2 whites seriously injured. The black mob was eventually dispersed by "a large force of special police." The *Boston Evening Transcript* disparaged the wire reports as propaganda, but its charge that the Southern wires were controlled by Southern Democrats had less power than the imagery in the reports themselves.[44]

In September 1874, Carl Schurz tied "the Southern Disturbances" to a government controlled by special interests. First a radical Republican who had helped to construct the Republican vision of a free labor South, then one of the framers of the Liberal Republican party, Schurz now attacked the use of federal offices to support and perpetuate "rapacious and corrupt" Southern state governments. Equating "the anarchy of power . . . the lawlessness of authority" with the anarchy of the Ku Klux Klan, he charged that both were "just as dangerous to the Republican institutions and to the welfare of the nation." Schurz tied the civil rights bill to his view of political corruption, condemning the measure as unconstitutional. African-Americans should not agitate for extra legislation, he said, but should "trust to the means they already have to make themselves respected, and to leave all else to the gradual progress of public opinion, which has already outgrown many a prejudice that a few years ago was still deemed invincible."[45]

The civil rights bill was rescued from oblivion only by Democratic wins in the 1874 elections. Republican congressmen's desire to consolidate Reconstruction before the Democrats arrived barely outweighed party members' fears that the measure was an attempt of corrupt politicians to harness the black vote by offering African-Americans extraordinary benefits that would undermine their willingness to work. When the lame-duck Congress reconvened in December 1874, House Republican leader Benjamin Butler tried to pass a bill protecting freedmen at the polls and an army appropriations bill to shore up stalwart Republicans in the South. Democrats filibustered. Butler was unable to get a suspension of the rules to maneuver around them as fifteen Republicans joined the opposition, worried that Butler's attempt to suspend the rules was simply a means "to get through a lot of jobbing measures under cover of Civil Rights and protection of the South." With his reputation as a special-interest broker, Butler had a terrible time getting the civil rights bill off the Speaker's table. Finally Republicans agreed to let Butler take it to the floor in late January.[46]

The galleries were full as the House discussed the bill in early February. After omitting provisions for integrated schools, churches, and cemeteries, the House passed the bill on February 5 by a vote of 162 to 100. While African-Americans in favor of a civil rights bill were horrified at the sacrifice of the school clause, all but the most radical Republicans approved the omission. "The bill . . . is worthy [of] the support of every congressman who wishes to deal equitably with the citizens of the United States, white and black," wrote even the *Boston Evening Transcript*. "This measure simply provides for the education of the blacks, and does not force their children into association with white scholars," at the same time demanding that the schools be equal. "The Republicans can stand upon such a platform as that," the *Transcript* chided unwilling party menbers. "The great desire and solicitude of the people are to support 'civil rights' and so execute in good faith the constitutional pledges of the nation." After initial reluctance, the Senate passed the school amendment by a vote of 38 to 62, and despite Democratic plans to talk the bill to death, the Senate repassed the civil rights bill without further amendment on February 27, 1875, with Democrats in the opposition. Grant signed the civil rights bill into law on March 1, 1875.[47]

While some radical papers like the *Boston Evening Transcript* defended the bill—wondering "[i]f the blacks and whites cannot shave and drink together . . . how can they remain tolerably peaceful in the same community?"—its passage drew fire from conservative and moderate Northern Republicans who still read into the measure a larger political story of the corruption of a growing government by those determined to advance through government support rather than through productive labor. The *New York Times* noted that Northern African-Americans were "quiet, inoffensive people who live for and to themselves, and have no desire to intrude where they are not welcome." In the South, however, it continued, "there are many colored men and women who delight in 'scenes' and cheap notoriety." It was these people, the "negro politician, . . . the ignorant field hand, who, by his very brutality has forced his way into, and disgraces, public positions of honor and trust—men . . . who have no feeling and no sensibility," who would "take every opportunity of inflicting petty annoyances upon their former masters." The author concluded that the law would not be enforceable, and that "it is a great mistake to seek to impose new social customs on a people by act of Congress." Noticing the immediate efforts of Southerners to circumvent the law by giving up public licenses and legislating against public disturbances, the *San Francisco Daily Alta California* agreed that the act was likely to produce more trouble than equality, and reiterated that social equality must be earned rather than enforced by law.[48]

The true way for African-Americans to achieve equality, Republicans argued, was to work. The *New York Times* approvingly quoted an African-American minister in the South who reiterated the idea that laborers must rise socially only as they acquired wealth and standing. The *Times* recorded his warning that "character, education, and wealth will determine their position, and all the laws in the world cannot give them a high position if they are not worthy of it." Even a correspondent for the staunchly Republican *Cincinnati Daily Gazette* reflected that "Sambo . . . can go to the hotels, ride in first-class cars, and enjoy a box in the theater. To what good is all this? . . . He needs now, to be let alone, and let work out his own destiny, aided only as his wants make him an object of charity."[49]

Press reports of challenges to the new Civil Rights Act downplayed the desire of prosperous African-Americans to enjoy the same rights as their white counterparts and emphasized instead the idea of disaffected, poor African-Americans backed by demagogues using the law to intrude into the society of those who had achieved success through hard work. Associated Press reports highlighted stories of African-Americans forcing themselves forward—and sometimes being pushed to do so by white instigators. The *Boston Evening Transcript* and the *San Francisco Daily Alta California* both reprinted a report from Chattanooga that "[a] white man tried to hire a negro to seat himself" at a hotel dining table, but the black man, "fearful of the consequences," refused. Three days later the Boston newspaper reported a Missouri story that "a desperado named Hall took a negro into a saloon . . . and attempted to place him on an equality with the white man, under the civil-rights bill." The bartender and Hall argued before the bartender chased out the first black man and shot another who tried to interfere. When "several negroes," turned away from a Montgomery, Alabama, theater, had the theater owner arrested, a reporter concluded: "The negroes are notorious politicians, and two of them were defeated by their own color at the last election for county officers." The *Birmingham (New York) Republican* reprinted the story of a black man who believed the Civil Rights Act gave him the right to ride free on the railroads. Benjamin Butler himself wrote a public letter, snapping that the new law did not permit an African-American "to force himself into any man's shop, or into any private man's home, or any eating-house, boarding-house or establishment." Any belief to the contrary exhibited "ignorance as well as, in some cases, . . . insufferable prejudice and malignity."[50]

Some African-Americans who identified themselves as members of the "better classes" echoed their white counterparts' dislike of the new law. The *San Francisco Daily Alta California* reprinted the opinion of a black barber in Georgia who opposed the measure. "I keep a barber shop for white men—" he said, "have shaved no negroes, and even under the Civil Rights bill no negro can have his face scraped or wool oiled in my shop. I am a colored man, but still I am a white man in principle; and I want my colored friends to know that, in their places, I am their friend, and that out of their places I am not their friend."[51]

And yet, angry as Northerners were at the image of poor blacks who challenged segregation with new legislation rather than by following the traditional path of advancement through hard work, they appeared to be willing to accord equality to more prosperous African-Americans who challenged discrimination without the benefit of the Civil Rights Act. By 1880, Northern Republicans reported that "the color line is being rapidly broken," and the *New York Times* covered the full black participation in a Virginia political convention, concluding that "the members of the Republican Convention are as free from molestation or insult as they would be in Worcester, Mass." Worried that angry black Republicans might join a reform organization, Democrats were treating African-Americans with respect. Even the local hotels had been desegregated for the occasion, and when the black delegates ate at various tables in a local dining room, "a large number of stanch Democrats, men and women, who were present, went on with their dinners as if the scene was not an unusual one."[52]

Republican approval of equality achieved naturally rather than by legislative fiat extended outside of politics. When the Pennsylvania Supreme Court upheld a lower court's decision that a black Philadelphia couple ejected from a theater was entitled to damages as well as the costs of their tickets, the *Philadelphia Daily Evening Bulletin* approved that "the manifest spirit of the Fifteenth Amendment" was gradually coming to be conceded everywhere and cheerfully predicted "the end of all this class of proscription in this State in the color line." The *New York Daily Tribune* complained that it had taken four years for the couple to get justice, but thought that their ultimate vindication indicated the approach of racial equality. In 1879, the *Boston Journal* and *New York Times* reported positively on the marriage of prosperous black lawyer A. H. Grimke to a white minister's daughter, commenting that the couple moved "in the best ranks of Boston society." In May 1880, the *New York*

Times cheerfully reported the admission of "educated gentleman" John F. Quarles to the New York bar. In September 1880, the *Times* reprinted an article from the *Boston Traveller* on marriage in Massachusetts; the article mentioned without comment twenty-three marriages of black men to white women.[53]

In 1880, the prominent civil rights case of West Point cadet Johnson C. Whittaker dramatically illustrated the stance of Northern Republicans toward civil rights. A former slave from South Carolina, Whittaker was appointed a cadet at West Point in 1876. White cadets mercilessly harassed and ostracized Whittaker, who was the only African-American at West Point after Henry O. Flipper graduated in June 1877. In April 1880, Whittaker was found gagged and bound to his bed, his ears slashed with a razor. Whittaker told his superiors that he had been attacked by three masked assailants whom he assumed were other cadets. West Point operated on a code of honor; each white student at the academy denied that he knew anything of the attack. Accused of faking the incident to gain sympathy from his teachers and from reformers, Whittaker asked for a court of inquiry to look into the case.[54]

The public took up the Whittaker case and worried it in the newspapers. When the story first broke, Northerners of both parties deplored the event. The *Detroit Evening News* claimed that "the whole country was on his side. Both parties in congress [*sic*], and every newspaper of every shade of politics" supported Whittaker. The *New York Daily Tribune* agreed that "the justice with which the Whittaker case has been regarded" indicated the "complete reversal of popular prejudice into fair dealing," and the *New York Herald* reflected that his story was "very generally believed to be true." "On no question has the will of the American people been more definit[e]ly and emphatically expressed than on the abolition of color caste," Jane Grey Swisshelm wrote in a letter to the *Chicago Tribune*. The editor of the *Tribune* agreed that the government should have protected Whittaker from "insult and outrage." The *New York Times* mocked bigots by reporting the scientific discovery by Professor David C. Comstock that African-American brains were, in fact, superior to white American brains. Suggesting that "the supposed inferiority of the negro brain is without foundation," the *New York Times* sneered that "[i]t would be a good idea for some expert to take the measurements of the heads of the whole corps of Cadets, and compare the average with the head of Whittaker."[55]

But then, at the end of May, Northerners abruptly deserted the black cadet. After extensive testimony by "expert witnesses" who insisted that a warning letter sent to Whittaker was in his own handwriting, the West Point court of inquiry unanimously concluded that Whittaker had inflicted the injuries upon himself and dishonorably discharged him. The modern scientific evidence swung even Republicans around to support the decision—as did the *New York Herald*'s reprint of purported facsimiles of the note and samples of Whittaker's handwriting—but it could not have done so had the explanation for his actions not seemed so plausible. The *New York Herald* reported "a general feeling of satisfaction at the result. 'I told you so' is the universal declaration," it wrote, "and it is uttered in no mean spirit, but joy and congratulation at the triumph of truth over fraud."[56]

The Northern interpretation of the Whittaker case revealed the pervasive fear that, not content with equality, African-Americans were deliberately exploiting popular sympathy to win extraordinary concessions so they would not have to work for their own success. By 1880, even moderate Republicans were complaining that "unprincipled adventurers" led the Southern stalwart Republicans as they "massed and wielded the colored vote," by promising African-Americans jobs and special-interest legislation, thus subverting society by elevating "rascality and ignorance." Southern Republicans needed the strong arm of the federal government to put down their opponents, and they maintained Northern Republican support for government intervention by circulating trumped-up stories of Southern white atrocities against freedpeople. There was a direct connection between such discredited Southern governments and Cadet Whittaker: his chief counsel, Daniel Chamberlain, had been the Republican governor of South Carolina from 1874 to 1877, and was associated with the regime attacked by the Tax-payers' Association.[57]

The Whittaker case seemed to mirror this negative image of Southern freedpeople. Whittaker initially appeared deserving, a black man trying to succeed and prevented by malicious whites. Then, the prosecution charged, to gain sympathy from his teachers and from reformers, to obtain an additional year at West Point so he could graduate, and "to be looked upon as a martyr for his capital in future life," he had staged a brutal attack on himself. Admitted to evidence were long letters he had written after the attack to a friend and to his mother, suggesting that he would appeal to Congress for aid in receiving justice; the prosecution accused him of writing the letters for publication in newspapers to "excite popular sympathy on his behalf."[58]

It appeared that, not content with equality, Whittaker had reached for additional action on his behalf by trumping up a racial incident. The *New York Herald* called him "a clumsy trickster and deceitful rogue" and claimed that Whittaker hoped to become distinguished as a victim, since he was incapable of gaining distinction through "more honorable and manly channels." Excoriating the white West Point cadets who pressed on "a boy of excellent character" "the weight of brutal, vulgar caste prejudice," the *Philadelphia Inquirer* nonetheless agreed with the *New York Herald* and blamed Whittaker for his "mad, criminal act," reflecting that it would probably keep black men from West Point for years to come. That fact that anyone was able to believe that an otherwise intelligent and upstanding cadet had lashed himself to his bed, slashed his ears, and then successfully hidden the razor from all investigators indicated just how primed Northerners were to attribute to African-Americans extraordinary efforts to garner sympathy in order to extract concessions so they could gain without work.[59]

Democrats made the point explicitly, using the Whittaker affair to reiterate their argument that stalwart Republicans favored African-Americans. The Democratic *Washington Post* published a letter from "a lady clerk" who wanted to know if Whittaker's counselor Professor Richard T. Greener would be docked pay from his job at the Treasury Department for the time he had volunteered to spend at the trial, trying "to stir up hostility between the two races."

> Whilst we poor lady clerks are paid but $40 or $60 a month, and not allowed to be absent one hour from our posts without having our pay cut down, even when sick, this favored negro man can spend days and weeks away from his desk defending negro murderers and fomenting ill-feeling against innocent people, with a full salary and official favor. What a blessed privilege it is to be a black man and a voter these days!

The *Washington Post* chortled that Republican senators had indeed been prepared to use the "Whittaker outrage" to push more legislation on behalf of African-Americans, but with Whittaker's conviction it was clear that they had "made a more conspicuous display of asinine qualities" than usual.[60]

While Republicans continued after the Whittaker trial to berate

Southerners for their benighted attitudes toward African-Americans, their protests were increasingly suspect as simple election rhetoric to shore up the Southern Republican organization. In August 1880, for example, the Republican Congressional Committee prepared a campaign document charging the Southern Democratic governments with defying the constitutional amendments, abusing black convicts in the South because there "the deepest prejudice prevails against the colored men," even falsely imprisoning men whose labor was wanted. Southern Democrats had burned black schools in the early years of Reconstruction; now they used state funds for white schools and taxed poor African-Americans for the scanty funds used to educate black children, charged the *New York Times.* As Republicans attacked white Southerners, though, skeptics could not help noticing the timing of their attacks . . . and their solution for Southern prejudice. In election seasons, Republicans vociferously called for the defeat of Democrats to break up the solid South, which was "a menace to the harmony and well-being of the Nation and a tremendous obstacle to the progress of the Southern States." Republican defense of black rights hardly seemed like a disinterested defense of principle.[61]

In 1883, the U.S. Supreme Court considered five civil rights cases, one each from Tennessee, New York, Kansas, Missouri, and California. On October 15, 1883, the court decided that the Civil Rights Act of 1875 was unconstitutional because federal authority could overrule only state institutional discrimination, not private actions; Justice John Marshall Harlan of Kentucky cast the only dissenting vote. With the decision, Northern Republicans stated that they had never liked the law, because it removed African-Americans from the tenets of a free labor society, using the government to give them benefits for which others had to work. The *New York Times* declared that African-Americans "should be treated on their merits as individuals precisely as other citizens are treated in like circumstances" and admitted that there was, indeed, "a good deal of unjust prejudice against" them. But the *Times* remained skeptical that legislation could resolve the problem. Even newspapers like the *Hartford Courant,* which supported the law, said it did so only because it proved that Americans were sincere in their quest for equal rights. Three days later that newspaper mused that the law had been necessary only for "the reorganization of a disordered society," and that freedpeople no longer needed its protection. The *Philadelphia Daily Evening Bulletin* agreed that public sentiment had changed so dramatically that the law was now unnecessary. Even the radical African-American *Cleveland Gazette,* which mourned the court's decision, agreed that the law was a dead letter anyway. The *New York Times* welcomed the decision, going so far as to charge the law with keeping "alive a prejudice against the negroes . . . which without it would have gradually died out."[62]

Instead of supporting the Civil Rights Act, Republicans reiterated the idea that right-thinking African-Americans wanted to succeed on their own. The *New York Times* applauded the public address of the Louisville, Kentucky, National Convention of Colored Men that concentrated largely on the needs of Southern agricultural labor and referred not at all to civil rights. That the convention had pointedly rejected chairman Frederick Douglass's draft address, which had included support for civil rights legislation, made the *Times* conclude that most attendees were "opposed to the extreme views uttered by Mr. Douglass," and that the great African-American leader should retire, since his "role as a leader of his race is about played out."[63]

Despite the *Times*'s conclusion, African-Americans across the country protested the decision both as individuals and in mass meetings, reflecting, "It is a mercy that Charles Sumner is not alive to mourn for his cherished Civil Rights bill." At a mass meeting in Washington, D.C., Frederick Douglass admonished that the decision "had inflicted a heavy calamity on the 7,000,000 of colored people of this country, and had left them naked and defenceless against the action of a malignant, vulgar and pitiless prejudice." When the African Methodist Episcopal (AME) Church Conference of Western States, in session in Denver, discussed the decision, delegates made "incendiary" speeches and "[a] Bishop declared that if the negroes' rights were thus trampled upon a revolution would be the result."[64]

In the face of repeated white insistence that the reversal of the law not only was the correct constitutional decision but also would have no effect on race relations, black protests of the decision raised the specter of African-Americans determined to manipulate the government for their own ends. Protests calling the reversal an insult were "silly," reported the *New York Times.*

A decision of the Supreme Court of the United States can hardly be an "insult" to anybody, and sensible negroes will not regret the sweeping away of the ineffective protection of an unconstitutional act of Congress. The behavior of the colored people under this decision will furnish a very good test of their fitness to share in the work of constitutional self-government. We hope they will have the good sense to see that this decision deprives them of none of their rights, and to accept it in that spirit of acquiescense [*sic*] with which all law-abiding people in this country receive the decisions of the courts.

When a Connecticut convention of black citizens protested the reversal, the *Times* reporter noted that "[t]he colored people here were not, as a rule, in sympathy with the convention, not believing in the efficacy of legislative action."[65]

Moderate and conservative Republicans and Democrats agreed that the decision simply removed extraordinary legislation on African-Americans' behalf. The *Chicago Tribune* offered "A Word to the Colored Men," which the *Philadelphia Daily Evening Bulletin* reprinted, disparaging black protests and insisting that the decision simply gave them the same rights as everyone else. Their hearts should not sink about "a decision which says that they shall not enjoy exceptional privileges." Pointing out that neither Jews nor Irish-Americans nor any other American had a right to contest exclusion from a hotel, the article claimed that African-Americans "claimed under the Civil Rights bill a right and privilege which was denied to the Jews. This is inconsistent with the spirit of the laws and of the Constitution." African-Americans were now "like other citizens, accorded the respect to which their abilities, industry, and character entitle them." The article endorsed the idea that "[d]eeds to lands, mechanics' certificates, and commercial paper must be the civil-rights bills of the future." The *Hartford Courant* also used the example of Jews excluded from Hilton's hotel at the famous Saratoga resort, and reiterated that with the overturning of the Civil Rights Act the African-American "is exactly in the position of the white man. He has exactly the same rights and the same means of enforcing them." The Democratic *Hartford Weekly Times* echoed its Republican counterpart, arguing that managers of hotels, boardinghouses, and saloons could refuse anyone they wished. It was "foolish" of Hilton to refuse Jews from his hotel at Saratoga, "but no one questioned his right. No person, black or white, male or female, has a right to force himself or herself upon the premises and the bed and board of the owner of a hotel or a saloon."[66]

Republicans and Democrats agreed that the only way for African-Americans to garner more rights was to work to deserve them, as all others did in America's free labor system. The *Philadelphia Daily Evening Bulletin* repeated this view:

> [F]urther advancement depends chiefly upon themselves, on their earnest pursuit of education, on their progress in morality and religion, on their thoughtful exercise of their duties as citizens, on their persistent practice of industry, on their self-reliance, and on their determination to exalt themselves, not as proscribed or despised Africans, but as American men clothed with the privileges of citizenship in the one great republic of the earth. They have it in their power to secure for themselves, by their own conduct, more really important "rights" than can be given to them by any formal legislation of Congress.

The Democratic *Hartford Weekly Times* agreed, and asserted that true black leaders, "not men like Fred. Douglass, who are 'professional' colored men, and who have been agitating something and been paid for it all of their lives," approved of the decision. "They say there is no such thing as social equality among white men, and that the colored man cannot get it by law, but by the way he conducts himself."[67]

Republican and Democratic newspapers highlighted those African-Americans who cheerfully told their neighbors "to acquire knowledge and wealth as the surest way of obtaining our rights." From Baltimore came the news that "Mr. John F. Cook, a colored man of character, who deservedly enjoys the respect of this entire community, who has held and administered with marked ability for years the responsible office of Collector of Taxes for the District of Columbia," told a reporter that he had no fears of white reprisals after the decision, expecting whites to accord to African-Americans "what legislation could never accomplish." "These are golden words, and if all men of his race were like Mr. Cook there would never be any trouble on this subject," concluded the Republican *Philadelphia Daily Evening Bulletin*.[68]

Even many Northern Democrats painted their own picture of an egalitarian free labor society that had no need of a civil rights law. First they restated the idea that Republican efforts for African-Americans had simply been a ploy to control the government by marshalling the black vote. Trying to make new ties to African-American voters, the Democratic *San Francisco Examiner* emphasized that Republicans had only wanted to use the black vote to create a Republican empire and that the reversal showed that Republicanism no longer offered advantages to black citizens. A reporter noted that members of the black community had said that "it was about time to shake off the Republican yoke and act in politics as American citizens, not as chattels of a party who cared but for their votes."[69]

While the rhetoric of the *San Francisco Examiner* repeated long-standing Democratic arguments, it also reinforced the idea that some hardworking African-Americans had indeed prospered in America, and that these upwardly mobile blacks were fully accepted even in Democratic circles. In San Francisco, the paper noted, "there are . . . many intelligent and educated men and women of African descent." Using the Republican pattern of according prosperous African-Americans names, descriptions, and their own words, it interviewed the Reverend Alexander Walters, whom it described respectfully as an educated and well-traveled young man, and happily printed both his assertion that in cities across the nation and "in the West . . . race prejudice has died out," and his prediction that the court's decision would drive black voters from the Republican party. Similarly, it quoted P. A. Bell, "the veteran editor of the *Elevator*, the organ of the colored people," as saying that in California—a Democratic state—"we people are treated just as well as if there were fifty Civil Rights bills."[70]

With the overturning of the 1875 Civil Rights Act, mainstream Republicans and Democrats, black and white, agreed that there must be no extraordinary legislation on behalf of African-Americans, who had to work their way up in society like everyone else. Stalwart Republicans who advocated additional protection for black citizens were seen as either political demagogues who wanted the black vote to maintain their power or misguided reformers duped by stories of white atrocities against freedpeople. Northern black citizens who advocated civil rights legislation, like Frederick Douglass, were either scheming politicians who, like their white counterparts, needed the votes of uneducated African-Americans, or they were disaffected workers who believed in class struggle and wanted to control the government in order to destroy capital.

Southern blacks seemed to be the worst of all these types. They appeared to want to increase the government's power solely in order to be given what others had earned, and to do so, they were corrupting government by keeping scheming Republican politicos in office. Perhaps the most telling signal that Northerners believed Southern black workers were determined to jump straight from the cotton fields to prominence came from the *New York Times*. In 1885, it reported that poor, lazy African-Americans were hoping literally to turn white. As one man's skin turned white in large patches, according to the *New York Times*, his ignorant neighbors in Macon, Georgia, rejoiced "dat de Lawd done 'termined to make white folk outen de niggers."[71]

5

The Black Exodus from the South, 1879–1880

Despite their fear of disaffected African-Americans who seemed unwilling to work and who apparently hoped to capture control of a growing government, Republicans had never abandoned their support of freedpeople who believed in rising through hard work. In the face of increasing industrialization, Republicans clung tenaciously to the idea that the American economy rested on the small farmer, and they championed freedpeople who tried to buy their own land and who thus seemed to be following the traditional American avenue to economic success. Numbers of freedpeople acquired land in the years from 1865 to 1920, especially in the upper South, where by 1890 one out of every three African-American farmers owned his or her own land. Although their holdings were small and these farmers were not, in general, prosperous, the numbers were not lost on Northerners anxious to prove that black Americans could indeed rise in a traditional way.[1]

In 1879, political events conspired to reinforce the Republican idea of the hard-working African-American. The story began in Louisiana, where Democrats had "redeemed" the state in 1877 and guaranteed their supremacy in the 1878 elections with widespread fraud and intimidation of Republican voters. With their votes suppressed, Louisiana freedpeople were discontented, afraid of what the future might bring under Democratic rule, and they determined to leave the South. Republicans in the North railed against the white tactics in Louisiana. While *Harper's Weekly* ran Thomas Nast's devastating cartoons portraying illiterate Southern whites demanding an "eddikashun qualifukashun" in order for freedmen to vote, congressional Republicans organized a committee to investigate the Louisiana elections. The committee, dominated by Republicans, reported repeated outrages against black voters, although many of its witnesses insisted that the election had been peaceful.[2]

Republicans of all stripes were furious at the tales coming from the South, and on January 16, 1879, Senator William Windom of Minnesota introduced a resolution calling for the organization of "a committee of seven Senators" to inquire "as to the expediency and practicability of encouraging and promoting . . . the partial migration of colored persons from those States . . . where they are not allowed to freely and peacefully exercise and enjoy their constitutional rights as American citizens, into such States as may desire to receive them and will protect them in said rights." His suggestion seemed prescient when, a few weeks later, the Democratic Louisiana legislature called for a revision of the state constitution. Who knew what that could mean for the freedpeople? Some Southern African-Americans had been actively exploring the possibility of leaving the South since at least 1876, but it was the Windom resolution and the threat of a new Louisiana constitution, coming after the committee testimony about election outrages, that Northerners believed started the great black exodus out of the South in 1879.[3]

Windom's suggestion that African-Americans should leave the South instantly received attention. The Democratic *Washington Post* interviewed Windom on January 18, presenting without political commentary his plan to "scatter" the black population of the South both to improve its condition and to end Southern repression of a black voting majority. Less than a week later, the *Cincinnati Daily Gazette* ran a headline declaring that Windom's "Invitation to Colored Men" was "Bearing Results." It reported that on January 22, delegations of African-Americans from six Southern states told Windom that African-Americans had been discussing leaving the South, and that a hundred thousand dissatisfied black people "could be induced to leave their homes if they had even moderate assurance that they would improve their condition." The delegates were joined by African-American congressional representatives from South Carolina, Richard H. Cain, Robert Smalls, and Joseph H. Rainey, "all of whom said they were disposed to favor Mr. Windom's scheme, provided he was in earnest." He assured them he was, and added that "he had no political purpose to accomplish by his resolution."[4]

National issues in 1879 made Northern Republicans, independents, and even some moderate Northern Democrats sympathetic to the anger behind Windom's resolution. In the spring of 1879 it seemed to Northerners that aggressive Southern Democrats were once again on a mission to take control of the nation. While the South retained congressional representatives based on its entire population, it appeared that, in Louisiana at least, black people were kept from the polls. Thus the unreconstructed Democrats enjoyed more power than they deserved under the Fourteenth Amendment, which apportioned congressional representation by population. This was a big problem for Northerners by 1879, since most of the South had been "redeemed" in 1877 and was now controlled by Democrats, who were often led by the same men Southerners had followed out of the Union in 1860. Reflecting on the situation, *Harper's Weekly* warned that the South "can not expect that the people of other States will quietly see their votes nullified by fraud and terror."[5]

Worse, also in the spring of 1879, congressional Democrats tried to control the 1880 presidential election by forcing a change in government elections policy. They attached to appropriations bills riders prohibiting the use of the army to guard the Southern polls, repealing the test oath for jurors, and repealing the law providing for federal supervision of elections. This left Republicans the choice of either bowing to Southern demands or voting against appropriations bills and thus leaving the government unfunded. Republicans refused to pass the bills, forcing a special session of the next Congress—the Forty-sixth—to reconsider the same questions in March 1879. Both houses of Congress were then Democratic, and they took up their fight directly with President Rutherford B. Hayes, forcing him either to veto appropriations bills or bow to their will. It appeared to Northerners that Southern Democrats were determined to nullify the role of the president and force him to do their bidding. Their actions were "revolutionary," Northern Republicans worried. "Public feeling . . . as to the present alarming crisis . . . is becoming very deeply interested, and is growing into a powerful and even angry excitement," a correspondent assured President Hayes. "The matured and deliberate purpose of these men is to destroy the Government."[6]

In the last days of the congressional session, as debate dragged on into the night and tempers flared, Democrats exacerbated Northern fears by passionately defending the Confederate president Jefferson Davis as a "great patriot" who should be returned to the U.S. Senate. Congress had agreed to pension soldiers of the Mexican War when Republican leader

George F. Hoar of Massachusetts rose to except Mexican War veteran Davis from the bill. Hoar probably intended his amendment to defeat the entire measure, but it was also a rebuke to the Democrats forcing the rider issue under the rubric of states' rights. Certainly his opponents believed the action was a "punishment of the people of the South . . . vicarious[ly] in the person of Jefferson Davis." They leaped to Davis's defense, lauding his patriotism, and pointing out that "other men who went quite as far as he did are not only not punished but are received into the highest stations in this Government." Mississippi senator Lucius Q. C. Lamar, the man who had written Mississippi's ordinance of secession, spoke of Davis's "exalted character." Comparing the Confederate president to Abraham Lincoln, U. S. Grant, and William T. Sherman, Southern Democrats insisted that they could not be false to their great leader.[7]

To Northern onlookers, the Democratic defense of Davis tainted the entire Southern population with continuing disloyalty. The Northern press plastered its pages with outrage at the "Confederates" in Congress. The *Boston Journal* looked at the support for Davis and the rider fight and concluded that Southern senators in Congress were "laboring under the impression that the associates of Mr. Davis are soon to control the government." Usually a strong proponent of sectional reconciliation, the *New York Times* presented what purported to be an interview with a Southern Democratic congressman outlining the plan his people were implementing to control the Union. Even moderate Democratic newspapers in the North fretted that unrepentant rebels planned to conquer the nation through legislative maneuvering. "If the officers and men who did the fighting on the Union side from 1861 to 1865 could have foreseen that in 1879 the Confederates would have a majority in both branches of Congress, it would have been pretty hard to prevent them from stacking arms and quitting the service," lamented one newspaper.[8] So prevalent was the Northern anger at Confederates in Congress that a popular rhyme had the young daughter of a crippled Union veteran asking her father why he had fought and lost his legs. Thinking of the "Confederate brigadiers" in Congress, he answered sadly that he "didn't know." Keenly aware of the upcoming election year, Northern newspaper editors and Republican politicians warned their readers and constituencies that Southerners must not be allowed to take over the presidency.[9]

Republican papers launched an all-out attack on the wealthy Southern white leaders who stood poised to take over the nation. They reported disparagingly and in minute detail the murder of a Georgia businessman by one of his peers, using the event as an illustration of the true nature of leading Southerners. While the Georgia press reported that the murder came out of an old feud maintained by the victim, hot-headed Robert Alston, the *New York Times* disagreed. It reported that everyone who had followed Georgia politics knew that Colonel "Bob" Alston was murdered because he was "too humane for his fellow citizens," as he had wished to reform the convict leasing system in the state under which convicts, usually ex-slaves, were horribly abused.[10]

Ironically, two weeks before his death the murdered man had written a letter to the *New York Daily Tribune* "to prove that life and liberty were as secure in Georgia as in any State in the Union, and to invite all the world to come and test the civilization of . . . the South." The *Cincinnati Daily Gazette* concluded that "the civilization down there won't bear the test just yet" and continued to run stories of duels in which "Prominent Citizens" were killed, commenting cheerfully that "if this . . . goes on, the prominent citizens of the South will, in time, become an extinct race." Thomas Nast captured the North's impression of the South in a cartoon for *Harper's Weekly*. In the drawing, two white Southerners sat on a porch under signs noting the black migration and the Alston murder. Reaching for the guns in their breast pockets, the "gentlemen" remark that "[t]hings are very dull. Let's have a shooting match." The caption read: "Nothing Else to Do."[11]

When, beginning in March, the Northern press began to take notice of a "Hegira," an "Exodus of Southern Colored People from the South," the movement made utter sense to Northern observers. In March and April of 1879, more than 6,000 freedpeople poured out of Louisiana, Mississippi, and Texas, up the Mississippi River, through St. Louis, and into Kansas. In the next year almost 15,000 more followed. Pushed by the fear of what might happen in their newly redeemed states, most of the early "Exodusters," as they were called, emigrated under the impression that they would receive free passage to Kansas and government assistance to help establish them in farming. The ex-slaves moved in small groups, with no general leader, all acting out of a faith that things could only get better if they left the South. Their hopes for government aid and free transportation were dashed, but ultimately most of the emigrants who survived the wrenching relocation did, indeed, enjoy a better life in

Kansas than their peers did in the deep South. In the last decades of the nineteenth century, black Kansans enjoyed greater economic, civil, and political rights than black Southerners.[12]

In the 1879 Exodus, a mass of uneducated and impoverished freed-people were emigrating on a millennial faith, but Northern Republicans filtered the Exodus through their own ideas about workers and saw instead a redemption of the idea that some African-Americans embraced traditional ideas about American workers. They were leaving intolerable conditions that threatened their lives and property, and were setting out to improve their fortunes as farmers in the West. Northerners described black emigrants in the same terms that they talked about white laborers who were trying to work their way up. The West was a haven for all men who were "strong" and "self-helpful"; anyone able to "do well in the East" was "pretty certain to do better in the West, because of less competition and capital and many more opportunities there." According to the *New York Times,* the emigrants were leaving Southern conditions that were "unfortunately only too strongly like those which have driven many a foreigner across the seas, to seek in our land the liberty to labor for himself and his family." The Exodusters were acting as good laborers, trying to improve their economic situation through their own efforts. The Northern Republican and independent press presented them in an extraordinarily positive light.[13]

In 1879, Northern attitudes toward Southerners and workers provided a backdrop against which Exodusters could shine. Northern Republican and independent observers contrasted the emigrating African-Americans with the unrepentant, violent, and grasping white Southerners. The congressional rider fight continued until July as the Democratic Congress passed one piece of legislation after another designed to force the government to bow to Southern demands for the removal of all federal troops from the South. President Hayes vetoed five bills, attacking the rider policy as "radical, dangerous, and unconstitutional." Suggesting that the old Confederate theory of state's rights was behind the rider attempts, he drew popular approval by insisting that the national government was superior to the states." The *New York Times* reported a Southern plot to seize the government and, failing that, to recommence the Civil War.[14]

Disaffected workers also made the Exodusters look good. In 1877, 20 percent wage cuts on the Baltimore and Ohio Railroad touched off a strike in West Virginia that erupted into a nationwide riot that shut down most of the nation's railroads, destroyed $10 million in property, and left 100 dead. It revealed, noted Allan Pinkerton, head of the infamous Pinkerton Detective Agency and author of the 1878 book *Strikers, Communists, Tramps and Detectives,* "that we have among us a pernicious communistic spirit which is demoralizing workingmen, continually creating a deeper and more intense antagonism between labor and capital, and so embittering naturally restless elements against the better elements of society, that it must be crushed out completely, or we shall be compelled to submit to greater excesses and more overwhelming disasters in the near future."[15]

Pinkerton was not the only one obsessed with striking workmen, communism, and anarchy. Newspapers ran frequent articles about communist actions, and cartoonists used communists as a favorite subject. One cartoon in *Harper's Weekly* showed men with skulls instead of heads, dressed in togas, one carrying a sword. They were communists, and "communism," explained the cartoon, "means the abolition of inheritance. The abolition of the family. The abolition of religion and the abolition of property." Another showed a "happy communist" examining a report that concluded that American wages were higher and the cost of living lower than in other countries. He complained: "I don't see Dry Champagne quoted." Yet another indicated that communists had solved the labor problem. It showed a man lying on a bed reading a paper, smoking and drinking while his wife sadly sewed piecework by the window. In another cartoon, an "intelligent workman" explained, "I am able, and always have been, to take care of myself and mine . . . real working-men are not rioters [or] strikers."[16]

Changing immigration patterns exacerbated the Northern fears of disaffected workers. By 1880, the increase in immigration was "alarming," according to the *San Francisco Daily Alta California.* The *New York Herald* agreed, worrying about "UNPRECEDENTED IMMIGRATION," as it entitled an article that predicted at least 400,000 newcomers every year. The *Herald's* numbers were almost accurate; from 1877 to 1890 more than 6.3 million immigrants arrived in America. The new immigrants hailed from different countries than those who had come before them, as increasing mechanization and pogroms drove people from southern and eastern Europe, and Americans eyed the newcomers warily. The *New*

York Herald called them "a motley crowd that is literally a congress of all nations." They had "strange faces, fantastic dresses, queer dialects and baggage and personal effects as odd as their owner." Northerners associated the newcomers with labor radicalism and worried that increasing numbers of immigrants who believed in class conflict would overawe the harmonious American free labor system. In comparison to disaffected white workers and these new immigrants, the black emigrants who were peacefully leaving an oppressive situation to improve their lives seemed model Americans in 1879.[17]

Northern Democrats initially heeded the opinions of Southern Democrats, using their anecdotes to paint a picture of dull ex-slaves who hoped to thrive on government subsidies in Kansas. Southerners noted the quasi-religious nature of the Exodus and disparaged the "various delusions" that had begun the movement; the Democratic *Washington Post* reported that the emigrants believed that the government would provide them with free transportation to Kansas, money, land, mules, and plows. It admonished that it was "cruel and wicked" to foster African-American hopes for government support when what freedmen needed was "to learn that they must work for their livelihoods." Democrats snarled that freedpeople mirrored disaffected workers everywhere. "It is with men here, without regard to race, as it is everywhere else," wrote A. J. Gilkey of Mississippi to the *New York World.* "Those who are sober, industrious and frugal can keep their noses off the grindstone. Those who are otherwise cannot."[18]

In contrast to early Democratic reports, Republican newspapers denied that popular enthusiasms dictated the Exodus, maintaining that black people were migrating to allow them to become free Americans. Their motives, wrote the *Cincinnati Daily Gazette,* were "peace, law and order, the security of property, the rights of man, and a chance to better their state." Black Americans were leaving the violent South to go where their lives were safe, they could own land, their children could go to school, and they could vote without danger. "The discontent among the black people of the South is deep, and not unreasonable," commented the *New York Times.* Southern freedmen were permitted "only the humblest rights of a human being." "Neither prosperity nor political freedom can be enjoyed by the blacks in the cotton-growing regions of Louisiana and Mississippi," it later concluded.[19]

According to Republican beliefs about political economy, the Exodusters were good workers, behaving precisely as they ought to. Exodusters reaffirmed the Republican belief in the efficacy of agriculture as the basic occupation of individuals in America's political economy. During the central months of the Exodus, a group of prominent New Yorkers revealed the persistence of the idea that farming was the foundation of the American success story when they blamed unemployment on "the rush to the professions, the commercial, mechanical, and other industrial avocations," and reiterated that "full and general cultivation of the soil . . . [assured] the highest prosperity." Exodusters were fulfilling the American prescription for prosperity. "Many farmers, now prosperous in the West, began without money or friends, and have worked their way to independence and comfort," the *New York Times* reported in 1879. "Energy, enterprise, thrift, perseverance" would bring success.[20]

Northern Republicans denied that emigrants hoped for government aid, asserting instead that Exodusters claimed only the homestead that the government offered to all settlers to allow them to begin their ascent to prosperity. Senator Windom even stated that his emigration scheme had been "simply a proposition to give the colored man the same opportunity that the white man had of getting land by actual settlement, and making a community of his own." The *Lawrence (Kansas) Journal* added that freedpeople "have a pretty correct notion of the Homestead laws. They want to get on to Government land." While many Kansans deplored the influx of impoverished freedpeople, the *Journal* editors, in any case, were happy to have them join the free labor economy of Kansas, for the state badly needed workers. Once they found homes, the editors wrote, they would dramatically increase the state's production. Republican politico Thurlow Weed actually called the Exodus "this great struggle of the colored race to better their condition, and find for themselves homes and liberty."[21]

African-Americans moving to Kansas to farm mirrored the Republican plan for gradual economic advancement through hard work. *Harper's Weekly* reported that the emigrants were "nearly all agricultural laborers, and few have any thing [sic] save their own hands to enable them to gain a living in a strange country." They had scattered through Kansas, where, in the settled counties, "they rent land, farm on shares, or work for wages. In some instances they are also able to buy improved farms or small unimproved tracts at from five to ten dollars an acre." On the frontier, they homesteaded or bought cheap railroad lands and, "in the first instance subsist by working for wages on the farms of the more prosperous white emigrants, afterward doing something for themselves." *Harper's Weekly* highlighted Exodusters who had prospered in the South before moving to Kansas. "To get away I sold six thousand dollars' worth of property for a nineteen-hundred-dollar note," it reported one man's lament. The paper portrayed the emigrants as ideal American workers, worrying only that they had been so successful that others less motivated to work might be encouraged to follow them.[22]

During the Exodus, Republicans living in the East compared the suffering freedpeople with the good Chinese workers being hounded in California by gangs of disaffected thugs. "Working-men" on the West Coast hated the competition from Asian immigrants and both agitated for their exclusion and physically attacked the Chinese workers themselves. Republicans in the East defended the Chinese, maintaining that they were model workers opposed by men hoping to extort high wages for poor work in a tight labor market. The "Chinaman" worked with "thoroughness, and for wages which a 'hoodlum' [that is, a mob member] would refuse with loathing and contempt," claimed the *New York Times*; he did not drink, fight, gamble, or swear; he was frugal, and, saving his money, scorned to accept the free lunches offered in bars— of which white workers cheerfully availed themselves. The *Times* concluded that the Chinese were "industrious, orderly, and frugal," all qualities lacking in their attackers. Comparing the Exodusters with the persecuted Chinese, several Thomas Nast cartoons in *Harper's Weekly* placed these groups on the side of "real working-men," while on the other side were "rioters, strikers, and blamers," or, in the South, lazy white Southern terrorists.[23]

As freedpeople appeared to follow the ideal pattern of free laborers, Republicans characterized the actions of white Southerners as an attack on the free labor system. Admiring the African-Americans who appeared to take seriously their position as free laborers, Republican observers were predisposed to sympathize with those forced to leave their homes for a better future. The *New York Times* indicted all of the South, not just Louisiana and Mississippi with their history of political attacks on freedpeople, for making life intolerable for the ex-slaves. Across the South, "employers of labor" were "neither just nor humane" to the freedpeople. The traditional enemies of free workers—a hostile government and avaricious "landlords"—held in virtual slavery "a deserving class of a grade above the laborer." Cheated by his employer and neighborhood store-owner alike, the freedman was helpless, for an ex-slave who objected to his treatment was blacklisted by "the employers," and, once unemployed, was at the mercy of vagrancy laws, which could sentence him to hard labor, virtually remanding him to slavery. The fear of such a scenario kept workers "in abject subjection to their masters." The issue was not political, wrote the *Times,* but "industrial." Not only did Southern black workers have significant reasons for discontent, but also they would not be true free workers if they could put up with such treatment without rebelling.[24]

Northerners scoffed at the Southern insistence that African-American workers were content until lured away from their homes by radical Republicans, insisting instead that the Exodus was the natural reaction of free workers to unfree conditions. "Obviously," opined *Harper's Weekly,* "if they had good wages and employment, and felt secure of all their rights, they would stay at home. . . . [A]ll the intelligent white leaders in the States concerned are arraigned by this great exodus." The *New York Times* concluded that migration from the South would continue so long as "the laborer, white or black, is oppressed. While labor is considered servile, and the condition of the laborer made irksome, there will be discontent and flight." Thomas Nast's April 26 cover for *Harper's Weekly* summed up the Republican disdain of the idea that African-American workers were well treated in the South. "Massa," says one of a group of respectable freedpeople going West, "I leave you because you 'kill us with Kindness.'"[25]

Stories of planters' attempts to keep African-American workers in the South at gunpoint convinced moderates that previous tales of Southern atrocities, which moderates had dismissed as political propaganda, were true. Support for the Southern freedpeople increased accordingly. Reporting that a mob had lynched a woman who had affirmed her plan to join her husband in Kansas, *Harper's Weekly* mused that such stories "appear to be well authenticated. . . . They seem to establish the fact that the worst revelations that have hitherto been made have fallen far short of the truth in regard to the relations between the whites of the South and the enfranchised slaves." It did not help the Northern image of Southern whites when, in October 1879, John T. Butler of South Carolina brought North a pack of hounds and "a negro named Sam" to demonstrate how fugitive slaves used to be pursued and how convicts were still hunted in the South. His aim, he said, was to show that the practice was humane, that the dogs were used simply to find the fugitives. *Harper's Weekly* called his demonstration absurd, and Thomas Nast drew a devastating cartoon of it, implying that the South was downplaying the current outrages there just as it downplayed slave hunting.[26]

The Exodusters won the sympathies of many Northerners, both white and black, who offered financial as well as moral support. In March, the *New York Times* hinted that "the friends of humanity may find it necessary to organize machinery to transport to regions where freedom is a reality, not a shadow, the hapless people who are denied their rights." Relief societies organized across the North and widely solicited funds with circulars. Instead of seeing their poverty as proof that emigrating freedpeople were lazy, Republican observers blamed their neediness first on their stunted existence in the South and then on the attempts of their landlords to keep them, forcing emigrants to flee "through woods and swamps, carrying nothing with them, as in former times, when flying from slavery." A relief circular declared that "there is no class of people in this country whose claims upon public sympathy and charity are so genuine as these poor colored people, who are driven out of their native States, empty, and almost heart-broken." Organizations in Boston and New York had large rallies to raise funds for Exodusters. "God help the oppressed blacks," concluded a note accompanying a twenty-five-dollar donation to a relief society. *Harper's Weekly* agreed, publishing a "touching appeal" for help that concluded: "We trust this appeal will meet with a hearty and immediate response, and that something practical may be done to relieve the suffering of these poor and deserving people."[27]

Everyone in America, North and South, black and white, was aware that a black exodus from the South endangered the Southern economy. Senator William Windom explained that his plan was actually intended to put pressure on the South. As early as March, prominent Louisiana politician P. B. S. Pinchback reported that "the exodus has assumed alarming proportions, which threatens to depopulate the State of her laborers," and the *Chicago Tribune* reported gleefully that with the loss of their workers, "the Southern whites are beginning to howl." By April, reports circulated in the North that emigrants were kept in the South at the point of guns—if they were lucky; stories circulated of lynching of Exodus "ringleaders." In May, a New Orleans correspondent of the Democratic *New York World* reported, "The emigration of the negroes has become a very serious matter," and planters began to explore again the possibility of importing Chinese workers to replace the emigrating freedpeople. The *New York Times* mused that the South was "expelling bone and sinew," and *Harper's Weekly* worried that "[l]abor, and with it wealth and power, are flying from the Southern States. . . . [I]t is vitally important to the Southern section of the Union to stop the Exodus which is draining its life-blood away." Cartoonist Thomas Nast portrayed the solid South as a man whose hands—literally—were running off to the West by themselves, leaving the Southern body behind. Radical Wendell Phillips cheerfully summed up Northern ideas about the effect of the Exodus: "Without laborers the Southern acres are worth nothing. Even a Southerner will come to his senses, or if he never had any senses, obtain some, when he is starved."[28]

Observers also noted that the emigration would hurt the South politically. If the black population left the South, the region's representation would be readjusted. A political tract from a Boston emigration society advised Southern African-Americans to get out of the South "as soon as possible, and before the next census shall be taken." Be "counted out in rebeldom and in where you go and make your homes," so that the thirty-five congressional representatives from the solid South would be "blotted out" with "Republicans from your own new homes," it counseled. The *New York Times* considered it "a just punishment of the arrogant politicians who rule the ex-slaveholding States" to see their region "dwindle in political importance and in material strength in consequence of their short-sighted and tyrannical policy."[29]

By the end of April 1879, white Southerners were so anxious about the Exodus that prominent planters and officials, including the governor of Mississippi and the president of the Vicksburg Cotton Exchange, called for a convention of blacks and whites in Vicksburg, Mississippi, "to take into consideration the present agitation." They invited "leading colored men" to join them, and, led by men like Senator Blanche K. Bruce of Mississippi, African-Americans outnumbered whites at the convention by at least six to one. Meeting on May 5, the Mississippi Valley Labor Convention, as it was called, had about five hundred delegates from "every county and parish on the Mississippi River between Helena, Arkansas, and New Orleans." At the convention, leading white planters joined prominent African-Americans, including ex-Senator

Hiram Revels, six former members of the Mississippi legislature, three members of the Louisiana legislature, and various black officeholders. Aware that planters had arrived at the convention with a resolution declaring that the cause of the Exodus was not political oppression, the African-American delegates caucused and agreed to abstain from voting on resolutions, but five of the thirteen members of the committee on resolutions were black and were perceived by reporters as "good leaders" who "seem[ed] to know what they want." "A lively fight is looked for over the report of the Committee on Resolutions," the *New York Times* noted.[30]

While the Northern press had paid very little attention to the numerous black conventions that discussed the Exodus, newspapers noticed the Vicksburg convention. Moderate and conservative Republicans, independents, and moderate Democrats all applauded it. The focus of their attention reflected their orientation. Black conventions around the time of the Exodus were basically labor conventions, but the Vicksburg convention bowed to the idea of an interdependent South that would join the North in a political economy in which labor and capital worked together for national prosperity. The convention's temporary chairman greeted the delegates with a speech declaring that "they had been called together by the old question which had disturbed the world ever since industry had been organized—capital and labor." Then the temporary chairman and ex-Governor Henry S. Foote of Mississippi both counseled "white and colored to shut their eyes to the past and, hand in hand, work together for the future prosperity of their native land."

The Vicksburg convention affirmed a Northern vision of a new South. On the one hand, delegates rejected the attempt of radical former Mississippi governor Foote to get planters to shoulder the blame for the political and physical harassment of African-Americans and to set up arbitration boards with the power to prosecute breaches of contract. On the other hand, they attributed the exodus not only to the credulity of ignorant freedpeople, who believed that Kansas was "a promised land, where their wants would be supplied, and their independence secured, without exertion on their part," but also to the low price of cotton and the previous year's partial crop failure, and to the region's "vicious system of credit."

The convention's solution to the South's difficulties was strikingly similar to that of Republicans at the end of the war. It resolved "[t]hat the interests of planters and laborers, landlords and tenants are identical; and that they must prosper or suffer together." It insisted that planters and landlords must "devise and adopt some contract system with laborers and tenants by which both parties will receive the full benefit of labor governed by intelligence and economy," and called for reformation of the region's credit system. It also affirmed that national and state constitutions guaranteed African-Americans "absolute legal equality with the white race," and, declaring that "the colored race shall be accorded the practical enjoyment of all rights, civil and political," the convention's members pledged "to use whatever of power and influence they possess" to protect black voting.[31]

Northern Republicans, independents, and moderate Democrats all cheered the convention's emphasis on industrial cooperation in the South. The Democratic *New York World* reported that the spirit of the convention was "harmonious," and that "[t]here seems to be a general willingness among both colored and white delegates to make concessions"; the *New York Herald* praised the convention for outlining an industrial program that bypassed conservative Southern Democratic politicians. The *New York Times* pointed out that the Vicksburg convention "may be classed among the signs of the time." It was "significant" that planters "practically affirm the industrial and commercial interdependence of whites and blacks." "If the action of the Mississippi Valley Labor Convention . . . shall be practically and generally sustained in the Southern States," wrote *Harper's Weekly*, "[i]t will be by far the most significant and beneficent event since the war. . . . Let [Southerners] put these words into deeds, and the 'Southern Question' will disappear."[32]

Laboring freedpeople condemned the Vicksburg convention and refuted its resolutions point by point at their own meetings, as they repeated their fears of white violence, but the convention's conclusions were not far from those expressed by prosperous African-Americans in the mainstream newspapers. Black leaders at the convention itself opposed the Exodus. They were joined by the National Conference of Colored Men, which gathered together "leading colored men" in Nashville and met the same day as the Vicksburg convention. The leaders of the Nashville convention ultimately accepted the Exodus but did not encourage it, despite enthusiasm for it from the floor, and after rejecting a resolution that was critical of the Vicksburg convention, the Nashville convention instead applauded the efforts of the planters at the Vicksburg convention "to effect an adjustment of the labor troubles existing in that section of the country," and called for "similar action in the future." Primarily, they counseled that African-American leaders "should endeavor to inculcate in the . . . minds [of freedpeople] a sufficient amount of independence to say to the country and the people by whom they are surrounded, If our labor is valuable, then it should command respect." Prominent leader Frederick Douglass joined the opposition to the Exodus and argued that African-Americans should stay in the South and work for their rights there. (Advocates of the Exodus cuttingly asked Douglass why he did not stay in the South himself).[33]

The Vicksburg convention confirmed Northern Republicans in their belief that some African-Americans were acting exactly as free laborers should, and that when they did so, their condition—and also that of the South—improved dramatically. Exodusters were using the only real bargaining chip of free workers—their labor. As they moved away from their oppressors to new employment, recalcitrant Southerners had to accede to the demands of the remaining workers. "The migration is . . . to some extent, a revolt of labor, which can be fully overcome only by an acknowledgement of its obligations on the part of capital," pointed out a writer for the *New York Times*. As early as April, the *Times* reported that planters anxious to retain their workers were offering them more favorable terms than in the past. It seemed the Exodusters were gaining their point. Self-interest could convince "[e]ven the most bumptious and cantankerous fire-eater . . . that fire-eating burns only his own brawling mouth," commented the *New York Times*.[34]

The apparent determination of the Exodusters to act as traditional free laborers reinforced positive Republican images of black labor. Everyone admitted that emancipation had not "demoralized" the ex-slaves, maintained the *New York Times*. "They are good and willing workers. They crave education for their children and comfort for themselves. They are anxious to become owners of land, and their industry and thrift as such are attested wherever opportunities for satisfying the desire are found." African-Americans who were not doing well were simply paralyzed by ignorance, the *Philadelphia Inquirer* explained, just as ignorant whites found it hard to succeed. "It is not that a certain class of the population is black and another class white that causes different material conditions in the South," it instructed its readers, "but that a certain portion are ignorant and degraded."[35]

Republican newspapers reinforced the idea that African-American workers could succeed if given an honest chance, by reporting that the emigrants to Kansas were doing well. "Western farmers are glad to help them make new homes on free soil," reported the *New York Times*. One-fifth of them, about three thousand, the *Philadelphia Inquirer* said, had bought land and were "making good progress in farming." Most of the rest were succeeding as laborers, and "few of them have become a positive burden on charity." All but 700 were "working for their living." White Kansans had welcomed the emigrants, it reported, and if the labor market was not flooded by another influx from the South, they would do well.[36]

Critically, at the same time that the Exodus reaffirmed Republican support for good black workers, it also forced Democrats to come to their defense. With the Exodus, it became imperative for Southern and Northern Democrats, as well as Northern Republican supporters of black labor, to see ex-slaves as successful workers. Only by arguing that the South presented great opportunities for black people could the South hope to retain its labor supply and convince the North that it was not, in fact, a benighted region begging for military supervision. In June 1879, the Democratic *New York World* maintained that shiftless freed-people lived in "idleness, ignorance and filth," but extolled "a good minority" that was "thrifty and industrious":

> There is a class which manages to save; and when a certain amount has been accumulated, go off and buy a small farm on the prairie and begin raising corn and cotton, and finally become apparently well-off. Scattered over the prairies are many of these small farmers, owning their own teams, land and cabins, of course, raising tobacco, corn and cotton, and making a very good livelihood. . . . This class of colored people, being orderly and well-to-do, are much respected by the whites.[37]

Southerners repeated this picture to demonstrate that African-Americans were not, in fact, being forced away. Georgia was especially proud of its record on black land ownership, claiming that African-Americans owned more than 300,000 acres in the state in 1879 and held more than $5 million in property, both real and personal, distributed "in small lots among the negroes of all classes and all sections." The *Norfolk (Virginia) Public Ledger* also reported African-American prosperity. In 1870, it recorded, 26 African-Americans in Norfolk owned $21,000 worth of real estate; by 1878, 141 African-Americans owned $115,000 worth. Black people were buying homes and investing their money, and their educational improvement matched "their desire to accumulate wealth." "There are now hundreds of colored families in Norfolk where the daily papers are regularly taken and eagerly read." A Virginia correspondent to *Harper's Weekly* commented that "[t]his statement is but a small concession of their great steps forward."[38]

Thanks to the black Exodus from the South in 1879, the entire Northern public was presented with a picture of successful black workers to contrast to the idle misfits of the early 1870s. *Harper's Weekly* agreed with a foreigner visitor's conclusion that the freedpeople's position was good; they were on their way toward becoming a comfortable, well-to-do population, and had good relations with the whites, with whom their lives were interdependent. Ideally, African-Americans should "stay at home and make the best of an excellent situation," it declared, while it admonished Southern whites to "do all you can to keep these people; conciliate them and make the most of them."[39]

At the end of 1879, the migration of a group of North Carolina freedpeople to Indiana put a new political spin on the idea of freedpeople moving to acquire land and better themselves. Since Indiana had gone Democratic in the previous election by about five thousand votes, Democratic politicians charged that the black migration into the state had been organized by the Republicans, who planned to import enough Republican voters to capture the state in 1880. Democrats tried to cast as a nefarious political plot what Republicans saw as a salutary lesson being forced on the South. Ultimately the Democrats' efforts reconciled the beliefs of Northern Republicans and Democrats about the nation's black community.[40]

On December 18, 1879, the day before the Senate adjourned, Democratic senator Daniel W. Voorhees of Indiana brought up for consideration a resolution calling for a Senate investigation of the factors inducing African-Americans to emigrate from the South, especially from North Carolina to Indiana. In response, William Windom threatened the South with increased government action when he submitted an amendment to the resolution providing that if the investigating committee found that the Exodus had been caused by Southern white cruelties or injustices to the freedpeople, the committee would "report to Congress what congressional action might be necessary to guarantee to all citizens full rights under the Constitution." Another part of his amendment repeated his support for migration of African-Americans out of the South. After a fierce partisan battle, the Senate organized a committee to investigate the causes of the Exodus. Three of the five men on the committee were Democrats: Zebulon B. Vance of North Carolina and George H. Pendleton of Ohio supported Chairman Voorhees of Indiana. Republicans Henry W. Blair of New Hampshire and William Windom acted as spoilers.[41]

The committee began to take testimony on January 19, 1880, and examined more than 150 witnesses from North Carolina, Georgia, Alabama, Mississippi, Louisiana, Texas, Missouri, Kansas, and Indiana (at a cost, incidentally, of about $30,000). The committee heard testimony that would not, it later admitted, be received in a court, but they listened to "hearsay" and opinion "with a view to ascertaining, if possible, the real state of facts in regard to the condition of the Southern colored people, their opinions and feelings, and the feelings and opinions of their white neighbors."[42]

From the beginning, all Northerners recognized the Exodus Committee as a Democratic political agent for the 1880 election. Accordingly, Republicans treated it with great disdain and reiterated that freedpeople were leaving bad conditions in the South not to stack Northern political contests but to make a good living for themselves elsewhere. The *New York Times* explained that Indiana farmers were anxious to employ freedpeople, especially as young white men left for the West or were lured away by the big city. Settling "colored families" on one's farm solved the midwestern labor crisis and was rapidly gaining popularity. Black hired hands would work in winter and summer. Their wives were competent nurses, laundresses, gardeners, dairymaids, and even field hands, if necessary, relieving the overworked wife and daughters of the farmer. Their children could run errands and do light work. A freed family made a farmer independent of outsiders. "I would take them even if ordinary farm laborers were plenty," the *New York Times* reported one farmer as saying, "which they are not." Republican observers reported that there was a demand for another ten or twenty thousand black men—and presumably their families—in Indiana.[43]

Voorhees's position on black emigration to Indiana was especially weak in two ways, both of which Republicans used to bolster the idea that migrating black Southerners were typical American workers. First, the midwestern Democratic party was full of migrants from other states as well as immigrants from other countries, in a period when massive immigration brought, for example, more than 53,000 foreign immigrants to New York in a single month in 1880. Newspapers did not miss the illogic of an attack on black emigration by a group of white immigrants. "What right had Mr. Hendricks [a Democratic Senator] to emigrate from . . . Ohio, to this State?" asked the *Indianapolis Daily Journal* in an article gleefully reprinted by the *Chicago Tribune*. "What right had Senator Voorhees' parents to emigrate from Virginia to this State? . . . What right had thousands of poor Irishmen, with nothing in the world but the shirts on their backs, to come here straight from the old country and become Democratic voters years before they were citizens? . . . If some able Democrat will answer these questions, then we will tell him by what right the colored American citizens emigrate from North Carolina to Indiana." *Harper's Weekly* made devastating use of this point, highlighting Thomas Nast's engraving of a newly arrived Irish immigrant demanding of an Exoduster in Kansas: "An' what right have you, sure, to be afther laving your native place an' coming here? Spake!"[44]

Voorhees's argument that black emigrants coming to Indiana were politically motivated was also vulnerable because the exodus to Kansas—a Republican state—continued in 1880. In January the *Philadelphia Inquirer* noted that the spring flood out of the South had begun early, as emigrants with money were already passing through St. Louis on their way to Kansas. The *Chicago Tribune* also noted the continued migration to Kansas and emphasized that the travelers were not politically motivated, but, like sensible white immigrants, were moving to secure their rights, better crops, and an education for their children. Indeed, one of the migrating African-Americans predicted that "[i]t won't be long before you see poor white people—honest, hard-working men—leaving Texas" too.[45]

In June 1880, Vance and Voorhees reported from the Exodus Committee. By this time, the committee had been largely discredited, and it was no accident that Voorhees chose to release the report immediately before the assembling of the Republican Convention for nominating a presidential candidate. Politicians ignored everything but the convention in Chicago; Washington "had gone wild" over it, and the House and Senate chambers were "deserted." Newspapermen of all political persuasions remained mesmerized by the machinations in Chicago, and few gave more than a nod to the conclusions of the committee.[46]

The majority report, signed by the Democrats on the committee, said just what everyone expected. It asserted that Northern politicians and railroad men had prompted emigration from North Carolina to Indiana and that stories of recent outrages on African-American voters were unfounded. While the majority admitted that Southern storekeepers did sometimes gouge sharecroppers, it commented that it was not aware "of any spot on earth where the cunning and the unscrupulous do not take advantage of the ignorant." The condition of African-Americans in the South was good, it concluded, much better than it would be in the North, with its cold climate and inhospitable inhabitants who were "not accustomed to them, their ways, habits of thought and action, their idiosyncrasies, and their feelings."[47]

Predictably, the minority report, signed by the Republicans on the committee, disagreed with the conclusions of the Democrats. It recorded the Republican counters to Voorhees's program, attributing the freedpeople's emigration to "the intolerable hardships, injustice, and suffering inflicted upon them by a class of Democrats in the South," rather than to the machinations of Republican politicians and railroad men. After making a partisan attack on the Democrats, who were profiting politically from the suppression of the black vote, it called for the government to protect black Southerners. Voorhees's report was weak, agreed the *Philadelphia Daily Evening Bulletin*. "Almost any theory will suit a man who finds himself in a tight place; but [his] explanation of a movement which forced tens of thousands of men and women to fly from their homes, will strike the average reader as being a little thin."[48]

Despite the disagreement between the two reports from the committee, though, in a sense the testimony gathered by the Senate Exodus Committee reconciled the Northern Democratic and Republican visions of the black community. With illuminating interviews, the testimony presented a picture of a black community divided between the African-American "better classes" and disaffected black workers. The Democratic majority on the committee interviewed many successful black men who denied any antagonism from their white neighbors, as well as unhappy workers who complained about their lot. Importantly for the national discussion of the freedpeople, the Associated Press reported the testimony in some detail as the committee sat.

In its dispatches the Associated Press highlighted testimony like that of Charles N. Otuy (or Otey), "slightly colored," the college-educated editor of the *Washington Argus* and principal of Howard University School. Otuy claimed that the emigration from the South to Indiana was of "the most ignorant of the country people," who had been deluded into moving with the promise of high wages and a new suit of clothes. Otuy insisted that he and "other prominent colored men" agreed that conditions in North Carolina were "on the whole, highly favorable" for freedmen and that there was no reason to leave. Calling attention to "colored lawyers who have made a name at the bar, doctors who have lucrative practice, farmers who own their own farms and [carry] their own cotton to market," Otuy reported that "every intelligent colored man" in North Carolina opposed emigration to Indiana.[49]

Similarly, James E. O'Hara, a prominent black lawyer who had moved from New York to North Carolina in 1862, and who was in Washington to push his claims to a congressional seat, insisted that all the black press in North Carolina and "nearly all of our prominent colored people are opposed to [emigration] except these few men here about Washington." He explained that the situation of African-Americans in North Carolina was comparable to that of whites. Both suffered from the poverty of the region, but they also prospered equally. He estimated that in his county alone, African-Americans owned 20,000 acres of land, and that "they make as much . . . as their white neighbors do." Farms, he said, ran "from 20 or 25 acres up to 300 or 400," and many more freedpeople owned smaller lots. In counties where black farmers did not own as much land, he attributed their poverty to the fact that they were not following the true path to prosperity. "The colored people over there do not seem to want to get up and acquire real estate," he complained. They "like fine horses, and I have known some colored men to pay $300 and $500 for a horse and buggy in the fall, but in our county I have always advised them to get a small home and pay for it, no matter how small it was."[50]

O'Hara clearly believed that the Exodusters were a poor, worthless set. He explained that those who were leaving were "the floating class" of people, not the "industrious colored men" or anyone who has "any great desire to acquire a home." Those who considered leaving believed that the government was sponsoring the emigration and would both provide a new suit of clothes to emigrants and guarantee wages of a dollar a day.

As soon as they heard that the government was not, in fact, involved, their interest died. Exodusters' complaints that African-Americans were not placed on juries reflected, he said, that only "persons of good moral character . . . persons who have the most at stake in a community, the most responsible persons" were chosen to be jurors. Because "colored men" were "generally ignorant," few had "the requisite moral character for jurors." The discrimination he saw in the South was not based on race, he said, but illustrated that "a poor man, or an ignorant man, in any community, is at a disadvantage."[51]

Nettled when Henry Blair implied he was testifying for political advantage, O'Hara snarled that "quite a number" of men considering emigration had visited him "to ask what the government was going to do for them." They "had been informed that they were to receive new clothing when they got here to Washington, and were to receive $1.50 a day for their labor in Indiana." O'Hara had told them that "the government could do nothing for them"; hearing this, they had decided not to move. O'Hara went on to show that his beliefs were those of his mainstream peers: "I have stated that Congress will not and ought not to give them anything. I am one of those who think the American negro ought to be left to work out his own destiny, and that he has been a foundling and a ward too long already."

Napoleon Higgins reinforced the testimony of Otuy and O'Hara. A black farmer who had been free before the war, Higgins had bought since the war 485 acres of farm land and a town lot; he estimated the two to be worth about $6,000. His farm had produced more than $3,000 worth of cotton the previous year. Other African-Americans in his county had also done well, he told the committee. Eight or so of them combined owned 1,500 acres; many more were small landholders. Higgins told the committee that he gave his hands rations, a garden patch, and a house, as well as $8 to $10 a month, and assured them that "a no-account hand don't get much, and a smart one gets good wages." Higgins thought his rights were well protected in the South. He could vote as he pleased, he sat on juries, and he believed that laborers were hired without discrimination in pay. Those who complained of ill-treatment at the hands of the courts were those who disliked the outcomes, he thought, not actual victims of discrimination. Higgins told the committee that he had "spoke to them and told them, lots of times, that . . . the only way to avoid [conviction] was to quit stealing." "If a man is a smart man, he gets in just the same as a white man," Higgins said with regard to tenantry, although his words clearly applied to his whole testimony.[52]

In contrast to men like Higgins and O'Hara were witnesses like Samuel L. Perry of North Carolina, a key Exodus organizer. An uneducated man, Perry's testimony was ungrammatical, and the story he told revealed his lack of prominence in the black community; he recounted much time spent waiting to see more influential men, who would not help him or sometimes even meet him; he was chronically broke; he confessed that he "ha[d] not read the papers lately." Perry described himself in a way that fitted the mainstream definition of a worthless lower-class schemer. He was thirty, and had left his home plantation after the war to move to eastern North Carolina "to get rich in raising cotton." Failing there, he now hoped for free lands, despite the fact that he was, by his own admission, doing "pretty well" as a hired laborer. He earned $11 to $12 a month and board, "more than anybody else," but complained that whites treated black workers only as "servants," although he agreed with his questioner that "any man who owes money to another man is a sort of servant." Perry placed himself in a black working class, and he directly identified the split in the black community, telling the committee that "there is a class of colored people, that is, I mean there are two grades, there are some colored people if he has got good white friends he will get along all right, but there are few of that kind. These higher classes, that is, not the majority there, it is not the general kind among the colored people."[53]

Perry's testimony reinforced the negative Northern image of the disaffected poor black voter. He told the committee that "the general feeling . . . among the class of colored people" he "associated with" was that they were being cheated out of their rights. Immediately hitting on the sensitive issue of black office-holding (and all that it implied), he explained: "We know we used to have a good many colored officers down there; since, we have lost all that. We do not think it has been done fairly. . . . There is some that have a different idea; but we do not believe it was done fair. And we think we used to have in these different States all these colored members we was to have in these different States and do not get them; all that we think is unfair." Perry also complained that Southerners had driven from the region the Northern men who had been "running the schools and the churches and paying for it out of their own pocket"; men that freedpeople "naturally" liked. By his own account Perry himself was a politician; one who had been turned out of office unfairly, he suspected. "I happened to have a right smart due of politics, and could hold up tolerably well among the laboring class of people there, and I didn't care about the balance of the niggers, those big niggers, so I was getting along."[54]

Perry's words made him appear to be an illiterate, lazy operator, disliked by prosperous members of the black community, the sort of man Northerners thought should be stripped of political power. What he did not say also confirmed his bad impression: it was clear that he was disingenuous about at least one financial transaction, and his protestations of ignorance only made his evasion more apparent. Even more damning was his admission that the railroad that transported emigrants was to pay him a kickback of a dollar for every person who traveled; he complained that the railroad had reneged on the deal and that it should pay him. "They don't do fair at all," he said.

Perry's excoriation of Southern conditions was so obviously open to a class interpretation rather than a racial one that he identified it himself. After explaining his dissatisfaction with the South, he confessed that whites had always treated him well: "they never treated me bad," he said, "I always had fair play." He confirmed that he and his acquaintances had no fear of violence or a resurgence of the Ku Klux Klan. Perry explained that "both white and colored people" complained of a road law that required ten days of work from every man between eighteen and forty, because they wanted to be paid for their work with tax money levied on men with property. People of both races—"all the poor people"—also complained of a tenant law that mortgaged crops to landlords. Further, Perry told the committee that he had "several white men's names, who said if I saw places for them to write to them and they would come [to Kansas]."

Reprinted in the papers, the testimony before the Exodus Committee presented to the Northern public a picture of, on the one hand, a group of upwardly mobile, enterprising, increasingly prosperous African-Americans, and, on the other hand, a group of lazy, barely articulate, uneducated freedpeople who wanted the government to cater to them. While Republicans argued that the Exodusters were the laudable freedpeople and Democrats championed those African-Americans who remained in the South, both sides shared the same general picture of the South's black population. Upwardly mobile black people who appeared to embrace the idea of success through hard work were welcome in the American community; those who seemed to cavil at their lot and hope for a windfall to maintain them were not.

While the Republicans and Democrats on the Exodus Committee placed blame for the South's problems in different places, the two groups outlined similar prescriptions for future action. The committee's majority concluded that Congress and the states had enacted all possible constitutional legislation for the benefit of the colored people of the South. African-Americans stood "upon a footing of perfect equality before the law," and had been "given the chance to work out their own civilization and improvement." It admonished that they had to be taught to depend on themselves and to cultivate the friendship of their white neighbors. Once friendship and harmony were fully attained, "there [would be] nothing to bar the way to their speedy civilization and advancement in wealth and prosperity, except such as hinder all people in that great work."[55]

Although skeptical that the conclusions of the committee were true in the deep South, the Republican *Philadelphia Inquirer* admitted that it was "not disposed to carp at the conclusions which the Democratic majority have [sic] arrived at." Reflecting that the report had "a considerable color of fairness and truth," the *Inquirer* agreed that the Southern black population currently enjoyed all the privileges guaranteed to American citizens. The *New York Times* disparaged the committee's report as a partisan setup, but it also reprinted with only mild skepticism the observations of the Reverend W. F. Hatfield, whose recent trip to the South had convinced him that white Southerners were doing all they could "to lift up the colored men to the rank of intelligent, useful, and moral citizens." Their efforts were paying off, as "the colored people are industrious, happy, and contented, and do not strive for higher wages or shorter hours. Many of them own farms in Georgia and Virginia, work them with zeal, and are encouraged by their old masters."[56]

By 1880, it seemed that Republicans and Democrats in the North had reached an agreement on the nation's approach to freedpeople. They opposed the political influence of African-Americans who wanted to use the government to redress societal inequalities. If permitted, the political "supremacy" of this sort of disaffected black man would subvert the government and thus the nation by harnessing it to the will of the indigent masses, who would use their power to confiscate wealth. At the same time, the 1879 Exodus forced Democrats to argue that African-Americans were not systematically oppressed and to join Northern Republicans in championing those who appeared to be succeeding in American life through hard work. By 1880, Northerners saw the black population as divided into a large mass that wanted to dominate and subvert the government, and a small but growing group of hard workers who were making rapid progress toward complete equality in American society.

6

The Un-American Negro, 1880–1900

By 1880, Northern Republicans and Democrats shared a belief that there were two sorts of African-Americans, paralleling the two types of American worker. During the 1870s, with the prevalence of labor agitation, civil rights legislation, and fear of the corruption of the American political system, Northern Americans of the "better classes" had discussed at length the attributes of workers. The Southern African-American stood in these debates as a symbol of the typical American laborer. Prosperous African-Americans represented the traditional worker who rose through hard work by accumulating wealth. Other freedpeople represented the disaffected worker who believed in a societal conflict between labor and capital and who planned to advance by dominating the government and using it to confiscate the wealth of others. In the 1880s and 1890s, Northerners who did not identify with a labor interest joined together to eliminate from power the disaffected African-Americans who seemed to threaten the core values of American society.

The fifteen years since the Civil War had established in the minds of prosperous Northerners the characteristics of disaffected black workers that made them dangerous to America. From Democrats in 1867 had come the argument that black voters would swing critical elections, thus creating a government beholden to their special interests. Republicans had attached to that argument the fear that those interests would reflect the ideas of those who believed that society was not, in fact, harmonious but was an ongoing struggle between labor and capital. If people who believed in this alternate system of political economy elected representatives who would do their bidding, they would change the nature of American government. Rather than simply facilitating individual production, the government would begin to support disadvantaged groups in society. The American system of free labor based on individual enterprise would collapse as the government became a broker between different interests. America would no longer strive for the equality of opportunity that permitted excellence but would content itself with the equality of condition that guaranteed mediocrity.

Only once after 1867 had the disaffected black population seemed to threaten directly to commence such an attack, with the widely unpopular Civil Rights Act of 1875, so the idea of black subversion of the government remained largely theoretical until the 1880s. Indeed, in 1879 the popular mainstream magazine *North American Review* ran a special issue on African-American suffrage, surveying the opinions of a wide range of prominent Americans, from old Southern Democrats like Wade Hampton and Lucius Q. C. Lamar to black spokespersons like Frederick Douglass and radical reformers like Wendell Phillips. While most warned that African-Americans must not fall into the thrall of demagogues who promised them government support, all but the irascible maverick politician Montgomery Blair agreed that black suffrage was an established fact of American life that could not be challenged. Republicans congratulated themselves on the Southern Democratic acceptance of black suffrage, and even the Democratic *Washington Post* commented that "there is nothing novel or startling in . . . their propositions." In the 1880 presidential election more than 70 percent of eligible African-Americans voted in the border states and 50 to 70 percent voted in the deep South. But the peculiar formulation of the dangers of black control of government made the place of African-Americans in public life precarious. In the right conditions, Northerners could easily turn against those African-Americans who appeared to be trying to dominate the government.[1]

The 1880s created exactly those conditions. By that time industry had begun to dominate the American landscape, and in 1880 nonagricultural workers outnumbered agricultural workers for the first time in American history. Conflict between wage earners and employers intensified. The 1880s and 1890s saw new levels of worker protests and strikes, and increasing discussion of an inherent conflict between labor and capital. Unskilled workers earned only $1.25 to $1.50 for ten hours of work, and laborers agitated for better hours and better pay. Increasingly their protests erupted into violence. In the twenty years between 1880 and 1900, 6.5 million workers launched 23,000 strikes. Reformers horrified by corporate capitalism offered dramatic solutions. In 1879, Henry George's *Progress and Poverty* demanded a national "single tax" on land made valuable because of its location near sites others had developed; his book became one of the nation's best-sellers, "single-tax" clubs were organized all over the country, and, with workers' support, George nearly became New York City's mayor in 1886.[2]

After the Great Railroad Strike of 1877, the "better classes" of Northerners worried that what they called "communism" and "socialism" were poised to take over the nation. "The Socialists, or, in other words, the Communists," reported the *Chicago Tribune* about a local election in 1879, held "anti-American principles and policies." This "alien organization" was "an enemy to everything that is peculiarly American and national," and was mounting a serious effort to "expel from the government . . . the American portion of the population." The *Philadelphia Inquirer* worried that "[t]he activity and pertinacity with which the adherents of Communism carry on their operations is remarkable." It explained that communism, socialism, and nihilism were "outgrowths of that rabid and vicious Commune of Paris, which rose in 1870 . . . into appalling proportions." The Commune's "emissaries, its refugees and its banished outlaws have propagated throughout every country of Europe and into the United States the vicious notions which were suppressed in France by fire and blood." On the heels of a socialist congress in Pittsburg, in January 1880 anti-Chinese sentiment brought workingmen to power in California, making mainstream Northerners tremble that politicians in the far West felt obliged to cater to disaffected workers. Newspapers from the *New York Herald* to the *Detroit Evening News* reported the San Francisco board of supervisors' condemnation of the elected governor, Isaac S. Kalloch, who had, the board reported, "tried to engender a wicked and brutal feeling among the poor against the rich inciting them to lawlessness . . . he has advised them to be in readiness for bloodshed and violence."[3]

The nation's disaffected workers seemed primed to take over the government—if not by force, then by politics. Prominent labor organizer and Knights of Labor leader Terrence V. Powderly himself wrote an article in the *North American Review* in 1882 that reassuringly called for better communication between employers and laborers and for laws that benefited each, but then asserted that necessity had taught "working-men" that they must organize politically "in order to compel politicians to perform their duty faithfully." *Harper's Weekly* felt obliged to oppose workers' unity in politics, for, still adhering to traditional ideas of free la-bor, it insisted that "differences in wealth . . . are due to natural differences of cleverness and of opportunity." "A contest of classes," it said, was "one of the most dangerous and anarchical forms of politics," be-cause it "announces that the interests of a certain class, not of the whole community, are to be the object of political action."[4]

More than ever, it seemed the workers' call for influence in politics dovetailed with the reviled spoils system, in which politicians main-tained power through an extensive patronage system, by parceling out jobs to their often illiterate and sometimes criminal supporters. New York's Democratic Tammany Hall was infamous under Boss William Marcy Tweed, but spoilsmen came from both parties and all states. "Pro-fessional politicians" owed their very existence to "the distribution of the offices among their friends," as a writer for *Century* put it. Politico and "philosopher" George Washington Plunkitt proudly told a reporter, "What tells in holdin' your grip on your district is to go right down among the poor families and help them in the different ways they need help. . . . If there's a family in my district in want I know it before the charitable societies do . . . [and] I can always get a job for a deservin' man." The *Detroit Evening News* scathingly dubbed men like Plunkitt "petty political mendicants." "In public life," wailed University of Mich-igan geologist and racial theorist Alexander Winchell in an 1883 *North American Review* article entitled "Communism in the United States," "the man who holds the largest and longest caucus-levees and practices the sharpest managerial tactics generally succeeds in holding the scepter of power. Alas, what qualifications for statesmanship are these!"[5]

Reformers had been demanding the end of political "Butlerism" since at least 1870, but their calls for the reform of the spoils system went no-where until the system reached a terrible conclusion. In July 1881 a dis-appointed office seeker, Charles Guiteau, shot President James Garfield. In the two and a half months that Garfield lingered between life and death, the country had plenty of time to deplore the practice that had finally put a bullet in the president's back. Garfield's painful death in September gave a powerful push to the idea of a purified government, and in 1883, congressmen who had previously guarded their patronage zealously now agreed that the spoils system had to be purged. Congress passed the Civil Service Act, which required that certain federal jobs be filled according to merit, through competitive exams overseen by a bipartisan civil service commission. Only about 10 percent of all federal jobs fell under this system at first, but the president was allowed to expand the list of civil service jobs.[6]

The Civil Service Act was a start, but the corruption of America's political system remained frightening to many in the 1880s as the federal government entered a period of new growth. In 1871 there were 53,000 civilians on the federal payroll; by 1881 the number was 107,000; it climbed to 166,000 in 1891 and to 256,000 in 1901. Democrats continued to charge, as they had since the Civil War, that Republicans were bent on empire building, but Democratic politicians' commitment to small, evenhanded government was suspect, and not only because it bolstered the repression of Southern African-Americans. While officially the Democratic party called for "[t]he old Democratic doctrine of equal and just laws for all with no special privileges for the few," Democrats were as greedy for government largess as Republicans. In 1879, a Democratic senator from South Carolina anxious for the improvement of the Savannah River above Augusta told a friend to get constituents to sign petitions asking for navigation improvements. If they did, he foresaw "a handsome appropriation." He also backed the construction of a U.S. courthouse in Greenville and wrote, "If the people there are smart and will back me up I shall get an appropriation for that purpose." In 1880, a writer for the *Atlantic Monthly* noted that Democratic opposition to "the centralizing tendencies of the republican [sic] party" reflected their political weakness, not their principles. "Let them once get possession of the administration at Washington, and they will change their tone. . . . The party in power always favors a strong government and the party out of power opposes it." Indeed, the Democratic administrations of Grover Cleveland from 1885 to 1889 and 1893 to 1897 did not reduce the growing government.[7]

There was a price for river appropriations, for new schools, for an eight-hour workday, and so on, and Northerners who did not identify themselves with a labor interest learned that they were the ones paying it. In 1883, three years after the Senate Exodus Committee's report and the same year that the Supreme Court overturned the Civil Rights Act of

1875, Yale political and social scientist William Graham Sumner wrote a manifesto for those who believed in the old free labor version of political economy, attacking what he perceived as the nation's dangerous drift toward an unhealthy political system. *What Social Classes Owe to Each Other* was a defense and a justification for the average American, whom he named "the Forgotten Man." The book crystallized the conviction that a stronger government must not undermine America's free labor system, and it identified those who adhered to that conviction as a distinct group in American society. Reflecting twenty years of public debate, Sumner explained the erosion of the old war-era version of society by using the ex-slaves as an example of the stereotypical American who could either succeed or fail according to his abilities.

Just as the men who divined America's political economy in the 1840s and 1850s had done before him, Sumner took it upon himself to explain to his readers how society worked. Unable to see that competition for jobs in a flooded labor market meant below-subsistence wages for many unskilled workers, he reiterated the old adage that the one duty of every man and woman was "to take care of his or her own self." This was especially easy in America, he wrote, where fertile land and unprocessed natural resources offered unskilled labor better rewards than skilled labor received. "The people who have the strong arms have what is most needed, and, if it were not for social consideration, higher education would not pay," Sumner asserted. As unskilled labor collected capital—which he said was simply "human energy stored or accumulated"—society could advance, developing different trades and professions, building churches, cities, and higher civilization.[8]

Sumner assured his readers that this time-honored system offered people "chances of happiness indescribably in excess of what former generations have possessed." At the same time, it offered "no such guarantees as were once possessed by some, that they should in no case suffer." Americans had "right at hand" a perfect example of how the system worked. Ex-slaves had lost their claims to "care, medicine, and support" when they were freed, and "now work and hold their own products, and are assured of nothing but what they earn." "Individual black men may seem worse off," he wrote, but "will any one say that the black men have not gained?" As Sumner indicated, black Americans were the perfect example of how America's economy worked: they were free to make their own way up in society, or to fall down into degradation and death.[9]

But according to Sumner, this natural system was endangered. Re-calling Northern discussions of disaffected workers, both black and white, he presented a portrait of America that struck a chord with members of the "better classes" fed up with the claims of those who had not succeeded. He explained that by using the terms "the poor and the weak," "humanitarians, philanthropists, and reformers" fastened "the negligent, shiftless, inefficient, silly, and imprudent" upon "the industrious and the prudent as a responsibility and a duty." Borrowing heavily from discussions of freedpeople, Sumner attacked reformers for stirring up discontent that discouraged individuals from working for a living. He maintained that reformers worried about the inevitable inequalities in society, seeing "wealth and poverty side by side," noting "great inequality of social position and social chances," and they set out to remedy the inequalities they did not like. But, explained Sumner,

> In their eagerness to recommend the less fortunate classes to pity and consideration they forget all about the rights of other classes; they gloss over all the faults of the classes in question, and they exaggerate their misfortunes and their virtues. They invent new theories of property, distorting rights and perpetrating injustice, as any one is sure to do who sets about the re-adjustment of social relations with the interests of one group distinctly before his mind, and the interests of all other groups thrown into the background.[10]

Who was to fund the elevation of these "dead-weights on the society"? Sumner put a new name on the moderate Northerner who rejected the idea of a societal class conflict that must be remedied by legislation. He was "the Forgotten Man," a "worthy, industrious, independent, and self-supporting" person—for he was "not infrequently a woman"—told by reformers that he must take care of the lazy "good-for-nothing," usually through taxation levied by the state. It had become, Sumner deplored, "quite disreputable to be respectable, quite dishonest to own property, quite unjust to go one's own way and earn one's own living." Denigrating the self-made man, "social doctors" took money from the prosperous and flocked about those who had done nothing to rise above poverty, promising to the lazy man government aid "to give him what the other had to work for."[11]

Blind to the reality that the new industrial economy limited an individual's ability to rise on the old free labor model, Sumner's Social

Darwinistic version of the old Republican worldview justified, and depended on, the rejection of those workers who proved themselves incapable of providing for themselves. No longer did a free labor society promise all a competency; now it recognized unsuccessful workers and abandoned them as worthless. The policy of state welfare promised devastation for the nation, Sumner wrote. It made poverty the "best policy. If you get wealth, you will have to support other people; if you do not get wealth, it will be the duty of other people to support you." The "amateur social doctors" who proposed to cure "poverty, pain, disease, and misfortune" with their own peculiar prescriptions had caused a "vast number of social ills which never came from Nature." "The greatest reforms which could now be accomplished would consist in undoing the work of statesmen in the past," he wrote. "All this mischief has been done by men who sat down to consider the problem . . . What kind of a society do we want to make?" Sumner insisted that laissez-faire—"Mind your own business"—was the only sound plan for society.[12]

Significantly, Sumner's prescription for a laissez-faire government was not as pure as his book indicated. By the 1880s, both state and national governments were intervening actively in the economy, developing American business. They promoted industry generally by maintaining a high tariff to protect American goods from foreign competition; they aided business specifically by funding railroads and other development projects requiring a deeper capital pool than individuals could provide. Critically, though, the government provided benefits only to those involved in developing the nation. Because mainstream Americans had never perceived the government's role as including legislation that protected individuals, but did believe it should promote business, Sumner could argue that the government was laissez-faire without seeing that it was, in fact, relatively activist.

The endangered heroes of Sumner's work were those people who believed in the idea of self-reliance and success through hard work. The Forgotten Man and the Forgotten Woman were the real productive strength of the country, he declared. "The Forgotten Man works and votes—generally he prays—but his chief business in life is to pay. His name never gets into the newspapers except when he marries or dies. He is an obscure man. He may grumble sometimes to his wife, but he does not [drink heavily], and he does not talk politics at the tavern. . . . The Forgotten Man is not a pauper. It belongs to his character to save something. Hence he is a capitalist, though never a great one." Sumner reiterated to his readers that the Forgotten Man was footing the bill for "every extension of the paternal theory of government." He reminded readers that human history was "one long story of attempts by certain persons and classes to obtain control of the power of the State, so as to win earthly gratifications at the expense of others." Fundamentally, though, there were only two things that concerned government. "They are," he explained, "the property of men and the honor of women. These it has to defend against crime." In the next twenty years, "Forgotten Men and Women" made sure American government did the job Sumner ascribed to it.[13]

Sumner's defense of the Forgotten Man recognized the existence of a distinct group of Americans who were angered and frightened by the seemingly incessant demands for economic and social legislation made in the name of labor and of African-Americans. These Americans of the "better classes," who hailed from both major parties and the independent persuasion as well, were disturbed by the claims of workers. African-Americans added to these demands with their insistence that government be strengthened "to protect the lives and property and the rights of the humblest of our fellow-citizens," and renewed calls for civil rights legislation and educational funding for Southern schools. These demands were especially irritating after 1880, when the rest of the nation, North and South, seemed to be entering a new era of reconciliation and prosperity that included all individuals, white and black, who were willing to work.[14]

By the 1880s the nation seemed to be recovering from its war wounds and from the recession of the mid-1870s, becoming more prosperous every day. The North was doing well economically, as postwar businesses grew into their new corporate structures. Production increased dramatically with the invention of new processes; in 1880, Pittsburgh blast furnaces produced more than a million tons of steel for the first time; refrigeration made the meat-packing industry a year-round business; cutting machines and sweat shops created ready-made clothing. Improved transportation systems enabled businesses to expand across the nation; new managerial systems guaranteed that the huge corporations that grew up were not tied to the talents or the lifespan of a lone proprietor. In this competitive world, prices dropped at the same time that the num-

ber of products available for consumption burgeoned. To unskilled laborers, who were pinched as employers tried to cut expenses, and to
farmers who were squeezed off their land as national markets corpo-
ratized agriculture, the postwar world looked harsh indeed; but to those
served by the new system, America seemed to be an economic wonder.

Beginning about 1880, the South finally seemed to be picking up economic steam, too, as the New South began to unite with the North's industrial might. Railroads were opening up the South's interior to new
markets; 161 cotton mills were operating in the South by that year, and
the number would jump to 400 in the next twenty years. Cotton production rose as fertilizers rejuvenated old land and as farmers worked their
land more intensively. The tobacco industry took off, too, as new technologies improved cigarette production, and smoking them became
America's new fad. Positive Northern reports on the Southern economy
missed that the new prosperity for some came at the expense of others,
as mills hired white workers almost exclusively and large landowners
pushed small farmers into tenantry.[15]

The dismal picture of the 1870s gave way in the 1880s to cheerful reports of Southern recovery. "All the intelligent men with whom I have
talked believe that the whole of Southern Virginia, and especially its
tidewater portions, has within the last few years entered upon an era of
greater prosperity than it has ever before known," wrote one observer;
"this prosperity affects all classes, and has few serious drawbacks." The
prosperous New South had a distinctly Northern cast, with Northern
capital and immigrants, railroads, crop diversity, and new frame houses
with "city-made chairs, tables, bedsteads, &c.," where "children now
read and intelligently discuss the news of the day for and to parents who
never enjoyed the privilege of reading for themselves." "The Yankees
ought to be satisfied," a Southerner told a former abolitionist touring the
South, for "every live man at the South is trying with all his might to be a
Yankee." Aside from the panic years of 1893 and 1894, newspapers happily enumerated a growing list of Southern mills and factories. The
changes seemed "little short of miraculous" to those who had not seen
the South since the war.[16]

Along with the economic reconciliation of the sections came the re-
newal of good feelings. As early as 1868 former Confederate and Union
soldiers honored their dead foes on Decoration Day; by the 1880s, both
sides were actively putting their war experiences behind them with large

celebrations of Memorial Day, soldiers' reunions, and the erection of statues memorializing the dead. From 1884 to 1887, *Century* published a series entitled "Battles and Leaders of the Civil War," written by men from both sides, who were asked to avoid political issues. The introduction to the series commented that "the passions and the prejudices of the Civil War have nearly faded out of politics, and its heroic events are passing into our common history where motives will be weighed without malice, and valor praised without distinction of uniform." U. S. Grant's popular tour of the South in early 1880 highlighted this sectional reconciliation.[17]

By 1884, Northerners of all political persuasions who believed in the idea of working for success were coalescing around the idea of black and white people working their way up together. Labor in general enjoyed high employment (despite low wages); the *Philadelphia Evening Bulletin* noted in 1880 "the existing 'boom' in labor and business." Mainstream Northerners continued to believe that right-thinking African-Americans could work their way up in American society in the North and the South, despite the prevalent racism that almost everyone recognized. The migration of black professionals out of the redeemed Southern states and into the North in the late 1870s encouraged this idea by strengthening the Northern urban black communities and increasing the numbers of prosperous African-Americans there.[18]

Missing the general trend toward agricultural consolidation that was strangling small farmers everywhere and forcing up the rate of tenancy and sharecropping in the South, newspapers also pointed happily to the apparent subdivision of Southern plantations into small farms, reflecting that "[t]he hard-working farmer, who follows the plow himself, is gradually crowding out the luxurious planter." "Any Southern planter, white or black, with brains and industry, may own his land . . . after a few years," said the *New York Times*. Mainstream Northerners applauded the efforts of General S. C. Armstrong at Hampton Agricultural and Normal Institute, where young African-Americans were not only provided with industrial training but were also "trained to shun towns and aspire to the ownership of land in the country, where they can establish decent, thrifty homes for themselves and become the leaders of their people toward everything that will make them good citizens." From the *Philadelphia Evening Bulletin* came the assurance that African-Americans would continue to advance "on their persistent practice of industry, on their self-reliance, and on their determination to exalt themselves, not as pro-scribed or despised Africans, but as American men clothed with the privileges of citizenship in the one great republic of the earth."[19]

The mainstream African-American community echoed the view of its white counterpart. In 1882, pathbreaking black historian George Washington Williams published his formidable *History of the Negro Race in America*. In his drive for "the truth," he wrote a compelling portrait of a small community of prosperous black citizens and warned that freedmen should not participate in politics until they had acquired land and education. The masthead of the *Maryville (Tennessee) Republican* declared "We Seek the Reward of Industry, Integrity and Honest Labor," while the black newspaper admonished that a man's failure was almost always a result of "neglect and even contempt of an honest business." In 1883, pointing to the tiny but growing prosperous black community, the black editor of the *Charleston (South Carolina) New Era* called for African-Americans to stop wasting their time and money on frivolities and buckle down to work. He preached that "nothing can be accomplished, by waiting for somebody to do something for you. . . . The wisest plan is to get to work yourself. . . . [S]ave up the odd pennies, and buy a lot, build thereon, a cabin if you can do no better." The *Vidalia (Louisiana) Concordia Eagle* advised couples who wished to prosper to limit their possessions to their "current conditions" rather than to indulge in wasteful show. The African-American former minister to Haiti, the Honorable John M. Langston, addressed a black audience gathered to celebrate the anniversary of emancipation on January 1, 1886. "The negro problem is to be solved by the negro himself in his cultivation of intelligence, virtue, wealth, and good understanding," he declared.[20]

Republicans and Northern Democrats both noted the increasing numbers of wealthy and professional African-Americans, and indeed, in North Carolina, for example, black-owned credit-rated firms increased fourfold between 1880 and 1905. Northerners championed the hard-working, often prosperous African-Americans who were buying land and establishing businesses in the North as well as in the South. Following what had become established practice, newspapers recorded the names of these black people, and often described them or quoted from them. To the *New York Times* from Indiana in 1886, for example, came the story of Miss Grace Brewer of Vincennes. The sole graduate of her public school that year, Brewer was "lionized" by both the black and white townspeople, who crowded her graduation, presented her with flowers, music, and a special poem, and applauded her "roundly" as her teacher "highly complimented her for her studious efforts."[21]

By the 1880s there was a highly visible portion of the black community, North and South, that perceived itself as a part of the American "better classes." It valued education, religion, temperance, and hard work. Holding themselves apart from the lower levels of black society, these prosperous African-Americans worshipped in their own churches, organized their own fraternal and women's clubs, published their own newspapers, and participated in local politics. By 1880 there was even a notable "black aristocracy" of prosperous, light-skinned African-Americans who associated with good white society in the North and South on terms approaching equality. Typified by wealthy congressman Blanche K. Bruce of Mississippi and Washington, D.C., whose wedding attracted national attention with its fancy display and elite guest list, the community appeared to be almost fully assimilated into mainstream American culture. In 1883, a correspondent for the *Hartford Courant* examined the black elite in an article entitled "Classes among Colored People"; after describing the wealth, education, and culture of the elite community, he recorded one woman's "conversation upon the difficulty of obtaining competent domestics."[22]

In contrast to the hardworking and successful black individual in mainstream thought was a mass of lazy black ne'er-do-wells who appeared to want the government to provide for them and elevate their social status. In the 1880s the nation was increasingly preoccupied with workers who believed in a conflict between labor and capital managed by demagogic labor leaders who promised to deliver the wealth of their employers to the mob. At the same time, farmers pinched by competition in the new national markets blamed railroads and middlemen for declining profits, and demanded government action. Popular worries about the growing power of angry workers and farmers gave special resonance to the image from the 1870s of disaffected field hands controlled by demagogues who promised confiscatory legislation. "There can be no security for private or public credit . . . where the . . . majority is without property and so ignorant that any artful demagogue can indoctrinate his followers in . . . bottomless sophistries," snarled the *Boston Evening Transcript* about life in the South. Reformers and new black leaders representing the apparently disaffected black workers of the 1880s still ad-

vocated class legislation that would aid African-Americans. Labor leader
and former abolitionist Wendell Phillips remained active, writing a famous article in the *North American Review* in 1879 calling for government guarantees of land to the freedpeople and for federal protection of
black voters. He continued to sound the ideas that had been so frightening in 1872. "Treason should have been punished by confiscating its
landed property," he wrote. "Land should have been divided among the
negroes, forty acres to each family." In *Century* in January 1885, reformer George Washington Cable went further. He warned that ignoring
the calls for justice to African-Americans would "presently yield the red
fruits of revolution."[23]

Cable's words highlighted just how imminent a workers' revolution
appeared to be in the 1880s, as industrialization created an urban under-
class and prominent black leaders tied African-Americans explicitly to
the struggle between labor and capital. In 1883, Frederick Douglass told
an audience: "Events are transpiring all around us that enforce respect of
the oppressed classes . . . the ideas of a common humanity against privi-
leged classes . . . are now rocking the world. . . . They are causing despots to tremble, class rule to quail, thrones to shake and oppressive associated wealth to turn pale." America, he warned, must take notice.
Former slave and editor of the *New York Globe* T. Thomas Fortune
voiced the underlying fear of the mainstream community. When the
government freed the slaves and gave them the vote, he wrote in 1884 in
his famous book *Black and White: Land, Labor and Politics in the South,*
"it added four million men to . . . the laboring masses. . . . It also added
four millions of souls to what have been termed . . . 'the dangerous
classes'—meaning . . . the vast army of men and women who . . .
threaten to take by force from society that which society prevents them
from making honestly." He indicted "the bloody story of the terrible mis-
carriage of the 'Reconstruction policy,'" and attacked the government for
neglecting land redistribution. "The hour is approaching," he warned,
"when the laboring classes of our country, North, East, West and South,
will recognize that they have a *common cause,* a *common humanity* and a
common enemy." He called for them to unite and work for "the uplifting
of labor [and] the more equal distribution of the products of labor and
capital."[24]

As the nation began to prosper, William Graham Sumner's description
of the Forgotten Man encapsulated the Northern "better classes"—white

and black, Republicans, independents, and Democrats—who began to close ranks against those who seemed to reject the idea of working for success. Frederick Douglass's 1883 call for a national black convention to voice the complaints of the race, for example, drew the response from a group of Georgia African-Americans that "the convention was desired by a few designing men who were after an easy living at the expense of the people." Repudiating the gathering, the Georgia men placed themselves firmly in the mainstream camp. "The true policy of the colored race was to ignore politics and conventions," they said, "and work out each family its own fortune, and that when colored men by industry and economy were self-sustaining citizens, that fact would bring them more power than all conventions in the world."[25]

The willingness of some African-Americans to abandon the stalwart Republicans and join the independents or Democrats reinforced the difference between those who seemed to have joined mainstream America and those who rejected the idea of working their way up, expecting instead to use the political system to confiscate wealth from others. Since the tax crisis of 1871, independents and Democrats had insisted that the solution to the race tension in the South was to split the black vote along class lines. So long as African-Americans were irrevocably in the Republican camp, Southern Democrats had every reason to suppress their vote. If the black vote were split, though, both parties would work to attract the best elements of that population. The mobs working with Republican demagogues for government support would no longer be powerful enough to warrant suppression.

By the early 1880s, the strategy of a split vote appeared to be working, as Southern splinter groups tried to break from the major parties and join with successful African-Americans to seize control of their states. By 1880, independent movements had organized in South Carolina, Georgia, and Arkansas. In 1879, independents in Virginia—called "Readjusters" because they hoped to reapportion and change the payback schedule for the state's debt—captured a majority of the Virginia legislature, and they sent their leader, ex-Confederate general William Mahone, to the Senate in 1880. The majority of Northerners welcomed the apparent movement of the "better classes" into reform or independent political action, at least in part because independent candidates always endorsed "a free vote and a fair count" and campaigned for black votes. Many leading African-Americans endorsed independent action, especially after 1883, when the Republican Supreme Court struck down civil rights legislation. In fact the Republican and independent movements in the South were vital in the 1880s. In seven states, they polled at least 40 percent of the vote in those years.[26]

Since the election of 1872, Northern Democrats had also been anxious to attract black voters, and by the 1880s, they had reached an accord with many African-Americans who were increasingly distancing themselves from a Republican party they felt was unresponsive to their needs. When the Republican Supreme Court found the Civil Rights Act unconstitutional in 1883, Northern Democrats jumped to attract angry Republicans to their standard. The Democratic *San Francisco Examiner* courted the black vote after the decision, and carefully reported the pithy comment of the AME minister Reverend Robert Seymour that "the black man has a good case for divorce from the Republican party on the ground of desertion." Northern Democrats allied themselves with independents and called for nonpartisan issues like civil service reform and economy in the government, which could attract all of the "better classes." They were led by men like New York governor Grover Cleveland, who appeared to have a color-blind dedication to principle and who broadened black appointments to office.[27]

Independents and Democrats of both races and from both sections seemed to be coalescing around a union of the "better classes" as the solution to America's political troubles, but Northern Republicans were in a quandary. Should they allow the destruction of their party organization in the South and recognize these former Democrats who had allied with blacks? Or should they hold tight to the Southern wing of their own party, despite its increasing weakness and association with corruption? Republican president Garfield died before his policy was clear, but his vice president, Chester A. Arthur, who declared himself "constantly bored by these so-called Southern Republicans, who excel in office begging," encouraged the independents, who appeared to have the support of both blacks and whites of the better classes and who promised to keep the South progressing. Prominent newspapers like the *Chicago Tribune,* the *Hartford Courant,* the *Cincinnati Commercial Gazette,* and the *Washington National Republican* supported Arthur and the independents, as did almost every black newspaper in the country as well as prominent black spokespersons like Robert B. Elliott, Blanche K. Bruce, and Fred-

erick Douglass (but not T. Thomas Fortune). U. S. Grant himself reflected that independents in Virginia would place the state "in a condition to invite immigration of people who will add greatly to the
resources as well as to the population of the State. The interests of all
citizens will then become so great that no fear need be entertained of
bad government, no matter which political party may have the
ascendency."[28]

While many moderate and conservative Republicans tentatively supported the independent movement, stalwart Republicans did not. By refusing to accept the Southern independent movement, they underlined
the connection between the Republican establishment and the disaffected Southern black workers. When Garfield's death in September
1881 left the presidency in the hands of the unpopular New Yorker and
man-about-town Chester Arthur, this enabled long-time leader of the
Republican party James G. Blaine to see his way clear to the 1884 presidential nomination. Blaine championed the stalwart Republicans in the
South, and by upholding them he identified the national Republican
party with the corruption of government. As the rest of the North increasingly turned toward civil service reform to curb the sort of patronage that had led to Garfield's assassination, the regular Republican organization seemed a machine for employing worthless men who, in turn,
guaranteed the election of their bosses to office. It did not help their image that prominent Republican senator John J. Ingalls of Kansas said
publicly that he would not vote to confirm a Democratic Cleveland
appointee because he was determined to keep African-Americans in
the Republican party. According to a disgusted New York Times editor,
Ingalls said "he should vote against his confirmation for the sole reason
that he was a Democrat and that it would be bad politics to put so good a
colored Democrat in office."[29]

At the same time, African-American Republican agitation for recognition within the party seemed to underscore the connection between
stalwarts and what many believed was the dangerous advancement of
blacks. In 1880, for example, the Philadelphia Inquirer ran an article entitled "Colored Republicans Claiming Their Rights." It told readers that
African-Americans were insisting that the party accept black delegates to
the national Republican convention. The Detroit Evening News ran what
purported to be an interview with James C. Richardson, a black delegate to the state Republican convention, who confessed that he drank

heavily, accepted bribes, and did little productive work. The segment of the black population represented by men like T. Thomas Fortune worked to organize African-Americans to vote for "the party that would return them the most benefits," and argued that "the colored men possessed the balance of power in electing a President." At a national African-American convention Frederick Douglass also called for government redress of wrongs and for much wider black office-holding. In 1884, black Americans emphasized the connection between black voting and a corrupted government when they overwhelmingly supported stalwart Republican John A. Logan of Illinois, nationally infamous for his corruption and spoilsmanship, for the Republican presidential nomination, thanks to his support for legislation promoting black rights. Logan's spot as the Republican vice-presidential candidate made the Republican ticket appear a thorough capitulation to corruption.[30]

The election of the reform Democrat Grover Cleveland in 1884 and his peaceful inauguration in March 1885 indicated that Americans were worried enough about disaffected African-Americans and their leaders corrupting the government that they were willing to return the Democrats to power. Republicans horrified by a ticket headed by Blaine and Logan had pulled away from the party to organize formally as the Independent Republicans (scornfully dubbed "Mugwumps" by their opponents). They voted with Democrats for the taciturn and businesslike New Yorker, despite the fact that before the election, stalwart Republicans had spread the word that a Democratic president would destroy the rights of African-Americans, overturn the Fourteenth and Fifteenth Amendments, and perhaps even return freedpeople to slavery. The Republicans' defeat was a "revolution" that indicated "the practical disappearance from our politics of what was known as the Southern question," according to the New York Times.[31]

When Cleveland promised in his inaugural address to protect black rights, but then commented that African-Americans must improve themselves and accept the "duties, obligations, and responsibilities" of citizenship, readers attributed to his laconic words the popular idea of black success through hard work rather than legislation. Cleveland's ideas won the approval of Northerners reaching from the state senate of racist Indiana, which resolved that it "heartily concur[red] in [his] sentiments," to a black New Yorker who reflected that Cleveland's approach to race questions put at rest sectional feeling. "As a representative of the

Colored Race," William Gross told the president that his references to African-Americans had been "well received" in New York. He hoped that his race would profit by the president's speech, he wrote, and that "all suggestions as to their improvement will be met by their endeavour to become useful and Intelligent Citizens." "The Southern question has entered for the last time as a decisive element into our national elections," recorded the *New York Times* with relief; "the attention of the country in the future not only may be, but must be, directed to other matters. And it is in this more than in anything else that consists the very great gain the country has won."[32]

Cleveland's inaugural address also indicated that mainstream dislike of Southern black Republicans was part and parcel of concern about the general corruption of the government. Cleveland himself loathed the "d—d everlasting clatter for offices," and charged the American voter with the responsibility to cast his ballot for the good of the nation, then to scrutinize public servants to assure their fidelity and usefulness. He also promised a more limited government and lower taxes to reduce the financial demands of the government on individuals. Finally, he endorsed civil service to protect citizens from "the incompetency of public employees who hold their places solely as the reward of partisan service, and from the corrupting influence of those who promise and the vicious methods of those who expect such rewards."[33]

The mainstream accord on race relations of the 1880s lasted until 1888, when a new stalwart Republican effort to protect black voting in the South rekindled the arguments of the past decade. In that year, the election of President Benjamin Harrison gave the Republicans control of the House and Senate for the first time since 1874. Every Republican presidential platform since 1872 had pledged to protect Southern African-American voting, but the pledges had come to naught. In 1874, after Democrats had captured the House of Representatives, Benjamin F. Butler proposed a "Force Bill" to prevent intimidation of Southern voters by giving the federal government control over Southern elections. The bill was delayed so long in the House that the Senate was able to kill it at the end of the congressional session. For the next fourteen years, Republicans could do nothing but call for suffrage protection in their political platforms. With the election of Harrison, who strongly favored an elections bill, Republican politicians renewed their attempts to pass a bill that would give black voters in the South federal protection. The two-year fight over a federal elections bill recalled the past twenty years of debate over black Americans and set the stage for the ultimate denigration of the black worker.[34]

The renewed agitation of stalwart Republican politicians for strong federal elections laws strengthened the image of blacks as disaffected workers primed to take over America. This fear echoed the South Carolina tax crisis of 1871 to 1874, but the extremes of labor agitation in the preceding ten years and the recent agricultural protests added an edge of hysteria to the older ideas. In an article in the *Forum* entitled "What Negro Supremacy Means," well-regarded tax reformer and ex-Confederate general Wade Hampton explained the evils of an "infusion of [a] large mass of ignorant voters" into politics. Drawing from James S. Pike's description of South Carolina during Reconstruction, Hampton explained that in those years the lowest elements of society "took control of the government." Organized by demagogues whom they supported in exchange for offices, jobs, and cash, he said, African-Americans had instituted a program of confiscation by imposing high taxes on the wealthy. Any new program to guarantee black voting would again put the government into the hands of the poor and ignorant, Hampton warned, which would "involve total and absolute ruin to the South, and infinite and irreparable loss to the whole country." "Negro supremacy" endangered property by threatening extensive patronage and legislation that favored workers.[35]

While stalwart Republican politicians wanted an elections bill, Northern Democrats and independents, and even many Republicans, believed that the proposal for an elections bill was an attempt to throw political power back to the black masses in the South. Before Harrison's election in 1888, a judge from Cincinnati protested the renewed call for the defense of black voting with telling repetition that recalled the tax debates of the 1870s. "Shall we . . . compel the Southern States to submit to the rule of ignorant field-hands?" he wrote to the *Cincinnati Daily Gazette.* Using the phrase "ignorant field-hand" four times in his letter, he worried that in the South "the intelligent white man is outnumbered five to one by the ignorant field-hand. . . . The problem . . . is a question between the rights of Civilization and the Constitution." "The white voters, as a class, are the more intelligent, masterful, and powerful, and they are the property owners," agreed *Harper's Weekly.* Recalling the government of South Carolina and Louisiana in the 1870s, E. L. Godkin of the *Nation* maintained that Southerners were "resisting the restoration of a regime which they intelligently believe would not only prevent industrial progress, but put their civilization itself in some peril." Quoting from Phillips's *North American Review* article, Southern Democrats recalled threats of confiscation by men who followed Phillips, and even pro-black reformers remembered early Reconstruction as a time when the freedpeople "fell into the arms of unscrupulous leaders and covered not a few pages of history with a record of atrociously corrupt government." Supporters of black rights warned the African-American man that he must say "that he does not want 'Negro supremacy,' . . . [or] . . . any office."[36]

Southern Democrats were careful to emphasize that their objection to black voting was based on their fear of rule by disaffected black workers. In the first Southern history of Reconstruction, *Why the Solid South? or Reconstruction and Its Results,* which was published in 1890 and "respectfully dedicated . . . to the business men of the North," prominent Southerners, led by Congressman Hilary A. Herbert of Alabama, explained that black voting was solely an attempt of demagogic Republicans to secure allies in the South. The authors paid tribute to this vision of American society as they revised the past, describing the infamous Black Codes of the immediate postwar years as an attempt to cope with the freedpeoples' idleness as they waited "for Government aid." Comparing Alabama's Black Codes to the vagrancy and apprenticeship laws throughout the North, Herbert insisted that they were simply "laws to remedy the labor situation." Similarly, the authors recalled James S. Pike's description of the South Carolina government in 1873, with its insistence that "[t]he intelligent property owners of the state" had "no influence on legislation" and concluded that the only bright spot in Southern Reconstruction was "the heroic determination of the better classes in the several states to restore good government." Aware that Northern businessmen hated the idea of an elections law, Herbert and his colleagues emphasized that renewed enforcement of black voting would put "in peril" "not only the properties of Southern, but of Northern men also—railroad stocks, state bonds, city bonds, county bonds, mining and manufacturing interests . . . if . . . negro domination should be again enforced at the South, many a princely fortune would vanish into air." Not only Southern but also national prosperity would crumble.[37]

Opponents of the elections bill forced Northerners to confront the idea of laborers taking over their communities—an idea that had cogent force in the wake of ever increasing labor violence. In 1886, a bomb popularly believed to have been thrown by an anarchist at a labor rally in Chicago's Haymarket Square touched off a riot that left seven police officers and four civilians dead, and seventy officers and numerous civilians wounded. Northerners remained frightened of such violence so close to home. E. L. Godkin challenged the Northern community to imagine "how it would behave if it suddenly found all its great interests, both moral and material, placed at the mercy of a majority composed of half-barbarous laborers acting through the forms of law." He suggested that no Northerner would sacrifice "either himself or his property or the social organization in which he was born and lived" to the principles of universal suffrage or obedience to the legislature.[38]

The idea of a new elections bill permitted Democrats, independents, and moderate Republicans to emphasize the idea of poor African-Americans controlled by political demagogues who catered to them. In October 1888, the *New York Times* wrote that a Colored Industrial Fair in Baltimore exhibited shoes, clothes, furniture, horseshoes, carpets, boats, carriages, jellies, bread, vegetables, and cereals made or grown by ex-slaves, but warned that although such industrial fairs showcased the best of African-Americans' work, "the great mass of the race are still uneducated and are yet to be modernized. Many of them do not know the name of the President of the United States. It is this ignorance that demagogues have handled so well." Before the 1890 elections, a leading Republican wrote a ten-page paean to the previous year of Republican government, ignoring African-Americans until the end of his article, when he barely nodded to them with the statement that the government "acknowledges its obligation to educate for the ballot those to whom the nation has given it, and its duty to open wide the gates of opportunity for all the people in every walk of life." Exaggerating this sentence, a Democrat claimed that the Senator had referred "to the colored people as the only ones to whom his party is under obligations."[39]

Many interpreted the proposed elections bill as a method by which professional politicians could maintain their political army in the South. The *New York Times* ran a Southern letter maintaining that "an exceptional negro improves greatly in character, manners, and good sense," but "the overwhelming mass of them are coarse, vulgar, and impure, and yet they are characterized above all things by the ambition to associate with the whites and to take office. They seem to deem it their political right to mingle freely in their homes with the most refined gentlemen and ladies, and to govern—a function for which they are singularly unfit." These "vulgar negroes" were thrust by their political bosses into office in exchange for political support. In July, the *Times* reprinted what purported to be a letter from just such a man, who chortled that "[i]f Mr. Harrison is re-elected, and if we get possession of the State offices as we expect to do . . . we will show the world that the colored people have some rights in Mississippi. . . . We have the numbers and the will."[40]

From 1888 to 1890, the image of the discontented black masses eclipsed the cheerful view of rising African-Americans that had obtained in the early 1880s. While the press still made much of the increasing property ownership among a growing community of prosperous blacks—one man maintained that a black college in Tennessee felt obliged to preach sermons "against excessive eagerness to make money"—even previous supporters of African-American workers began to redefine them in the face of the new agitation. *Harper's Weekly* claimed that "the new generation of colored people grown up since the war" felt a "half-sullen discontent" because the kindly relations of master and slave had been replaced by the new economic world in which "the freeman stands to his employer in the hard, practical relation of the wage receiver." "Imprudence and improvidence are among the most characteristic traits of the negro," wrote the *New York Times*; African-Americans still hoped that they would be "taken care of without any exertion of their own." By 1890, the *New York Times* had completely revised the Republicans' positive postwar stance on black workers, reflecting that "[t]he great trouble in the South has always been the idleness and consequent worthlessness of a large part of the negro population." Changing attitudes played out in everyday life. In January 1890, a black leader in Detroit, Robert A. Pelham, Jr., lamented that a "recent wave of prejudice . . . seems to have struck Detroit within the past year."[41]

The apparent attempt to create a political army of disaffected workers in the South promoted Northern fears not of racial domination but of government controlled by the masses, who, using it to promote their own interests, would change the very nature of American society. Mainstream Northerners had heard a great deal about socialism throughout the 1880s, and it sounded much like William Graham Sumner's warnings about the plot against the Forgotten Man. By the mid-1880s, it had become clear that lifelong wage laborers were a new group in society that was there to stay. Laborers appeared to have fewer and fewer chances to rise now, and they would have even fewer chances as industry continued to concentrate. Increasingly, urban workers appeared to constitute a cohesive group with its own interests.[42]

At the same time, many other Americans with special interests were turning to the government for aid, seeking specific welfare legislation. Notably, the Grand Army of the Republic (GAR) was demanding federal pensions for army veterans and their dependents. The GAR had been organized by stalwart Republican John A. Logan of Illinois, who was almost as infamous as Benjamin Butler as a spoilsman, to turn Civil War veterans into a political machine, and it wielded enormous power in the 1890s as a lobbying group. The pension struggle became a symbol of interest groups' attempts to harness the government to their own imperatives.[43]

Those opposed to government expansion into social welfare saw socialism in workers' organizations and the pension movement and predicted the death of American government if they succeeded. The plan of socialists, reformer Washington Gladden explained, was to increase use of the government and "paternal" legislation, to the ultimate end of the nationalization of capital. The government would become all: "every citizen would be directly and consciously in the employ of the government." In 1890, *Harper's Weekly* reminded readers that "paternal government," which brought the "interfering hand of public authority" everywhere, led to "overtaxation, extravagance, corruption, jobbery, and all forms of tyranny and injustice"; it was "not agreeable to . . . Americanism." William M. Sloan agreed in *Century* that "the essentials of American life" had been "reversed" as "socialism of an extreme and dangerous type"—in the shape of both patronage and direct legislation, which was itself a form of spoilsmanship—had taken over the nation.[44]

While the elections bill was under debate, newspaper accounts of political organizing by blacks fed a popular fear that the mass of African-Americans hoped to use the national government to attain prosperity. In February 1890, a convention of black Americans in Washington elected P. B. S. Pinchback—infamous for his role in the corrupt Reconstruction government of Louisiana—president of its national organization, and issued an address calling for black voters to support only candidates who were "known to be in favor of justice to the colored American citizens." It also called for congressional emendation of judiciary laws to integrate juries, and passage of an education bill, an elections bill, a civil rights bill, and a bill reimbursing depositors of the failed Freedman's Savings and Trust Company, which, although endorsed by prominent public figures, had legally been a private institution mismanaged by its directors. The Nation castigated the African-American politicians at the convention for holding blacks apart from the rest of the nation and demanding "the enactment of class legislation in their behalf." It warned that the meeting would "strengthen the growing resentment" against those who demanded extraordinary rights. Quoting from the 1883 decision overturning the Civil Rights Act, it insisted that it was time for the African-American to "cease to be the special favorite of the laws."[45]

An elections bill would have been menacing enough on its own, but stalwart Republicans compounded the threat with another bill designed to benefit African-Americans. In March 1890, the Republican House began to debate once again an education bill for federal funding of schools. Education bills had passed the Senate in 1884, 1886, and 1888, but the House had killed them all. Now, with a Republican House, an education bill appeared to have a chance of passing. The Blair Education Bill, sponsored by stalwart Republican senator Henry W. Blair of New Hampshire, called for the expenditure of $77 million over eight years for education. While the wording of the bill made it apply to the entire country, it was defended and popularly known as a bill to provide schools for the Southern freedpeople. Because the money was to be apportioned according to illiteracy rates, about 75 percent of it would go to the South. The bill had wide African-American support, except among those like T. Thomas Fortune, who wanted a stronger bill that would combat school segregation. "I do not know of a single colored man in the State of Mississippi who does not ardently wish that this measure should pass," insisted Senator James Z. George of Mississippi. Certainly young Eva Chase favored it; she published a poem in the Washington Bee entitled, "God bless Senator Blair for his Educational Bill."[46]

The "bill to promote mendicancy," as it was known, was widely unpopular in the North because it proposed to use the government to provide extraordinary benefits for African-Americans. "Nobody Wants It," declared an article in the St. Paul Pioneer Press, reprinted approvingly by the Nation. Harper's Weekly opposed the bill, arguing that it would cause an "inevitable demoralization of the community." "The strength of the American system is local self-government," editor George William Curtis wrote. "Whatever strengthens that promotes the general welfare. Whatever teaches the State to look to the national government for results which it should owe to its own industry, sacrifice, intelligence, and energy is a general misfortune." He approved of General Samuel C. Armstrong's motto: "Take out the self-help, and the rest is not worth much." A Massachusetts educator agreed: "In this country it is the duty and privilege of the individual to provide for himself and take care of himself, and not depend upon the Government to do it." The nation's chief opponent of the Blair Bill, editor Edward P. Clark of the *New York Evening Post,* warned that "the disposition to fall back upon the General Government for everything" was "the most alarming tendency in American character at the present time. Unless it is arrested there is, it seems to me, grave danger for our future as a nation." In March 1890, the Senate defeated the bill.[47]

In April 1890, the month after the North had rejected the Blair Bill, the House asked Massachusetts representative Henry Cabot Lodge to reconcile the many elections bills presented to the new Congress, despite the fact that *Harper's Weekly* claimed that the idea of an elections bill was universally unpopular. Profoundly influenced in his youth by his family's friend Charles Sumner, whom many believed had personally set up the Reconstruction governments to enact redistributive legislation for freedmen and to provide himself with a solid constituency, Lodge produced a strong new bill. It provided for federal supervision of elections in cities of more than 20,000 inhabitants, and in entire congressional districts upon the request of at least 100 voters. Even Republicans criticized the bill; the Republican caucus agreed to introduce the bill by only one vote, and *Harper's Weekly* said the measure was "neither wise nor patriotic." While the House debate was fierce, it was tightly controlled by the caucus rule and by House speaker Thomas B. Reed, who manipulated the House rules to suit his needs. When the bill passed the House with all but two Republicans voting for it—some complaining bitterly of the "keen sting of the caucus lash"—it appeared that stalwart Republican politicos had forced it through to maintain their base of support among black Southerners. A combination of independents, Democrats, and Republicans bottled the bill up in the Senate, where it ultimately died.[48]

The national upheaval over the elections bill and the Blair Education Bill convinced Northerners that they must keep the government from the hands of those who wanted to create a paternalistic government catering to those unwilling to work. Mainstream Northerners turned to the disfranchisement of those who did not share the antigovernment self-help ideology of mainstream Americans. Disfranchisement, advocates claimed, would not mean that a few would oppress the majority, but that the majority would be protected from "all political evils" as it was guided "toward the blessings of higher national and individual prosperity." From the *New York Times* came the conclusion that

> [t]he political evils arising from negro suffrage could be cured if any Southern State could be brought to impose a qualification for voters, which should apply equally to voters of both races. It is ignorance and improvidence that are dangerous, not black ignorance and black improvidence. An educational test or a property test, or a combination of both, would insure the elimination from politics of these dangerous evils, and so long as the tests were impartial and impartially applied, there could be no ground of complaint in the enforcement of such a test.

Harper's Weekly agreed that the South needed to develop a legal restriction of the suffrage to avoid race discrimination. In 1890, Mississippi obliged those adhering to this idea by adopting a new constitution that imposed an education qualification on the suffrage.[49]

Stalwart Republicans challenged the new Mississippi constitution, but the solution seemed correct to most other Republicans, Democrats, and independents. Southerners insisted that they would count any "intelligent and reasonable ballot . . . cast by black hands." From "an old Republican and graduate of Yale now resident in Mississippi" came the news that "'the refined, highly cultivated, and thoroughly conscientious and better class in New England and the North' have practically the same ends in view with a similar class in the Southern States." Noting that "the better class of colored citizens" enabled "a 'law and order' victory . . . over the liquor interest" in his town, the author explained that "negro rule as such is unreasonable and unintelligent, and could not be tolerated, as it would not be tolerated in New York or New England."[50]

With this assurance that disfranchisement was based not on race but on a true understanding of America's best interests, Northerners of the "better classes" backed the new Mississippi constitution. Cleveland, with his positive record on race, endorsed it. In 1891, independent newspapers like the *Buffalo Enquirer* along with the *Boston Evening Transcript* maintained that most African-Americans were making "wonderful progress," and that education qualifications would only disfranchise the disaffected black masses. *Century* suggested that ballot reform would actually benefit African-Americans by encouraging them to seek education, thus starting them on their road to "general intelligence and personal independence." The *Kansas City Star* explained: "the negro is making steady and rapid advancement both in respect to material prosperity and moral and intellectual development. The American negroes have already attained a degree of prosperity which their most sanguine friends did not dream of twenty-five years ago. . . . The negro is working out his own salvation and if he is let alone he will come into the possession of all the rights and privileges which await his higher development by logical processes."[51]

The sense that disaffected African-Americans had to be purged from politics before they corrupted the government became a conviction in 1892, when election-year debates cemented Northern acquiescence in black disfranchisement. The election of 1892 pitted high-tariff Republicans, led by President Benjamin Harrison, against low-tariff Democrats, led by the renominated ex-president, Grover Cleveland. The prominence of the tariff issue presented a problem to Northern Democrats, many of whom wanted a protective tariff. It also worried Southern Democrats, who knew that if the growing Southern Alliance, made up of angry farmers, drew votes away from the Democrats, the split might permit black votes to carry the Republicans to power in Southern states.[52]

To unite the Democrats behind Cleveland, Charles A. Dana of the *New York Sun* ignored the tariff issue and focused on the stalwart Republicans' continuing call for a federal elections bill as the critical issue of the campaign. He recalled the Louisiana debacle of the early 1870s, claiming that Republican policy "leads back to negro domination . . . the Federal Lieutenant of infantry dispersing, under orders from Washington, the Legislature elected by the sovereign voters of a free state," and tied the bill to Reconstruction South Carolina's "fraud, force, legislation for plunder, taxation that is confiscation, disaster and ruin to the new prosperity of the New South. The blackest ink is not black enough to describe the consequences of the Force bill policy, once successfully put into operation by the politicians who have devised it," he concluded. Blind to the rhetorical power of the Force Bill campaign, the *Philadelphia Evening Bulletin* found Dana's efforts to push "the 'Force Bill' Bogy" "amusing."[53]

But the threat of "negro supremacy" in the South, with its overtones of socialism and control of the state by the masses, was not amusing to most Northerners. In the summer of 1892 Northerners were even more vulnerable to fears of a socialistic government than they had been two years before. In July, Homestead, Pennsylvania, exploded in a labor struggle in which strikers, angry about wage cuts and firings, took control of Andrew Carnegie's ironworks and, after a bloody struggle, joined with sympathetic citizens to run the town. "Labor War Begun," ran the headline in the *Philadelphia Evening Bulletin*.[54] "Society and civilization are at bay" in Homestead, read *Harper's Weekly*. "A strong mob had been organized and armed, by determined leaders, for the purpose of interfering with property rights, and hindering the peaceful employment of labor; and had threatened death to any man who should assert the rights they wished to destroy." Led by demagogues, it explained, "a mob is in control." For four months newspapers covered the 1892 strike, printing not only that strikers had killed three of the Pinkertons hired to drive them away, but also that they had tried to poison the town's food supply and that one striker had singled out Carnegie's managing partner for assassination.[55]

Northerners had also seen the specter of black mobs, as men like T. Thomas Fortune had risen to prominence in the Northern black community. Influenced by radical economic theories, and a fiery advocate of black rights, Fortune represented the disaffected black worker agitating for black advancement. In 1887 he organized the National Afro-American League to fight for the protection of black voting, the end to lynching, equalized school funding, and equal rights to transportation and public accommodation. "We propose to accomplish our purpose by the peaceful methods of agitation, through the ballots and the courts," he announced, "but if others use weapons of violence . . . it is not for us to run away from violence." The league's first convention in 1890 passed over Fortune as too radical to be its president; nonetheless the organization was still too much for most Northerners. The *Nation* said the convention advocated "class legislation," and the *St. Louis Republic* denied that the convention represented "the decent negroes of the South." In April 1892, when a large crowd of African-Americans gathered to protest a Southern lynching, the majority of the crowd was initially well ordered. When T. Thomas Fortune got up and listed the long history of white oppression of black Americans, however, the mood changed. "What are you going to do about it?" he asked the crowd. "Fight! Fight!" shouted his audience. The protestors decided to take their grievances directly to President Harrison, drawing popular attention to the idea that African-Americans expected their complaints to be addressed directly by the federal government.[56]

Mainstream Northerners of all parties opposed an elections bill in the 1892 campaign. At the National Democratic Convention, Senator John M. Palmer of Illinois, who had fought for integrated schools in his state, denounced a "force bill." The New York Times reflected that stalwart Republicans seemed determined to pass such an unpopular bill to give them control of the government: "The more public opinion is shown to be against it the more the Republican managers will be eager to pass it, in order to get that control of Southern voting machinery that would enable them to defy public sentiment." The Negro National Democratic Committee met with men from seventeen states claiming to be Republicans, and as a group they determined to turn away from the Republican party. The New York Times ran a letter from John T. Shuften, "a leading colored man" of Orlando, Florida, "a lawyer of ability and possessing marked influence with his race," explaining that he was deserting the Republican party, which wanted an elections bill solely to shore up the eroding Republican political machine in the South.[57]

With its continuing call for elections laws, the Republican ticket of 1892 seemed to threaten to create a government that would be controlled by the disaffected black masses. The Republican party, lamented Harper's Weekly, "has become the party whose distinctive idea is the perversion of taxation from the support of government to the enrichment of a class for private ends." In addition, opponents of Harrison continued to hammer home the idea that he was the leader of a corrupt organization designed to put poor blacks into office. Immediately after Harrison's nomination, the New York Times ran a story that he had brought a South Carolina delegate to his convention with a promise of the postmastership of Charleston, for which the man "was not capable of discharging the duties."[58]

The Democratic platform in 1892 explicitly called for state control of elections, and when Democrat Grover Cleveland was elected to a second term—the only president to lose his office for a term and then regain it—it seemed the people had spoken. Beneath their fear of a growing federal government and their call for state control of elections was a very real fear that the lower classes would seize control of the national government and institute redistributive legislation. They believed such legislation would undermine the true basis of American society, the willingness to work one's way up economically and socially. *Century* reflected this national anxiety in November 1892 when it ran two accounts of the Paris Commune recalling the arson, snipers, "wanton destruction," and "blood-stained scenes" of workers' rule in Paris twenty years before. *Harper's Weekly* believed that, with Cleveland's victory, Civil War issues were finally settled; the federal government would no longer expand to interfere in individual's lives. William Graham Sumner's individualism, it seemed, was winning out over the idea of an active federal government.[59]

The rhetoric of the 1892 election confirmed that a dangerous mass of disaffected black workers who rejected the core American value of working for success sought to change the nature of American government. Supporting federal legislation in their behalf, they represented the dangers of a strong "paternal" federal government. The fact that some Southern African-Americans had joined the Populist movement of discontented farmers anxious for government aid cemented the conviction that black Americans wanted an activist government operating on behalf of "the people," against the wealthy. In their 1892 platform, after all, the Populists demanded that the government respond directly to the needs of the people. Written by Ignatius Donnelly, a maverick politician known for his violent novel about class warfare, *Caesar's Column*, the platform maintained "that the power of government—in other words, of the people—should be expanded . . . as rapidly and as far as the good sense of an intelligent people and the teachings of experience shall justify, to the end that oppression, injustice, and poverty shall eventually cease in the land."[60]

In 1893, a student of Populism explained that early government aid to freedpeople had threatened to rewrite the nature of the American government, leading ultimately to heresies like that of the Populists. During the war, "the government . . . became not merely a creation of the people to execute their will . . . but an active, powerful force, superior to the people, a thing to appeal to, to be relied upon, to be regarded as a father." After the war, "the American people found a host of new offices created by the exigencies of the war, the race and reconstruction questions, and clamoring multitudes of idle men." Instead of cutting back, then, "the policy adopted served only to hasten the propagation of socialistic ideas." A hostile New Orleans lawyer was more explicit, charging that during Reconstruction the freedman "was made the ward of the nation," enjoying benefits given to no other race. This "Negro domination" threatened Southern civilization during Reconstruction and in 1893, he said, it dictated the repeal of the Fifteenth Amendment.[61]

The depression of 1893 to 1897 cemented fears that disaffected workers planned to change the government. Beginning in February 1893, as panic selling on the New York Stock Exchange reflected glutted markets, uncertain currency values, declining exports, and low agricultural prices, the depression left 2 million unemployed by 1894. The numbers continued to rise as banks failed and businesses went bankrupt; by 1895, one worker in five was unemployed. As state and private relief organizations were unable provide enough relief, the unemployed increasingly asked for federal government aid. In the spring of 1894, Jacob Coxey led "the Tramps' March on Washington," from Massillon, Ohio. Five hundred men, women, and children made up "Coxey's Army," which offered the president "a petition with boots on" for a road-building program to provide government jobs. The "army" attracted national attention and raised national fears. It was dispersed by 100 mounted police when it reached the White House, and Coxey was promptly arrested for trespassing, but the march had made clear a popular demand for government action on behalf of those left behind in the world of corporate capitalism.[62]

In the years after 1894, mainstream Americans pulled their government out of the reach of those they perceived to be disaffected workers who believed in a conflict between labor and capital. In February 1894, a Democratic Congress repealed all federal elections laws. The immediate results appeared fortuitous. Thanks to the disappearance of the Force Bill issue and to an economic panic, Southern states began to split their vote for the first time since 1872. Reflecting on a split vote in Alabama, *Harper's Weekly* reported that the most important thing about the election was that "a very large number of colored men voted on the Democratic side. This means not only that many negroes have concluded to identify themselves as much as possible with the most respectable and influential class of the Southern whites . . . [but also that] the trouble about the negro vote in the South may now be considered to be in the course of natural and ultimate adjustment." The *New York Times* reflected that the "eminent leaders of the white race in the South . . . are in essential harmony with the best expression of the judgments of the wiser leaders of the colored race." Specifying that the "wiser leaders" were not "the colored men who are professional politicians and whose opinions are influenced by disappointed ambition for office," the *Times* emphasized the recent declaration of a black conference of "representative colored men" held in Tuskegee, Alabama. The declaration said that African-Americans were progressing, and called for "self-help and self-reliance." It urged African-Americans to buy land, educate their young, and erase debt. The *Times* noted the absence of a call for an elections bill, an education bill, or "the need of offices or of votes." The next year, the *New York Times* rejoiced that the Republican "Southern machine" would be broken up and fall to pieces.[63]

Also in 1894, mainstream Americans launched a major attack on workers. In the summer of that year, a strike that began at George Pullman's Palace Car Company in Pullman, Illinois, spread across the country and stopped trains nationwide. Those nervous about workers applauded as President Grover Cleveland obtained an injunction against the strike and sent several thousand special deputies to Illinois to end it. Dr. James Weir, Jr., a self-identified psychologist from Kentucky, went so far as to argue that strikers' methods proved their degeneration. He branded "communism, socialism, and nihilism" atavistic, and declared that "[c]ivilization, in its purity, demands an individualism totally inconsistent with . . . communism and socialism." Equating the "congenital criminal" and the labor agitator—although the latter was "far the more dangerous to society"—he advocated killing off the treacherous labor organizers. In 1895, the Supreme Court spoke for mainstream Americans when it handed down *In re Debs*, which, by declaring illegal the forcible obstruction of interstate commerce, virtually outlawed striking. "We hold that the government of the United States . . . [has] . . . jurisdiction over every foot of soil within its territory, and [acts] directly upon each citizen," declared the court, but rather than aiding individuals, that strength would be used to thwart the growing power of disaffected workers.[64]

The Northern conviction that the mass of African-Americans were disaffected workers not only dictated disfranchisement but also justified discrimination against black Americans in general by attributing to them the laziness, ignorance, and violence associated with those who rejected the free labor ideal. When a black correspondent to the *New York Times* complained that employers discriminated against black workers, the *Times* answered him by quoting an employer at a Southern mill, who had said that African-Americans would have the jobs "if the negroes would work as white men work." They were certainly intelligent enough to learn the work, but even when they did, he said, "they still have to overcome the race dislike for continuous labor." A few were good workers, but the rest were prone to "take frequent, unexpected, and unexplained holidays," and "the habit of loafing was too common." If black workers cultivated "the habits of industry and regularity" in the South, said the employer, they could break into the Northern market successfully. Once resolved to be "industrious, . . . the negroes of this country could press their demand for equality of treatment as labourers with much better prospect of success than . . . [through] . . . mistaken political legislation."[65]

Other students of the "race question" argued that, because the government had coddled the ex-slaves, their development into good free workers had been stunted. "Work is the most important factor in the development of personality," wrote Jasper C. Barnes, and since African-Americans had never had to work to achieve the fruits of citizenship, but rather had been given them, they were morally deficient. An angry Southerner reported in 1900 that government stewardship had ruined the ex-slaves: "We delivered the African man over to the nation in 1865 orderly, fairly industrious, without vices, without disease, without crime. In the hands of the nation he has become disorderly, idle, vicious, diseased; three times more criminal than the native white and one and a half times more criminal than the foreign white consisting largely of the scum of Europe."[66]

Like the recidivist white strikers, these deficient workers were seen as permanently disabled. In *Harper's Monthly Magazine,* former slave owner Robert Bingham declared that education was useless for helping blacks, for they were unable to learn; industrial training was useless because they were no good with tools. Massachusetts native Henry M. Field's popular 1890 account of the South, *Bright Skies and Dark Shadows,* insisted that African-Americans must be unable to rise, or the past decades of equality would have created a prosperous black community. "It is disappointing and discouraging to find that, with all these opportunities, they are little removed from where they were a hundred years ago," he wrote. When A. H. Grimke, a black lawyer in Boston, countered Field's argument with a long list of black professionals, Field pointed out that they were all "mulattoes" with the best white blood of the South in their veins. "But putting every one of these to the account, how far could a dozen or two of isolated individuals, go to prove the capacity of a whole race, the mass of whom are still far, far behind?" Instead of succeeding on their own, African-Americans had been forced into prominence by being "given" the rights of citizenship and protected by the government.[67]

The branding of African-Americans as disaffected workers trying to take over the government not only confirmed Northern acquiescence in disfranchisement and discrimination but also mixed dangerously with racism to destroy the Northern image of black Americans as potential equals in American society. Persistent racism combined with the idea that deficient black workers were unable to survive in a free labor society to popularize the view that African-Americans were profoundly inferior to the Forgotten Man who succeeded in America. Democratic extremists had been arguing for decades that African-Americans were "inferior being[s], not entitled, by natural justice or humane policy, to the rights of citizenship," but they had been dismissed by mainstream thinkers. Now, using the example of politics, Henry A. Scomp argued in the *Forum* that black people automatically took positions opposite to those of whites on all issues, including those of basic civilization. He argued that the mass of African-Americans automatically opposed themselves to "the Caucasian's faith, education, social virtues, patriotism, and energy." African-Americans were restive, Scomp wrote, "roaming over the land with no regular occupation, no property, and no visible means of support." "Sooner or later," he worried, "a deplorable collision must come." He called for measures to "dispel the clouds . . . before they break, and perhaps deluge America with such a torrent of blood at the end of the nineteenth century as flooded France at the end of the eighteenth." "Upon the correct solution [of the race question]," agreed

Thomas Nelson Page, depends "the progress and security, if not the very existence, of the American people." African-Americans, it appeared, were not only opposed to mainstream Northerners in politics but also opposed to everything else for which Americans stood.[68]

This growing sense of African-Americans as "other" carried beyond politics. Beginning in 1889, lynchings of African-Americans in the South increased dramatically. Popular myth rooted the hangings and burnings of African-American men in their attacks on white women. The actual circumstances of lynchings indicate that they were rooted in economic and social tensions, but many Northerners saw alleged African-American attacks on white women as a logical extension of the black assault on American government. What Southerners feared, after all, was "Negro supremacy." While to an old Southern Democrat such as Wade Hampton in 1888, that still meant only control of the government by influencing elections, those too young to remember the political history of Reconstruction to which he referred could easily read into the accusation a black struggle for racial domination.[69]

Henry Litchfield West made explicit the connection between politics, rape, and lynching when he wrote "The Race War in North Carolina," published in the *Forum* at the end of the century. He explained that, in Wilmington, "ministers, lawyers, doctors, merchants, railroad officials, cotton exporters, and . . . the reputable, taxpaying, substantial men of the city" had determined to enforce "white supremacy" because "thriftless, improvident" African-Americans held a majority at the polls. In 1896, blacks had joined with Populists to take control of the city, he said, organizing an incompetent police force and appointing magistrates who permitted crime; "property was not safe," he claimed, and "women were assaulted on the streets." The article went on to link a government of black officeholders with insults to white "girls," who were forced to deal with the men in their capacity as government officials. To combat African-American government, West wrote, "[t]he Negro . . . was pilloried as the quintessence of all that was brutal and dangerous"; newspapers highlighted stories of black men assaulting white women and "highly esteemed" citizens. In 1898, the white vigilante committees in Wilmington terrorized black citizens into complete submission after leaving ten African-Americans dead and forcing Republicans to resign their elected offices. "We . . . will never again be ruled by men of African origin," declared the white Democrats in the city.[70]

A letter to *Century* in 1891 argued that Northerners accepted lynching because it represented an impulse of law and order at a time when government, controlled by the nation's worst elements, no longer protected life and property. Referring to a riot in Cincinnati sparked by the acquittal of a murderer "of unusual brutality and undoubted guilt," the author blamed the mob rule on the fact that "we . . . allow . . . the least intelligent and least moral elements of the . . . population" to govern, and "they make and administer laws to suit their own tastes." Eventually "the laws cease to give the community that protection upon which its existence depends," and lynching and mob rule result. In 1896, a writer for the *New York Times* stripped the rationalization from this argument and pithily summarized its application to the South. Southern lynch mobs operated under the assumption that "if anything goes wrong, it is always safe . . . to kill a negro," he said, "and that any negro will do."[71]

The suggestion that the mass of African-Americans opposed civilization became an increasingly mainstream idea after 1890; even some members of the black "better classes" accepted lynching. A black minister from Montgomery, for example, argued that "[t]here never was a respectable colored man lynched in the South. . . . [I]n the lynchings I have known about, the victims were always men in the community no one could say a good word for. They came out from the slums at night, like the raccoon, and stole back again." The *Montgomery Enterprise* noted approvingly that two brothers convicted of murder were lynched "in an orderly manner" by "Best Citizens." "Twenty leaders of the lynching were among the prominent and wealthy men of the city," it wrote. Prominent African-Americans probably felt the need to differentiate themselves from those who were associated with anti-American values. A subscriber to the Colorado Springs *Western Enterprise* opposed anti-lynching activism with a rationale that significantly tied him firmly to the view of the "better classes": he reiterated the argument that individuals could stop lynching "by industry and economy." Critically, the tolerance of prominent blacks for lynching vindicated the idea that the practice was based not on race but on the attempt of the respectable community to weed out its undesirables.[72]

In fact, Northerners tried hard to hold on to the idea of class rather than racial divisions in America. Successful African-Americans protested the growing tendency to lump together all blacks by color. In an address to the New York City Nineteenth Century Club in 1893, African-American professor and minister Reverend Joseph C. Price complained of "the theory that all colored men and women belonged to the same class." There were "different classes of colored men and women as well as different classes of whites," he reminded listeners. Prejudice against African-Americans was not about color, he said, but about "color only as it stood for a condition. If ignorance was the real cause, then intelligence must be the remedy. In education must be found the response to all the leading objections raised against the colored man." A female reformer also tried to reinforce class divisions, reminding readers of the *Chautauquan* that wealthy black women moved "in a society of their own; a class as distinctly marked as the 'upper four hundred' in Manhattan," and should not be classified with the poor black maids.[73]

While on the one hand Northern race lines after 1890 became much clearer than they had ever been before, on the other hand Northerners continued to defend the rights of the prominent African-Americans who were increasingly visible as they ran businesses, held fetes, and bought summer homes. In 1895, even as segregation became widespread in the North, a survey of "first-class hotels" in New York City revealed that they were quite willing to take "any colored man who came, behaved like a gentleman, and had the price." In 1896, an article by Dr. T. J. Morgan reprinted in the *Baltimore Afro-American* declared that as African-Americans had steadily grown in "wealth, culture, self-respect and power," public opinion among "thoughtful white people" had changed, making them "cheerfully" concede privileges which fifty years before would have been thought impossible.[74]

By the end of the century, mainstream Americans were solidifying their attack on the mass of African-Americans even while they accepted the equality of a few select individuals. In 1896, the Supreme Court handed down its *Plessy v. Ferguson* decision permitting segregation in public facilities and echoing the civil rights debates by declaring that "[if] the two races are to meet upon terms of social equality, it must be the result of natural affinities, a mutual appreciation of each other's merits and a voluntary consent of individuals" rather than through legislation outlawing segregation. In June of the same year, Harvard University conferred an honorary degree on Booker T. Washington, principal of the Tuskegee Normal and Industrial Institute. This was the first time Harvard had ever conferred a degree on an African-American, and the event was widely praised. Significantly, Washington was a champion of the idea that black Americans must work their way up to prosperity, leaving political and social issues to sort themselves out after African-Americans had achieved economic success.[75]

Ordinary civic organizations also supported African-Americans of the "better classes" even as racism increased against African-Americans in general. In January 1896, the Chicago Woman's Club admitted to membership Mrs. F. B. Williams, "a refined and educated woman but a mulatto." The club had struggled over the issue but finally concluded that "admission to the Woman's Club should not be on the ground of color, creed, or any line but that of fitness and personal character." Similarly, the St. Louis businessmen issued a circular before the Republican convention of the same year, requesting all public places "to accord to the respectable colored men . . . such treatment as any reputable and respectable person would receive." In spite of the *Plessy* decision, prominent North Carolina black minister Charles Pettey felt able to declare in 1897: "We as a race are enjoying the brightest rays of Christian civilization." Race was important in late nineteenth-century America, but it was less important than one's position in the community as either a disaffected worker trying to force himself forward with government help or a prosperous individual who had achieved his own success.[76]

Prominent African-Americans echoed the belief that hard-working black citizens were welcome in America. Booker T. Washington led the chorus, but his voice was only one among many, especially as his own disciples and others similarly trained fanned out across the nation to spread the message of self-help. "The better thinking Negro has forgiven the white man; and the better thinking white man has forgotten the Negro as a slave!" wrote G. W. Lowe in the *Helena (Arkansas) Reporter.* An article in the *Little Rock (Arkansas) American Guide* agreed that an African-American got along fine in the South "when he manifests a disposition to work and conduct himself in a manner becoming a good citizen. Neither the shiftless negro nor the shiftless white man meets with any success in the South." If one were willing to work, there was plenty to do at good wages. The black population would prosper, it said, "if left alone by the meddlesome, fanatical reformers of the East." In the *Montgomery Enterprise*, J. H. Phillips told the black man to save money to become "a substantial citizen, a man." Phillips sadly accepted the idea that the men of the emancipation generation had depended on others for their needs rather than practicing "self-help," but he joyfully announced that the twentieth century broke "upon us as a people full of encouragement, and determined to act our part as men."[77]

There was truth in the argument that some African-Americans were welcome in American society. At the end of the nineteenth century, members of the black upper class interacted with whites regularly on an equal basis. In Detroit, for example, the children of black and white community leaders mingled at the Detroit high school before going on to the Detroit College of Law, the Detroit College of Medicine, or the University of Michigan at Ann Arbor. Black leaders were members of the city's political and social clubs; their wives joined elite white women in reform clubs. Black professionals served a white clientele; black and white businessmen worked together on new ventures. Unlike their identification of nonelites, newspapers and other printed materials rarely identified prosperous African-Americans as "colored."[78]

Far from representing the entire black population, however, these prominent African-Americans insisted on their distinction from poor blacks. While the majority of black Americans remained in the South, tied to farm tenancy in the region's devastating crop-lien system, at the turn of the century an article from a nationally circulated column reprinted in African-American newspapers identified the characteristics of "the genteel negro." In a defense whose very stridency indicated the increasing tendency to lump all black Americans together, the article explained, "There are thousands of Negroes . . . all over the South who are as refined in their ways and as pure in their lives as are the blue blood aristocracy of the South. An indecent, uncleanly, boisterous Negro is as repugnant to them as he is to the most refined white man or woman. With this element, the respectable Negro holds no communication, save as he comes in contact with him in his daily work." The article reiterated that "respectable, well-behaved Negroes" were "opposed to lawlessness and disorder." It was unjust, then, for whites to enact Jim Crow legislation, they said, "making us suffer for the disorder, bad manners and offensiveness of the lower classes." "Refined Negro men and women" should not have to ride in railroad cars with "the lower and baser classes."[79]

In the fall of 1896, Americans of the "better classes" joined together to reject presidential candidate William Jennings Bryan, whom opponents had labeled as a radical promoting socialistic ideas. Bryan had run on a Democratic platform calling for the expansion of the currency; condemning trusts, monopolies, and a high tariff that protected business;

and attacking the use of injunctions against organized labor declared constitutional by *In re Debs* the previous year. The Populists had endorsed Bryan, and the rhetorical contributions to the campaign of men like Minnesota's Ignatius Donnelly, with his violent imagery and apocalyptic threats, had further tarnished the candidate in the eyes of mainstream Americans who labeled Bryan an "anarchist" and a "revolutionist." As Bryan had stumped the nation, making 600 speeches in 29 states and traveling 13,000 miles in 14 weeks, his Republican opponent William McKinley, running on a hard money platform, had simply stayed at home while his managers attacked Bryan's radicalism. When McKinley won and the Republicans retained control of Congress, it seemed the nation had rejected a radical reworking of American government. The vote was close enough, though, to keep some people nervous.

Individualism "is at a higher point than it has ever before reached," claimed a writer for the *Forum* in 1897, but Americans still needed to worry:

> Many of those persons who advocated the emancipation of the Southern slave, and who contended with the ballot and the sword for his freedom to choose his vocation and enter into competition with the white laborer, now abandon the ideal of competition and adopt that of socialism. They would argue that it is better, not only for the colored man, but for the white man, to give up individual adventure, and to accept such an organization of society as would determine the career of each member of it and apportion to him his share of the productions of the whole. A small percentage of the citizens of the United States hold this theory of socialism in the full application of its principle; but very many have adopted some parts of the scheme, perhaps without seeing the drift of the reform which they would introduce into the community.

It was imperative to keep the mass of African-Americans from the polls, lest they should reinstate "the politics of reconstruction times, with 'a bayonet behind each ballot,' as President Harrison said of the Force bill he wanted to put upon the South to keep his party in office," warned the *New York Times*. Even African-Americans opposed to the contraction of the suffrage agreed that "there are many negroes who owing to their lack of education and position in life, are victims of the political briber, are for sale, a most abominable condition of political prostitution." The identification of poor African-Americans with the destruction of the government had pervaded American society.[80]

By 1903, each Southern state had enacted education, literacy, or property requirements for suffrage, and as black voting dropped dramatically, it seemed to Northerners that the new system was working, excluding the black masses and safeguarding the federal government from the "paternalism" that would destroy the nation. The new suffrage restrictions curtailed white voting as well as black. When Louisiana's new voting law went into effect on January 1, 1898, only 9.5 percent of African-Americans and 46.6 percent of whites were registered to vote. A year before, the numbers had been 95.6 percent of African-Americans and 103.2 percent of whites. Similar laws in the North guaranteed that the government was purged of those who would subvert it.[81]

By the 1890s, black political activity symbolized the growing danger of an un-American system of class conflict taking over the nation. Northerners who rejected the idea of a conflict between labor and capital and who wanted desperately to preserve a traditional American belief in working one's way up the economic ladder joined together during the last two decades of the century. Anxious to purge the nation of unbelievers, they first acquiesced in black disfranchisement, then accepted the idea that African-Americans, who only thirty-five years before had seemed to be ideal American workers on their way to prosperity, were instead bound by race into permanent semibarbarism.

Epilogue

Booker T. Washington Rises Up from Slavery, 1901

At the turn of the century, America's most prominent African-American, Booker T. Washington, acknowledged the potency of the assault on African-Americans as disaffected workers when he wrote *Up from Slavery*. This masterful autobiography countered the idea that African-Americans were harbingers of socialism aiming to reap benefits through special-interest legislation. In *Up from Slavery*, Washington attempted to reclaim the positive wartime image of the Southern African-American worker and, in so doing, to argue for black Americans' eventual equality in America. Using his own extraordinary journey from slavery to international prominence as a symbol for African-Americans in general, the erudite and crafty "Wizard of Tuskegee" appropriated the Northern worker myth and made it central again to the African-American experience. He painted his own life as the ideal of what Northerners had hoped would happen to freedpeople after the war. In a sense, *Up from Slavery* was a black person's version of Horatio Alger's *Ragged Dick*.

Up from Slavery was ostensibly the story of the founding of Tuskegee Institute in Tuskegee, Alabama, after the war. Washington had cooperated with a biographer before, and together they had produced a shoddy autobiography of the man himself, designed for consumption by the poor blacks among whom Washington worked. But this autobiography was quite different. Washington worked hard on it himself, and deliberately intended it for Northern white readers, whom he hoped to interest in the school. A clever political and fund-raising tract as much as it was the story of a life, *Up from Slavery* was meticulously crafted both to attract

225

mainstream Americans and to swing them toward Washington's way of thinking. After serializing the book in *Outlook* from November 1900 to February 1901, Washington published *Up from Slavery* in 1901.

Washington began his book by emphasizing that his vision of the South was biracial. Suggesting that he was the voice for both African-Americans and whites in the South, Washington insisted that he—and the black community—harbored no bitterness toward whites. Regarding the rumor that his father was a white man who had lived on a plantation near his mother, the tall, handsome man with piercing gray eyes and bi-racial features commented that "I never heard of his taking the least interest in me or providing in any way for my rearing." Far from resenting this parental slight, he charitably concluded that his father "was simply another unfortunate victim of the institution which the Nation unhappily had engrafted upon it at that time."[1] By extension, Washington's black community had charitable feelings toward Southern whites, who also had been stunted by slavery. He recalled the loyalty of slaves toward their white families during the Civil War and recounted stories of freed-people supporting former owners during Reconstruction. "I have long since ceased to cherish any spirit of bitterness against the Southern white people on account of the enslavement of my race," he wrote (7–9).

Downplaying the idea that he was in any way a gifted individual, Washington insisted on his typicality in his first chapter, entitled "A Slave among Slaves." His life began with no extraordinary promise, he wrote, "in the midst of the most miserable, desolate, and discouraging surroundings" that were "typical" for slave quarters. His early years were "not very different from those of thousands of other slaves," a round of work, hunger, privation, sweltering heat, and bitter cold. Sprung from anonymity, his only acknowledged tie to a past was his mother. She, too, despite her "large fund of good, hard, common sense which seemed to enable her to meet and master every situation," faded into near invisibility in a narrative that told the story of a typical life (1, 3, 7).

Washington identified even one of the defining characteristics of his life, an insatiable quest for learning that marked him apart from his con-temporaries, with the more typical quest of most other freed slaves for an education. Recounting his long and finally successful struggles with a spelling book, his arrangements for night tutoring, and his sabotage of an employer's clock to get himself to school on time, Washington im-pressed on his readers that he was only one of many. If you were not there, he wrote, you cannot "form any exact idea of the intense desire which the people of my race showed for an education. . . . [I]t was a whole race trying to go to school." From young to old, they crowded the makeshift schoolrooms. "Day-school, night-school, Sunday-school, were always crowded, and often many had to be turned away for want of room" (18–19).

After establishing his own moderation and typicality, Washington quickly indicated to his readers that his life's story would be based on the values associated with the North immediately after the Civil War. Echoing Northern postwar sentiment, his tale began with his conviction that slavery had stunted the whites as badly as the slaves, causing "labour, as a rule, to be looked upon as a badge of degradation, of inferiority." White boys were not taught trades, girls did not learn housework. Just as Northern Republicans had predicted, Washington confirmed that, with emancipation, "the slaves were almost as well fitted to begin life anew as the master," for while whites did not know how to work, most slaves "had mastered some handicraft, and none were ashamed, and few unwilling, to labour." He told of the important lesson his mother had taught him when she refused to go into debt for a "store-bought" cap and had made him one herself. She "had strength of character" to decline to try to impress her neighbors and to live within her means. Washington noted that "several" of the boys with store-bought caps who used to make fun of him "have ended their careers in the penitentiary, while others are not able now to buy any kind of a hat" (10–11, 20).

Reviving immediate postwar ideas, Washington went so far as to suggest that African-American boys were the nation's purest adherents to a free labor ideology. The obstacles with which young black men had to contend was an "advantage," he suggested, "as far as real life is concerned," because African-American men had to work harder and better than white youths to succeed. From "the hard and unusual struggle through which he is compelled to pass, he gets a strength, a confidence" alien to those with easier paths. Washington claimed to be saddened by "members of any race claiming rights and privileges, or certain badges of distinction, on the ground simply that they were members of this or that race, regardless of their own individual worth or attainments." Unlike those misguided people, he recognized that "mere connection with what is known as a superior race will not permanently carry an individual forward unless he has individual worth, and mere connection with what is regarded as an inferior race will not finally hold an individual back if he possesses intrinsic, individual merit." The universal and eternal law of human nature was that merit, "no matter under what skin found," is eventually "recognized and rewarded" (23–24).

Significantly, the mentors and tutors Washington singled out as the most influential in his development were not people like his brother John, whose kindness helped shield the young Washington from some of the cruelties of slavery and whose wages helped to fund the boy's education; all were Northerners. The lessons they taught reflected the immediate postwar free labor ideas of the Republican party. Mrs. Viola Ruffner "was a 'Yankee' woman from Vermont" with a widespread reputation "for being very strict with her servants." Working for her as a houseboy in 1867 and 1868, Washington soon came to understand, he recalled, that her "strictness" was simply a devotion to cleanliness, promptness, system, honesty, and frankness. She insisted that work be done well, that the house and yard must be kept in good repair. From Mrs. Ruffner, Washington learned his lifelong habit of neatness. "The lessons that I learned in the home of Mrs. Ruffner were as valuable to me as any education I have ever gotten anywhere since," he noted (26).

It was the teaching of Mrs. Ruffner that enabled Washington to impress another Northern woman enough to get himself admitted to Hampton Normal and Agricultural Institute in Virginia. When Washington arrived at the school in 1872, he was tired, ragged, dirty, and broke. Unsure of his potential, the head teacher, Miss Mary F. Mackie, devised an unusual entrance examination for the young man. She asked him to sweep a recitation room. Thanks to Mrs. Ruffner, Washington knew how to clean thoroughly enough to please even Miss Mackie, another "'Yankee' woman who knew just where to look for dirt." Mackie admitted Washington to the school because he could work according to Northern standards, and he did not permit the reader to miss the significance of the event. While white men advanced in American society through family connections or knowledge, freedmen would enter by working, not by superior intellectual prowess or exceptionality. "The sweeping of that room was my college examination, and never did any youth pass an examination for entrance into Harvard or Yale that gave him more genuine satisfaction." Washington emphasized too that "hundreds" of other African-Americans "found their way to Hampton and other institutions after experiencing something of the same difficulties that I went through" (31).

From Mrs. Ruffner, Washington had learned to work; from Miss Mackie he learned "the dignity of labour." In his position as Hampton's janitor, Washington worked with Miss Mackie for two weeks one fall to prepare the building for the school year. During those two weeks, he recalled, "I was taught a lesson which I shall never forget." Mackie, who "was a member of one of the oldest and most cultured families of the North," worked at his side washing windows, cleaning rooms, performing the menial housekeeping tasks necessary to get the school in order. Washington could not comprehend at first "how a woman of her education and social standing could take such delight in performing such service, in order to assist in the elevation of an unfortunate race." After finally coming to understand, he concluded that, since his time with Miss Mackie, "I have had no patience with any school for my race in the South which did not teach the dignity of labour" (42).

Washington's most influential mentor at Hampton, though, was not Miss Mackie but was the head of the school, General Samuel C. Armstrong. Washington's hero worship for the former Union general was so overwhelming that he did not describe Armstrong's influence on him explicitly. Rather, Washington spoke of Armstrong generally as "the noblest, rarest . . . strongest, and most beautiful character that it has ever been my privilege to meet," "a perfect man," even "superhuman"; a man who was revered by his African-American students; "a type of that Christlike body of men and women who went into the Negro schools at the close of the war by the hundreds to assist in lifting up my race." Washington did not need to explain to his readers that General Armstrong was a former Union general who had devoted himself to establishing Hampton as the most prominent freedmen's school after the war, basing it on the idea of free labor and self-help, and explicitly rejecting the idea of government legislation to benefit the freedpeople (32–34, 43).

During his Hampton years, Washington absorbed other free labor values, as well. He learned the elements of Northern society: regular mealtimes, tablecloths, napkins, toothbrushes, sheets, and, critically, the use of the bathtub. He extolled the value of the bath, "not only in keeping the body healthy, but in inspiring self-respect and promoting virtue." Another Northern woman, Miss Nathalie Lord, from Portland, Maine, taught him "how to use and love the Bible," so that he learned to "make it a rule to read a chapter or a portion of a chapter in the morning, before beginning the work of the day." Washington also received less spiritual edification during the Hampton years. A summer at home looking for work during a strike in the local coal mines made him hate strikes. He explained that the men seemed to go on strike whenever they got a little money saved. Weeks spent out of work consumed all their savings, often leaving them in debt, and forced them to go back to work at the same wages, worse off than before. Washington attributed strikes to labor agitators, musing that "[b]efore the days of strikes in that section of the country, I knew miners who had considerable money in the bank, but as soon as the professional labour agitators got control, the savings of even the more thrifty ones began disappearing" (39–40).

Altogether, according to the account of his life in Up from Slavery, Washington's time at Hampton inculcated him with the values Northern Republicans hoped to have instilled in freedpeople after the war. He had come to the school with the idea, generally prevalent among ex-slaves, he said, that an education was a route to "a good, easy time, free from all necessity for manual labour." But his Northern instructors taught him the lessons of a free labor society. At Hampton, he reported, he "not only learned that it was not a disgrace to labour, but learned to love labour, not alone for its financial value, but for labour's own sake and for the independence and self-reliance which the ability to do something which the world wants done brings." Washington took care to point out that he was only one of Hampton's three or four hundred students, all of whom were "tremendously in earnest," many so determined to learn that they studied even as they provided for families (36, 43).

According to Up from Slavery, Washington immediately put his Northern education to work in a way bound to win the approbation of Northern readers. After graduating from Hampton, he took a job as a waiter in a summer resort in Connecticut, where he quickly discovered that waiting tables took skills he did not have. Demoted to busing tables, he had to learn to be a waiter before being restored to that higher position. Washington's description of his experiences as a waiter were peculiarly significant in the face of a campaign bruited in the Boston Evening Transcript in the mid-1870s. In the summer of 1874, wealthy white male and female college students "acted as waiters at public tables, at fashionable places of summer resort," to underscore the honor of manual labor. Washington did not write idly about waiting tables.[2]

Having established his credentials as a traditional free laborer, Washington turned immediately to what he called "the Reconstruction Period," the years from 1867 to 1878, which he contrasted dramatically with the free labor ideal. During this time, he maintained, "two ideas were constantly agitating the minds of the coloured people." These were "the craze for Greek and Latin learning, and . . . a desire to hold office." Washington tapped into the complaint prevalent among mainstream Northerners after 1871 that African-Americans wanted education solely to "be free from most of the hardships of the world, and, at any rate, [to] live without manual labor." In 1873, for example, the radical *Boston Evening Transcript* had published a letter from one teacher of the freedpeople who admitted that his classes studied Latin. "Heaven forgive the author of this sin!" Arthur Sumner added.[3] This black quest for Greek and Latin had no purpose, Washington wrote, except to "make one a very superior human being" (47).

Ignoring his own brief flirtation with the ministry, he again echoed mainstream attitudes when he caricatured uneducated African-American ministers who received the "call" to preach as soon as they learned to read, in order to avoid work. In 1867, *Harper's Weekly* published an account of a "colored theological school" in Georgia, recounted by Miss Julia A. Shearman of Brooklyn, who was teaching in the state. Shearman explained that the school consisted of "about forty ministers, of different ages, from the white-headed father in Israel to the young licentiate, every one [*sic*] with a book in his hand, and eager to study." Shearman seemed torn between, on the one hand, her respect for these men, so anxious to learn that they welcomed correction from each other and from the female teachers, and, on the other hand, amusement that any people so ignorant could be "ministers"—she herself put the word in quotation marks. Shearman wrote: "[N]ow picture, if you can, *a ministers' spelling class!* Imagine my feelings as I called on the Rev. Mr. ——— to spell w-o-r-l-d, and the Rev. Mr. ——— to spell b-e-a-s-t-s; a difficult word, by-the-way, both to spell and pronounce, and over which every one tripped and fell!"[4]

Washington's views of politics echoed mainstream Northern anxieties about African-Americans in the early 1870s. He worried that "[t]he ignorance of my race was being used as a tool with which to help white men into office," while there were men in the North who "wanted to punish the Southern white men by forcing the Negro into positions over the heads of the Southern whites." Recounting that in Alabama he was pressured by freedmen to vote as they did, he reported that one man told him: "We can't read de newspapers very much, but we knows how to vote, an' we wants you to vote jes' like we votes. . . . We watches de white man, and we keeps watching de white man till we finds out which way de white man's gwine to vote; an' when we finds out which way de white man's gwine to vote, den we votes 'xactly de other way. Den we knows we's right." Meanwhile, political agitation made black people neglect "the more fundamental matters of perfecting themselves in the industries at their doors and in securing property." Like all but the radical wing of the Republican party in 1867, Washington suggested that "it would have been wiser if some plan could have been put in operation which would have made the possession of a certain amount of education or property, or both, a test for the exercise of the franchise" for both whites and blacks. He recounted the story of a former state lieutenant governor who ended up carrying bricks for a living, reflecting that "the coloured people, so largely without education, and wholly without experience in government, made tremendous mistakes, just as any people similarly situated would have done" (49–50, 65).

Washington also lamented that, during Reconstruction, "our people throughout the South looked to the Federal Government for everything, much as a child looks to its mother." He chided "a large class" of lazy African-Americans in postwar Washington who wanted federal offices. In contrast to the "substantial, worthy citizens" in the black community, like Senator Blanche K. Bruce, these men were "superficial" and without foundation. Contrasting his mother's example and echoing Horace Greeley's criticisms in 1872 and 1873, Washington recalled that during a sojourn in the national capital he saw young black men "who were not earning more than four dollars a week spend two dollars or more for a buggy on Sunday to ride up and down Pennsylvania Avenue in, in order that they might try to convince the world that they were worth thousands. I saw other young men who received seventy-five or one hundred dollars per month from the Government, who were in debt at the end of every month. I saw men who but a few months previous were members of Congress, then without employment and in poverty." He saw the daughters of laundresses going "to the bad," because they had been educated away from their mothers' trade at the same time they had learned to want expensive dresses, hats, and shoes. "In a word," he concluded, "while their wants had been increased, their ability to supply their wants had not been increased in the same degree" (49, 52–53).

Washington's prescription for these lazy spendthrifts was a formula straight out of the immediate post–Civil War Republican plan. He wished that he could spirit the majority of them "into the country districts and plant them upon the soil, upon the solid and never deceptive foundation of Mother Nature, where all nations and races that have ever succeeded have gotten their start,—a start that at first may be slow and toilsome, but one that nevertheless is real." He wished that the girls had been given "the most thorough training in the latest and best methods of laundrying and other kindred occupations," at the same time as they had been given mental training to improve the strength and culture of their minds. While most educated African-Americans determined "to prepare themselves to be great lawyers, or Congressmen, and many of the women planned to become music teachers," Washington concluded that "there was need for something to be done to prepare the way for successful lawyers, Congressmen, and music teachers" (53–55).

Hired in 1881 to take charge of a normal school for African-Americans in Tuskegee, Alabama, a town of 2,000 people, evenly split between the races in the Black Belt of the South, Washington found the South that most Northern Republicans had imagined in 1865, and that mainstream Americans still dreamed about in the early 1880s. In the countryside, the freedpeople outnumbered the whites by at least three to one. The town of Tuskegee was isolated, connected only by a branch railroad to the rest of the world. The white people there were educated and cultured, and while the "coloured people" were ignorant, they "had not, as a rule, degraded and weakened their bodies by vices such as are common to the lower class of people in the large cities." Here, too, though, the Northern plans for Reconstruction had been thwarted. The people planted cotton up to their doors, refusing to diversify crops even enough to provide their own food. African-Americans lived far beyond their means. Families lived in cabins, sleeping in one room, eating fat pork and corn bread at random times, sharing a single fork. Deeply in debt, these same families were paying for sixty-dollar sewing machines, fourteen-dollar clocks, and even a sixty-dollar organ, which no one could play. One of the saddest sights he saw on his tour of the region, Washington recalled, was "a young man, who had attended some high school, sitting down in a one-room cabin, with grease on his clothing, filth all around him, and weeds in the yard and garden, engaged in studying a French grammar" (63, 65–67, 71).

Race relations in Tuskegee were "pleasant"; the town's largest hardware store was "owned and operated jointly by a coloured man and a white man." In Tuskegee, Washington found ideal "types" of Southerners who made the new school a success; from them Washington "never sought anything in vain." Mr. George W. Campbell, an ex-slaveholder, now a merchant and banker, and Mr. Lewis Adams, an ex-slave, and a mechanic, shoemaker, harness-maker, and tinsmith, offered both financial and moral support to Washington's efforts to establish Tuskegee Institute. Equating the two men—a wealthy white man and an ex-slave—Washington claimed that Mr. Adams had "in a large degree, derived his unusual power of mind from the training given his hands," as he had mastered three trades in slavery. "If one goes to-day into any Southern town, and asks for the leading and most reliable coloured man in the community . . . in five cases out of ten he will be directed to a Negro who learned a trade during the days of slavery," he declared (63–64, 70–71).

Despite the whites' general goodwill toward their black neighbors, much of Tuskegee's white population "looked with some disfavour" upon the new school. They worried that it would cause race trouble and decrease the value of black labor as educated African-Americans left agriculture and domestic service. Washington explained that those who objected to the school "had in their minds pictures of what was called an educated Negro, with a high hat, imitation gold eye-glasses, a showy walking stick, kid gloves, fancy boots, and what not—in a word, a man who was determined to live by his wits." Whites nervous about the new school could not see how education "would produce any other kind of a coloured man." Indeed, when the school opened on July 4, 1881, the thirty students who applied for admission claimed to have studied Latin, Greek, grammatical and mathematical "rules," "banking and discount," geography, and "cube root," but most of them had "only the merest smattering of the high-sounding things that they had studied"; they did not have basic mathematical or literary skills. They could not set a table or perform a trade; they had no money in the bank. Most wanted to learn just enough to enter the relatively lucrative profession of teaching. Their chief ambition was "to get an education so that they would not have to work any longer with their hands" (69–74).

Together with Miss Olivia A. Davidson, who later became his second wife, Washington concluded that the school must teach students more than book learning. Students had to learn how to take care of their body, "how to bathe; how to care for their teeth and clothing . . . what to eat, and how to eat it properly . . . how to care for their rooms." Recognizing that 85 percent of African-Americans in the Gulf states were engaged in agriculture, Washington determined to "be careful not to educate our students out of sympathy with agricultural life"; making sure that they would not migrate from the country to cities where they would have to "live by their wits." Their education should make them go back "to the plantation districts," where they could "show the people there how to put new energy and new ideas into farming, as well as into the intellectual and moral and religious life of the people." He emphasized that "we wanted to give them such a practical knowledge of some one industry, together with the spirit of industry, thrift, and economy, that they would be sure of knowing how to make a living after they had left us" (74).[5]

Washington portrayed the construction of Tuskegee Institute as a model of the development of a free labor society as Northern Republicans understood it in the years during and immediately after the Civil War. As soon as he had obtained enough money to purchase land for the school through the help of sympathetic whites and the sacrifice of poor but determined freedpeople, he turned his attention to cultivating the land, not only to train the students but also "because we wanted something to eat." Echoing the theory of political economy that held that society developed agriculture first and then, with the sale of surplus food, men accumulated capital to develop other trades, Washington noted that "[a]ll the industries at Tuskegee have been started in natural and logical order, growing out of the needs of a community settlement." Washington also determined that the students would do all the work of the institute, despite the clear wishes of their parents and the students' own idea "that it was hardly the proper thing for them to use their hands, since they had come there, as one of them expressed it, 'to be educated, and not to work.'" He wanted the students "taught the latest and best methods of labour, so that the school would not only get the benefit of their efforts, but the students themselves would be taught to see not only utility in labour, but beauty and dignity; would be taught, in fact, how to lift labour up from mere drudgery and toil, and would learn to love work for its own sake." When students dragged their heels at clearing land for the first crops, Washington took a leaf from Miss Mackie's book, shouldered an axe, and "led the way to the woods." When the students "saw that I was not afraid or ashamed to work, they began to assist with more enthusiasm" (76, 80–81, 84, 87, 91).

Tuskegee students not only learned to work but also learned the lessons of Northern cleanliness that Washington had picked up from Mrs. Ruffner. Washington told readers that he had always insisted upon absolute cleanliness at Tuskegee. He taught that "people would excuse us for our poverty, for our lack of comforts and conveniences, but that they would not excuse us for dirt." He insisted on toothbrushes, baths, sheets, and nightclothes. Students had to clean and mend their clothes before each evening's inspection. Washington noted that these tactics brought about "a higher degree of civilization among the students" (102–103).

The students constructed their own school building and the furniture in it; they set up the kitchen and cooked. The utensils were scanty, the dining room was "very rough and uncomfortable," the cooking was done over a fire outdoors, and meals had no schedule. Everything was "so out of joint and so inconvenient" that for the first two weeks "something was wrong at every meal." The students were not always fed, and one woman, trying to get water from a well with a broken rope, complained that "[w]e can't even get water to drink at this school." But, Washington emphasized in an echo of free labor theory, "gradually, by patience and hard work, we brought order out of chaos, just as will be true of any problem if we stick to it with patience and wisdom and earnest effort." In the end, the trials were beneficial. Using the troubled construction of the kitchen as a symbol of African-American life, Washington mused:

> I am glad that our students had to dig out the place for their kitchen and dining room. I am glad that our first boarding-place was in that dismal, ill-lighted, and damp basement. Had we started in a fine, attractive, convenient room, I fear we would have 'lost our heads' and become 'stuck up.' It means a great deal, I think, to start off on a foundation which one has made for one's self. . . . When our old students return to Tuskegee now, as they often do, and go into our large, beautiful, well-ventilated, and well-lighted dining room, and see tempting, well-cooked food—largely grown by the students themselves—and see tables, neat tablecloths and napkins, and vases of flowers upon the tables, and hear singing birds, and note that each meal is served exactly upon the minute, with no disorder, and with almost no complaint

coming from the hundreds that now fill our dining room, they, too, often say to me that they are glad that we started as we did, and built ourselves up year by year, by a slow and natural process of growth. (94–95)

Washington illustrated the effects of hard work by emphasizing the enormous difference between the early Tuskegee and the school of 1900. The school's first animal was a blind horse donated by a local white man; by 1900, Washington noted, the school owned "over two hundred horses, colts, mules, cows, calves, and oxen, and about seven hundred hogs and pigs, as well as a large number of sheep and goats." Having begun with classes held in a shanty, the school boasted nineteen buildings constructed within twenty years, built almost entirely by students. Even Washington's efforts on behalf of Tuskegee were an example of success through hard work. The Tuskegee principal spent much of his time on the road drumming up funds for his fledgling institution. In the early years, times were hard. He recounted one occasion when he found himself on a fund-raising tour in Providence, Rhode Island, without a penny for breakfast, eventually buying food with a quarter he found in the street. By the end of the century, Washington had received a check for $50,000 from railroad magnate Collis P. Huntington. It was not "good luck" that had brought that sort of check, nor was it from simply begging for the charity that lazy men sought. "It was hard work. Nothing ever comes to one, that is worth having, except as a result of hard work." When Huntington had been reluctant to support the institution, Washington had become increasingly determined to prove to him that the school was valuable. His donations increased proportionately. The investment came not from the whim of the wealthy man, Washington insisted, but from his own hard work (81, 88, 110–111).

What did this free labor vision mean for race relations? With the "farm work reasonably well started," Washington turned to brickmaking, not only because Tuskegee Institute needed bricks for buildings but also because the town had no brickyard and "there was a demand for bricks in the general market." After three costly failures, the determined Washington pawned his watch for funds to try again, finally establishing an enterprise that would sustain the institute. He recalled that his brickmaking enterprise taught him an important lesson in race relations. White people who had no sympathy for movements to elevate freedpeople came to buy the bricks simply because they were good bricks.

Unsympathetic whites in the neighborhood noticed that "we were supplying a real want in the community" and began to support a black school that added "to the wealth and comfort of the community." They began to trade with the African-Americans at the school; business interests intermingled. This trade helped to establish a foundation for easy race relations in the neighborhood of the school. Welcome in new communities, Tuskegee-trained brickmakers found that they, too, contributed to "pleasant" race relations. The same was true of Tuskegee's other students. "The man who learns . . . to build and repair wagons and carts is regarded as a benefactor by both races in the community where he goes. The people with whom he lives and works are going to think twice before they part with such a man" (89–91).

Human nature recognizes merit, Washington reiterated, and "the visible, the tangible . . . goes a long ways in softening prejudices. The actual sight of a first-class house that a Negro has built is ten times more potent than pages of discussion about a house that he ought to build, or perhaps could build." Washington's critique of black education fell squarely in line with Republican theories of free labor and the gradual development of society, applying the accepted formula of free labor to race issues. He made these implications explicit:

> The individual who can do something that the world wants done will, in the end, make his way regardless of race. One man may go into a community prepared to supply the people there with an analysis of Greek sentences. The community may not at that time be prepared for, or feel the need of, Greek analysis, but it may feel its need of bricks and houses and wagons. If the man can supply the need for those, then, it will lead eventually to a demand for the first product, and with the demand will come the ability to appreciate it and to profit by it. (90–91)

Washington maintained that Southern whites treated him well, thanking him for the work he was doing. He also emphasized that he never forced himself forward in social situations, and implied that his reticence guaranteed that he was very well treated. As an example, he told the story of a train trip through Georgia, when two Northern white ladies insisted that Washington accompany them for dinner despite his reluctance. Finally released, he went to the smoking car to see "how the land lay." To his astonishment, every man, whom he presented as "nearly every one of them a citizen of Georgia," introduced himself and thanked Washington for his efforts to rebuild the South (100).

In public speeches in the North and South, Washington tapped the postwar Northern hopes for the South when he described his vision of the nation. The Wizard of Tuskegee gave credit to Southerners for all they had done to help freedpeople. He advocated bringing the races together and cultivating "friendly relations" rather than encouraging bitterness. In a veiled but obvious reference to voting, he encouraged the African-American man to "more and more consider the interests of the community in which he lived, rather than seek alone to please some one who lived a thousand miles away from him and from his interests." Finally, he echoed the long-standing mainstream mantra that

> the whole future of the Negro rested largely upon the question as to whether or not he should make himself, through his skill, intelligence, and character, of such undeniable value to the community in which he lived that the community could not dispense with his presence. . . . [A]ny individual who learned to do something better than anybody else—learned to do a common thing in an uncommon manner—had solved his problem, regardless of the colour of his skin, and that in proportion as the Negro learned to produce what other people wanted and must have, in the same proportion would he be respected.

Using an example that echoed those printed in the postwar Northern Republican newspapers, Washington told the story of a graduate of Tuskegee whose knowledge of chemistry and agriculture had enabled him to grow 266 bushels of sweet potatoes per acre where his neighbors produced only 49. Anxious for advice, white farmers "honoured and respected him because he, by his skill and knowledge, had added something to the wealth and the comfort of the community in which he lived." Washington's theory of education, which fit perfectly with postwar Republican political economy, would not confine African-Americans "for all time to farm life—to the production of the best and the most sweet potatoes—but . . . if he succeeded in this line of industry, he could lay the foundations upon which his children and grandchildren could grow to higher and more important things in life" (117–120).

Relying on the postwar idea that from economic prosperity would come social and political advantages, Washington took public stands on voting and social rights that, taken out of context, seemed regressive. He insisted on voting rights, but advocated the impartial suffrage that most Republicans had wanted until they were forced into a stronger policy by Southern white opposition to any black rights at all. Although he be-

lieved in universal suffrage in principle, he wrote, the South had peculiar conditions that called for the protection of the ballot by education or
property restrictions so long as they were applied "with equal and exact
justice to both races." Again echoing the free labor prescription for success, Washington scorned Jim Crow legislation but opposed agitation
against it, since pressure simply increased resistance. He told African-
Americans to depend "upon the slow but sure influences that proceed
from the possession of property, intelligence, and high character for the
full recognition of his political rights." For those who adhered to a traditional belief in the nature of American society, voting and social rights
were natural outgrowths of economic success. Forcing them before economic development was useless, and potentially counterproductive.
"The time will come when the Negro in the South will be accorded all
the political rights which his ability, character, and material possessions
entitle him to" (51, 58–60, 137–139).

Washington closed *Up from Slavery* by using the story of Tuskegee and
its founder as a type for the progress of freedpeople to the upper levels of
American society, clinging tightly to the old idea that a free labor society
permitted everyone to succeed. Twenty years before, he recalled, he had
made his first "humble effort" at Tuskegee, "in a broken-down shanty
and an old hen-house, without owning a dollar's worth of property, and
with but one teacher and thirty students." The school now owned 2,300
acres of land and sixty-six buildings, and it ran thirty industrial depart-
ments designed to turn out students with skills and with the understanding "that labour is dignified and beautiful—to make each one love
labour instead of trying to escape it." The school owned more than
$700,000 worth of property and boasted a million dollar endowment.
Its enrollment had swelled to 1,400 students from twenty-seven states
and from foreign countries, taught by 110 instructors and officers. For
ten years the school had hosted the annual Negro Conference to study
the needs of America's black population; in 1900, Washington and
T. Thomas Fortune—unlikely friends—had organized the National Negro Business League to promote black professional activities. Like his
school, Washington himself was an example of success through hard
work. In the book's final paragraph, Washington noted the difference between the young ex-slave in 1881 whose poverty had forced him to sleep
under a sidewalk in Richmond, Virginia, and the prominent man of
1900, correspondent of presidents, honored by Harvard, the first Afri-

can-American speaker ever in a segregated facility, speaking to the Richmond City Council, the state legislature, state officials, and his original hosts, the African-Americans of the city (182–187).

In 1901, Booker T. Washington tried to reclaim for the entire black community the vision of upwardly mobile African-Americans succeeding in American society. But he was fighting a holding action that ultimately failed. In the early twentieth century, the progressive idea of big business and big labor brokered by a big government eclipsed the free labor theory of the nineteenth century. As it did so, white Americans increasingly perceived a color line in society rather than a division between those who believed in individualism and those who believed in class activism. In 1915, D. W. Griffith's *The Birth of a Nation* signaled the popular acceptance of an America segregated by color when it immortalized on film the revisionist, racist history that had been specific to the late 1890s. Using powerful cinematic innovations, the film showed noble white supremacists organizing to curb the vicious black rapists who controlled government with the help of misguided radical Republicans. Historian-turned-president Woodrow Wilson showed the movie at the White House and mused: "It's like writing history with lightning. And my only regret is that it is all terribly true."[6]

It was not, of course, "terribly true," although it was certainly terrible that such dramatic revisionism had come to be accepted as truth. Although the twentieth century forgot it, the struggle between the theory of a society based on free labor and one based on class conflict mediated by legislation had profoundly affected race relations in nineteenth-century America. Seeing ex-slaves as abstract figures in a free labor society, Northerners had ignored the devastating effects of poverty, racism, and economic dislocation in the postwar black experience. When the majority of the Southern African-Americans could not overcome the overwhelming obstacles in their path to economic security, Northerners saw their failure as a rejection of free labor ideals, accused them of being deficient workers, and willingly read them out of American society. So strong was this Northern image of African-Americans that it overrode the reality of nineteenth-century life.

Perceiving ex-slaves as stereotypical free workers immediately after the war, Northern Republicans championed the freedpeople and expected them to rebuild the South as they worked their way up in American society. When hostile white Southerners blocked blacks' entry into the free labor world by hampering their freedom and harassing them, Northern Republicans fought to give black men the vote to enable them to protect their own interests.

The conjunction of black suffrage, labor unrest, and government expansion established the framework of political debate for the rest of the century at the same time that it began to undermine Northern Republican support for Reconstruction. In response to black suffrage, Democrats angry at Republican expansion of the government developed the racist argument that black voters would control the Republican "empire." To stay in power, Republicans would cater to black voters with special-interest legislation, and, more important, with patronage and government jobs paid for by taxpayers. The government would become a vehicle for the support of the ex-slaves.

Northern Republicans were not worried about a Republican empire harnessed to hard-working freedpeople, but, increasingly nervous about the growing power of laborers who seemed unwilling to engage in productive labor, moderate and conservative Republicans feared that radical freedmen who called for land redistribution and increased government services hoped to use the government to confiscate wealth. Applying the Democratic construct to their fear of those who believed in economic conflict, Republicans began to associate with labor radicals the black workers who seemed to reject hard work in favor of confiscatory legislation or patronage. Filtering through this worldview the political events of the early 1870s in South Carolina and Louisiana, as well as civil rights agitation, Republicans came to agree with Democrats that the mass of ex-slaves hoped to survive off government largess, rather than through hard work.

By 1880, oblivious to the effects of the dramatic economic changes on individual advancement in American society, Northerners both white and black who saw themselves as members of the "better classes" believed there were two groups of African-Americans. They contrasted the apparently disaffected workers who believed in a societal conflict between labor and capital and who wanted the government to support them against those few prominent African-Americans who seemed to be prospering on their own. Northerners who did not identify with a labor interest lived in fear that government might fall into the thrall of those who rejected the free labor ideal. Legislation in favor of disaffected workers would subvert the government and the very basis of the nation;

prosperous individuals would flee from confiscation, and the poor would prefer handouts to work. The free labor society that made America different from the rest of the world would collapse.

Northerners' determination to keep apart government and the individual dictated their abhorrence of the "spoils system," their obsession with political corruption, and their acceptance of the peculiar government activism that permitted government aid to business but insisted on a strict "laissez-faire" approach to the disadvantaged. A system by which politicians parceled out jobs in exchange for political support meant a world in which men would opt for the ease of government sinecures rather than productive labor that actually benefited the nation. This system also created "corruption" everywhere, as politicians passed pork-barrel legislation to fund their patronage lists, offered incentives—from free holiday turkeys to cold cash—for votes, and, ultimately, saw government service as simply an avenue to the power that would enable them to line their own pockets. The "better classes" worked hard to divorce the government from those who rejected productive labor in favor of government support, even as they used the government to help those entrepreneurs who seemed actually to be developing the nation's productivity.

The growing fear of those who wanted government redress of economic inequalities led the "better classes" of Northerners to mythologize individualism in American society. According to the wartime idea of free labor, all could rise to a competency at least. By the early postwar years, men like Horatio Alger had developed the "rags-to-riches" idea, which suggested that even the poorest could rise to wealth so long as they refused to be sucked into class activism and instead practiced the individual virtues of hard work and economy. In the 1880s, this idea evolved into William Graham Sumner's Social Darwinism, which wrote off those who did not rise as lazy malcontents who refused to exert themselves in productive labor and were thus unworthy leeches on American society. By the 1890s, these disaffected workers appeared to threaten to take over the American government as they voted into office politicians beholden to them. Seemingly unable to survive in a free labor system, they appeared inferior to those who could. And it seemed they would have to lose the vote before they destroyed American society. To late nineteenth-century Northerners, the mass of African-Americans represented those who threatened to commandeer the government.

From 1888 to 1892, the efforts of stalwart Republicans to defend black voting in the South convinced Northerners that disaffected African-Americans sought to harness the government for their own advancement. Although mainstream Northerners continued to praise traditionally successful African-Americans, most concluded that the majority of African-Americans were ignorantly determined to dominate a strong American government for their own interests and must be disfranchised to protect traditional America. Northerners were also willing to entertain the leap from that position to the next, advanced by conservative Southerners, that African-Americans were alien to civilized American values and should be segregated to protect the sensibilities of the "better classes." Northerners could now adopt more easily the contention of academics that African-Americans were biologically inferior to white Americans. When lynchings increased after 1888, Northern outrage was muffled as the "better classes" of Americans—black as well as white—accepted the idea that black men deserved hanging for their apparent attacks on traditional American society. Northern willingness to accept Southern restrictions on African-American voting only increased as conservatives argued that efforts to tie the government to special interests, like those of the Populists, were the logical outgrowth of government efforts on behalf of the freedpeople.

The social, economic, and political suppression of the "mass" of African-Americans after 1892 coincided with the birth of the Progressive movement, which demanded that the American government redress the excesses of the nation's new industrial society. Progressives backed government legislation to establish basic safety standards in factories, minimum wages and maximum hours, clean food and water, and so on. There was a logical connection between disfranchisement and the Progressive movement. Having removed from political power those who represented the use of government in the service of disaffected laborers, Americans could now entertain ideas of a government that worked to ameliorate the abuses of the industrial system without fearing the triumph of socialism.[7]

In the years after the Civil War, mainstream Northerners increasingly perceived the mass of African-Americans as adherents of a theory of political economy in which labor and capital were at odds and in which a growing government would be used to advance laborers at the expense of capitalists. For these Northerners, the majority of ex-slaves became the face of "communism" or "socialism," as opponents dubbed this view of political economy. The support of part of the black population for the free labor ideal assured mainstream Northerners that all Americans could indeed prosper if they only tried. Ultimately, Northerners turned against African-Americans not because of racism, although they were certainly racist. Northerners turned against freedpeople after the Civil War because African-Americans came to represent a concept of society and government that would destroy the free labor world. Black citizens, it seemed, threatened the core of American society.

Notes

Preface

1. C. Vann Woodward, *The Strange Career of Jim Crow* (New York: Oxford University Press, 1955). See also J. Morgan Kousser, *The Shaping of Southern Politics: Suffrage Restriction and the Establishment of a One-Party South, 1880–1910* (New Haven: Yale University Press, 1974), which ties the death of black voting to political events; Joseph H. Cartwright, *The Triumph of Jim Crow: Tennessee Race Relations in the 1880s* (Knoxville: University of Tennessee Press, 1976), which ties disfranchisement to specific political imperatives in the 1880s; and Michael Perman, *The Road to Redemption: Southern Politics, 1869–1879* (Chapel Hill: University of North Carolina Press, 1984). On racism, see Joel Williamson, *The Crucible of Race: Black-White Relations in the American South since Emancipation* (New York: Oxford University Press, 1984); Howard N. Rabinowitz, "From Exclusion to Segregation: Southern Race Relations, 1865–1890," in Donald G. Nieman, ed., *African-American Life in the Post-Emancipation South, 1861–1900* (New York: Garland Publishing, 1994), pp. 341–350; George Fredrickson, *The Inner Civil War: Northern Intellectuals and the Crisis of the Union* (New York: Harper & Row, 1965); George Fredrickson, *The Black Image in the White Mind: The Debate on Afro-American Character and Destiny, 1817–1914* (New York: Harper & Row, 1971). For recent cultural studies arguing that nineteenth-century America was a "white republic" whose constantly reconceived racism subordinated peoples defined as "others" while it served the economic, psychological, and social needs of whites, see Alexander Saxton, *The Rise and Fall of the White Republic: Class Politics and Mass Culture in Nineteenth-Century America* (1990; reprint, London: Verso, 1996). Herbert Hill, "The Problem of Race in American Labor History," *Reviews in American History*, 24 (1996): 180–204; Noel Ignatiev, *How the Irish Became White* (New York: Routledge, 1995); David Roediger, *The Wages of Whiteness* (London: Verso, 1991). The *Journal of the Early Republic* published a "Special Issue on Racial Consciousness and Nation Building in the Early Republic" 19 (Winter 1999): 577–777; see articles by David R. Roediger, Daniel K. Richter, Lois E.

Horton, Joanne Pope Melish, Jon Gjerde, James Brewer Stewart, Lacy K. Ford, Jr., James P. Ronda, and David Brion Davis. For a more complex portrait of the interplay of racism and society, see Barbara Jeanne Fields, "Ideology and Race in American History," in J. Morgan Kousser and James McPherson, eds., *Region, Race and Reconstruction: Essays in Honor of C. Vann Woodward* (New York: Oxford University Press, 1982), and Edward L. Ayers, *The Promise of the New South: Life after Reconstruction* (New York: Oxford University Press, 1992).

2. Vincent P. DeSantis, *Republicans Face the Southern Question—The New Departure Years, 1877–1897* (Baltimore: Johns Hopkins Press, 1959); Stanley P. Hirshson, *Farewell to the Bloody Shirt: Northern Republicans and the Southern Negro, 1877–1893* (Bloomington: Indiana University Press, 1962); and William Gillette, *Retreat from Reconstruction, 1869–1879* (Baton Rouge: Louisiana State University Press, 1979) argue that Northern Republicans abandoned African-Americans because they were driven by the need to build up a Southern constituency. For the argument that Republican support for African-Americans was principled but unpopular, see LaWanda and John H. Cox, "Negro Suffrage and Republican Politics: The Problem of Motivation in Reconstruction Historiography," *Journal of Southern History*, 33 (August 1967): 303–330; Glenn M. Linden, "A Note on Negro Suffrage and Republican Politics," *Journal of Southern History*, 36 (August 1970): 411–420. Xi Wang refined these interpretations in his powerful book, *The Trial of Democracy: Black Suffrage and Northern Republicans, 1860–1910* (Athens: University of Georgia Press, 1997).

3. On reformers and society, see David Montgomery, *Beyond Equality: Labor and the Radical Republicans, 1862–1872* (New York: Alfred A. Knopf, 1967). John G. Sproat, *"The Best Men": Liberal Reformers in the Gilded Age* (New York: Oxford University Press, 1968). Michael Les Benedict, "Reform Republicans and the Retreat from Reconstruction," in Eric Anderson and Alfred A. Moss, Jr., *The Facts of Reconstruction: Essays in Honor of John Hope Franklin* (Baton Rouge: Louisiana State University Press, 1991), pp. 53–77. On corruption, see Mark Wahlgren Summers, *The Era of Good Stealings* (New York: Oxford University Press, 1993). On civil service reform, see Ari Hoogenboom, *Outlawing the Spoils: A History of the Civil Service Reform Movement, 1865–1883* (Urbana: University of Illinois Press, 1961).

4. For an example of prejudicial stereotypes, see *Harper's Weekly*, February 20, 1869, p. 123, which shows Cupid drawn as an Irishman, a Frenchman, a German, an Englishman, an African, and a Yankee. Labor historians examining race relations among American workers have established that workers' allegiances were not uniformly divided by race but changed according to circumstances. Similarly, historians exploring the importance of gender

relations to post–Civil War America have illuminated the effect of family and gender patterns on postwar life and politics. For historians who argue that race relations were inseparable from political, class, gender, and social tensions, see David Herbert Donald, "A Generation of Defeat," in Walter J. Fraser, Jr., and Winfred B. Moore, Jr., eds., *From the Old South to the New: Essays on the Transitional South* (Westport, Conn.: Greenwood Press, 1981), pp. 3–20; Fields, "Ideology and Race"; Ayers, *Promise of the New South;* Glenda Elizabeth Gilmore, *Gender and Jim Crow: Women and the Politics of White Supremacy in North Carolina, 1896–1920* (Chapel Hill: University of North Carolina Press, 1996); Amy Dru Stanley, *From Bondage to Contract: Wage Labor, Marriage, and the Market in the Age of Slave Emancipation* (Cambridge: Cambridge University Press, 1998); Martha Hodes, *White Women, Black Men: Illicit Sex in the 19th-Century South* (New Haven: Yale University Press, 1977). Peter Rachleff's *Black Labor in Richmond, Virginia, 1865–1890* (Philadelphia: Temple University Press, 1984), Eric Arnesen's *Waterfront Workers of New Orleans: Race, Class, and Politics, 1863–1923* (New York: Oxford University Press, 1991), and Daniel Letwin's *The Challenge of Interracial Unionism: Alabama Coal Miners, 1878–1921* (Chapel Hill: University of North Carolina Press, 1998) reveal that that there was no uniform practice of either antipathy or acceptance characterizing black and white workers' contacts in the late nineteenth century. See also Eric Arnesen, "Up from Exclusion: Black and White Workers, Race, and the State of Labor History," *Reviews in American History,* 26 (1998): 146–174.

5. On press and public opinion, see Thomas C. Leonard, *The Power of the Press: The Birth of American Political Reporting* (New York: Oxford University Press, 1987); Donald A. Ritchie, *Press Gallery: Congress and the Washington Correspondents* (Cambridge: Harvard University Press, 1991); Mark Wahlgren Summers, *The Press Gang: Newspapers and Politics, 1865–1878* (Chapel Hill: University of North Carolina Press, 1994); and Mary P. Ryan, *Civic Wars: Democracy and Public Life in the American City during the Nineteenth Century* (Berkeley: University of California Press, 1997), especially pp. 12–14. See also *Harper's Weekly,* May 11, 1867, pp. 293–294.

6. William Ghormley Cochrane, "Freedom without Equality: A Study of Northern Opinion and the Negro Issue, 1861–1870," Ph.D. diss., University of Minnesota, 1957, pp. 158–159, 188–189. *Washington Post,* January 21, 1879, p. 2. *Harper's Weekly,* March 7, 1868, p. 146. On the importance of newspapers, see also *New York Herald,* July 10, 1867, p. 4. *Harper's Weekly,* April 22, 1865, and March 11, 1865. Rival was *North American Review. Harper's New Monthly Magazine* (January 1866), in Cochrane, "Freedom without Equality," p. 170.

7. Menahem Blondheim, in *News over the Wires: The Telegraph and the Flow of*

Public Information in America, 1844–1897 (Cambridge, Mass.: Harvard University Press, 1994), has shown how the city-based telegraph news services standardized national news; Summers, *The Press Gang,* pp. 18–21, explains how newly widespread railroad systems delivered city newspapers across the countryside.

8. On Northern conditions before the war, see Jeremy Atack and Fred Bateman, *To Their Own Soil: Agriculture in the Antebellum North* (Ames: Iowa State University Press, 1987), pp. 3–4, and Jeremy Atack, "The Agricultural Ladder Revisited: A New Look at an Old Question with Some Data for 1860," *Agricultural History,* 63 (Winter 1989): 1–25. Compare Dongyu Yang, "Farm Tenancy in the Antebellum North," in Claudia Goldin and High Rockoff, eds., *Strategic Factors in Nineteenth-Century American Economic History* (Chicago: University of Chicago Press, 1992), pp. 135–156.

9. For an overview of the transformation of the economy, see James West Davidson, William E. Gienapp, et al., *Nation of Nations,* vol. 2 (New York: McGraw-Hill, 1990), pp. 642–713.

10. Historians have noted the plasticity of the late nineteenth-century electorate and attributed it to religious or ethnic tensions, or to the reorganization of the political system. See, for example, Paul Kleppner, *The Cross of Culture: A Social Analysis of Midwestern Politics, 1850–1900* (New York: The Free Press, 1970) and *The Third Electoral System, 1853–1892: Parties, Voters, and Political Cultures* (Chapel Hill: University of North Carolina Press, 1979); Richard Jensen, *The Winning of the Midwest: Social and Political Conflict, 1888–1896* (Chicago: University of Chicago Press, 1971); Richard Jensen, "The Religious and Occupational Roots of Party Identification: Illinois and Indiana in the 1870s," *Civil War History,* 16 (December 1970): 325–343. On popular disenchantment with political parties, see Michael E. McGerr, *The Decline of Popular Politics: The American North, 1865–1928* (New York: Oxford University Press, 1986). For contemporary analysis of independents, see, for example, B. A. Hinsdale to J. A. Garfield, January 27, 1879, and J. A. Garfield to B. A. Hinsdale, January 30, 1879, in Mary L. Hinsdale, ed., *Garfield-Hinsdale Letters: Correspondence between James Abram Garfield and Burke Aaron Hinsdale* (Ann Arbor: University of Michigan Press, 1949), pp. 396–398. See also *New York Times* reprinted in *Harper's Weekly,* April 19, 1879, p. 302, and November 29, 1879, p. 934; *Boston Herald,* quoted in *Harper's Weekly,* August 30, 1879, p. 682; and *Washington Post,* March 9, 1879, p. 2. See also M. C. Butler to R. R. Hemphill, March 13, 1880, M. C. Butler MSS, Duke University Library. See also *Century Magazine,* October 1890, p. 951. For a review of the divisions in Republican thought in the nineteenth century, see Richard E. Welch, Jr., *George Frisbie Hoar and the Half-Breed Republicans* (Cambridge, Mass.: Harvard University Press, 1971).

11. On Southern tourism, see Nina Silber, *The Romance of Reunion: Northerners and the South, 1865–1900* (Chapel Hill: University of North Carolina Press, 1993).

Prologue

1. Booker T. Washington, *Up from Slavery* (1901; reprint, New York: Oxford University Press, 1995), pp. 121–125. The Atlanta Address is printed on pp. 127–131. The definitive biography of Booker T. Washington is Louis R. Harlan, *Booker T. Washington: The Making of a Black leader, 1856–1901* (London: Oxford University Press, 1972), and Louis R. Harlan, *Booker T. Washington: The Wizard of Tuskegee, 1901–1915* (New York: Oxford University Press, 1983).
2. On Jim Crow, see Washington, *Up from Slavery,* pp. 58–60, 97–98.
3. Ibid., pp. 141, 132, 173–182.
84. For an encapsulation of this argument for black industrial education, see *Nation,* February 20, 1873, p. 131.

1 The Northern Postwar Vision, 1865–1867

1. William E. Gienapp, "The Republican Party and the Slave Power," in Robert H. Abzug and Stephen E. Maizlish, eds., *New Perspectives on Slavery and Race in America* (Lexington: University Press of Kentucky, 1986), pp. 51–78.
2. On similarities of Republican and Democratic ideas about free labor, see James L. Huston, "Facing an Angry Labor: The American Public Interprets the Shoemakers' Strike of 1860," *Civil War History,* 28 (September 1892): 197–212. On the attributes of the free labor system and its shortcomings, see Eric Foner, *Free Soil, Free Labor, Free Men: The Ideology of the Republican Party before the Civil War* (New York: Oxford University Press, 1970); Gabor S. Boritt, *Lincoln and the Economics of the American Dream* (Memphis: Memphis State University Press, 1978); Heather Cox Richardson, *The Greatest Nation of the Earth: Republican Economic Policies during the Civil War* (Cambridge, Mass.: Harvard University Press, 1997); James L. Huston, *Securing the Fruits of Labor: The American Concept of Wealth Distribution, 1765–1900* (Baton Rouge: Louisiana State University Press, 1998). Abraham Lincoln, Message of the President, December 3, 1861, *Congressional Globe,* 37th Cong., 2nd sess., Appendix, p. 4.
3. On this distinction, see Iver Bernstein, *The New York City Draft Riots: Their Significance for American Society and Politics in the Age of the Civil War* (New York: Oxford University Press, 1990), pp. 172–190, and Sean Wilentz,

Chants Democratic: New York City and the Rise of the American Working Class, 1788–1850 (New York: Oxford University Press, 1984). On rise of a working class by 1850 and its characteristics, see Richard B. Stott, *Workers in the Metropolis: Class, Ethnicity, and Youth in Antebellum New York City* (Ithaca, N.Y.: Cornell University Press, 1990). On American applications of the ideas of Ricardo and Malthus, see Huston, *Securing the Fruits,* pp. 153–161.

4. See Joel H. Silbey, *A Respectable Minority: The Democratic Party in the Civil War Era, 1860–1868* (New York: W. W. Norton & Co., 1977); Bruce Collins, "Ideology of Ante-Bellum Northern Democrats," *Journal of American Studies,* 11 (April 1977): 103–121; Jean H. Baker, *Affairs of Party: The Political Culture of Northern Democrats in the Mid-Nineteenth Century* (1983; reprint, New York: Fordham University Press, 1998), pp. 143–258.

5. See Huston, *Securing the Fruits,* pp. 302–303. David Roediger has attributed this negative image of the black worker as at the heart of worker racism in America; see David R. Roediger, *The Wages of Whiteness: Race and the Making of the American Working Class* (London and New York: Verso, 1991).

6. *Philadelphia Daily Evening Bulletin,* May 28, 1861, p. 4. See also *Philadelphia Public Ledger,* May 30, 1861, p. 2. *New York Times,* May 12, 1861, p. 4. See also *Indianapolis Daily Journal,* May 16, 1861, p. 2. *New York Times,* September 1, 1861, p. 4. *Philadelphia Daily Evening Bulletin,* November 27, 1861, p. 4, and December 3, 1861, p. 4. *Chicago Tribune,* August 22, 1861, p. 2. *New York Times,* December 6, 1861, p. 2. For the development of this idea, see Richardson, *Greatest Nation of the Earth,* pp. 210–217.

7. *New York Times,* January 13, 1865, p. 4, and February 21, 1865, p. 1.

8. *Congressional Globe,* 37th Cong., 2nd sess., Appendix, pp. 156–157. See Washington column in *Philadelphia Daily Evening Bulletin,* April 5, 1862, p. 5. See also news from the *Washington Republican,* May 10, 1862, in *Chicago Tribune,* May 14, 1862, p. 2. Letter of William Still, Corresponding Secretary of S.C. and Statistical Association of the Colored People of Pennsylvania, in *Philadelphia Daily Evening Bulletin,* April 7, 1862, p. 1. *Indianapolis Daily Journal,* December 7, 1863, p. 2. *Cincinnati Daily Gazette,* April 3, 1862, p. 1, and April 5, 1862, p. 2. *Chicago Tribune,* December 18, 1861, p. 2. *Philadelphia Daily Evening Bulletin,* January 10, 1862, p. 4, including quotation from *New York World.* See also *Chicago Tribune,* January 21, 1862, p. 2; *New York Times,* March 14, 1862, p. 3. Compare George M. Fredrickson, *The Black Image in the White Mind: The Debate on Afro-American Character and Destiny, 1817–1914* (1971; reprint, Middletown, Conn.: Wesleyan University Press, 1987), pp. 168–171.

9. *Cincinnati Daily Gazette,* September 25, 1862, p. 2. *New York Daily Tribune,* March 11, 1862, p. 4.

10. Reynolds Farley, *Growth of the Black Population: A Study of Demographic*

Trends (Chicago: Markham Publishing Co., 1970), pp. 41–45. On Northern black life in midcentury, see Emma Lou Thornbrough, *The Negro in Indiana before 1900: A Study of a Minority* (1957; reprint, Bloomington: Indiana University Press, 1993); David A. Gerber, *Black Ohio and the Color Line, 1860–1915* (Urbana: University of Illinois Press, 1976); Douglas Henry Daniels, *Pioneer Urbanites: A Social and Cultural History of Black San Francisco* (Philadelphia: Temple University Press, 1980); Leonard P. Curry, *The Free Black in Urban America 1800–1850: The Shadow of the Dream* (Chicago: University of Chicago Press, 1981); Robert R. Dykstra, *Bright Radical Star: Black Freedom and White Supremacy on the Hawkeye Frontier* (Cambridge, Mass.: Harvard University Press, 1993); George A. Levesque, *Black Boston: African American Life and Culture in Urban America, 1750–1860* (New York: Garland Publishing, 1994). On keeping African-Americans out of the North, see, for example, July 27, 1860, speech of Jackson Grimshaw at Clinton, Illinois, in *Chicago Tribune,* August 1, 1860, p. 2. For lengthy exchanges between O. O. Howard and his wife, Lizzy, about their cook, Julia, see the O. O. Howard MSS, Bowdoin College Library, letters of January 8, 1864; January 14, 1864; July 24, 1864; September 4, 1864; September 22, 1864; October 2, 1864; October 14, 1864; November 27, 1864. For a portrait of Northern African-American life in the nineteenth century, see Nick Salvatore, *We All Got History: The Memory Books of Amos Webber* (New York: Times Books, 1996).

11. Francis Wayland to Rev. L. Peck, February 19, 1862, Francis Wayland MSS, John Hay Library, Brown University. Andrew Johnson, January 21, 1864, in Jon L. Wakelyn, ed., *Southern Unionist Pamphlets and the Civil War* (Columbia: University of Missouri Press, 1999), p. 265. Lincoln signed the bill March 3, 1865.

12. James W. Grimes, *Congressional Globe,* 38th Cong., 1st sess., pp. 3300, 2972, 2974. On private versus government sponsorship of education, see *Chicago Tribune,* October 8 1867, p. 2. On the Freedmen's Bureau and non-discrimination, see Herman Belz, "The Freedmen's Bureau Act of 1865 and the Principle of No Discrimination According to Color," *Civil War History,* 21 (September 1975): 197–217. *Chicago Tribune,* August 28, 1865, p. 2.

13. *New York Times,* February 1, 1865, p. 4. *Congressional Globe,* 38th Cong., 1st sess., pp. 2989–2990. *New York Times,* January 20, 1865, p. 4. Ibid., July 24, 1868, p. 4. James M. Ashley, *Congressional Globe,* 38th Cong., 2nd sess., p. 141.

14. For Northern reaction to the end of the war, see, for example, Walt Whitman, *Specimen Days in America* (London: The Walter Scott Publishing Co., Ltd., n.d.), pp. 101–102, and Charles I. Glicksberg, *Walt Whitman and the Civil War* (Philadelphia: University of Pennsylvania Press, 1933), pp. 174–175.

15. On Democratic ideas, see Baker, *Affairs of Party.* On Johnson's predilections,

see his "First Annual Message," December 4, 1865, in James D. Richardson, *Messages and Papers of the Presidents* (Washington, D.C.: Government Printing Office, 1897), vol. 6, pp. 353–371, especially pp. 353–356. For a good history of Reconstruction politics, see Brooks D. Simpson, *The Reconstruction Presidents* (Lawrence: University Press of Kansas, 1998).

16. There has been much debate about who the radicals were and what their program was. Howard K. Beale, *The Critical Year: A Study of Andrew Johnson and Reconstruction* (New York: Harcourt, Brace and Co., 1930), argued that the radicals were fanatics that completed the work of the abolitionists. T. Harry Williams, *Lincoln and the Radicals* (Madison: University of Wisconsin Press, 1941), claimed that the radicals were the driving force in Congress during the Civil War. He said that they wanted "instant" emancipation, confiscation of property, the enlistment of black soldiers, and civil and political equality for African-Americans to give Republicans control of Southern politics and the Southern economy. In *Lincoln Reconsidered* (New York: Alfred A. Knopf, 1956), David H. Donald countered that the radicals agreed only about what they opposed; they shared no social and economic goals. Irwin Unger, *The Greenback Era: A Social and Political History of American Finance* (Princeton: Princeton University Press, 1964), Robert P. Sharkey, *Money, Class, and Party: An Economic Study of Civil War and Reconstruction* (Baltimore: Johns Hopkins Press, 1959), Stanley Coben, "Northeastern Business and Radical Reconstruction: A Re-examination," *Mississippi Valley Historical Review,* 46 (1959): 69–90, and Glenn M. Linden, "'Radicals' and Economic Policies: The House of Representatives, 1861–1873," *Civil War History,* 13 (March 1967): 51–65, agreed with Donald, establishing that the radicals shared no economic program. See also Glenn M. Linden, "'Radicals' and Economic Policies: The Senate, 1861–1873," *Journal of Southern History,* 32 (May 1966): 189–199. In his *Andrew Johnson and Reconstruction* (Chicago: University of Chicago Press, 1960), Eric McKitrick also pointed out that the radical label was wielded by the Democrats to brand all Republicans as fanatics. Edward L. Gambill's "Who Were the Senate Radicals?" *Civil War History,* 11 (September 1965): 237–244, analyzed voting cohesion to create a useful spectrum of politicians of both parties, from those advancing Reconstruction measures to those opposing them. He concluded that moderate Republicans held the balance of power in the Senate during the critical year of 1866. Glenn M. Linden's "'Radical' Political and Economic Policies: The Senate, 1873–1877," *Civil War History,* 14 (September 1968): 240–249, further argued that "radical" cohesion had broken by 1873, when all Republicans voted as a bloc. Harold Hyman, ed. *The Radical Republicans and Reconstruction, 1861–1870* (Indianapolis: Bobbs-Merrill 1967), concluded that radicals wanted to promote African-American suffrage and

conditions, and that while most Americans shared that goal in the 1860s, they did not do so in the 1870s. My understanding of the radicals is shaped by these later interpretations. Radicals wanted black economic and political equality in America but shared no other goals; most Northern Americans agreed with them immediately after the war. Despite Democrats' constant harping on the radicalism of the Republican party, while radicals were vocal, moderates always controlled Congress. Radical power waned dramatically after 1870.

17. *Daily Ohio State Journal,* April 24, 1865, p. 2.

18. Richardson, *Messages and Papers of the Presidents,* 6: 310–312. James M. McPherson, *Ordeal By Fire: The Civil War and Reconstruction* (New York: Alfred A. Knopf, 1982), p. 505. For complaints about "The Great Pardoner," see *Philadelphia Daily Evening Bulletin,* January 10, 1867, p. 4.

19. See Dan T. Carter, *When the War Was Over: The Failure of Self-Reconstruction in the South, 1865–1867* (Baton Rouge: Louisiana State University Press, 1985) and Michael Perman, *Reunion without Compromise: The South and Reconstruction, 1865–1868* (Cambridge: Cambridge University Press, 1973). On Southern justification for Black Codes, see *Harper's Weekly,* March 9, 1867, p. 146. On Johnson's leniency as a cause of Southern defiance, McKitrick, *Andrew Johnson and Reconstruction,* p. 211.

20. For Schurz's correspondence with Edwin Stanton and Charles Sumner about the mission, see Frederic Bancroft, ed., *Speeches, Correspondence and Political Papers of Carl Schurz,* vol. 1: October 20, 1852–November 26, 1870 (New York: G. P. Putnam's Sons, 1913), pp. 264–265, 267–268.

21. Carl Schurz, *The Reminiscences of Carl Schurz,* vol. 3 (New York: Doubleday, Page & Company, 1908), p. 206. "Message of the President of the United States . . . Accompanied by a Report of Carl Schurz on the Condition of the South." Sen. Ex. Doc. 2, 39th Cong., 1st sess., December 19, 1865, pp. 13–15, 37–38, 40.

22. Schurz, "Report on the Condition of the South," pp. 21, 28–29.

23. Ibid., pp. 16–24, 38, 52, 69.

24. Ibid., p. 60, dated August 27, 1865.

25. "Letter of General Grant concerning Affairs at the South," in Schurz, "Report," pp. 106–108.

26. William S. McFeely, *Grant: A Biography* (New York: W. W. Norton & Company, 1981). On Grant's letter and tour of the South, see Brooks D. Simpson, "Grant's Tour of the South Revisited," *Journal of Southern History,* 54, no. 3 (August 1988): 425–448. On the Schurz and Grant reports, see James G. Blaine, *Twenty Years of Congress* (Norwich, Conn.: The Henry Bill Publishing Company, 1893), vol. 2, 147–154.

27. For acceptance of Johnson's views by a prominent Republican, see Henry

Ward Beecher to Charles G. Halpine et al., August 30, 1866, in *Beecher's "Cleveland Letters"* (n.p., 1884). Richardson, *Messages and Papers of the Presidents,* 6: 353–371.

28. On inadequacy of moderate ideas about Reconstruction, see Perman, *Reunion without Compromise.*

29. Soldiers' quotations are in Julie Saville, *The Work of Reconstruction: From Slave to Wage Laborer in South Carolina, 1860–1870* (Cambridge: Cambridge University Press, 1994), p. 25; General Tillson is quoted in *Augusta Loyal Georgian* [an African-American paper] January 20, 1866, p. 1. On the transition from slave to free labor, see, for example, Victor B. Howard, *Black Liberation in Kentucky: Emancipation and Freedom, 1862–1884* (Lexington: University Press of Kentucky, 1983), pp. 91–107.

30. William D. Kelley, "The South: Its Resources and Wants: Embracing his Addresses to the citizens of New Orleans, Address at Montgomery, Alabama, and His Address to His constituents." (Washington, D.C.: Union Republican Congressional Executive Committee [1867?]). See also Lawrence N. Powell, *New Masters: Northern Planters during the Civil War and Reconstruction,* (New Haven: Yale University Press, 1980); and Lawrence N. Powell, "The American Land Company and Agency: John A. Andrew and the Northernization of the South," *Civil War History,* 21 (December 1975): 293–308.

31. *Chicago Tribune,* October 4, 1867, p. 2. Although they had no faith in the power of free black labor, even Democrats believed that the South had been "blessed . . . by munificent Nature, she has but to plant and behold her crops brought to perfection, with one-fourth of the labor required elsewhere" (*New York World,* July 30, 1867, p. 2).

32. Gilbert C. Fite, *Cotton Fields No More: Southern Agriculture, 1865–1980* (Lexington: University Press of Kentucky, 1984), pp. 30–47.

33. This tendency was not lost on Democratic papers like the *New York World,* which charged: "'Physicians, heal yourselves.' If voting the Republican ticket will cure . . . evils in the South, why are they not cured in the North? . . . If Radical State governments could lift the laboring people out of poverty, the Northern laborers ought, by this time, to be very prosperous and contented" (May 24, 1867, p. 2).

34. For Northern attempts to implement the free labor ideal in the South, see William F. Messner, *Freedmen and the Ideology of Free Labor: Louisiana, 1862–1865* (Lafayette: University of Southwestern Louisiana Press, 1978); Steven Joseph Ross, "Freed Soil, Freed Labor, Freed Men, John Eaton and the Davis Bend Experiment," *Journal of Southern History,* 44 (May 1978): 213–232; Eric Foner, "Reconstruction and the Crisis of Free Labor," in *Politics and Ideology in the Age of the Civil War* (Oxford: Oxford University Press, 1980), pp. 97–127; Paul A. Cimbala, "The 'Talisman Power': Davis Tillson,

The Freedmen's Bureau, and Free Labor in Reconstruction Georgia, 1865–1866," *Civil War History,* 28 (June 1982): 153–171. *New York Times,* November 15, 1867, p. 4.

35. Powell, *New Masters,* p. 32. *New York Times,* November 15, 1867, p. 4. *Philadelphia Inquirer,* July 26, 1867, p. 4. Quotation from *New York Herald* in *Harper's Weekly,* June 1, 1867, p. 339.

36. *Philadelphia Inquirer,* June 20, 1867, p. 4, and August 24, 1867, p. 4. *Statement of the United States Mutual Protection Company for Encouraging Settlements in the Southern States* (Boston: n.p., 1865), p. 5.

37. Kelley, "The South: Its Resources and Wants," p. 15. On Kelley's speeches in general, see *Harper's Weekly,* June 1, 1867, p. 339. *Philadelphia Inquirer,* June 13, 1867, p. 4, and August 21, 1867, p. 4. See, for example, *New York Daily Tribune,* January 31, 1867, p. 4. *New York Times,* January 20, 1865, p. 4.

38. *Philadelphia Inquirer,* June 21, 1867, p. 4. *Boston Evening Transcript,* April 18, 1871, p. 2. *New York Daily Tribune,* January 7, 1867, p. 4.

39. *Harper's Weekly,* March 16, 1867, p. 163, and March 23, 1867, p. 179. Schuyler Colfax to Friend Wheeler, December 20, 1866, Schuyler Colfax MSS, Library of Congress. S.R. No. 16 for Southern relief was changed in the House to use monies already appropriated for the Freedmen's Bureau. For an account of one relief effort, see Anne Middleton Holmes, *The New York Ladies' Southern Relief Association, 1866–1867* (New York: 1926). On a Southern relief meeting at Cooper Union, where Henry Ward Beecher and Horace Greeley spoke, see *New York Daily Tribune,* January 22, 1867, p. 4. On Southern Famine Relief Commission, see ibid., February 27, 1867, p. 4. *Harper's Weekly,* February 15, 1868, p. 99; May 2, 1868, p. 276; March 16, 1867, pp. 173–174; January 12, 1867, p. 19. *Philadelphia Inquirer,* March 6, 1868, p. 4; April 14, 1868, p. 4; April 16, 1868, p. 4.

40. On parade issue, see *Harper's Weekly,* May 18, 1867, p. 309, May 25, 1867, pp. 323, 324.

41. In the 1890s, the New South movement became associated with Henry W. Grady of the *Atlanta Constitution* with the publication of his *The New South* (1890). In *The Road to Reunion, 1865–1900* (Boston: Little, Brown and Co., 1937) Paul H. Buck argued that the ideals of the New South promoted sectional reconciliation; W. J. Cash's *The Mind of the South* (New York: Alfred A. Knopf, 1941) saw the New South as a triumph of the South's heroic values. C. Vann Woodward's *Origins of the New South* (Baton Rouge: Louisiana State University Press, 1951) disagreed, arguing that New Southerners were dishonest businessmen who repressed the Southern African-American population; Jonathan M. Wiener, *Social Origins of the New South, Alabama 1860–1885* (Baton Rouge: Louisiana State University Press, 1978), added that the New South was not new but simply an extension of continuing planter ide-

ology. Gaines M. Foster's *Ghosts of the Confederacy: Defeat, the Last Cause, and the Emergence of the New South, 1865–1913* (New York: Oxford University Press, 1987) explored the use of Southern mythology to ease the transition from Old South to New. See also James Tice Moore, "Redeemers Reconsidered: Change and Continuity in the Democratic South, 1870–1900," *Journal of Southern History,* 44 (August 1978): 357–378; Harold D. Woodman, "Sequel to Slavery: The New History Views the Postbellum South," *Journal of Southern History,* 43 (November 1977): 523–545; James C. Cobb, "Beyond Planters and Industrialists: A New Perspective on the New South," *Journal of Southern History,* 54 (February 1988): 45–68. For an examination of Grady's world and ideas, see Harold E. Davis, *Henry Grady's New South: Atlanta, A Brave and Beautiful City* (Tuscaloosa: University of Alabama Press, 1990). *Harper's Weekly,* March 23, 1867, p. 179, and April 6, 1867, p. 210, 211, on Joseph E. Brown. *Chicago Tribune,* July 20, 1867, p. 2. *New York Times,* August 13, 1867, p. 4. On policies of these New Southerners, see Michael Perman, *The Road to Redemption: Southern Politics, 1869–1879* (Chapel Hill: University of North Carolina Press, 1984), pp. 7–17, 68–70, 239–242.

42. See Schurz, "Report," and *New York Times,* August 13, 1867, p. 4. Sidney Andrews, *The South since the War* (Boston: Ticknor and Fields, 1866), pp. 5–6. See Peter Kolchin, "The Business Press and Reconstruction," *Journal of Southern History,* 33 (May 1967): 183–196. *New York Times,* November 2, 1865, p. 4.

43. *Philadelphia Inquirer,* August 5, 1867, p. 4. *Harper's Weekly,* July 6, 1867, p. 419.

44. See Steven Hahn, "Emancipation and the Development of Capitalist Agriculture: The South in Comparative Perspective," in Kees Gispen, ed., *What Made the South Different* (Jackson: University Press of Mississippi, 1990), p. 86; Gavin Wright, *Old South, New South: Revolutions in the Southern Economy since the Civil War* (New York: Basic Books, 1986), p. 107; and Harold D. Woodman, "Class, Race, Politics, and the Modernization of the Postbellum South," *Journal of Southern History,* 63 (February 1997): 3–22. Powell, *New Masters,* p. 146. On scarcity in the South, see, for example, *Philadelphia Inquirer,* June 17, 1867, p. 4. *Harper's Weekly,* March 7, 1868, p. 147.

45. *Chicago Tribune,* September 3, 1865, p. 2. *New York Times,* November 12, 1865, p. 4. *Cincinnati Daily Gazette,* July 2, 1867, p. 1. See also *Philadelphia Daily Evening Bulletin,* January 26, 1867, p. 4, and January 28, 1867, p. 4. On Southern white responses to emancipation, see Perman, *Reunion without Compromise;* James L. Roark, *Masters without Slaves: Southern Planters in the Civil War and Reconstruction* (New York: W. W. Norton & Co., 1977); Carter, *When the War Was Over.*

46. On the importation of Chinese laborers, see *New York World*, August 2, 1867, p. 2, and *New York Times*, October 5, 1873, p. 4. For a devastating indictment of this attempt, see *New York Herald*, July 27, 1867, p. 4. For a firsthand account of Southern atrocities, see affidavit of Roda Ann Childs, in *Augusta Loyal Georgian*, October 13, 1866, p. 3. On Southern violence, see George C. Rable, *But There Was No Peace: The Role of Violence in the Politics of Reconstruction* (Athens: University of Georgia Press, 1984). *New York Times*, November 12, 1865, p. 4. *Philadelphia Daily Evening Bulletin*, February 2, 1867, p. 6.

47. In his famous "Crime against Kansas" speech, Charles Sumner had used the sexual abuse of a black woman to symbolize the plight of slaves; reflecting this theme, *Harper's Weekly* illustrated the incident by showing a crowd of leering white men beating a shapely young black woman (*Harper's Weekly*, January 12, 1867, pp. 18–19). *Harper's Weekly*, September 7, 1867, p. 563, and September 14, 1867, p. 577. *Philadelphia Inquirer*, August 22, 1867, p. 4. For another story indicating that "the rebellion is not crushed yet," see "Justice," from Macon, Georgia, December 12, 1866, in *Harper's Weekly*, January 5, 1867, p. 13.

48. *New York Times*, August 13, 1867, p. 4. *Philadelphia Inquirer*, April 18, 1867, p. 4. See also ibid., August 20, 1867, p. 4. This theme continued throughout the 1870s; see, for example, *Cincinnati Daily Gazette*, February 27, 1873, p. 4.

49. *New York World*, March 19, 1867, p. 4. *Philadelphia Inquirer*, August 2, 1867, p. 4; August 13, 1867, p. 4; August 21, 1867, p. 4.

50. Charles H. Gilchrist, Jackson, Mississippi, September 17, 1865, in Schurz, "Report," p. 69. *Philadelphia Inquirer*, April 18, 1867, p. 4. *Ashtabula (Ohio) Sentinel*, quoted in *Nation*, August 19, 1869, p. 143. Philadelphia *Inquirer*, August 24, 1867, p. 4. *Harper's Weekly*, November 2, 1867, p. 691. *Philadelphia Daily Evening Bulletin*, February 19, 1867, p. 4.

51. *Harper's Weekly*, February 23, 1867, p. 114. See also *New York Daily Tribune*, January 26, 1867, p. 4; February 23, 1867, p. 4; and *Philadelphia Daily Evening Bulletin*, February 19, 1867, p. 4.

52. Roger L. Ransom and Richard Sutch, *One Kind of Freedom: The Economic Consequences of Emancipation* (Cambridge: Cambridge University Press, 1977), pp. 44–51.

53. Frederick Law Olmstead, *The Cotton Kingdom: A Selection* (Indianapolis: The Bobbs-Merrill Company, 1971). All quotations in Loren Schweninger, *Black Property Owners in the South, 1790–1915* (Urbana: University of Illinois Press, 1990), pp. 144–145.

54. See article from *New York World* reprinted in *New York Daily Tribune*, January 30, 1867, p. 4. *New York Times*, September 9, 1865, p. 4. See also *Philadelphia Inquirer*, August 7, 1867, p. 4. *Cincinnati Daily Gazette*, July 2, 1867,

p. 1. *Philadelphia Inquirer,* August 29, 1867, p. 4. *New York Times,* November 15, 1867, p. 4. *Chicago Tribune,* October 12, 1867, p. 2. See also *Harper's Weekly,* August 3, 1867, p. 492. *Philadelphia Inquirer,* August 7, 1867, p. 4. *New York Times,* September 23, 1865, p. 4.

55. *Cincinnati Daily Gazette,* May 30, 1867, p. 1. *Harper's Weekly,* March 9, 1867, p. 14; January 11, 1868, p. 18.

56. *New York Times,* August 10, 1865, p. 4. *Chicago Tribune,* July 20, 1867, p. 2, and November 3, 1867, p. 2. *Boston Evening Transcript,* January 18, 1873, p. 3, and January 24, 1873, p. 3. Edward Atkinson in "The Reign of King Cotton," p. 454, in Willie Lee Rose, *Rehearsal for Reconstruction: The Port Royal Experiment* (London: Oxford University Press, 1964), p. 229. Schurz, "Report," p. 25. On education, see engravings in *Harper's Weekly,* May 25, 1867, p. 321. For importance of education in a free labor South, see Richard B. Drake, "Freedmen's Aid Societies and Sectional Compromise," *Journal of Southern History,* 29 (May 1963): 175–186.

57. *New York Times,* November 16, 1865, p. 4. *Chicago Tribune,* February 22, 1868, p. 2.

58. See Judy Hilkey, *Character Is Capital: Success Manuals and Manhood in Gilded Age America* (Chapel Hill: University of North Carolina Press, 1997); Irvin Wyllie, *The Self-Made Man in America* (New York: Free Press, 1954). Horatio Alger, Jr., *Ragged Dick: Or, Street Life in New York with the Boot-blacks* (New York: Signet Classic, 1990), pp. 77–78.

59. *Harper's Weekly,* April 27, 1867, p. 257. Ibid., January 11, 1868, pp. 28–29. On Keep, see also ibid., February 1, 1868, p. 67.

60. Ibid., January 11, 1868, pp. 28–29. For a list of the rules for becoming rich, see *New York Daily Tribune,* February 18, 1867, p. 4. For advice to young men wanting to farm, see ibid., March 13, 1867, p. 4.

61. *New York Daily Tribune,* January 30, 1867, p. 4. *Cincinnati Daily Gazette,* May 24, 1867, p. 2; see also *Philadelphia Inquirer,* May 21, 1867, p. 1. Southern Democratic newspapers reported that the speech was "incendiary," and Kelley was attacked by a mob in Mobile. (See cartoon, *Harper's Weekly,* June 1, 1867, p. 341.) Quotation from *New York Herald,* in *Harper's Weekly,* June 1, 1867, p. 339.

62. *Harper's Weekly,* March 30, 1867, pp. 193–194. For another "farm school," see *Boston Evening Transcript,* October 25, 1873, p. 2.

63. *Harper's Weekly,* April 6, 1867, p. 212, and March 23, 1867, pp. 178–179.

64. *New York World,* January 29, 1867, p. 2.

65. *Ashtabula (Ohio) Sentinel,* quoted in *Nation,* August 19, 1869, p. 143. *Harper's Weekly,* August 10, 1867, pp. 504–505. *Nation,* July 15, 1869, p. 45.

66. *New York Times,* quoted in *Harper's Weekly,* September 14, 1867, p. 579. *Philadelphia Inquirer,* July 26, 1867, p. 4. *Chicago Tribune,* March 31, 1871, p. 2.

2 The Mixed Blessing of Universal Suffrage, 1867–1870

1. For an exploration of this concept, see James L. Huston, *Securing the Fruits of Labor: The American Concept of Wealth Distribution* (Baton Rouge: Louisiana University Press, 1998), especially pp. xiii and 330–336. For both Republican and Democratic discussion of this idea, see *Philadelphia Press,* in *Washington Chronicle,* February 28, 1869, p. 2, and *Washington Post,* March 3, 1879, p. 2.

2. Carl Schurz, "Report on the Condition of the South," Sen. Ex. Doc. 2, 39th Cong., 1st sess., December 19, 1865, pp. 42–44. See also *New York Daily Tribune,* January 9, 1867, p. 4, and resolutions of National Equal Rights Convention of Colored Men, reported in ibid., January 14, 1867, p. 4.

3. See, for example, *New York Times,* October 12, 1865, p. 4. *Augusta Loyal Georgian* [African-American], February 17, 1866, p. 2; and October 12, 1866, p. 2.

4. *New York World,* December 13, 1867, p. 2, and June 14, 1867, p. 4. James D. Richardson, *Messages and Papers of the Presidents, 1789–1897,* vol. 6 (Washington, D.C.: Government Printing Office, 1897), pp. 359–360. On black suffrage debate, see Xi Wang, *The Trial of Democracy: Black Suffrage and Northern Republicans, 1860–1910* (Athens: University of Georgia Press, 1997), pp. 18–48. See also William Gillette's classic *The Right to Vote: Politics and the Passage of the Fifteenth Amendment* (Baltimore: Johns Hopkins Press, 1965), which covers the debates leading up to the Fifteenth, as well as the amendment itself. Edward Bates quotation in Wang, *Trial of Democracy,* p. 22.

5. Schurz, "Report," p. 43. *Philadelphia Inquirer,* April 4, 1867, p. 4. *Cincinnati Daily Gazette,* April 25, 1867, p. 2. See also *Philadelphia Inquirer,* March 1, 1867, p. 3.

6. On early postwar Republican attention to tension between labor and capital, see, for example, *New York Times,* July 26, 1865, p. 4.

7. On eight-hour-day movement, see Philip S. Foner, *History of the Labor Movement in the United States* (New York: International Publishers, 1947), pp. 377–382; on workers' organizations, see pp. 344–346; on the National Labor Union, see pp. 370–375. On the National Labor Union and the Labor Reform party, see David Montgomery, *Beyond Equality: Labor and the Radical Republicans, 1862–1872* (New York: Alfred A. Knopf, 1967), pp. 135–196. *Cincinnati Daily Gazette,* January 18, 1871, p. 2. On the Republican party and workers, see Montgomery, *Beyond Equality.* For Republican defense of the party's pro-labor history, see *Cincinnati Daily Gazette,* May 3, 1867, p. 2. *New York Times,* July 26, 1865, p. 4. A. C. Cameron in *Workingman's Advocate,* April 21, 1866, quoted in William Ghormley Cochrane, "Freedom without Equality: A Study of Northern Opinion and the Negro Issue, 1861–

1870," Ph.D. diss., University of Minnesota, 1957, p. 369. Foner, *Labor,* pp. 371–374.

8. A British observer at the end of the war commented that America had no distinct "working class." Samuel Smith, *Reflections Suggested by a Second Visit to the United States of America, Being a Paper Read before the Liverpool Philomatic Society,* March 13, 1867 (Liverpool: David Marples, 1867), pp. 10–12.

9. *Chicago Tribune,* May 16, 1867, p. 2. See also *Philadelphia Inquirer,* March 21, 1867, p. 4, for description of "good" workers. For a discussion of this debate, see Martin J. Burke, *The Conundrum of Class: Public Discourse on the Social Order in America* (Chicago: University of Chicago Press, 1995).

10. For a description of the new president pro tem, see *Philadelphia Daily Evening Bulletin,* March 2, 1867, p. 4.

11. *Harper's Weekly,* January 19, 1867, p. 34. See similar argument over black suffrage in Washington, D.C., in *Harper's Weekly,* January 19, 1867, p. 35. Speech of Reverend Henry Ward Beecher before the Brooklyn Fraternity, in *New York Daily Tribune,* February 14, 1867, p. 8. Beecher's speech also called for women's suffrage. *Harper's Weekly,* April 25, 1868, p. 258. In contrast to this argument, Republicans who supported black suffrage but opposed women's suffrage—which had been agitated for for a much longer time than black suffrage and which had prominent supporters as well—argued that the majority of women really did not want to vote. The cause was being pushed by a few outspoken people who did not represent the majority, newspapers reported. "A few of the strong-minded, to whom, by some mistake of nature, the wrong sex was assigned, are clamorous upon the subject," the *Philadelphia Inquirer* claimed, "but they do not reflect the opinions or the wishes of the great majority of women who are satisfied with their condition, and believe themselves to be well represented by their fathers, husbands, sons and brothers." *Philadelphia Inquirer,* April 12, 1867, p. 4; August 27, 1868, p. 4; and November 20, 1868, p. 4. See also quotation from *New York Daily Tribune* in *Washington Chronicle,* April 10, 1870, p. 2.

12. On Wilson and suffrage, see *New York World,* November 26, 1867, p. 4. *Cincinnati Daily Gazette,* May 15, 1867, p. 2. *Harper's Weekly,* September 7, 1867, p. 562. See also *Harper's Weekly,* April 13, 1867, p. 238; May, 4, 1867, p. 275; and May 11, 1867, p. 304. Compare to *New York Herald,* which opposed African-American suffrage on racial grounds and applauded the English Reform movement. *New York Herald,* July 29, 1867, p. 4; July 31, 1867, p. 4.

13. H. L. Trefousse, *Benjamin Franklin Wade: Radical Republican from Ohio* (New York: Twayne Publishers, 1963), pp. 281–282. *New York Daily Tribune,* November 27, 1866, p. 4; February 2, 1867, p. 4; February 4, 1867, p. 4; Feb-

ruary 6, 1867, p. 4. *Philadelphia Daily Evening Bulletin,* January 11, 1867, p. 4. On *New York Times,* see *New York World,* November 26, 1867, p. 4. On impartial suffrage, see *Boston Evening Transcript,* April 18, 1871, p. 2. Schurz, "Report," p. 43. On moderate opposition to black voting, see Cooper Union Address [of Republicans], February 28, 1866, reprinted in *New York World,* November 8, 1867, p. 2.

14. *Columbus (Ohio) Crisis,* March 27, 1867, p. 65. *Philadelphia Inquirer,* March 13, 1867, p. 4. See also ibid., May 30, 1867, p. 4. *Chicago Tribune,* February 23, 1867, p. 2.

15. Thaddeus Stevens, *Congressional Globe,* 39th Cong., 2nd sess., p. 252. James G. Blaine, *Twenty Years of Congress,* vol. 2 (Norwich, Conn.: The Henry Bill Publishing Company, 1893), p. 262.

16. *New York World,* March 19, 1867, p. 4. For an examination of attempts to organize African-American voting, see Victor B. Howard, *Black Liberation in Kentucky: Emancipation and Freedom, 1862–1884* (Lexington: University Press of Kentucky, 1983), pp. 146–155.

17. *Chicago Tribune,* March 27, 1867, p. 1. *Harper's Weekly,* April 6, 1867, p. 211. *New York World,* quoted in *Chicago Tribune,* April 17, 1867, p. 2.

18. *New York Times,* May 29, 1867, p. 4. *Chicago Tribune,* March 27, 1867, p. 1. Ibid., March 30, 1867, p. 2. See also *Wilmington (N.C.) Dispatch,* quoted in *Chicago Tribune,* April 11, 1867, p. 2.

19. *Harper's Weekly,* April 6, 1867, p. 211; May 4, 1867, p. 275; May 11, 1867, p. 291; September 21, 1867, p. 595. *Philadelphia Inquirer,* April 2, 1867, p. 4. *New York Times,* April 27, 1867, p. 4. See articles from the *New York Daily Tribune* and *New York Times* reprinted in *Washington Chronicle,* March 24, 1867, p. 2.

20. *Chicago Tribune,* January 25, 1867, p. 2. *Cincinnati Daily Gazette,* April 25, 1867, p. 2. See also Thomas Nast's cartoon in *Harper's Weekly,* April 6, 1867, p. 224. *Harper's Weekly,* April 6, 1867, p. 211.

21. *New York World,* April 9, 1867, p. 2. *Chicago Tribune,* March 30, 1867, p. 2, and April 11, 1867, p. 2.

22. General Swayne, assistant commissioner of Freedmen's Bureau in Alabama, quoted in *Harper's Weekly,* January 11, 1868, p. 18. *Cincinnati Daily Gazette,* April 29, 1867, p. 2. *Harper's Weekly,* April 20, 1867, p. 242. *Philadelphia Inquirer,* March 20, 1867, p. 4. See also *Washington Chronicle,* March 24, 1867, p. 1, letter reprinted from *Philadelphia Press.* See also *Philadelphia Inquirer,* March 6, 1867, p. 4, and March 26, 1867, p. 4.

23. *New York World,* April 5, 1867, p. 4. On April 19, 1867 (p. 2), the *Chicago Tribune* satirized the Democratic attempts to woo black voters. *Chicago Tribune,* March 30, 1867, p. 2. *Harper's Weekly,* May 4, 1867, p. 274. On Wilson, see Ernest McKay, *Henry Wilson: Practical Radical* (Port Washington,

N.Y.: Kennikat Press, 1971). *Philadelphia Inquirer,* June 13, 1867, p. 4. See
also *Philadelphia Inquirer,* April 23, 1867, p. 4. *Chicago Tribune,* March 30,
1867, p. 2. Wilson did threaten confiscation if the South did not accept the
Military Reconstruction Act. See *Philadelphia Inquirer,* April 22, 1867, p. 4.
For a transcript of Wilson's speech in Augusta, Georgia, see *Augusta Loyal
Georgian,* May 9, 1867, p. 2.

24. *Columbus (Ohio) Crisis,* May 8, 1867, p. 116. The definitive study of the
Union League is Michael W. Fitzgerald, *The Union League Movement in the
Deep South: Politics and Agricultural Change during Reconstruction* (Baton
Rouge: Louisiana State University Press, 1989). *Harper's Weekly,* June 6,
1867, p. 355. On Wilson's views, see interview with Wilson in *New York
Herald,* July 2, 1867, p. 5.

25. On prosperous African-Americans, see Robert C. Kenzer, *Enterprising
Southerners: Black Economic Success in North Carolina, 1865–1915* (Charlottesville: University Press of Virginia, 1997); see especially pp. 9–34 on
landownership. On the characteristics of black political leadership in South
Carolina, see Thomas Holt, *Black over White: Negro Political Leadership in
South Carolina during Reconstruction* (Urbana: University of Illinois Press,
1977). For a biography of a prosperous black family during the nineteenth
century, see Michael P. Johnson and James L. Roark, *Black Masters: A Free
Family of Color in the Old South* (New York: W. W. Norton, 1984); on the
family's decision to become Democrats, see pp. 325–328. On the American
black "elite" after 1880, see Willard B. Gatewood, *Aristocrats of Color: The
Black Elite, 1880–1920* (Bloomington: Indiana University Press, 1990).
Compare Alywn Barr, "Black Legislators of Reconstruction Texas," *Civil War
History,* 32 (December 1986): 340–351, which argues that African-American legislators in Texas voted for pro-labor measures regardless of their own
socioeconomic status. For a description of delegates to the Georgia Freedmen's Convention, see *Augusta Loyal Georgian,* January 20, 1866, p. 3. For
the entire list of the convention's resolutions, see ibid., January 27, 1866,
p. 1. Emma Lou Thornbrough, ed., *Black Reconstructionists* (Englewood
Cliffs, N.J.: Prentice-Hall, 1972), excerpts the resolutions. On black leaders,
see Eric Foner, *Freedom's Lawmakers: A Directory of Black Officeholders during Reconstruction* (Baton Rouge: Louisiana State University Press, 1996);
Howard N. Rabinowitz, "Three Reconstruction Leaders: Blanche K. Bruce,
Robert Brown Elliott, and Holland Thompson," in Leon Litwack and August Meier, eds., *Black Leaders of the Nineteenth Century* (Urbana: University
of Illinois Press, 1988), pp. 191–217; and Howard N. Rabinowitz, ed.,
Southern Black Leaders of the Reconstruction Era (Urbana: University of Illinois Press, 1982).

26. In *Philadelphia Inquirer,* April 19, 1867, p. 4 (AP wire). Nell Irvin Painter has

identified these differences in black community representatives as ones between "representative colored men," who manipulated whites by mimicking white values; and "executors," who voiced the communally decided wishes of the black community. Nell Irvin Painter, *Exodusters: Black Migration to Kansas after Reconstruction* (New York: Alfred A. Knopf, 1977), pp. 15–16 and 22–23.

27. On grassroots African-American political activity, see Eric Foner, "Black Reconstruction Leaders at the Grass Roots," in Litwack and Meier, eds., *Black Leaders*, pp. 219–234. *Harper's Weekly*, April 6, 1867, p. 211. *Philadelphia Inquirer*, April 15, 1867, p. 4. See same story in *Washington Chronicle*, April 14, 1867, p. 1. *Harper's Weekly*, April 27, 1867, p. 259. Nashville meeting reported in *Harper's Weekly*, April 27, 1867, p. 259; *Chicago Tribune*, April 19, 1867, p. 3; and originally in *Cincinnati Daily Gazette*, April 14. Similar meetings reported in *Philadelphia Inquirer*, May 4, 1867, p. 4, for example. Fitzgerald, *Union League*, pp. 43, 60–61. Loren Schweninger, *James T. Rapier and Reconstruction*, (Chicago: University of Chicago Press, 1978), p. 47.

28. *Chicago Tribune*, March 27, 1867, p. 1. See also *Columbus (Ohio) Crisis*, April 3, 1867, p. 77. *Philadelphia Inquirer*, April 19, 1867, p. 4. *New York Herald*, July 8, 1867, p. 4; July 16, 1867, p. 5; July 17, 1867, p. 5.

29. Fitzgerald, *Union League*, pp. 16–23. *Philadelphia Inquirer*, May 23, 1867, p. 4. See also *Cincinnati Daily Gazette*, April 30, 1867, p. 2.

30. On black workers' organization, see Peter J. Rachleff, *Black Labor in the South: Richmond, Virginia, 1865–1890* (Philadelphia: Temple University Press, 1984). Philip Foner, *History of the Labor Movement in the United States* (New York: International Publishers, 1947), pp. 395–396. William C. Hine, "Black Organized Labor in Reconstruction Charleston," *Labor History*, 25 (1984): 504–517, reprinted in Donald G. Nieman, ed., *African American Life in the Post-Emancipation South, 1861–1900*, vol. 4: *African Americans and Non-Agricultural Labor in the South, 1865–1900* (New York: Garland Publishing, 1994). Jerrell H. Shofner, "Militant Negro Laborers in Reconstruction Florida," *Journal of Southern History*, 39 (August 1973): 397–408. On South Carolina freedmen, labor, and politics, see Julie Saville, *The Work of Reconstruction: From Slave to Wage Laborer in South Carolina, 1860–1870* (Cambridge: Cambridge University Press, 1994). On interracial labor cooperation at a later period, which is suggestive for an earlier time as well, see Rick Halpern, "Organized Labor, Black Workers, and the Twentieth-Century South: The Emerging Revision," in Melvyn Stokes and Rick Halpern, eds., *Race and Class in the American South since 1890* (Oxford: Berg Publishers, 1994), pp. 43–76. *Montgomery Advertiser*, July 28, 1867; and see the examination of agricultural workers' revolt in Fitzgerald, *Union League*, pp. 165–169. See, for example, *Philadelphia Inquirer*, May 13, 1867, p. 8.

31. *New York World*, May 24, 1867, p. 2. *Baltimore Sun*, July 1, 1867, p. 2.

32. William H. Chafe has attributed the later demand of African-Americans for office as a search for "tangible recognition" from the white community. With no institutional protection or justice, they looked to political parties to set the tone for society by according them status. See William H. Chafe, "The Negro and Populism: A Kansas Case Study," *Journal of Southern History*, 34 (August 1968): 402–419. *Harper's Weekly*, April 27, 1867, p. 259. *Harper's Weekly*, May 4, 1867, p. 275, and May 25, 1867, p. 323. On African-American demands for office-holding, see Howard, *Black Liberation*, pp. 155–159. *New York World*, July 12, 1867, p. 2. On demands for black police officers in Richmond, see *New York Herald*, July 10, 1867, p. 5. *Columbus (Ohio) Crisis*, May 27, 1867, p. 131. *Harper's Weekly*, May 11, 1867, p. 291.

33. See reports in *New York Herald*, July 18, 1867, p. 11. Fitzgerald, *Union League*, pp. 66–71. *Columbus (Ohio) Crisis*, May 22, 1867, p. 132. *Philadelphia Inquirer*, August 29, 1867, p. 4.

34. *Harper's Weekly*, September 14, 1867, p. 579; April 27, 1867, p. 259; September 21, 1867, p. 595; February 8, 1868, p. 96.

35. *Columbus (Ohio) Crisis*, March 13, 1867, p. 52. Compare Mark Wahlgren Summers, *The Era of Good Stealings* (New York: Oxford University Press, 1993).

36. On the size of government in 1865, see Ari Hoogenboom, *Outlawing the Spoils: A History of the Civil Service Reform Movement, 1865–1883* (Urbana: University of Illinois Press, 1961), p. 1. For Democratic rhetoric about taxation and the rich, see, for example, *Columbus (Ohio) Crisis*, March 20, 1867, p. 60,

37. *Columbus (Ohio) Crisis*, March 20, 1867, p. 60; and April 13, 1867, p. 76. *New York Daily Tribune*, January 11, 1867, p. 4. See also ibid., March 15, 1867, p. 4, on high costs of government.

38. *Baltimore Sun*, July 16, 1867, p. 1; July 19, 1867, p. 2; July 22, 1867, pp. 2 and 4; July 24, 1867, p. 2. *St. Paul Pioneer Press*, November 3, 1868, in Cochrane, "Freedom without Equality," p. 369.

39. For a larger examination of the role of the Civil War debt and Republican taxation on what became civil service reform, see Sherman S. Rogers, "George William Curtis and Civil Service Reform," *Atlantic Monthly* (January 1893): 15–25. For an alternative version of origins of civil service reform, see Hoogenboom, *Outlawing the Spoils. New York World*, July 9, 1867, pp. 2 and 4; July 12, 1867, p. 2; September 3, 1867, p. 2. See also *Baltimore Sun*, July 15, 1867, p. 2, which linked demoralized African-Americans to murder of white men.

40. *New York World*, August 16, 1867, p. 2, and November 1, 1867, p. 2.

41. Ibid., August 16, 1867, p. 2; November 1, 1867, p. 2; May 22, 1867, p. 2.

42. Ibid., July 12, 1867, p. 2, and November 22, 1867, p. 2. On black influence in the Southern Republican party and on party policy, see Michael Perman, *The Road to Redemption: Southern Politics, 1869–1879* (Chapel Hill: University of North Carolina Press, 1984), pp. 22–56.

43. *Baltimore Sun,* July 12, 1867, p. 2. *New York Herald,* July 17, 1867, p. 4; July 18, 1867, p. 11. See also ibid., July 26, 1867, p. 4.

44. *New York World,* July 26, 1867, p. 4. *Cincinnati Daily Gazette,* May 30, 1867, p. 1. *Chicago Tribune,* May 16, 1867, p. 2.

45. *New York Times,* February 5, 1866, p. 4; May 13, 1867, p. 4; April 25, 1867, p. 4; August 13, 1867, p. 4.

46. Ibid., January 16, 1868, p. 2, and February 6, 1868, p. 2. *Columbus (Ohio) Crisis,* May 22, 1867, p. 130.

47. *New York Times,* May 29, 1867, p. 4. *Philadelphia Inquirer,* May 21, 1867, p. 1. *Chicago Tribune,* October 8, 1867, p. 2. *Washington Chronicle,* March 24, 1867, p. 2. See also *Philadelphia Inquirer,* March 27, 1867, p. 4. *Harper's Weekly,* April 13, 1867, p. 238.

48. On demagogues, see *New York Times,* June 20, 1867, p. 4; *Boston Evening Transcript,* February 16, 1871, p. 2; *Chicago Tribune,* May 16, 1867, p. 2.

49. *Philadelphia Inquirer,* August 13, 1867, p. 4. See also *New York Herald,* July 26, 1867, p. 4. James M. McPherson, *Ordeal by Fire: The Civil War and Reconstruction* (New York: Alfred A. Knopf, 1982), p. 535. *Harper's Weekly,* October 12, 1867, p. 642; September 7, 1867, p. 563; August 31, 1867, p. 547; August 3, 1867, p. 483. For a negative account of black majorities registering to vote, see *New York Herald,* July 1, 1867, p. 2.

50. *Chicago Tribune,* May 25, 1867, p. 2. *New York Times,* June 8, 1867, p. 4. See also *Harper's Weekly,* May 25, 1867, p. 323. Ibid., September 7, 1867, p. 563. *New York Times,* June 27, 1867, p. 4. *New York Herald,* July 16, 1867, p. 8.

51. See Philip Foner, "A Labor Voice for Black Equality: The *Boston Daily Evening Voice,* 1864–1867," in Philip Foner, *Essays in Afro-American History* (Philadelphia: Temple University Press, 1978), pp. 112–133. Labor historians have contributed immeasurably to our understanding of the interplay of race and class in the minds of American workers. From an older understanding that either ignored issues of race altogether or argued that labor unions systematically excluded African-Americans, we have come to see the rich intersection of race and class and their impact on communities and culture. While some recent historians, notably Alexander Saxton, Herbert Hill, Noel Ignatiev, and David Roediger, still adhere to the idea that deep racist exclusion dominated white labor's approach to African-Americans, other labor historians have moved toward a more nuanced picture of the postwar world of industry. Most recently, Peter Rachleff's *Black Labor in Richmond,*

Virginia, 1865–1890 (Philadelphia: Temple University Press, 1984); Eric Arnesen's *Waterfront Workers of New Orleans: Race, Class, and Politics, 1863–1923* (New York: Oxford University Press, 1991) and Daniel Letwin's *The Challenge of Interracial Unionism: Alabama Coal Miners, 1878–1921* (Chapel Hill: University of North Carolina Press, 1998) have explored the wide range of relationships between black and white workers, revealing that there was no uniform practice of either antipathy or acceptance characterizing workers' contacts in the late nineteenth century. For a full review of labor historians' approaches to issues of race and class, see Eric Arnesen, "Up from Exclusion: Black and White Workers, Race, and the State of Labor History," *Reviews in American History,* 26 (1998): 146–174. On Republican struggle with workers' organization, see Montgomery, *Beyond Equality.*

52. Trefousse, *Wade,* pp. 285–289. *Harper's Weekly,* July 6, 1867, p. 418. *New York Times,* June 20, 1867, p. 4. On scandalized reactions to the Wade speech, see *Baltimore Sun,* July 9, 1867, p. 2; *New York Herald,* July 8, 1867, p. 4, and July 16, 1867, p. 6. See also article from *Cincinnati Commercial,* reprinted in *New York Herald,* July 8, 1867, p. 6. The vast majority of historical literature on socialism and communism in America concentrates on the twentieth century (see, for example, Guenter Lewy, *The Cause That Failed: Communism in American Political Life* [New York: Oxford University Press, 1990]), but American radicalism had been alive and well since at least 1864. See Philip S. Foner, *The Workingmen's Party of the United States: A History of the First Marxist Party in the Americas* (Minneapolis: M.E.P. Publications, 1984). *Harper's Weekly,* October 26, 1867, p. 674.

53. *New York Times,* November 10, 1867, p. 4. *Harper's Weekly,* August 17, 1867, p. 514. African-Americans in Washington, D.C., had voted in June (*Harper's Weekly,* June 29, 1867, p. 403). McPherson, *Ordeal by Fire,* pp. 535–536. *New York World,* November 1, 1867, p. 2. *New York Times,* November 10, 1867, p. 4. Ibid., November 2, 1867, p. 4. On *New York Times* and black suffrage, see *New York World,* October 15, 1867, p. 4. *New York Times,* October 31, 1867, p. 4. On constitutions, see, for example, ibid., November 15, 1867, p. 4. *Chicago Tribune,* August 13, 1867, p. 2.

54. Michael Les Benedict, "The Rout of Radicalism: Republicans and the Election of 1867," *Civil War History,* 18 (December 1972): 334–344. Michael Les Benedict, *A Compromise of Principle: Congressional Republicans and Reconstruction, 1863–1869* (New York: W. W. Norton & Company, 1974), pp. 257–278. James G. Blaine to Israel Washburn, Jr., September 12, 1867, in Gaillard Hunt, *Israel, Elihu, and Cadwallader Washburn: A Chapter in American Biography* (New York: The Macmillan Company, 1925), p. 121. On Republican radicalism until 1867, see Peyton McCrary, "The Party of Revolution: Republican Ideas about Politics and Social Change, 1862–1867," *Civil War History,* 30 (December 1984): 330–350.

55. *Harper's Weekly,* January 18, 1868, p. 34. *New York Times* quoted in *Harper's Weekly,* September 14, 1867, p. 579. See also *Chicago Tribune,* October 5, 1867, p. 2; October 6, 1867, p. 2. See also *Harper's Weekly's* pointed praise of the black government of Liberia (*Harper's Weekly,* January 25, 1868, pp. 61–62).

56. *Harper's Weekly,* January 18, 1868, p. 34.

57. On Democrats and taxation, see *Philadelphia Inquirer,* July 8, 1868, p. 4.

58. *New York World,* March 19, 1867, p. 4.

59. *Philadelphia Inquirer,* August 8, 1868, p. 4. *Columbus (Ohio) Crisis,* March 20, 1867, p. 60, and April 24, 1867, p. 97. *Philadelphia Inquirer,* September 18, 1868, p. 4. *Harper's Weekly,* February 22, 1868, p. 115. *New York World,* November 1, 1867, p. 2. Referenda for black suffrage had failed miserably in the Northern states in the years since the war, thanks largely to Northern Democratic prejudice against black Americans. For Democratic attempts at racist legislation in 1868, see *Chicago Tribune,* May 14, 1868, p. 2. Ohio Democrats passed a "visible admixture" law prohibiting suffrage for anyone who looked like he had African blood (*Philadelphia Inquirer,* August 21, 1868, p. 4). Southern newspaper quoted in *Harper's Weekly,* April 18, 1868, p. 243.

60. *Philadelphia Inquirer,* August 17, 1868, p. 4; August 10, 1868, p. 4; August 20, 1868, p. 4; September 22, 1868, p. 4.

61. On the Democratic Convention and platform, see Edward L. Gambill, *Conservative Ordeal: Northern Democrats and Reconstruction, 1865–1868* (Ames: Iowa State University Press, 1981), pp. 137–143; *North American Review,* 107 (October 1868): 445–465; *Philadelphia Inquirer,* July 9, 1868, p. 4.

62. *Harper's Weekly,* April 11, 1868, p. 226. *Philadelphia Inquirer,* October 8, 1868, p. 3. Jay Cooke's letters in ibid., March 21, 1868, pp. 1–2, and March 23, 1868, p. 4.

63. *Harper's Weekly,* February 22, 1868, p. 115; February 8, 1868, p. 82; April 11, 1868, p. 226. *Chicago Tribune,* March 14, 1868, p. 2. For an attack on Democratic currency ideas, see *New York Daily Tribune,* January 10, 1867, p. 4, and speech of Justin Smith Morrill (R-Vt.) in Congress on January 24, 1867, reprinted in *New York Daily Tribune,* January 25, 1867, p. 2.

64. John Bigelow to [?] Hargreaves, February 26, 1868, Bigelow MSS, New York Public Library.

65. *New York Times,* June 21, 1868, p. 4. Henry Wilson and Galusha Grow in *Philadelphia Inquirer,* September 28, 1868, p. 2. See also J. W. Patterson in ibid., September 29, 1868, p. 8.

66. *Harper's Weekly,* May 9, 1868, pp. 290–291. *Philadelphia Inquirer,* April 1, 1868, p. 4; July 18, 1868, p. 4.

67. On Ku Klux Klan, see *Harper's Weekly,* April 18, 1868, p. 243, and *Montgomery Daily Mail,* quoted in *Harper's Weekly,* March 14, 1868, p. 163. *Chicago*

Tribune, April 10, 1868, p. 2. *Philadelphia Inquirer,* April 7, 1868, pp. 2–3, 4. *Harper's Weekly,* February 29, 1868, p. 130. Ibid., March 21, 1868, p. 178; March 28, 1868, p. 195; April 11, 1868, p. 227.

68. *Harper's Weekly,* April 25, 1868, p. 258. On whites who voted Republican in the South, see Allen W. Trelease, "Who Were the Scalawags?" *Journal of Southern History,* 29 (November 1963): 445–468. Chicago *Tribune,* April 16, 1868, p. 2; August 14, 1868, p. 2; January 16, 1868, p. 2; February 22, 1868, p. 2.

69. *Chicago Tribune,* August 9, 1868, p. 2. *North American Review,* 107 (July 1868): 167, 173–174.

70. *Harper's Weekly,* April 4, 1868, p. 211. General Swayne, assistant commissioner of Freedmen's Bureau in Alabama, quoted in ibid., January 11, 1868, p. 18. See illustration of freedpeople gathering firewood, ibid., March 14, 1868, p. 173. *Chicago Tribune,* July 14, 1868, p. 2.

71. *Harper's Weekly,* March 7, 1868, p. 147. *Philadelphia Inquirer,* April 9, 1868, p. 2, and September 17, 1868, p. 4; see also August 15, 1868, p. 4.

72. *Chicago Tribune,* February 1, 1868, p. 2. Ibid., February 22, 1868, p. 2. Patterson quoted in *Philadelphia Inquirer,* September 29, 1868, p. 8.

73. McPherson, *Ordeal by Fire,* pp. 536. For an analysis of the constitutional conventions, see Jack B. Scroggs, "Carpetbagger Constitutional Reform in the South Atlantic States, 1867–1868," *Journal of Southern History,* 27 (November 1961): 475–493. *New York Times,* August 28, 1868, p. 4. Ashley in ibid., August 22, 1868, p. 1.

74. On Georgia story, see, for example, *Philadelphia Inquirer,* July 27, 1868, p. 4; September 4, 1868, p. 1; September 5, 1868, p. 4; September 9, 1868, p. 4.

75. On Grant as moderate rebuke to radicals, see James G. Blaine to Israel Washburn, Jr., September 12, 1867, in Hunt, *Washburn,* p. 121, and William Schouler to Israel Washburn, Jr., October 26, 1868, in ibid., p. 123. Republicans began immediately to resurrect hard money policies. (See, for example, *Philadelphia Inquirer,* February 18, 1869, p. 4.) *New York Times,* November 5, 1868, p. 4.

76. *Philadelphia Daily Evening Bulletin,* January 29, 1869, p. 4.

77. *New York Times,* December 17, 1868, p. 4, and January 16, 1869, p. 4.

78. From *Philadelphia Press,* in *Washington Chronicle,* February 21, 1869, p. 2, and February 28, 1869, p. 2. *New York World,* January 15, 1869, p. 4. *Philadelphia Daily Evening Bulletin,* January 29, 1869, p. 4. *Philadelphia Inquirer,* November 9, 1868, p. 4; November 10, 1868, p. 4. From *Philadelphia Press,* in *Washington Chronicle,* April 25, 1869, p. 1. On Democrats' hopes to work with Grant, see Perman, *Road to Redemption,* pp. 6–9.

79. *Harper's Weekly,* February 6, 1869, p. 81, 85.

80. *New York Times,* January 12, 1869, p. 1, and January 16, 1869, p. 1. On ver-

sions of the amendment, see also *New York Times,* January 24, 1869, p. 1. On Fifteenth Amendment, see John M. Matthews, *Legislative and Judicial History of the Fifteenth Amendment* (1909; reprint, New York: Da Capo Press, 1971).

81. On support for suffrage, see *New York Times,* February 15, 1869, p. 4, and February 19, 1869, p. 4. Ibid., January 31, 1869, p. 1. For the vote, see ibid., January 31, 1869, p. 1. Synopses of debates on the measures appeared in the *New York Times* from January 24, 1869 (p. 1), to February 27, 1869 (p. 1).

82. In addition to the committee's amendment itself, see also Wilson's proposed amendments (*New York Times,* February 3, 1869, p. 1) and Warner's (ibid., February 4, 1869, p. 1). See review of Morton's speech, ibid., February 5, 1869, p. 1. Ibid., February 6, 1869, pp. 1 and 4, and February 19, 1969, p. 4.

83. See ibid., February 18, 1869, p. 1. *New York World,* January 1, 1869, p. 4. On savages, see ibid., January 3, 1869, p. 4. *New York Times,* February 19, 1869, p. 4. *Washington Chronicle,* February 21, 1869, p. 2.

84. See *New York Times,* February 5, 1869, p. 1. See also *Chicago Tribune,* June 12, 1868, p. 2, on tentative Northern Democratic support for black voting in the South in response to public pressure. See *Washington Chronicle,* March 14, 1869, p. 1, on the Georgia legislature's willingness to accept the amendment to prevent the expulsion of members ineligible under the Fourteenth Amendment and the reseating of black members. See also ibid., March 14, 1869, p. 2. In his introductory speech on the bill, Boutwell initially endorsed universal suffrage in part to preserve Republican domination of the government, to the great disgust of Democrats and even many Republicans; see *New York Times,* January 24, 1869, p. 1, and January 25, 1869, p. 4. On James Dixon's speech against the measure, see ibid., January 30, 1869, p. 1. Ibid., February 9, 1869, p. 1. Ibid., January 31, 1869, p. 1.

85. Stewart, *Congressional Globe,* 40th Cong., 3rd sess., p. 668. *Philadelphia Daily Evening Bulletin,* February 2, 1869, p. 4. Even Northern Republicans who remained unenthusiastic about African-American suffrage could look forward to the removal of the divisive suffrage question from the local political arena, where it had been an issue for years as Northern states fought over it in their own constitutions. See Phyllis F. Field, "Republicans and Black Suffrage in New York State: The Grass Roots Response," *Civil War History,* 21 (June 1975): 136–147; Phyllis F. Field, *The Politics of Race in New York: The Struggle for Black Suffrage in the Civil War Era* (Ithaca, N.Y.: Cornell University Press, 1982).

86. *Washington Chronicle,* May 30, 1969, p. 2. See letter from A. R. Calhoun, Post Commander, Post 19, GAR, May 14, 1869, in ibid., May 16, 1869, p. 2. See also ibid., May 16, 1869, p. 2. Ibid., August 29, 1969, p. 2. The reunion was held August 30.

87. On Georgia's vote on the Fifteenth Amendment, see ibid., March 14, 1869, pp. 1 and 2; March 21, 1869, p. 2. John W. Blassingame and John R. McKivigan, eds., *The Frederick Douglass Papers, Series One: Speeches, Debates, and Interviews*, vol. 4: *1864–1880* (New Haven: Yale University Press, 1991), pp. 266–267.

88. *Chicago Tribune*, February 4, 1870, p. 2. *New York World*, March 19, 1867, p. 4. Albion W. Tourgée, *A Fool's Errand by One of the Fools*, ed. John Hope Franklin (1879; reprint, Cambridge, Mass.: Harvard University Press, 1961), p. 169.

89. Elihu B. Washburne, in *New York World*, January 9, 1869, p. 6. Ibid., January 11, 1869, p. 4.

3 Black Workers and the South Carolina Government, 1871–1875

1. *Harper's Weekly*, May 18, 1867, p. 306. See also *Harper's Weekly*, January 19, 1867, p. 34.

2. *Boston Evening Transcript*, February 15, 1871, p. 2. *Chicago Tribune*, March 31, 1871, p. 2. *New York Times*, March 7, 1871, p. 4. *Chicago Tribune*, March 7, 1871, p. 2. For other positive images of black legislators, see *Boston Daily Evening Transcript*, February 1, 1871, p. 3.

3. *Boston Daily Evening Transcript*, January 28, 1871, p. 1.

4. *Scribner's Monthly*, 1 (December 1870): 214–215.

5. On press interest in the Franco-Prussian War and the Paris Commune, see Philip M. Katz, *From Appomattox to Montmartre: Americans and the Paris Commune* (Cambridge, Mass.: Harvard University Press, 1998), pp. 61–84. Republican newspapers further highlighted the events in Paris because the American ambassador to France, Elihu B. Washburne, who was the only foreign ambassador to remain in the city during the seige, was a Republican whose rectitude and statesmanship during the crisis made him a useful standard-bearer for a party suffering under administrative scandals.

6. Quotation from *Cincinnati Daily Gazette*, May 22, 1871, p. 2. Ibid., May 31, 1871, p. 2, reprinted from *New York World*; *Boston Evening Transcript*, October 24, 1871, supplement, p. 1. The unnatural role of women in the Commune gained much attention as a symbol of disorder. See *Cincinnati Daily Gazette*, June 13, 1871, p. 2; *Philadelphia Inquirer*, July 19, 1871, p. 4; *Boston Evening Transcript*, May 15, 1872, p. 1; *Chicago Tribune*, June 18, 1871, p. 2. On property confiscation, see, for example, *Philadelphia Inquirer*, August 30, 1871, p. 4; *Chicago Tribune*, May 4, 1871, p. 2. *Boston Evening Transcript*, October 20, 1871, supplement, p. 1.

7. Quotation in *Cincinnati Daily Gazette*, May 31, 1871, p. 2, reprinted from *New York World*. *Philadelphia Inquirer*, August 30, 1871, p. 4. *Chicago Tri-*

bune, May 4, 1871, p. 2. *Boston Evening Transcript,* October 20, 1871, supplement, p. 1.

8. See also *Cincinnati Daily Gazette,* April 4, 1871, p. 2. On fear of a workingman's political party, see, for example, *Philadelphia Inquirer,* August 2, 1871, p. 4, and August 10, 1871, p. 1; *Cincinnati Daily Gazette,* February 25, 1871, p. 4. Frank Norton, "Our Labor System and the Chinese," *Scribner's Monthly,* 2 (May 1871): 62. Chicago letter to the *Cincinnati Herald and Presbyter* quoted in *Cincinnati Daily Gazette,* December 12, 1871, p. 2. On the Chicago fire and fear of communists, see also Karen Sawislak, *Smoldering City: Chicagoans and the Great Fire, 1871–1874* (Chicago: University of Chicago Press, 1995), pp. 46–48. See also *Philadelphia Inquirer,* October 28, 1871, p. 3. Brace quotation is from Robert M. Fogelson, *America's Armories: Architecture, Society and Public Order* (Cambridge, Mass.: Harvard University Press, 1989), pp. xxx, 24.

9. *Boston Evening Transcript,* December 13, 1871, p. 2. *Philadelphia Inquirer,* October 25, 1871, p. 4. On the International Workingmen's Association, see Philip S. Foner, *History of the Labor Movement in the United States* (New York: International Publishers, 1947), p. 413. *Philadelphia Inquirer,* August 30, 1871, p. 4. See also *Cincinnati Daily Gazette,* April 4, 1871, p. 2.

10. *Boston Evening Transcript,* January 20, 1871, p. 1.

11. On the Republican party and the rise of this distinction between workers, see Iver Bernstein, *The New York City Draft Riots* (New York: Oxford University Press, 1990), pp. 172–190. *Philadelphia Inquirer,* October 25, 1871, p. 4. *Cincinnati Daily Gazette,* April 4, 1871, p. 2.

12. Since the war, Democrats had accused Republicans of favoring the rich. On Democrats, see Joel H. Silbey, *A Respectable Minority: The Democratic Party in the Civil War Era, 1860–1868* (New York: W. W. Norton & Co., 1977); Jean Harvey Baker, *Affairs of Party: The Political Culture of Northern Democrats in the Mid-Nineteenth Century* (Ithaca, N.Y.: Cornell University Press, 1983); Bruce Collins, "Ideology of Ante-Bellum Northern Democrats," *Journal of American Studies,* 11 (April 1977): 103–121. The 1868 Democratic call for the redemption of government bonds in greenbacks codified the dislike of the rich with a stab at wealthy bondholders. Belmont to McCook, June 5, 1871, Marble Papers, in Irving Katz, *August Belmont: A Political Biography* (New York: Columbia University Press, 1968), p. 195. *New York World,* September 14, 1871, p. 6. For Democratic speeches on labor, see *Congressional Record,* 42nd Cong., 2nd sess., 1871, pp. 102–105, 217–228, 251–258. On consolidation of New York City's Republican and Democratic elites in 1872, see Bernstein, *Draft Riots,* pp. 237–257.

13. *New York Times,* April 17, 1871, p. 4.

14. On freedmen in control of property interests, see *Philadelphia Inquirer,*

March 27, 1867, p. 4. On the South Carolina government in this period, see Thomas Holt, *Black over White: Negro Political Leadership in South Carolina during Reconstruction* (Urbana: University of Illinois Press, 1979), and W. E. Burghardt Du Bois, *Black Reconstruction in America* (New York: Russell & Russell, 1935), chap. 10, "The Black Proletariat in South Carolina," pp. 381–340.

15. Du Bois, *Reconstruction,* pp. 404–405. On land reform in South Carolina, see Carole K. Rothrock Bleser, *The Promised Land: The History of the South Carolina Land Commission, 1869–1890* (Columbia: University of South Carolina Press, 1969).

16. On actions of the state legislature, see Holt, *Black over White,* pp. 152–170. Quotations from Joel Williamson, *After Slavery: The Negro in South Carolina during Reconstruction, 1861–1877* (Chapel Hill: University of North Carolina Press, 1965), pp. 255.

17. Williamson, *After Slavery,* pp. 260–265.

18. *New York Times,* April 2, 1871, p. 4.

19. On controversy over Southern violence, see George C. Rable, *But There Was No Peace: The Role of Violence in the Politics of Reconstruction* (Athens: University of Georgia Press, 1984), pp. 14–15. *Cincinnati Daily Gazette,* March 22, 1871, p. 1; *Chicago Tribune,* March 22, 1871, p. 1, from the *New York Daily Tribune.* On Southern Democratic hatred of the Ku Klux Klan, see Michael Perman, *The Road to Redemption: Southern Politics, 1869–1879* (Chapel Hill: University of North Carolina Press, 1984), pp. 63–64.

20. For the popular outpouring of anger over Kershaw's speech, see *Cincinnati Daily Gazette,* March 22, 1871, p. 1; *Chicago Tribune,* March 22, 1871, p. 1, and March 23, 1871, pp. 2 and 3; *San Francisco Daily Alta California,* April 11, 1871, p. 2; *Virginia City (Nev.) Daily Territorial Enterprise,* April 18, 1871, p. 2, and April 19, 1871, p. 2. On the Ku Klux Klan Act, see Xi Wang, *The Trial of Democracy: Black Suffrage and Northern Republicans, 1860–1910* (Athens: University of Georgia Press, 1997), pp. 82–87.

21. William C. Hine, "Black Organized Labor in Reconstruction Charleston," *Labor History,* 25 (1984): 504–517, reprinted in Donald G. Nieman, ed., *African American Life in the Post-Emancipation South, 1861–1900,* vol. 4: *African Americans and Non-Agricultural Labor in the South, 1865–1900* (New York: Garland Publishing, 1994). On South Carolina freedmen, labor, and politics, see Julie Saville, *The Work of Reconstruction: From Slave to Wage Laborer in South Carolina, 1860–1870* (Cambridge: Cambridge University Press, 1994).

22. See Holt, *Black over White,* and Eric Foner, "Black Labor Conventions during Reconstruction," in Ronald C. Kent et al., eds., *Culture, Gender, Race, and U.S. Labor History* (Westport, Conn.: Greenwood Press, 1993), pp. 91–

102. Robert Somers, *The Southern States since the War, 1870–1871* (University, Ala.: University of Alabama Press, 1965), pp. 41–43. The *Cincinnati Daily Gazette* noted the South Carolina race-class identity in 1867. See *Cincinnati Daily Gazette*, May 15, 1867, p. 2.

23. The South Carolinians may have imitated the Citizens' Association of New York (see *New York World*, January 21, 1871, p. 2). On the Chamber of Commerce meeting, see Yates Snowden, ed., *History of South Carolina*, vol. 2 (Chicago: Lewis Publishing Company, 1920), p. 905. On convention's proceedings, see *Charleston Daily Courier*, May 9 through May 15, 1871; see also *Chicago Tribune*, May 11, 1871, p. 2. On composition of the convention, see *Savannah Morning News*, May 10, 1871, p. 2, and *New York Daily Tribune*, May 8, 1871, p. 1. For Kershaw's attitude about African-Americans and the convention, see *Charleston Daily Courier*, May 11, 1871, p. 1.

24. The approach of Northern Democrats reflected the new national Democratic strategy of regaining power by downplaying opposition to the Reconstruction laws. On Democratic policy, see Lawrence Grossman, *The Democratic Party and the Negro: Northern and National Politics* (Urbana: University of Illinois Press, 1976), pp. 23–30. Many other Northern newspapers had little to say about the meeting. For a list of Northern correspondents in Columbia, see *Charleston Daily Courier*, May 9, 1871, p. 1, and May 11, 1871, p. 2.

25. *New York Daily Tribune*, May 1, 1871, p. 1.

26. Following Greeley, the *Chicago Tribune* picked up and printed this article a week later (May 8, 1871, p. 2). See also *Chicago Tribune*, May 12, 1871, p. 2. Several papers had hinted earlier that the movement had a good basis for support in the North. See *Cincinnati Daily Gazette*, March 22, 1871, p. 2; *Chicago Tribune*, March 23, 1871, p. 2; *San Francisco Daily Alta California*, March 24, 1871, p. 2. For Democratic reaction to the article, see *New York World*, May 1, 1871, p. 4, and Savannah *Morning News*, May 6, 1871, p. 2.

27. First quotations from James S. Pike, *The Prostrate State: South Carolina under Negro Government* (New York: Loring & Massey, 1935), p. 179. *New York World*, May 13, 1871, p. 4. The *New York Times* (May 12, 1871, p. 2) reprinted the letter of South Carolina governor Scott to the convention. *New York Daily Tribune*, May 12, 1871, p. 5; May 11, 1871, p. 4; May 13, 1871, p. 5; May 10, 1871, p. 2; May 15, 1871, p. 1; May 17, 1871, p. 4.

28. On Phillips, see *New York Daily Tribune*, May 12, 1871, p. 4; *Philadelphia Inquirer*, August 30, 1871, p. 4; *New York Times*, May 10, 1871, p. 4. B. F. Butler, quoted in *New York Daily Tribune*, May 9, 1871, p. 5; *Cincinnati Daily Gazette*, May 11, 1871, p. 3; *Boston Evening Transcript*, May 9, 1871, p. 4. On Butler and the Commune, see *New York Daily Tribune*, June 26, 1871, p. 2.

29. *Chicago Tribune*, May 13, 1871, p. 2. Quotation from the *National Standard*, reprinted in the *Chicago Tribune*, June 19, 1871, p. 4.
30. *New York Daily Tribune*, June 10, 1871, p. 1.
31. *Chicago Tribune*, June 27, 1871, p. 2. See also ibid., June 26, 1871, p. 2.
32. For one of Phillips's speeches on Butler, see *New York World*, September 14, 1871, p. 7. David Montgomery, *Beyond Equality: Labor and the Radical Republicans, 1862–1872* (New York: Alfred A. Knopf, 1967), pp. 368–371. *Nation*, October 5, 1871, pp. 221–222. On laborers' attempts to establish themselves as a political force, see Bernstein, *Draft Riots*, pp. 243–257. On the support of the Massachusetts Irish community for Butler, see Dale Baum, "The 'Irish Vote' and Party Politics in Massachusetts, 1860–1876," *Civil War History*, 26 (June 1980): 117–141.
33. *San Francisco Daily Alta California*, November 4, 1871, p. 2.
34. On convention's conclusions, see *New York Times*, May 14, 1871, p. 1. *New York Daily Tribune*, May 1, 1871, p. 1.
35. *New York Daily Tribune*, May 31, 1871, p. 1; June 7, 1871, p. 4; June 8, 1871, p. 4.
36. Ibid., June 7, 1871, p. 5. *New York World*, September 27, 1871, p. 3.
37. *New York Daily Tribune*, June 2, 1871, p. 1; June 7, 1871, p. 8; June 8, 1871, p. 1; June 9, 1871, p. 1; June 10, 1871, p. 4. For more on strike, see *Cincinnati Daily Gazette*, June 13, 1871, p. 2.
38. *New York Daily Tribune*, September 15, 1871, p. 5.
39. *Philadelphia Inquirer*, October 23, 1871, p. 4.
40. Quotation from *Washington Chronicle*, reprinted in *Columbia (S.C.) Daily Union*, January 4, 1872, p. 2.
41. Robert Franklin Durden, *James Shepherd Pike: Republicanism and the American Negro: 1850–1882* (Durham, N.C.: Duke University Press, 1957), pp. 187–189. *New York Daily Tribune*, April 12, 1872, quoted in Durden, *Pike*, p. 189.
42. The classic book on Liberal Republicanism remains John G. Sproat, *"The Best Men": Liberal Reformers in the Gilded Age* (New York: Oxford University Press, 1968). On Democrats and the idea of a reform party, and on Liberal Republican editors, see Katz, *Belmont*, pp. 195–198. On the divisions in the election of 1872, see William Gillette, *Retreat from Reconstruction, 1869–1879* (Baton Rouge: Louisiana State University Press, 1979), pp. 56–72. On the press in the election of 1872, see Mark Wahlgren Summers, *The Press Gang: Newspapers and Politics, 1865–1878* (Chapel Hill: University of North Carolina Press, 1994), pp. 237–255. *New York Daily Tribune*, June 2, 1871, p. 5. For Southern politics in the 1872 election, see Perman, *Road to Redemption*, pp. 108–126.
43. *Chicago Tribune*, January 9, 1972, p. 4. *New York Daily Tribune*, January 19, 1872, p. 4. *Chicago Tribune*, January 26, 1872, p. 4.

44. In December 1871, a week after the commencement of the Forty-second Congress, Democrat John P. Shanks of Indiana introduced a bill to establish a bureau of labor, which the House promptly referred to the Committee on Education and Labor. *Congressional Record,* 42nd Cong., 2nd sess., 1871, p. 57. On December 13, 1871, the committee reported back a bill written by the driving force of the group, George F. Hoar. The new bill called for the appointment of a commission to study the wages and hours of labor in the United States, and the division of profits between labor and capital. For debates on bill, see *Congressional Record,* 42nd Cong., 2nd sess., 1871, pp. 102–105, 217–228, 251–258. Montgomery, *Beyond Equality,* pp. 373–374. *Nation,* June 13, 1872, pp. 381, 385–386. *Cincinnati Daily Gazette,* February 9, 1872, p. 2.

45. On mainstream interest in the black vote, see, for example, *Boston Evening Transcript,* July 18, 1872, p. 2, and July 22, 1872, p. 4. On black vote for Grant, see, for example, ibid., August 16, 1872, p. 2, and August 17, 1872, p. 8; James M. McPherson, "Grant or Greeley? The Abolitionist Dilemma in the Election of 1872," *American Historical Review,* 71 (October 1965): 43–61. Perman, *Road to Redemption,* pp. 145–146.

46. *Boston Evening Transcript,* July 18, 1872, p. 2. *Nation,* January 23, 1873, p. 50. On black repudiation of former abolitionist George W. Julian, see Emma Lou Thornbrough, *The Negro in Indiana before 1900* (1957; reprint, Bloomington: Indiana University Press, 1993), pp. 288–291.

47. For qualities of black "better classes," see Glenda Elizabeth Gilmore, *Gender and Jim Crow: Women and the Politics of White Supremacy in North Carolina, 1896–1920* (Chapel Hill: University of North Carolina Press, 1996); Willard B. Gatewood, *The Black Elite, 1880–1920* (Bloomington: Indiana University Press, 1990); David M. Katzman, *Before the Ghetto: Black Detroit in the Nineteenth Century* (Urbana: University of Illinois Press, 1973). Elliott, quoted in *Boston Daily Evening Transcript,* January 4, 1873, p. 6. See also *Nation,* January 23, 1873, p. 50.

48. Durden, *Pike,* pp. 201–202. The articles appeared in the *New York Daily Tribune,* March 29 and April 8, 10, 11, 12, 19, 1873. On Northern attention to South Carolina, see, for example, *Cincinnati Daily Gazette,* March 29, 1873, p. 4. On the book's popularity, see Durden, *Pike,* pp. 202–205.

49. *Nation,* January 9, 1873, p. 17, and January 30, 1873, p. 66. The Louisiana crisis still resonated in the newspapers as late as 1875. See *San Francisco Daily Alta California,* January 10, 1875, p. 2. For a brief review of Pinchback's Louisiana troubles in this period, see Maurine Christopher, *Black Americans in Congress* (New York: Thomas Y. Crowell Company, 1976), pp. 108–112. For selected documents concerning Pinchback's role in the Louisiana scandal, see Henry Clay Warmouth, *War, Politics and Reconstruction: Stormy Days in Louisiana* (New York: The Macmillan Company, 1930).

See also Perman, *Road to Redemption,* pp. 142–144.

50. For comparison of notebooks to text, see Durden, *Pike,* pp. 206–219. Pike, *Prostrate State,* pp. 10–13, 21.

51. Pike, *Prostrate State,* pp. 100–105, 53, 254, 179.

52. Ibid., p. 224, 254, 264.

53. Ibid., pp. 273–279.

54. *Cincinnati Daily Gazette,* April 16, 1873, p. 1, and April 17, 1873, p. 1.

55. For a discussion of the Colfax Massacre, see Eric Foner, *Reconstruction: America's Unfinished Revolution, 1863–1877* (New York: Harper & Row, 1988), p. 437. *Cincinnati Daily Gazette,* April 16, 1873, p. 1, and reprints from the *New Orleans Picayune,* April 8, and of the *Missouri Republican,* April 13, in *Cincinnati Daily Gazette,* April 17, 1873, p. 4. See also *Boston Evening Transcript,* April 16, 1873, p. 2.

56. *Nation,* January 22, 1874, p. 52. *Boston Evening Transcript,* March 30, 1874, p. 8, and May 26, 1874, p. 4. *Chicago Tribune,* February 18, 1874, p. 8.

57. *Philadelphia Inquirer,* April 17, 1873, p. 4. Ibid., March 31, 1873, p. 4. Ibid., April 4, 1873, p. 4. *Cincinnati Daily Gazette,* April 21, 1873, p. 4. For rhetoric against labor, see also *San Francisco Daily Alta California,* June 1, 1873, p. 2; August 27, 1873, p. 2; November 11, 1873, p. 2. See also *Philadelphia Inquirer,* June 19, 1873, p. 1, and December 24, 1873, p. 4. *Chicago Tribune,* January 5, 1874, p. 4.

58. *New York Times,* July 13, 1873, p. 4; see also ibid., May 6, 1874, p. 5.

59. *Columbia (S.C.) Daily Union,* January 7, 1873, p. 2. *Cincinnati Daily Gazette,* March 29, 1873, p. 4. *San Francisco Daily Alta California,* August 23, 1873, p. 1; August 25, 1873, p. 1. *Philadelphia Inquirer,* August 26, 1873, p. 4. *Boston Evening Transcript,* August 23, 1873, p. 2; August 29, 1873, p. 4. *New York Times,* August 26, 1873, p. 1; August 28, 1873, p. 1.

60. *Boston Evening Transcript,* January 12, 1874, p. 4. Elliott, in *New York Daily Tribune,* February 23, 1874, p. 7. Harriet Beecher Stowe, excerpt from *Palmetto Leaves,* in *Cincinnati Daily Gazette,* April 8, 1873, p. 2.

61. *Boston Evening Transcript,* September 29, 1873, p. 6. *San Francisco Daily Alta California,* October 9, 1873, p. 2, from the *New York World.*

62. Beecher article reprinted from *Christian Union* in *Charleston News and Courier,* January 6, 1874.

63. The Tax-payers had maintained a fight in the courts throughout 1873 against the validity of the state debt. See *Philadelphia Inquirer,* May 1, 1873, p. 1, and July 25, 1873, p. 1. On the convention, see *New York Daily Tribune,* January 14, 1874, p. 7. *Boston Evening Transcript,* January 14, 1874, p. 2. *New York Times,* January 14, 1874, p. 4. *Congressional Record,* 43rd Cong., 1st sess., 1874, p. 2653, Samuel J. Randall (Pa.).

64. *Boston Evening Transcript,* March 20, 1874, p. 8, identified Senator Chesnut, Governor Aiken, Governor Bonham, Governor Manning. *Philadelphia In-*

quirer, March 31, 1874, p. 1. *Congressional Record,* 43rd Cong., 1st sess., 1874, p. 2652.

65. House, *Petition of the Tax-Payers' Convention of South Carolina,* 43rd Cong., 1st sess., 1874, H. Misc. Doc. 233, pp. 1–2. *Philadelphia Inquirer,* April 1, 1874, p. 8. On 1874 Tax-payers' Convention as a fusion movement, see Perman, *Road to Redemption,* pp. 166–169.

66. *Congressional Record,* 43rd Cong., 1st sess., 1874, p. 2688. *Philadelphia Inquirer,* April 2, 1874, p. 2. *Boston Evening Transcript,* April 8, 1874, p. 2.

67. On Grant and delegation, see *Boston Evening Transcript,* March 31, 1874, p. 4; *Philadelphia Inquirer,* April 8, 1874, p. 1.

68. *San Francisco Daily Alta California,* June 16, 1874, p. 2.

69. *New York World,* April 9, 1874, p. 4. See discreetly edited letter from Colonel Richard Lathers to the *Washington Chronicle,* reprinted in the *New York World,* April 9, 1874, p. 2. *New York Times,* February 18, 1874, and February 17, 1874, p. 4. For a striking echo of Pike's opinion of immature African-American politicians and their quest for fame, see *New York Times,* January 24, 1875, p. 6. *Philadelphia Inquirer,* April 10, 1874, p. 4. The *Philadelphia Inquirer's* use of the word *class* meant "group." It did not have a specific economic connotation.

70. *Boston Evening Transcript,* February 13, 1874, p. 6.

71. *New York Times,* March 7, 1874, p. 3. For similar references to white workers, see, for example, *New York Daily Tribune,* January 13, 1874, pp. 4 and 5; January 14, 1874, p. 4. *Boston Evening Transcript,* January 14, 1874, p. 2.

72. *New York Times,* March 7, 1874, p. 3.

73. *New York Times,* March 7, 1874, p. 3. See also ibid., May 12, 1875, p. 5, and speech of Virginia Governor James L. Kemper on how African-Americans should act, printed in *San Francisco Daily Alta California,* May 19, 1874, p. 2. *Chicago Tribune,* January 2, 1874, p. 5.

74. *Charleston News and Courier,* January 12, 1874, p. 1. Ibid., January 9, 1874, p. 2; January 14, 1874, p. 1; January 15, 1874, p. 1.

75. *Harper's Weekly,* February 7, 1874. Ibid., March 14, 1874, cover. Columbia's use of "aping" was likely a reference to Darwinism and had the racial connotations of associating the African-American legislators with gorillas. Her words also refer to the pending civil rights bill. *Boston Evening Transcript,* May 23, 1874, p. 1.

76. On Butler as head of House, see *New York Daily Tribune,* March 3, 1874, p. 1. *Nation,* April 16, 1874, pp. 247–248. See also Ibid., August 27, 1874, p. 132.

77. *Scribner's Monthly,* 8, no. 2 (June 1874): 129–160. Edward King, "The South Carolina Problem: The Epoch of Transition," in ibid., p. 135.

78. *Boston Evening Transcript,* May 2, 1874, p. 6. *Cincinnati Daily Gazette,* March 16, 1875, p. 4. *San Francisco Daily Alta California,* July 8, 1875, p. 1.

79. *New York Times,* May 6, 1874, p. 5. Charles Nordhoff, *The Cotton States in*

the Spring and Summer of 1875 (New York: D. Appleton & Company, 1876), pp. 20–21.

80. *San Francisco Daily Alta California,* May 27, 1875, p. 1.

81. See Michael E. McGerr, "The Meaning of Liberal Republicanism: The Case of Ohio," *Civil War History,* 28 (December 1982): 307–323, which argues that Liberal Republicanism in Ohio was a throwback to Jacksonian Democracy, with a low-tariff, antimonopoly stand, but which also shows that Liberal Republicans did well in Democratic politics after the Liberal Republican movement failed. *San Francisco Daily Alta California,* July 8, 1875, p. 1.

82. *Beaufort (S.C.) Tribune,* quoted in *New York Times,* January 20, 1879, p. 4. *Boston Evening Transcript,* April 22, 1875, p. 4.

83. On South Carolina split, see *Boston Evening Transcript,* September 14, 1874, p. 2; *Nation,* October 1, 1874, p. 212. *Cincinnati Daily Gazette,* March 6, 1875, p. 4. *Boston Evening Transcript,* January 1, 1875, p. 4. Ibid., May 10, 1875, p. 4. On 1874 realignment and retrenchment, see Perman, *Road to Redemption,* pp. 135–164, 182–232.

84. See Edmund K. Drago, *Hurrah For Hampton! Black Red Shirts in South Carolina during Reconstruction* (Fayetteville: University of Arkansas Press, 1998). Tax protesters Wade Hampton and Martin Witherspoon Gary, for example, were former Confederate generals who were key "redeemers" in 1876. On Gary, Hampton, and the campaign, See Richard Zuczek, "The Last Campaign of the Civil War: South Carolina and the Revolution of 1876," *Civil War History,* 42, no. 1 (March 1996): 18–31. On Hayes's courting of progressive Southerners, see Perman, *Road to Redemption,* pp. 267–270.

4 Civil Rights and the Growth of the National Government, 1870–1883

1. *Harper's Weekly,* June 1, 1867, p. 338. See also address of William Henry Seward in New York on February 28, 1866, reprinted in *New York World,* November 8, 1867, p. 2. *New York World,* November 22, 1867, p. 4; and see reference there to similar article in *Louisville (Ky.) Courier* [Democratic]. On civil rights, see Herman Belz, *Emancipation and Equal Rights: Politics and Constitutionalism in the Civil War Era* (New York: W. W. Norton & Co., 1978), pp. 108–140.

2. See, for example, Paul E. Johnson, *A Shopkeeper's Millennium: Society and Revivals in Rochester, New York, 1815–1837* (New York: Hill and Wang, 1978).

3. *Cincinnati Daily Gazette,* May 30, 1867, p. 1. See also *Philadelphia Inquirer,* May 21, 1867, p. 1. "Resolutions of a Freedmen's Convention," in *Black Reconstructionists,* ed. Emma Lou Thornbrough (Englewood Cliffs, N.J.: Prentice-Hall, 1972), p. 33.

4. *New York World,* December 10, 1867, p. 2. *Columbus (Ohio) Crisis,* April 17, 1867, p. 94. *De Bow's Review,* quoted in *Chicago Tribune,* July 6, 1868, p. 2.

5. *New York Times,* August 22, 1868, p. 4. Ibid., May 14, 1869, p. 4.

6. Eric Foner, *Reconstruction: America's Unfinished Revolution, 1863–1877* (New York: Harper & Row, 1988), pp. 365–372. Brown quotation is on p. 369.

7. The definitive biography of Sumner is David Herbert Donald, *Charles Sumner* (New York: Da Capo Press, 1996). For earlier accusations that Sumner was going too far in his attempts to protect African-Americans, see Heather Cox Richardson, *The Greatest Nation of the Earth: Republican Economic Policies during the Civil War* (Cambridge, Mass.: Harvard University Press, 1997), pp. 233–234. Charles Sumner, *Congressional Globe,* 41st Cong., 2nd sess., May 13, 1870, p. 3434. *Congressional Globe,* 41st Cong., 2nd sess., July 7, 1870, p. 5314.

8. *New York World,* January 21, 1871, pp. 1 and 4.

9. *Chicago Tribune,* April 2, 1871, p. 2.

10. *Boston Evening Transcript,* January 16, 1872, p. 2.

11. Donald, *Sumner.* See article in *Boston Evening Transcript,* June 5, 1872, p. 2, which lists individuals and newspapers that censured Sumner for his attack on Grant. Ibid., August 13, 1872, p. 4. On Sumner and Douglass and the alignments in this election, see James M. McPherson, "Grant or Greeley: The Abolitionist Dilemma in the Election of 1872," *American Historical Review,* 71 (October 1965): 43–61. *Congressional Globe,* 42nd Cong., 2nd sess., p. 880, in Donald, *Sumner,* pp. 534–535. Michael Perman, *The Road to Redemption: Southern Politics, 1869–1879* (Chapel Hill: University of North Carolina Press, 1984), pp. 139–141, agrees that regular Republicans pushed the bill to cement black loyalty.

12. For Senate rejection of amendment, see *Congressional Globe,* 42nd Cong., 2nd sess., pp. 928–929, and 3268–3270. For an excellent summary of the 1872 fight over the measure, see Donald, *Sumner,* pp. 539–549. See also Bertram Wyatt-Brown, "The Civil Rights Act of 1875," *Western Political Quarterly,* 18 (June 1965): 769.

13. On Sumner, the civil rights bill, and the presidential campaign, see, for example, *Boston Evening Transcript,* July 13, 1872, p. 8; July 24, 1872, p. 4; July 31, 1872, p. 4. For Democratic accusations about the political motivations behind the civil rights bill, see, for example, *San Francisco Examiner,* October 25, 1883, p. 2.

14. See, for example, *Philadelphia Daily Evening Bulletin,* October 16, 1872, p. 4, and November 8, 1872, p. 4. *Boston Evening Transcript,* August 6, 1872, p. 4. Ibid., August 1, 1872, p. 2.

15. *Boston Evening Transcript,* July 31, 1872, p. 4. *Nation,* March 13, 1873, p. 173.

16. *Boston Evening Transcript,* July 31, 1872, p. 1. *Nation,* March 13, 1873, p. 173.

17. *New York Times,* November 1, 1873, p. 4. *Boston Evening Transcript,* August 14, 1873, p. 4. See also ibid., June 9, 1873, p. 8. *Philadelphia Inquirer,* August 8, 1873, p. 4. *San Francisco Daily Alta California,* February 15, 1873, p. 2, and August 16, 1873, p. 2.

18. *Cincinnati Daily Gazette,* April 16, 1873, p. 1, and reprints from the *New Orleans Picayune,* April 8, and the *Missouri Republican,* April 13, in *Cincinnati Daily Gazette,* April 17, 1873, p. 4. See also *Boston Evening Transcript,* April 16, 1873, p. 2. Ibid., April 22, 1873, p. 1. On fears of black organization for political offices, see, for example, *New York Times,* August 26, 1873, p. 1, and August 28, 1873, p. 1; *Boston Evening Transcript,* August 23, 1873, p. 2, and August 29, 1873, p. 4. *Boston Evening Transcript,* September 10, 1873, p. 2.

19. *Boston Evening Transcript,* February 27, 1873, p. 6. Ibid., September 30, 1873, p. 8.

20. On challenge to all-white juries, see *Boston Evening Transcript,* March 31, 1873, p. 8. For AP story on a Kentucky "Colored Educational Union," see ibid., February 19, 1873, p. 4. Douglas Henry Daniels, *Pioneer Urbanites: A Social and Cultural History of Black San Francisco* (Philadelphia: Temple University Press, 1980). *San Francisco Daily Alta California,* April 1, 1873, p. 1. Ibid., November 26, 1873, p. 4. *Boston Evening Transcript,* July 14, 1873, p. 4. *New York Times,* September 12, 1873, p. 5.

21. See, for example, *Boston Evening Transcript,* July 30, 1873, p. 2.

22. For a brief, comprehensive history of the civil rights bill, see *San Francisco Daily Alta California,* January 20, 1875, p. 1. For statement that the bill would never reappear, see *Philadelphia Inquirer,* January 6, 1874, p. 1.

23. *New York Daily Tribune,* January 7, 1874, p. 1. *San Francisco Daily Alta California,* November 26, 1873, p. 1, and December 10, 1873, p. 1. See *Chicago Tribune,* January 2, 1874, p. 3, in which prominent African-American county commissioner John Jones publicly demanded the passage of the bill, threatening black abandonment of the Republican party if it should not pass, but emphasized, "We are not demanding what is known as social rights. These social relations lie entirely outside the domain of legislation and politics."

24. *Philadelphia Inquirer,* January 7, 1874, pp. 1, 8. *New York Daily Tribune,* January 7, 1874, p. 6. *Chicago Tribune,* January 7, 1874, p. 4; January 8, 1874, p. 4; January 16, 1874, p. 2. See also *New York Daily Tribune,* January 9, 1874, p. 6, reprint of article from *New York Commercial Advertiser. Philadelphia Inquirer,* January 6, 1874, p. 4. *Nation,* January 8, 1874, p. 17.

25. *Philadelphia Daily Evening Bulletin,* May 25, 1874, p. 4.

26. *New York Daily Tribune*, February 19, 1874, p. 2. Ibid., January 3, 1874, p. 5. For the development of this argument, see George Washington Cable, "The Freedmen's Case in Equity," *Century*, 29 (January 1885): 409–419.

27. On dislike of the bill, see, for example, *Nation*, January 8, 1874, p. 17, and *Philadelphia Inquirer*, January 14, 1874, p. 4. On Democratic opposition to bill, see, for example, *Boston Evening Transcript*, January 23, 1874, p. 8. Jean H. Baker, *Affairs of Party: The Political Culture of Northern Democrats in the Mid-Nineteenth Century* (1983; reprint, New York: Fordham University Press, 1998), pp. 143–176. *Columbus (Ohio) Crisis*, March 27, 1867, p. 68. See also *Providence Daily Post*, which called Republicans "the party of centralization" (January 11, 1867, p. 1). *New York Times*, January 15, 1879, p. 4. *New York World*, May 1, 1874, p. 4.

28. *Harper's Weekly*, February 2, 1867, p. 66. On the party regularity of the justices, see James G. Blaine, *Twenty Years of Congress*, vol. 1 (Norwich, Conn.: The Henry Bill Publishing Company, 1884), p. 540. President Lincoln had appointed Chief Justice Salmon P. Chase and four of the other justices. On *Slaughterhouse Cases* and civil rights bill, see *Nation*, January 8, 1874, p. 17, and *New York World*, May 1, 1874, p. 4.

29. *Philadelphia Daily Evening Bulletin*, May 26, 1874, p. 3. *San Francisco Daily Alta California*, December 3, 1873, p. 1. Israel Washburn, in Gaillard Hunt, *Israel, Elihu and Cadwallader Washburn: A Chapter in American Biography* (New York: The Macmillan Company, 1925), pp. 149–151.

30. Article from *Cincinnati Daily Gazette*, reprinted in *New York Daily Tribune*, January 2, 1874, p. 8. *Worcester Spy*, reprinted in *New York Daily Tribune*, February 16, 1874, p. 7. See also report of Henry L. Dawes, in *Nation*, February 19, 1874, p. 115.

31. *Cincinnati Daily Gazette*, March 6, 1875, p. 4. For a discussion of patronage as social welfare, see Theda Skocpol, *Protecting Soldiers and Mothers: The Political Origins of Social Policy in the United States* (Cambridge, Mass.: Harvard University Press, 1992).

32. The *Chicago Tribune* highlighted the story of an African-American man traveling first class on a steamer from Detroit to Put-in-Bay, Ohio, who was awarded $100 in damages by a jury that agreed he had been illegally refused food—all this under existing legislation (*Chicago Tribune*, January 23, 1874, p. 8). *Philadelphia Inquirer*, March 18, 1867, p. 4. For an article comparing Jews and African-Americans as scapegoats, see also *Cincinnati Daily Gazette*, February 1, 1873, p. 2. The *Philadelphia Daily Evening Bulletin* bemoaned the "brutal folly" of prejudice that cursed the world, and noted that "the suffering that has been caused by it, in the case of the Jews for example, is incalculably great" (June 4, 1880, p. 4). *Chicago Tribune*, June 8, 1874, p. 4. Ibid., January 12, 1874, p. 4.

33. *Chicago Tribune,* January 2, 1874, p. 2. See also *New York Daily Tribune,* January 31, 1874, p. 6. In January 1874, New York City's Association for Improving the Condition of the Poor gave relief aid to 22,000 people (*Boston Evening Transcript,* February 13, 1874, p. 8). On unemployed laborers demanding help from the government, see *New York Daily Tribune,* January 6, 1874, p. 5; also ibid., January 24, 1874, p. 12. Congressional Committee on Education and Labor, quoted in *Philadelphia Inquirer,* January 8, 1874, p. 8. *Boston Evening Transcript,* May 20, 1874, p. 1.

34. *New York Daily Tribune,* January 2, 1874, p. 8. Ibid., January 1, 1874, p. 6. *Boston Evening Transcript,* July 30, 1874, p. 8.

35. *Boston Evening Transcript,* February 13, 1874, p. 8; *New York Daily Tribune,* January 10, 1874, p. 1; *Chicago Tribune,* January 12, 1874, p. 4.

36. Foner, *Reconstruction,* p. 366. General Swayne, assistant commissioner of the Freedmen's Bureau in Alabama, in *Harper's Weekly,* January 11, 1868, p. 18. The *Baltimore Sun* gave the New Orleans appropriation as $60,000 (July 18, 1867, p. 1). See article from *New York Post* in *Boston Evening Transcript,* March 7, 1873, p. 3; *Boston Evening Transcript,* April 11, 1873, p. 8; *Nation,* February 20, 1873, p. 131. *Boston Evening Transcript,* October 8, 1873, p. 4. *Harper's Weekly,* October 26, 1867, p. 675. *New York Daily Tribune,* February 16, 1874, p. 3.

37. *Boston Evening Transcript,* July 23, 1873, p. 8.

38. *New York Daily Tribune,* January 10, 1874, p. 1. See also January 15, 1874, p. 6. *Cherokee Advocate,* January 24, 1874, p. 2.

39. *San Francisco Daily Alta California,* July 15, 1874, p. 2.

40. *Philadelphia Inquirer,* January 20, 1874, p. 4. *New York Daily Tribune,* January 13, 1874, p. 4. On role of army in Reconstruction and Grant's eventual abandonment of its use, see James E. Sefton, *The United States Army and Reconstruction, 1865–1877* (1967; reprint, Westport, Conn.: Greenwood Press, 1980).

41. See *Chicago Tribune,* January 24, 1874, p. 4. *New York Daily Tribune,* March 12, 1874, p. 4. See also ibid., March 16, 1874, p. 6, and March 24, 1874, p. 1. For a critique of Butler, see George F. Hoar, *Autobiography of Seventy Years,* vol. 2 (New York: Charles Scribner's Sons, 1903), pp. 312, 329–363.

42. Donald, *Sumner,* p. 586. For a newspaper version of the conversation between Sumner and Hoar, see *Chicago Tribune,* March 12, 1874, p. 1. Ibid., March 12, 1874, p. 4, and March 17, 1874, p. 4. *San Francisco Daily Alta California,* March 14, 1874, p. 1. *Boston Evening Transcript,* March 31, 1874, p. 2; May 4, 1874, p. 8; May 8, 1874, p. 8; May 11, 1874, p. 8.

43. On passage of bill, see *Philadelphia Inquirer,* May 25, 1874, p. 1; *Boston Evening Transcript,* May 23, 1874, p. 1, 4. Ibid., May 25, 1874, p. 8. Article from *New York Times,* reprinted in *Philadelphia Daily Evening Bulletin,* May 26, 1874, p. 3. See also *Philadelphia Inquirer,* May 25, 1874, p. 4. *Boston Evening*

Transcript, May 22, 1874, p. 8; May 25, 1874, p. 8; June 8, 1874, p. 8; June 11, 1874, p. 8.

44. *Boston Evening Transcript,* August 2, 1874, p. 4; August 7, 1874, p. 2; August 8, 1874, p. 4.

45. Ibid., September 25, 1874, p. 2.

46. Ibid., January 1, 1875, p. 4. *Springfield (Mass.) Republican,* February 4, 1875, and January 28, 1875, in Wyatt-Brown, "Civil Rights Act," p. 773. See also ibid., pp. 771–774. *Boston Evening Transcript,* January 5, 1875, p. 8; January 27, 1875, p. 8.

47. *Boston Evening Transcript,* February 4, 1875, p. 2, and February 5, 1875, p. 8. *San Francisco Daily Alta California,* February 6, 1875, p. 1, and January 20, 1875, p. 1; also House Misc. Doc. 44, 43rd Cong., 1st sess. For another radical newspaper's approval of the bill, see *Cincinnati Daily Gazette,* March 4, 1875, p. 4. *San Francisco Daily Alta California,* February 7, 1875, p. 1. *Boston Evening Transcript,* February 19, 1875, p. 8. Matthew Carpenter of Wisconsin was the only Republican to vote nay. The *Boston Evening Transcript,* admonished that "[t]he course of the Democrats, North and South, against 'civil rights,' affords a good criterion for judging the exact value of their promises, in both sections, of equal rights to the colored man" (January 28, 1875, p. 4; see also ibid., February 6, 1875, p. 4; February 8, 1875, p. 4; February 9, 1875, p. 4). On passage, see ibid., March 4, 1875, p. 6.

48. *Boston Evening Transcript,* March 3, 1875, p. 4. *New York Times,* March 6, 1875, p. 4. *San Francisco Daily Alta California,* March 8, 1875, p. 2.

49. *New York Times,* June 21, 1875, p. 2. *Cincinnati Daily Gazette,* March 6, 1875, p. 5. See also ibid., March 8, 1875, p. 2.

50. *Boston Evening Transcript,* March 8, 1875, p. 2; March 11, 1875, p. 2; March 12, 1875, p. 8. *San Francisco Daily Alta California,* March 7, 1875, p. 1. *Birmingham (N.Y.) Republican* quoted in *San Francisco Daily Alta California,* April 4, 1875, p. 1. *San Francisco Daily Alta California,* April 4, 1875, p. 1, and March 21, 1875, p. 1. See also John Hope Franklin, "The Enforcement of the Civil Rights Act of 1875," reprinted in Donald G. Nieman, ed., *African-American Life in the Post-Emancipation South, 1861–1900,* vol. 4: *African Americans and Non-Agricultural Labor in the South, 1865–1900* (New York: Garland Publishing, 1994), pp. 103–113.

51. *San Francisco Daily Alta California,* April 4, 1875, p. 1.

52. *New York Times,* April 25, 1880, p. 1. See also ibid., July 30, 1880, p. 4.

53. *Philadelphia Daily Evening Bulletin,* May 11, 1880, p. 4. Compare this article to that in ibid., June 4, 1880, p. 4, which bemoaned continuing racism. *New York Daily Tribune,* May 20, 1880, p. 4. From *Boston Journal,* in *New York Times,* April 28, 1879, p. 5. *New York Times,* May 14, 1880, p. 3. From *Boston Traveller,* in *New York Times,* September 17, 1880, p. 3.

54. For an account of the Whittaker affair, see John F. Marszalek, *Assault at West*

Point: The Court-Martial of Johnson Whittaker (n. p.: John F. Marszalek, 1984).

55. *Detroit Evening News,* May 19, 1880, p. 2. *New York Daily Tribune,* May 20, 1880, p. 4, and May 21, 1880, p. 4. *New York Herald,* May 23, 1880, p. 10. *Chicago Tribune,* April 19, 1880, p. 6. Ibid., April 21, 1880, p. 4. See also ibid., April 24, 1880, p. 4. See personal account of his own ordeal from another black cadet, from the *St. Louis Globe-Democrat,* reprinted in *Chicago Tribune,* April 27, 1880, p. 3. *New York Times,* May 3, 1880, p. 4.

56. On handwriting testimony, see *New York Herald,* May 1, 1880, p. 10; May 4, 1880, pp. 5 and 6; May 5, 1880, p. 10; May 6, 1880, pp. 5 and 6; May 8, 1880, p. 5; May 9, 1880, p. 5; May 13, 1880, p. 5; May 14, 1880, p. 4; May 16, 1880, pp. 8 and 10. See also *New York Daily Tribune,* May 20, 1880, p. 4.

57. *Harper's Weekly,* January 4, 1879, p. 2.

58. *New York Herald,* May 16, 1880, p. 8.

59. Ibid., May 18, 1880, p. 6, and June 1, 1880, p. 6. *Philadelphia Inquirer,* May 31, 1880, p. 4. For review of case and findings, see *New York Herald,* May 30, 1880, p. 12.

60. *Washington Post,* June 2, 1880, p. 2. See also *New York Herald,* May 30, 1880, p. 10.

61. *New York Times,* August 28, 1880, p. 1; September 14, 1880, p. 4; September 17, 1880, p. 3; October 22, 1880, pp. 2 and 4; October 30, 1880, p. 4; November 26, 1880, p. 3.

62. *New York Times,* October 16, 1883, p. 4, and October 18, 1883, p. 4. *Hartford Courant,* October 16, 1883, p. 2, and October 19, 1883, p. 2. *Philadelphia Daily Evening Bulletin,* October 16, 1883, p. 4. *Cleveland Gazette,* October 20, 1883, p. 2.

63. *New York Times,* September 26, 1883, p. 1; September 28, 1883, pp. 4 and 5. The convention was held a month before the Supreme Court declared the Civil Rights Act of 1875 unconstitutional, during a period of agitation about the issue. Douglass was very vocal about his views. For Douglass's views on the reversal, see Frederick Douglass, *Life and Times of Frederick Douglass,* (New York: Library of America, 1994), pp. 966–980. See also *New York Times,* October 17, 1883, p. 4. For a brief discussion of the larger meaning of Douglass's opposition to the 1883 decision, see David W. Blight, *Frederick Douglass' Civil War: Keeping Faith in Jubilee* (Baton Rouge: Louisiana State University Press, 1989), pp. 221–222. On Douglass's speech to the convention, see *Cleveland Gazette,* September 29, 1883, p. 1. *New York Times,* September 29, 1883, pp. 1 and 4.

64. *Cleveland Gazette,* October 20, 1883, p. 2. *Boston Evening Transcript,* October 23, 1883, p. 2. *San Francisco Examiner,* October 19, 1883, p. 1. See also ibid., October 21, 1883, p. 8. For call to a meeting in Connecticut, see *Hartford Weekly Times,* December 13, 1883, p. 4.

65. For statements that the decision would change nothing for the worse, see, for example, *New York Times,* October 16, 1883, p. 4, and October 24, 1883, p. 1; *Philadelphia Daily Evening Bulletin,* October 18, 1883, p. 1. For negative portrayals of opposition to the decision, see, for example, *New York Times,* November 9, 1883, p. 5. Ibid., October 26, 1883, p. 4; December 31, 1883, p. 2.

66. Article from the *Chicago Tribune,* in *Philadelphia Evening Bulletin,* October 22, 1883, p. 1. *Hartford Courant,* October 19, 1883, p. 2. *Hartford Weekly Times,* October 25, 1883, p. 4. On Jews and Saratoga hotels, see also *New York Herald,* May 30, 1880, p. 12.

67. *Philadelphia Daily Evening Bulletin,* October 16, 1883, p. 4. *Hartford Weekly Times,* November 22,, 1883, p. 1.

68. Letter of Mrs. F. W. Corbin, in *Cleveland Gazette,* December 1, 1883, p. 4. *Philadelphia Daily Evening Bulletin,* October 17, 1883, p. 2.

69. *San Francisco Examiner,* October 17, 1883, p. 2; October 20, 1883, p. 2; October 28, 1883, p. 5. See also *Hartford Weekly Times,* October 18, 1883, p. 4.

70. *San Francisco Examiner,* October 17, 1883, p. 2.

71. *New York Times,* June 15, 1885, p. 1; see also ibid., June 16, 1885, p. 3.

5 The Black Exodus from the South, 1879–1880

1. In the lower South, fewer than 20 percent of African-American farmers owned their own land in 1920. See Loren Schweninger, "A Vanishing Breed: Black Farm Owners in the South, 1651–1982," *Agricultural History,* 63 (Summer 1989): 41–60.

2. For African-American organizing, see *New York Times,* January 2, 1879, p. 4. *Harper's Weekly,* January 18, 1879, p. 52.

3. *Congressional Record,* 45th Congress, 3rd sess., 1879, p. 483. On Southern African-Americans and the Exodus, see Nell Irvin Painter, *Exodusters: Black Migration to Kansas after Reconstruction* (New York: Alfred A. Knopf, 1977), pp. 82–117; 137–159. On effect of new constitution on emigration, see *New York Times,* April 24, 1879, p. 4.

4. *Washington Post,* January 20, 1879, p. 1. *Cincinnati Daily Gazette,* January 23, 1879, pp. 1, 4. On Windom and Exodus, see Robert S. Salisbury: *William Windom: Apostle of Positive Government* (Lanham, Md.: University Press of America, 1993), pp. 178–202.

5. *Harper's Weekly,* October 11, 1879, p. 803.

6. Wm. L. Helfenstein to R. B. Hayes, April 3, 1879, R. B. Hayes MSS, Library of Congress, on microfilm.

7. *Cincinnati Daily Gazette,* March 3, 1879, pp. 4 and 5; March 5, 1879, p. 7. George F. Hoar, *Congressional Record,* 45th Cong., 3rd sess., 1879, p. 2225. *Congressional Record,* 45th Congress, 3rd sess., 1879, p. 2226. On Lamar's

continuing affection for Davis, see George F. Hoar, *Autobiography of Seventy Years*, vol. 2 (New York: Charles Scribner's Sons, 1903), p. 177. *Congressional Record*, 45th Cong., 3rd sess., 1879, pp. 2227, 2238, 2230.

8. Article from the *Boston Journal*, reprinted in *Cincinnati Daily Gazette*, March 14, 1879, p. 5. *New York Times*, April 4, 1879, p. 5. See, for example, article from *Chicago Times* in *Cincinnati Daily Gazette*, March 24, 1879, p. 7, and *Chicago Times*, April 4, 1879, in William Henry Jewitt [?] to R. B. Hayes, April 5, 1879, R. B. Hayes MSS. See also *New York World*, June 3, 1879, p. 4. *Washington Post*, March 26, 1879, p. 2. The *Cincinnati Commercial* reflected that "[t]he Confederate crowd waiting for the little offices about the Senate is a melancholy spectacle" (quoted in *Washington Post*, March 29, 1879, p. 3).

9. *Washington Post*, April 1, 1879, p. 2. President Hayes received another poem written by Hank Wagoner of California and dedicated to "Benjamin Hill's Confederate Senate"; see Hank Wagoner to R. B. Hayes, April 1879, R. B. Hayes MSS. When a Republican newspaper asserted, "If George Washington were alive now, he would oppose many of the measures advocated by Southern leaders in Congress," a Democratic editor retorted that "if George Washington had lived to this day he would now be too old to take interest in public affairs, and would be mainly remarkable as the oldest person on earth" (*Washington Post*, January 17, 1879, p. 2). See, for example, *Cincinnati Daily Gazette*, March, 28, 1879, p. 4, and February 4, 1879, p. 4. See also articles from the *Chicago Times* and the *Chicago Tribune*, in *Cincinnati Daily Gazette*, March 5, 1879, p. 7. For a speech by John Sherman on Southern domination, see *New York Times*, July 25, 1879, p. 4. On "Confederates" in 1880 election, see C. Waggoner to Rutherford B. Hayes, April 3, 1879, R. B. Hayes MSS.

10. *Cincinnati Daily Gazette*, March 12, 1879, p. 4. Article from Augusta, Georgia, *Chronicle and Sentinel*, reprinted in *Cincinnati Daily Gazette*, March 18, 1879, p. 5. Article from *New York Times*, reprinted in *Cincinnati Daily Gazette*, March 15, 1879, p. 5. In 1887, an article in *Forum* echoed this argument, saying that Alston had been murdered by a lessee. See Rebecca L. Felton, "The Convict Leasing System of Georgia," *Forum* (January 1887): 484–490.

11. *Cincinnati Daily Gazette*, March 14, 1879, p. 4. See also article from *Philadelphia Press*, reprinted in *Cincinnati Daily Gazette*, March 14, 1879, p. 5. *Cincinnati Daily Gazette*, March 20, 1879, pp. 4 and 5. *Harper's Weekly*, April 5, 1879, p. 276.

12. The press had periodically noted the gradual migration out of the South since the war. See, for example, *San Francisco Daily Alta California*, February 22, 1873, p. 4. Painter, *Exodusters*, pp. 184–201, 256–261. For an African-American account of the Exodus, see the *Vidalia (La.) Concordia*

Eagle [African-American], March 27, 1879, p. 3. On Exodus, see Robert G. Athearn, *In Search of Canaan: Black Migration to Kansas, 1879–80* (Lawrence: Regents Press of Kansas, 1978). On Kansas life of Exodusters, see Randall Bennett Wood, *Black Odyssey: John Lewis Waller and the Promise of American Life, 1878–1900* (Lawrence: Regents Press of Kansas, 1981); Norman L. Crockett, *The Black Towns* (Lawrence: Regents Press of Kansas, 1979); and Jacob U. Gordon, *Narratives of African-Americans in Kansas, 1870–1992: Beyond the Exodust Movement* (Lewiston, N.Y.: E. Mellen Press, 1993).

13. *New York Times,* April 19, 1879, p. 4, and April 21, 1879, p. 4.

14. For a detailed discussion of the appropriations fight, see Ari Hoogenboom, *The Presidency of Rutherford B. Hayes* (Lawrence: University Press of Kansas, 1988), pp. 75–78. *New York Times,* April 4, 1879, p. 5. Ibid., May 5, 1879, p. 2.

15. Robert V. Bruce, *1877: Year of Violence* (Indianapolis: Bobbs-Merrill, 1959). Allan Pinkerton, *Strikers, Communists, Tramps and Detectives* (1878; reprint, New York: Arno Press, 1969), pp. 19–20.

16. *Harper's Weekly,* February 1, 1879, p. 92; September 6, 1879, p. 716; May 31, 1879, p. 428; March 8, 1879, p. 196.

17. *San Francisco Daily Alta California,* June 4, 1880, p. 2. *New York Herald,* May 1, 1880, p. 8.

18. *Cincinnati Daily Gazette,* April 2, 1879, p. 4. *Washington Post,* March 17, 1879, p. 1. Ibid., March 18, 1879, p. 2. See also conversation with Democratic planter from Louisiana, in *Harper's Weekly,* May 24, 1879, p. 402. A. J. Gilkey to *New York World,* June 13, 1879, p. 8. See also *New York World,* June 13, 1879, p. 4.

19. *Cincinnati Daily Gazette,* April 2, 1879, p. 4; April 4, 1879, p. 4. *New York Times,* March 18, 1879, p. 3. See also ibid., April 6, 1879, p. 6. *New York Daily Tribune,* in *Washington Post,* March 20, 1879, p. 2. *New York Times,* April 7, 1879, p. 4. See also ibid., April 24, 1879, p. 4.

20. *New York Times,* April 24, 1879, p. 2; April 19, 1879, p. 4.

21. *Cincinnati Daily Gazette,* March 28, 1879, p. 4. *Washington Post,* March 24, 1879, p. 3. On Kansans' dislike of Exodusters, see, for example, *New York Times,* April 27, 1879, p. 1. *Lawrence {Ks.) Journal,* April 22, 1879, reprinted in *New York Times,* April 29, 1879, p. 2. Thurlow Weed, speech at Cooper Union, in *New York Times,* April 24, 1879, p. 5.

22. *Harper's Weekly,* December 6, 1879, p. 950; May 17, 1879, p. 386.

23. *New York Times,* April 7, 1876; March 1, 1877, p. 4. *Harper's Weekly,* February 3, 1879. See, also, for example, ibid., March 29, 1879, p. 256; September 13, 1879, p. 721; November 22, 1879, p. 923. See also *Cincinnati Daily Gazette,* March 7, 1879, p. 4.

24. *New York Times,* September 23, 1879, p. 4.

25. For accusation that radicals were misrepresenting the causes of the Exodus, see, for example, *Washington Post,* March 27, 1879, p. 2. *Harper's Weekly,* May 26, 1879, p. 322. *New York Times,* October 6, 1879, p. 4. See also *Harper's Weekly,* May 17, 1879, p. 386, and *New York Times,* May 2, 1879, p. 4. *Harper's Weekly,* April 26, 1879, p. 321.

26. *Harper's Weekly,* May 17, 1879, p. 386; November 29, 1879, p. 934; November 1, 1879, p. 861.

27. *New York Times,* March 18, 1879, p. 3. For reports of relief funds flooding in, see *New York Times,* April 30, 1879, p. 1; May 6, 1879, p. 2. See, for example, *Cincinnati Daily Gazette,* April 2, 1879, p. 8. J. C. Hebbard to R. B. Hayes, April 1879, R. B. Hayes MSS. *Cincinnati Daily Gazette,* April 4, 1879, p. 4. Capt. George W. Williams et al., Headquarters of Cincinnati Refugee Relief Committee, to the Public, April 1879, in R. B. Hayes MSS. *New York Times,* April 24, 1879, p. 5; April 25, 1879, p. 5. *Harper's Weekly,* May 17, 1879, p. 386.

28. Speech of William Windom reported in *Washington Post,* March 24, 1879, p. 3. *Cincinnati Daily Gazette,* March 28, 1879, p. 4; April 2, 1879, pp. 4 and 8; April 7, 1879; p. 4. *Chicago Tribune,* March 29, 1879, p. 4; April 2, 1879, p. 12. *New York World,* May 3, 1879, p. 8. Article from the *San Francisco Chronicle,* in *New York Times,* April 28, 1879, p. 2. *New York Times,* April 30, 1879, p. 1; April 6, 1879, p. 6; March 30, 1880, p. 4. *Harper's Weekly,* April 26, 1879, p. 322; May 3, 1879, p. 356; November 29, 1879, p. 934; December 6, 1879, p. 950. Letter of Wendell Phillips, in *New York Times,* April 24, 1879, p. 5.

29. Circular of the Principia Club, quoted in *New York Times,* April 29, 1879, p. 1. See also speech of George S. Boutwell at rally in Boston, reported in *New York Times,* April 25, 1879, p. 5. *New York Times,* March 10, 1879, p. 4.

30. On Vicksburg convention, see Painter, *Exodusters,* pp. 216–220. *New York World,* May 6, 1879, p. 8. *New York Times,* May 5, 1879, p. 1; May 6, 1879, p. 2.

31. William Windom and Henry W. Blair, "The Proceedings of a Migration Convention and Congressional Action Respecting the Exodus of 1879," *Journal of Negro History,* 4 (January 1919): 51–92 (from http://www.jstor.org). See also *Harper's Weekly,* May 24, 1879, p. 403. *New York World,* May 7, 1879, p. 8.

32. *New York World,* May 6, 1879, p. 8. *New York Herald,* May 8, 1879, in Painter, *Exodusters,* p. 219. *New York Times,* May 8, 1879, p. 4. *Harper's Weekly,* May 24, 1879, p. 402.

33. Painter, *Exodusters,* pp. 220–223. On similarities between the Vicksburg and Nashville conventions, see article from *Boston Transcript,* May 7, 1879, reprinted in *New York World,* May 9, 1879, p. 2. *Proceedings of the National Conference of Colored Men of the United States* (Washington, 1879), in

Painter, *Exodusters*, p. 223. *New York World*, May 7, 1879, p. 8. *Washington Post*, February 13, 1879, p. 1. *New York Times*, May 5, 1879, p. 1. Letter from Frederick Douglass, printed in *Vicksburg Commercial Daily Advertiser*, May 7, 1879, reprinted in Windom and Blair, "The Proceedings of a Migration Convention and Congressional Action Respecting the Exodus of 1879," pp. 56–57. *New York Times*, April 24, 1879, p. 5.

34. *New York Times*, May 8, 1879, p. 4. See also *Harper's Weekly*, November 29, 1879, p. 934. *New York Times*, April 26, 1879, p. 1; July 3, 1879, p. 4; April 3, 1879, p. 4. Thomas Nast, incidentally, was not convinced by the Vicksburg convention. The May 31 cover of *Harper's Weekly* showed Southern whites welcoming African-Americans back to the South, but suggested that this was like the spider inviting the fly into her parlor (*Harper's Weekly*, May 31, 1879, p. 421).

35. *New York Times*, May 8, 1879, p. 4. *Philadelphia Inquirer*, January 16, 1880, p. 4.

36. *Philadelphia Inquirer*, January 2, 1880, p. 4.

37. *New York World*, June 9, 1879, p. 1.

38. On Georgia freedpeople's property holding, see article from *Atlanta Constitution*, November 28, 1879, reprinted in *New York Times*, December 1, 1879, p. 8. *Harper's Weekly*, May 31, 1879, p. 423.

39. *Harper's Weekly*, April 26, 1879, p. 322.

40. On African-American migration to Indiana and life there, see Emma Lou Thornbrough, *The Negro in Indiana before 1900* (1957; reprint, Bloomington: Indiana University Press, 1993), pp. 206–230.

41. *Congressional Record*, 46th Cong., 2nd sess., December 18, 1879, p. 155. The Democratic St. Louis *Post-Dispatch*, December 19, 1879, p. 4, snarled that "Senator Windom, the enemy of the negro race, is still busying himself in Washington with his scheme to transfer the negroes of the South to the fertile Northwest." *Report and Testimony of the Select Committee of the United States Senate to Investigate the Causes of the Removal of the Negroes from the Southern States to the Northern States*, 46th Cong., 2nd sess., Senate Report 693, p. iii; hereinafter cited as *Senate Exodus Report*.

42. *Senate Exodus Report*, pp. iii, ix.

43. *New York Times*, January 3, 1880, p. 5. *Philadelphia Inquirer*, January 26, 1880, p. 4. *New York Times*, January 5, 1880, p. 4; January 24, 1880, p. 4; February 7, 1880, p. 4; February 19, 1880, p. 4.

44. *San Francisco Daily Alta California*, June 4, 1880, p. 2. Article from *Indianapolis Daily Journal*, reprinted in *Chicago Tribune*, January 12, 1880, p. 3. *Harper's Weekly*, January 31, 1880, p. 65.

45. *Philadelphia Inquirer*, January 14, 1880, p. 8, and January 28, 1880, p. 1. *Chicago Tribune*, January 3, 1880, p. 9; January 27, 1880, pp. 3 and p. 4.

46. AP dispatch to *San Francisco Daily Alta California*, June 9, 1880, p. 4.

47. *Philadelphia Inquirer,* June 5, 1880, p. 1. *Philadelphia Daily Evening Bulletin,* June 5, 1880, p. 4. *New York Times,* June 3, 1880, p. 4. See also *New York Times,* June 5, 1880, p. 4. *Senate Exodus Report,* pp. vi–vii. For approbation of the report, see *Washington Post,* June 2, 1880, p. 1.

48. *Philadelphia Daily Evening Bulletin,* June 5, 1880, p. 4. See also continuing Republican stories of Southern atrocities: *New York Times,* August 18, 1880, p. 4; August 13, 1880, p. 4; September 7, 1880, p. 4; September 14, 1880, p. 4; and Gov. J. P. St. John, quoted in *New York Times,* December 9, 1880, p. 2.

49. AP report in *Philadelphia Inquirer,* January 27, 1880, p. 1, and in *Chicago Tribune,* January 31, 1880, p. 2.

50. *Senate Exodus Report,* pp. 49–71.

51. On black classes, see Willard B. Gatewood, Jr., "Aristocrats of Color: South and North, the Black Elite 1880–1920," *Journal of Southern History,* 54 (February 1988): 3–20, and his bibliographical footnote, p. 4.

52. *Senate Exodus Report,* pp. 261–263.

53. Ibid., pp. 280–303.

54. Ibid.

55. Ibid., pp. vii–viii. For a newspaper copy of the report, see *New York Times,* June 2, 1880, p. 2.

56. *Philadelphia Inquirer,* June 8, 1880, p. 4. *New York Times,* June 3, 1880, p. 4; June 5, 1880, p. 4; May 17, 1880, p. 8.

6 The Un-American Negro, 1880–1900

1. *North American Review,* 128 (March 1879): 225–283. *Washington Post,* February 17, 1879, p. 2. David Herbert Donald, *Liberty and Union* (Lexington, Mass.: D. C. Heath, 1978), p. 262.

2. James West Davidson, William E. Gienapp, et al., *Nation of Nations,* vol. 2 (New York: McGraw-Hill, 1990), pp. 670–673. Henry George, *Progress and Poverty* (New York: H. George & Co., 1879).

3. *Chicago Tribune,* March 30, 1879, p. 4. *Philadelphia Inquirer,* January 9, 1880, p. 4. For more on the association of the Communards and American labor unrest, see Philip M. Katz, *From Appomattox to Montmartre: Americans and the Paris Commune* (Cambridge, Mass.: Harvard University Press, 1998), pp. 161–183. *New York Times,* January 3, 1880, p. 1. *San Francisco Daily Alta California,* June 3, 1880, p. 2; see also ibid., June 10, 1880, p. 4. See also *Philadelphia Inquirer,* June 1, 1880, p. 4. *Detroit Evening News,* May 4, 1880, p. 1. See also *New York Herald,* May 5, 1880, p. 6, and May 10, 1880, p. 6.

4. T. V. Powderly, in *North American Review,* 135 (August 1882): 126. "The Organization of Labor," *Harper's Weekly,* September 13, 1879, p. 722.

5. *Century,* 39 (November 1889): 314. William L. Riordon, *Plunkitt of Tammany Hall* (1905; reprint, New York: Signet Classic, 1995), pp. 27–28. For a close examination of a specific boss's rule, see James A. Kehl, *Boss Rule in the Gilded Age: Matt Quay of Pennsylvania* (Pittsburgh, Pa.: University of Pittsburgh Press, 1981). *Detroit Evening News,* January 3, 1880, p. 2. *North American Review,* 136 (May 1883): 462–463. On Alexander Winchell, see *New York Herald,* May 10, 1880, p. 8, for a review of his book on the evolution of races.

6. For an account of the president's slow death from infection, see Harriet S. Blaine Beale, ed., *Letters of Mrs. James G. Blaine,* vol. 1 (New York: Duffield and Company, 1908), pp. 209–242.

7. Ballard C. Campbell, *The Growth of American Government: Governance from the Cleveland Era to the Present,* (Bloomington: Indiana University Press, 1995). Leonard D. White, *The Republican Era, 1869–1901: A Study in Administrative History* (New York: The Macmillan Company, 1958), p. 2. M. C. Butler to R. R. Hemphill, March 21, 1879, M. C. Butler MSS, Duke University. *Atlantic Monthly,* February 1880, p. 224, "The Strong Government Idea."

8. William Graham Sumner, *What Social Classes Owe to Each Other* (1883; reprint, New York: Arno Press, 1972), pp. 113, 127, 62, 64.

9. Ibid., p. 65.

10. Ibid., pp. 20–23. Compare Frederick Douglass's 1875 complaints about the "swarms of white beggars who sweep the country in the name of the colored man," *American Missionary,* 19 (September 1875): 197, quoted in Richard B. Drake, "Freedmen's Aid Societies and Sectional Compromise," *Journal of Southern History,* 29 (May 1963): 175–186.

11. Sumner, *Social Classes,* pp. 21–23, 126, 145–146, 131–132.

12. Ibid., pp. 24, 117–120. On Sumner, see Sidney Fine, *Laissez Faire and the General-Welfare State: A Study of Conflict in American Thought, 1865–1901* (Ann Arbor: University of Michigan Press, 1956), pp. 79–91.

13. Ibid., pp. 101, 149–151.

14. See resolutions of protest meeting, reprinted in *New York Times,* March 18, 1879, p. 2. On African-American call for schools funded by white taxes, see *Cleveland Gazette,* October 20, 1883, p. 2. James A. Garfield to Burke A. Hinsdale, December 30, 1880, in Mary C. Hinsdale, ed., *Garfield-Hinsdale Letters: Correspondence between James Abram Garfield and Burke Aaron Hinsdale* (Ann Arbor: University of Michigan Press, 1949), p. 469.

15. Davidson, Gienapp, et al., *Nation of Nations,* 2: 722–730.

16. *New York Times,* February 20, 1886, p. 3. From the *Sacramento Record-Union,* reprinted in *New York Times,* July 26, 1886, p. 2. *New York Times,* June 19, 1881, p. 4. T. W. Higginson, "Some War Scenes Revisited," *Atlantic*

Monthly, July 1878, pp. 1–9. *New York Times,* May 2, 1881, p. 4. See also ibid., August 31, 1881, p. 4.

17. Gaines M. Foster, *Ghosts of the Confederacy: Defeat, the Lost Cause, and the Emergence of the New South, 1865 to 1913* (New York: Oxford University Press, 1987), p. 71. *Century* (October 1884): 943–944, in Foster, *Ghosts,* pp. 69–70. See also Stephen Davis, "'A Matter of Sensational Interest': The *Century Battles and Leaders* Series," *Civil War History,* 27 (December 1981): 338–349. *Philadelphia Inquirer,* January 2, 1880, p. 1.; January 6, 1880, p. 8. David Blight, *Race and Reunion: The Civil War in American Memory* (Cambridge, Mass.: Harvard University Press, 2000).

18. *Philadelphia Evening Bulletin,* January 23, 1880, p. 1. On Northern prejudice, see *Scribner's Monthly Magazine,* 20, (June 1880): 304–305. Gilbert Osofsky, *Harlem: The Making of a Ghetto* (New York: Harper & Row, 1963), p. 20.

19. While landownership was increasing, tenancy was growing at a greater rate. See Gilbert C. Fite, *Cotton Fields No More: Southern Agriculture, 1865–1980* (Lexington: University Press of Kentucky, 1984), p. 5. *New York Times,* July 31, 1881, p. 6. See also ibid., September 30, 1881, p. 2. Ibid., November 14, 1881, p. 4. Ibid., February 20, 1886, p. 3. *Philadelphia Evening Bulletin,* October 16, 1883, p. 4.

20. George Washington Williams, *History of the Negro Race in America* (New York: G. P. Putnam's Sons, 1883). On Williams's thought, see William Toll, "Free Men, Freedmen, and Race: Black Social Theory in the Gilded Age," *Journal of Southern History,* 44 (November 1978): 571–596. *Maryville (Tenn.) Republican* [African-American], October 7, 1876. Bernard E. Powers, Jr., *Black Charlestonians: A Social History, 1822–1885* (Fayetteville: University of Arkansas Press, 1994), p. 177. *Vidalia (La.) Concordia Eagle* [African-American], October 2, 1875, p. 1. *New York Times,* January 2, 1886, p. 2.

21. *New York Times,* August 12, 1883, p. 6. On African-American economic advancement during Reconstruction, see Powers, *Black Charlestonians;* Robert Higgs, *Competition and Coercion: Blacks in the American Economy, 1865–1914* (Cambridge: Cambridge University Press, 1977); Michael P. Johnson and James L. Roark, *Black Masters: A Free Family of Color in the Old South* (New York: W. W. Norton & Co., 1984); Loren Schweninger, *Black Property Owners in the South, 1790–1915* (Urbana: University of Illinois Press, 1990); Willard B. Gatewood, *Aristocrats of Color: The Black Elite, 1880–1920* (Bloomington: Indiana University Press, 1990); Janette Thomas Greenwood, *Bittersweet Legacy: The Black and White "Better Classes" in Charlotte, 1850–1910* (Chapel Hill: University of North Carolina Press, 1994); Robert C. Kenzer, *Enterprising Southerners: Black Economic Success in North Caro-*

lina, 1865–1915 (Charlottesville: University Press of Virginia, 1997). Statistics in Kenzer, *Enterprising Southerners*, p. 49. *New York Times*, June 20, 1886, p. 1. See also ibid., April 13, 1881, p. 4. For the life story of a member of the black "better classes," see Nick Salvatore, *We All Got History: The Memory Books of Amos Webber* (New York: Times Books, 1996).

22. On the black "better classes," see Glenda Elizabeth Gilmore, *Gender and Jim Crow* (Chapel Hill: University of North Carolina Press, 1996); David M. Katzman, *Before the Ghetto: Black Detroit in the Nineteenth Century* (Urbana: University of Illinois Press, 1973), especially pp. 135–174; Gatewood, *Aristocrats of Color*, p. 8. *Hartford Courant*, October 12, 1888, p. 1.

23. *Boston Evening Transcript*, November 22, 1883, p. 4. Wendell Phillips, in *North American Review*, 128 (March 1879): 257–260. George Washington Cable, "The Freedmen's Case in Equity," *Century*, 25 (January 1885): 1, 4.

24. Frederick Douglass, April 16, 1883, "Twenty-first Anniversary of Emancipation in the District of Columbia." Fortune was the editor of the *New York Globe* until 1884, then of the *New York Freeman*, which became the *New York Age*. On Fortune, see I. Garland Penn, *The Afro-American Press and Its Editors* (1891; reprint, New York: Arno Press, 1969), pp. 131–138. See also Herbert J. Doherty, Jr., "Voices of Protest from the New South, 1875–1910," *Mississippi Valley Historical Review*, 42 (June 1955): 45–66. T. Thomas Fortune, *Black and White: Land, Labor, and Politics in the South* (New York: Fords, Howard, & Hulbert, 1884), pp. 38–40. Ibid., pp. 103, 238, 241–242, 175.

25. *New York Times*, August 18, 1883, p. 1.

26. On Northern Republican politics in this period, see Stanley P. Hirshson, *Farewell to the Bloody Shirt: Northern Republicans and the Southern Negro, 1877–1893* (Bloomington: Indiana University Press, 1962), pp. 94–98. J. Morgan Kousser, *The Shaping of Southern Politics: Suffrage Restriction and the Establishment of a One-Party South, 1880–1910* (New Haven: Yale University Press, 1974), pp. 21–27. Hirshson, *Bloody Shirt*, pp. 116–119. Speech of Reverend Alexander Walters of AME Zion Church, in *San Francisco Examiner*, October 17, 1883, p. 2. On the role of fusion parties in race relations, see Joseph H. Cartwright, *The Triumph of Jim Crow: Tennessee Race Relations in the 1880s* (Knoxville: University of Tennessee Press, 1976).

27. *San Francisco Examiner*, October 21, 1883, p. 8. See also *Hartford Weekly Times*, October 18, 1883, p. 2. Lawrence Grossman, *The Democratic Party and the Negro: Northern and National Politics, 1868–1892* (Urbana: University of Illinois Press, 1976), pp. 60–142.

28. On independents (Mugwumps), see Geoffrey Blodgett, *The Gentle Reformers: Massachusetts Democrats in the Cleveland Era* (Cambridge, Mass.: Harvard University Press, 1966). John G. Sproat, *"The Best Men": Liberal Re-*

formers in the Gilded Age (New York: Oxford University Press, 1968); Glenn C. Altschuler, *Race, Ethnicity, and Class in American Social Thought, 1865– 1919* (Arlington Heights, Ill.: Harlan Davidson, 1982); and George M. Fredrickson, *The Inner Civil War: Northern Intellectuals and the Crisis of the Union* (1965; reprint, Urbana: University of Illinois Press, 1993), pp. 194– 195. Hirshson, *Bloody Shirt*, p. 107. Thomas C. Reeves, *Gentleman Boss: The Life of Chester Alan Arthur* (New York: Alfred A. Knopf, 1975), pp. 308–313. Fortune supported Arthur in general, though. See *New York Freeman*, March 7, 1885, p. 2. U. S. Grant to James D. Brady, October 4, 1881, in *New York Times*, October 20, 1881, quoted in Hirshson, *Bloody Shirt*, p. 109.

29. Hirshson, *Bloody Shirt*, pp. 98–122. On civil service reform, see Ari Hoogenboom, *Outlawing the Spoils: A History of the Civil Service Reform Movement, 1865–1883* (Urbana: University of Illinois Press, 1961). *New York Times*, June 30, 1886, p. 4.

30. *Philadelphia Inquirer,* January 12, 1880, p. 1. *Detroit Evening News*, May 14, 1880, p. 4. Samuel J. Stokley at meeting of black New Yorkers, in *New York Times*, August 30, 1883, p. 5. *New York Times*, September 26, 1883, p. 1. James Pickett Jones, *John A. Logan: Stalwart Republican from Illinois* (Talla- hassee: University Presses of Florida, 1982), pp. 175–177. For the story of the downfall of a black stalwart Republican politician, see Gary R. Kremer, *James Milton Turner and the Promise of America* (Columbia: University of Missouri Press, 1991). Another, more complicated story is told in Randall Bennett Woods, *A Black Odyssey: John Lewis Waller and the Promise of Ameri- can Life, 1878–1900* (Lawrence: Regents Press of Kansas, 1981).

31. *New York Times*, January 24, 1886, p. 6.

32. State Senate of Indiana to Grover Cleveland, March 6, 1885; and William Gross [?] to Grover Cleveland, March 6, 1865, both in Grover Cleveland MSS, Library of Congress, on microfilm. *New York Times*, January 24, 1886, p. 6.

33. Cleveland quotation from H. Wayne Morgan, *From Hayes to McKinley: Na- tional Party Politics, 1877–1896* (Syracuse, N.Y.: Syracuse University Press, 1969), p. 253. James D. Richardson, *Messages and Papers of the Presidents*, vol. 8 (Washington: Government Printing Office, 1898), pp. 299–303.

34. On federal elections bill of 1890, see Vincent P. DeSantis, *Republicans Face the Southern Question: The New Departure Years, 1877–1897* (New York: Greenwood Press, 1959), pp. 198–215, and Xi Wang, *The Trial of Democ- racy: Black Suffrage and Northern Republicans, 1860–1910* (Athens: Univer- sity of Georgia Press, 1997), pp. 232–252.

35. On Hampton's popularity in the North, see *Detroit Evening News*, May 14, 1880, p. 2. Wade Hampton, "What Negro Supremacy Means," *Forum*, 5

(June 1888): 383–395. See also John T. Morgan, "Shall Negro Majorities Rule?" *Forum*, 6 (September 1888): 568–599.

36. Hon. William M. Dickson, letter to *Cincinnati Daily Gazette*, January 12, 1888, quoted in Henry Watterson, "The Hysteria of Sectional Agitation," *Forum*, 5 (April 1888): 134–145; see p. 136. *Harper's Weekly*, April 5, 1890, p. 254. E. L. Godkin, "The Republican Party and the Negro," *Forum*, 7 (May 1889): 246–257; see p. 255. Alfred H. Colquitt, "Is the Negro Vote Suppressed?" *Forum*, 4 (October 1887): 268–278; see p. 274. See also *New York Times*, July 26, 1886, p. 2. George W. Cable, "What Shall the Negro Do?" *Forum*, 5 (August 1888): 627–639; see pp. 630, 634.

37. On business and the elections bill, see Hirshson, *Bloody Shirt*, p. 221. *New York Times*, December 6, 1890, p. 4. Hilary A. Herbert et al., *Why the Solid South? or Reconstruction and Its Results* (Baltimore: R. H. Woodward & Company, 1890), pp. 23, 31–36, 86–103, 430, 440–442. See also Philip A. Bruce, *The Plantation Negro as a Freeman* (1888; reprint, Northbrook, Ill.: Metro Books, 1972), p. 244.

38. Godkin, "The Republican Party and the Negro," p. 256.

39. *New York Times*, October 14, 1888, p. 20; see also ibid., November 3, 1888, p. 3, and February 20, 1886, p. 3. Henry L. Dawes, "A Year of Republican Control," *Forum*, 9 (March 1890): 24–35; see p. 35. J. G. Carlisle, "Republican Promise and Performance," *Forum*, 9 (May 1890): 243–254; see p. 253.

40. *Harper's Weekly*, March 29, 1890, p. 234. *New York Times*, March 16, 1890, p. 14. Ibid., July 16, 1890, p. 4.

41. *Harper's Weekly*, January 25, 1890, p. 62. Charles Forster Smith, in *Century*, 42 (May 1891): 154–156. *Harper's Weekly*, January 11, 1890, p. 23. *New York Times*, December 9, 1888, p. 4. Ibid., May 19, 1890, p. 4. See also *Harper's Weekly* cartoons showing professional African-Americans as undereducated bunglers (*Harper's Weekly*, supplement, February 2, 1890, p. 152). Robert A. Pelham, Jr., in *Detroit Tribune*, January 5, 1890, p. 9, quoted in Katzman, *Before the Ghetto*, p. 93.

42. For description of socialism, see *Philadelphia Evening Bulletin*, October 16, 1883, p. 4. On economic changes and the ideological changes they demanded, see James L. Huston, *Securing the Fruits of Labor: The American Concept of Wealth Distribution, 1765–1900* (Baton Rouge: Louisiana State University Press, 1998), pp. 339–378.

43. Mary R. Dearing, *Veterans in Politics: The Story of the GAR* (Baton Rouge: Louisiana State University Press, 1952); Stuart McConnell, *Glorious Contentment: The Grand Army of the Republic, 1865–1900* (Chapel Hill: University of North Carolina Press, 1992). On pension fight, see McConnell, *Glorious Contentment*, pp. 139–165; on Logan, see ibid., pp. 193–200. On role of

veterans' benefits in changing American government, see Theda Skocpol, *Protecting Soldiers and Mothers: The Political Origins of Social Policy in the United States* (Cambridge, Mass.: Harvard University Press, 1992), and Patrick J. Kelly, *Creating a National Home: Building the Veterans' Welfare State, 1860–1900* (Cambridge, Mass.: Harvard University Press, 1997). On Cleveland's opposition to frivolous pension applications and his veto of Dependent Pension Bill in 1887, see Morgan, *From Hayes to McKinley*, pp. 254–258.

44. Washington Gladden, "The Strength and Weakness of Socialism," *Century*, 31 (March 1886): 737–749. On socialism, see also *Harper's Weekly*, May 31, 1890, p. 419; May 17, 1890, p. 378; May 10, 1890, p. 359; February 22, 1890, p. 134. Ibid., January 18, 1890, p. 42. William M. Sloan, "Pensions and Socialism," *Century*, 42 (June 1891): 179–188.

45. *New York Times*, February 7, 1890, p. 2. *Chicago Tribune*, February 7, 1890, p. 6. Eric Foner, *Reconstruction: America's Unfinished Revolution, 1863–1877* (New York: Harper & Row, 1988), pp. 531–532. Carl R. Osthaus, *Freedmen, Philanthropy, and Fraud: A History of the Freedman's Savings Bank* (Urbana: University of Illinois Press, 1976). *Nation*, February 13, 1890, p. 123.

46. Daniel W. Crofts, "The Black Response to the Blair Education Bill," *Journal of Southern History*, 37 (February 1971): 40–65.

47. *St. Paul Pioneer Press*, quoted in *Nation*, February 6, 1890, p. 101. See also *Keokuk (Iowa) Gate City*, ibid. *Chicago Tribune*, January 11, 1888, p. 4. Article from *Springfield (Mass.) Republican*, in *Boston Evening Transcript*, January 11, 1888, p. 6. *Harper's Weekly*, March 15, 1890, p. 199. Letter to the *New York Evening Post*, reprinted in *Chicago Tribune*, January 13, 1888, p. 4. Edward P. Clark to Grover Cleveland, February 26, 1887, Cleveland MSS. For debate over bill, see Hirshson, *Bloody Shirt*, pp. 192–200. Crofts, "The Black Response to the Blair Education Bill."

48. *Harper's Weekly*, February 1, 1890, pp. 78–79. Ibid., June 28, 1890, p. 494. On federal elections bill and debate, see Hirshson, *Bloody Shirt*, pp. 200–235.

49. Winchell in *North American Review*, 136 (1883): 119–134. *New York Times*, January 21, 1890, p. 4. See also *Harper's Weekly*, May 24, 1890, p. 399, and Washington Gladden, "Safeguards of the Suffrage," *Century*, 37 (February 1889): 621–628. *Harper's Weekly*, February 15, 1890, p. 119.

50. *Charleston News and Courier*, in *Harper's Weekly*, January 25, 1890, p. 62. *Harper's Weekly*, March 8, 1890, p. 174. See also ibid., January 25, 1890, p. 62.

51. Lawrence Grossman, *The Democratic Party and the Negro* (Urbana: University of Illinois Press, 1976), p. 158. "Ballot Reform as an Educator," *Century*, 41 (January 1891): 473. From *Buffalo Enquirer*, in *Public Opinion*, 11 (August 29, 1891): 506–507; from *Boston Evening Transcript*, in ibid., (October

3, 1891): 629–630; from *Kansas City Star,* in ibid. (October 3, 1891): 630. See also from *Atlanta Constitution,* November 29, 1892, in ibid., 14 (December 3, 1892): 200.

52. This was the basis for fear of the black vote during the time of Populism. Very few people seemed to worry that the Populists and the freedpeople would join together in this election.

53. On Dana's campaign, see Hirshson, *Bloody Shirt,* pp. 239–242. *Philadelphia Evening Bulletin,* July 9, 1892, p. 4.

54. *Philadelphia Evening Bulletin,* July 6, 1892, p. 3.

55. *Harper's Weekly,* July 16, 1892, p. 674.

56. Emma Lou Thornbrough, "The National Afro-American League, 1887–1908," *Journal of Southern History,* 27 (November 1961): 494–512. *Nation,* February 13, 1890, p. 123. See also *Chicago Tribune,* in *New York Age,* February 8, 1990. *New York Times,* April 5, 1892, p. 1.

57. Grossman, *The Democratic Party and the Negro,* p. 158. *New York Times,* March 15, 1892, p. 4. Ibid., June 22, 1892, p. 5. Ibid., August 22, 1891, p. 1.

58. *Harper's Weekly,* September 3, 1892, p. 842. *New York Times,* July 16, 1892, p. 1.

59. Archibald Forbes, "What I Saw of the Paris Commune II," *Century,* 45 (November 1892): 48–66; C. W. T., "What an American Girl Saw of the Commune," ibid., pp. 61–68. *Harper's Weekly,* November 19, 1892, p. 1106.

60. On African-Americans and Populism, see William H. Chafe, "The Negro and Populism: A Kansas Case Study," *Journal of Southern History,* 34 (August 1968): 402–419. Chafe makes the point that, in fact, African-Americans generally disliked the Populist message.

61. Frank Basil Tracy, "Menacing Socialism in the Western States," *Forum* (May 1893): 332–342; see p. 336. John C. Wickliffe, "Negro Suffrage a Failure: Shall We Abolish It?" *Forum* (February 1893): 797–804.

62. Davidson, Gienapp, et al., *Nation of Nations,* pp. 780–781. Fine, *Laissez Faire and the General-Welfare State,* pp. 289–396.

63. On repeal of elections laws, see Wang, *The Trial of Democracy,* pp. 253–159. On relationship between Populism and disfranchisement, see C. Vann Woodward, *The Strange Career of Jim Crow* (New York: Oxford University Press, 1955). See Edward P. Clark, "Solid South Dissolving," *Forum,* 22 (1896): 263–274. *Harper's Weekly,* August 20, 1892, p. 794. *New York Times,* March 8, 1892, p. 4. Ibid., June 1, 1893, p. 4.

64. James Weir, Jr., in *Century,* 48 (October 1894): 952–954. *In re Debs,* 158 U.S. 564, 599 (1895).

65. *New York Times,* August 13, 1895, p. 4.

66. Jasper C. Barnes, *The Influences of the Change of the Industrial Systems of the South on the Development of Personality in the Afro-American* (Wooster, Ohio:

The Herald Printing Co., 1900), pp. 2–4. Robert Bingham, "An Ex-Slave-holder's View of the Negro Question in the South," *Harper's Monthly Magazine* (European ed.), July 1900, p. 16.

67. Bingham, "An Ex-Slaveholder's View." Henry M. Field, *Bright Skies and Dark Shadows* (New York: Charles Scribner's Sons, 1890), pp. 144–147.

68. For continuing African-American calls for office, see, for example, *Baltimore Afro-American* [African-American], December 14, 1895, p. 2. See discussion in *New York Times*, January 5, 1880, p. 4. Henry A. Scomp, "Can the Race Problem Be Solved?" *Forum*, 8 (December 1889): 365–376; see pp. 369, 376. Thomas Nelson Page, "The Negro Question," in *The Old South: Essays Social and Political* (New York: Charles Scribner's Sons, 1892), p. 280.

69. See Joel Williamson, *The Crucible of Race: Black-White Relations in the American South since Emancipation* (New York: Oxford University Press, 1984); Edward L. Ayers, *Vengeance and Justice: Crime and Punishment in the Nineteenth-Century American South* (New York: Oxford University Press, 1984); George C. Wright, *Racial Violence in Kentucky, 1865–1940: Lynchings, Mob Rule, and "Legal Lynchings"* (Baton Rouge: Louisiana State University Press, 1990); W. Fitzhugh Brundage, *Lynching in the New South: Georgia and Virginia, 1880–1930* (Urbana: University of Illinois Press, 1993); W. Fitzhugh Brundage, ed., *Under Sentence of Death: Lynching in the South* (Chapel Hill: University of North Carolina Press, 1997). Wade Hampton, "What Negro Supremacy Means," *Forum* (June 1888): pp. 383–395. Hampton's article concentrated exclusively on politics and confiscation. In *Angels in the Machinery: Gender in American Party Politics from the Civil War to the Progressive Era* (New York: Oxford University Press, 1997), Rebecca Edwards notes that Democrats connected the expansion of the federal government to the violation of white women by black men. For another interpretation of the role of generational change in promoting racial tension, see David Herbert Donald, "A Generation of Defeat," in Walter J. Fraser and Winfred B. Moore, Jr., eds., *From the Old South to the New: Essays on the Transitional South* (Westport, Conn.: Greenwood Press, 1981), pp. 3–20. On generational change, see also C. Vann Woodward, *Origins of the New South, 1877–1913* (Baton Rouge: Louisiana State University Press, 1951); Ayers, *Vengeance and Justice*; Glenda Elizabeth Gilmore, *Gender and Jim Crow: Women and the Politics of White Supremacy in North Carolina, 1896–1920* (Chapel Hill: University of North Carolina Press, 1996), pp. 64–67.

70. Henry Litchfield West, "The Race War in North Carolina," *Forum*, 26 (January 1899): 578–591. For an examination of the connection between the fusion movement and lynching in North Carolina, see Gilmore, *Gender and Jim Crow*, pp. 77–118; quotation is from p. 111.

71. *Century*, 42 (June 1891): 313–314. *New York Times*, January 14, 1896, p. 4.

For a similar discussion of lynching, see Owen Wister, *The Virginian* (1902; reprint, New York: Signet, 1979), pp. 270–274.

72. Quotation in Edward L. Ayers, *Southern Crossing: A History of the American South, 1877–1906* (Oxford: Oxford University Press, 1995), pp. 108–109. *Montgomery Enterprise* [African-American] January 26, 1900, p. 4. *Colorado Springs Western Enterprise* [African-American], January 27, 1900, p. 2.

73. *New York Times*, January 13, 1893, p. 8. Olive Ruth Jefferson in the *Chautauquan*, in *Public Opinion*, 15 (August 12, 1893): 433.

74. Rayford Whittingham Logan, *Negro in American Life and Thought: The Nadir, 1877–1901* (New York: Dial Press, 1954), pp. 240–251. *New York Times*, March 7, 1890, p. 3; March 10, 1890, p. 5. Cartwright, *Triumph of Jim Crow.* See, for example, the *Baltimore Afro-American*, August 10, 1895, and November 11, 1895, p. 1. *New York Times*, June 19, 1895, p. 3. On avoiding racial divisions, see also George F. Hoar, *Autobiography of Seventy Years*, vol. 2 (New York: Charles Scribner's Sons, 1905), p. 159. *Baltimore Afro-American*, June 27, 1896, p. 1.

75. *Plessy v. Ferguson*, 163 U.S. 537, 551 (1896). *New York Times*, May 21, 1890, p. 1; June 25, 1896, p. 8.

76. *New York Times*, January 26, 1896, p. 27. Ibid., June 8, 1896, p. 5. For African-American reaction to the St. Louis businessmen's circular, see *Baltimore Afro-American*, December 14, 1895, p. 2. In Gilmore, *Gender and Jim Crow*, p. 20; quotation from *Star of Zion*, June 3, 1897.

77. On Washington and his national network, see *Denver Colorado Statesman* [African-American], January 27, 1900, p. 4. G. W. Lowe in *Helena (Ark.) Reporter* [African-American], February 1, 1900, p. 1. *Little Rock (Ark.) American Guide* [African-American], January 27, 1900, p. 1. J. H. Phillips, in *Montgomery Enterprise*, January 26, 1900, p. 1.

78. Katzman, *Before the Ghetto*, pp. 160–161.

79. "The Genteel Negro," in *Birmingham (Ala.) Wide-Awake* [African-American], January 24, 1900, p. 2, and *Montgomery Enterprise*, January 26, 1900, p. 2.

80. W. T. Harris, "Statistics *versus* Socialism," *Forum*, 24 (October 1897): 186–199; see p. 187. *New York Times*, June 28, 1896, p. 5. *Huntsville (Ala.) Star* [African-American], January 26, 1900, p. 2.

81. Kousser, *The Shaping of Southern Politics*, pp. 32, 49, 57.

Epilogue

1. Booker T. Washington, *Up from Slavery* (1901; reprint, New York: Oxford University Press, 1995), p. 2. Hereinafter pages are cited in the text.

2. *Boston Evening Transcript*, February 6, 1875, p. 4.

3. Letter of Arthur Sumner to Mrs. Cheney in *Boston Evening Transcript*, January 13, 1873, p. 7.

4. Shearman, in *Harper's Weekly*, April 13, 1867, p. 238. See also cartoon of uneducated African-American doctor and teacher, in *Harper's Weekly*, June 14, 1879, p. 464.

5. For an earlier argument that this was the right education for African-Americans, see *New York Times*, June 17, 1875, p. 4. For support for remedial education for the South in general, see *Philadelphia Inquirer*, May 1, 1867, p. 4. For move away from classical studies and toward vocational education in general, see *Philadelphia Daily Evening Bulletin*, March 1, 1867, p. 4, and *Philadelphia Inquirer*, August 29, 1868, p. 4.

6. Tim Dirks, "The Birth of a Nation," wysiwyg://5/http://www.filmsite.org/birt.html (June 5, 2000).

7. On progressivism and government activism, see Sidney Fine, *Laissez Faire and the General-Welfare State: A Study of Conflict in American Thought, 1865–1901* (Ann Arbor: University of Michigan Press, 1956), pp. 373–400. Compare Richard Schneirov, *Labor and Urban Politics: Class Conflict and the Origins of Modern Liberalism in Chicago, 1864–1897* (Urbana: University of Illinois Press, 1998).

Index

Abolitionists, 12, 58, 110, 192
African-American community, divisions in, 52–53, 57; in South Carolina, 90, 121; in Colfax Massacre, 108; and civil rights, 133–134, 146–147; and Exodus, 170–171, 176–181; after 1880, 194, 222
African-American politicians: and free labor theory, 49–50, 53; belief in economic conflict, 53; support of radical measures, 54; conflicts between, 57; as demagogues, 62, 142; in constitutional conventions, 66; in Congress, 84; in South Carolina, 89–90, 110
African-Americans: Northern, 12, 38; enfranchisement of, 78; demand for protection, 130; urban professionals, 193
African-American women, 11; as workers, 99, 115, 174; wealthy, 220; as teachers, 233
African Methodist Episcopal (AME) Church: and civil rights, 151; and black voting, 198
Alabama: and Carl Schurz, 18; politics in, 49, 50; and Wilson, 51; strikes in, 55; radical black meeting in, 56; vote for constitution, 71; black schools in, 138; and civil rights, 145; and Exodus, 174; Black Codes, 203; split vote in, 214; black conference in, 215; B. T. Washington in, 231–232
Alger, Horatio, 35, 243
Arkansas: and racial harmony, 120; fusion movement in, 197
Armstrong, Samuel C., 193, 208, 229
Arthur, Chester A., 198–199
Ashtabula (Ohio) Sentinel, 30, 39
Associated Press (AP): on black radicalism, 54, 68–69; on black riots, 56; on civil rights, 145; on Exodus, 176

Atlanta Constitution, 4
Atlantic Monthly, 187

Baltimore Afro-American, 220
Baltimore Sun: and black suffrage, 56; and corruption, 58; and black office-holding, 60
Beaufort (South Carolina) Tribune, 120
"Better classes": and black schools, 138; and communism, 185; and disaffected workers, 189, 191, 196–197; and disfranchisement, 210; and African-Americans, 242–244
"Better classes," black: and Elliott, 104; and Colfax Massacre, 108; and political independence, 119–120; resentment of segregation, 125, 133; and Grant, 128; and civil rights, 146; after 1880, 194–197, 200–201, 205, 217, 219–222
Birmingham (New York) Republican, 145
Birth of a Nation, The (film), 241
Black and White: Land, Labor and Politics in the South (Fortune), 196
Black Codes, 17; justification for, 19, 302; Northern dislike of, 28; as echo of slavery, 53
Blaine, James G., on Military Reconstruction Act, 48; on radicalism, 66; and 1884 election, 199–200
Blair, Henry W., 174, 178, 207
Blair Education Bill, 207–209
Boston Evening Transcript: and Atlanta Address, 4; and reconciliation, 26; and black suffrage, 47; and free black labor, 83–84; and black education, 84, 231; and Paris Commune, 86; and Internationals, 87; and disaffected workers, 88, 108; and